The Call of the Daimon

The Call of the Daimon

Aldo Carotenuto

Translated by
Charles Nobar

Chiron Publications · Wilmette, Illinois

Originally published in 1989 as *La Chiamata del Daimon: Gli orizzonti della verita dell'amore in Kafka*. ©1989, Gruppo Editoriale Fabbri, Bompiani.

Translation ©1993 by Aldo Carotenuto.

Library of Congress Catalog Card Number: 93-29052

Printed in the United States of America.
Copyedited by Carla Babrick.
Cover design by Michael Barron

Library of Congress Cataloging-in-Publication Data:

The call of the Daimon.
     p.   cm.
  ISBN 0-933029-83-7
   1. Kafka, Franz, 1883-1924—Criticism and interpretation.
PT2621.A26Z647 1994
833'.912—dc20   93-29052
                                                      CIP

ISBN 0-933029-83-7

For Caterina

Contents

Introduction

> *Truth is what everyone*
> *needs to live, but it can-*
> *not be received or*
> *acquired from anyone*
> *else. Everyone must con-*
> *tinually produce it from*
> *within himself, otherwise*
> *he perishes. It is impos-*
> *sible to live without*
> *truth. It may be that*
> *truth is life itself.*
> G. Janouch, Conversa-
> tions with Kafka, *p. 1131*

Kafka was a lonely and tormented man. "As alone as Kafka" is the way he put it to the young writer Janouch (1951, p. 1082) in the attempt to find the only adequate measure of his condition: the metaphor was not external but internal, mixed with his being. No human condition, not even that of Kaspar Hauser, to whom Janouch compares it, could be equally tragic. In a letter that Milena wrote to Max Brod (1937, pp. 258–59) after her relationship with Kafka had ended, she defined him as pure, a man without any refuge just because of his purity. Life was something quite different for him than it was for all other people: it was an enigma, a "mystical enigma." He was compelled to lift it toward the pure, the true, the immutable. But his ascension was not a means to an end, rather, it was an inner constriction dictated by his incapacity to accept compromise (Brod 1937, pp. 258–259). Reality, if it were interrogated by a pure heart, would have to give up its secret, and *truth* would issue forth in all its blazing light. Like the mad Parsifal and like the land surveyor K., he was compelled to leave everything behind and go off in search of truth. But what is the truth of which Kafka speaks? What are these mysterious horizons that he must reach? Life and love, guilt and innocence, the self and otherness, all curve and intersect to form these horizons.

Kafka had to resolve an enigma: he had to understand who he was and who the other was, that disquieting other which appeared in his writings, each time dressed in different garb — the defendant, the judge, the doctor, the insect, the dog, the powerful lord of the castle, and the crowded ranks of lovers, now fat, elephantine, and castrating women like Gardena or Brunelda, now thin and welcoming like Frieda, images of passion (Kafka 1914–1915a; 1916–1917a; 1912b; 1922a; 1922b; 1912–1914).

If the *other*, as an endopsychic image, represented a way of being that was unknown to him, if it was an incarnate possibility closed up at the center of the soul, then Kafka's countenance could do nothing but continually change with the mise-en-scène of his characters. He *was* Josef K. interrogating himself about his guilt (1914–1915a), but above all he was K., the land surveyor (1922b) who tried to measure, hence comprehend, the horizons of truth. His myth was that of the *search* and the *call*.

In his works, the unconscious speaks with the voice of a *deus absconditus* who thunders his law from afar, who, from an inaccessible place commands humanity to set out on a journey to meet him. In the Greek myth, the Sphinx devours all those who cannot solve her riddles. In this search, too, there is a mortal danger, because the truth does not want to be revealed, nor bring to light that which must remain buried in dark unknowing.

In the dream of a woman, a disquieting figure appears. The dreamer finds herself near the house of the man she loves. When she goes through the gate of that house, she realizes that she can never leave it again. The atmosphere is solemn, as if one were in a cathedral. Now the woman understands that a secret is being guarded there, a terrible secret that she must unveil. But all those who have attempted it have been discovered and killed.

There is a trapdoor and a stairway that lead to a dark, damp cellar. A woman is handling a corpse. Others, in decomposition, are hidden in the bowels of the building. The dreamer, however, manages to climb over the gate, taking with her a bit of paper on which the truth is written. But she has no time to read it. She knows she may be discovered from one moment to the next and tries to hide the paper in a high place, inaccessible and unimaginable. But she fears that no one will ever find it and that its message — like that of Kafka's emperor — will never reach its destination. Thus her sacrifice will have been for nought. The woman feels that she is under an obscure menace: no one can reveal the truth without dying. She is overcome by a terror that takes the form of madness. It is a terror of death, something like diabolical possession. The secret visage of the phantom may destroy her and take possession of her mind.

Kafka's search is the search for this secret that must be revealed and given to the world. The terror of the dream woman, her anguish, is like Kafka's. The mystery has something to do with otherness, with a past that cannot be remembered. In order to learn who he is, and who are the others he meets along his way, Kafka must lift the trapdoor, descend into the cellar and observe those corpses. He must encounter the daimon and challenge the law of silence. And this is what makes Kafka write: his books are the message he throws to the world in the hope that it will get across the gate, in the hope that someone will be able to read it. These texts, at times obscure — these dense metaphors in which everyone can find a different truth — are his testimony, are the note that he may not have had time to read, to work out to the end so that he would not remain a victim of his phantom. The *daimon*, once evoked, avenges himself on the writer, provoking insomnia and anguish in him and planting the seed of destruction, the illness that ended his life: tuberculosis of the larynx.

In his last days, Kafka could neither eat nor speak. His voice, like that of Josephine the singer (Kafka, 1924), became ever weaker. He had violated the taboo, and now he had to pay for his acts. The inability to communicate with the other became crystallized in the organic degeneration produced by his disease: only writing was left to him. Significantly, he was condemned in the end to use only this means of communication that for years he had preferred as a way of relating to others. The writer's last messages, in fact, were all notes written on bits of paper.

In all mystery rituals, those who violate the taboo are killed. Kafka had approached the labyrinthine world of the unconscious. Thus, vengeance was wreaked on him by that Dionysian element which Kafka never succeeded in putting into words, the ignored emotion that never appeared directly in his writings.

The truth that Kafka seeks is a truth where the sound of emotion becomes words — in which the other uncovers her face, in which the fragments of the soul can finally be pieced together so that an identity can take shape.

Kafka's works are "a voice from out of chaos" (Magris 1974, pp. 220–222). The writer's life perhaps can be described as the attempt to delineate that chaos and the absurd, the opening of that abyss of nothingness that seems intent on swallowing the individual. Faced with this prospect, the only possible solution seems to be that of questioning. The passion for questioning that distinguishes all his characters — and which compels the dog (Kafka 1971) to refuse food, to look at it only to analyze and understand it — contains the dramatic metaphor of the inability to approach life directly, to let it flow inside oneself. The dog knows he is different from all other dogs, because from the very beginning something was not right in him. In this "scientific" fast of his, which does not seem to interest any of the other animals around him, there takes place the drama of abandonment which then, in truth, is revealed to be self-abandonment.

> For it was clear that nobody troubled about me, nobody beneath the earth, on it, or above it; I was dying of their indifference; they said indifferently: "He is dying," and it would actually come to pass. And did I not myself assent? Did I not say the same thing? Had I not wanted to be forsaken like this? . . . Perhaps the truth was not so very far off, and I not so forsaken, therefore, as I thought; or I may have been forsaken less by my fellows that by myself, in yielding and consenting to die. (Kafka, 1971, pp. 311–312)

"No one takes care of me" is a phrase I hear repeatedly from my patients and for which, in many cases, there is only one bitter reply: "No one takes care of others." The feeling of being abandoned does not arise from the lack of people around us, from the lack of a smile, of a face that wears an expression of interest in our lives. Abandonment is an *inner* thing, and one doesn't fight it by means of an incongruous search for solidarity. Just in order to get relief from this distressing situation, the dog / Kafka decides to take a different road. Abandonment calls up the idea of searching. In spite of getting no answers to his questions, the animal's actions indicate the search for freedom as the only answer to the suffering from exclusion and solitude. This freedom, which in Kafka's case seems to find its source in art alone, makes of art the attempt to redeem an otherwise failed existence. In the thousands of pages of his diary, of his letters, as well as of his novels and stories, the Czech writer puts a visage on his inner chaos, confronts it, seeks an inner unity for it. And if the only reality which seems to open up is that of the vacuum, of loneliness, of the impossibility of loving, and of exile as of privation, his activity becomes the testimony of the "implacable exegesis of existence" (Magris 1974, p. 222).

To read Kafka is to question oneself continually, to discover vacuums and fractures and, like him, to desire a universe that seems eternally inaccessible. One's choice of an author is never accidental. Any interest we feel for someone or something reveals a part of our soul that has been projected onto them. This is not the first time that I have become interested in the human and artistic itinerary of a creative personality whose works can open new horizons to readers. My university seminars, in which many of my books have originated, have focused on Apuleius, Pasolini, Nietzsche—and now Kafka. My first encounter with the Prague writer goes back to the reading of my youth. Like Dostoyevski, Kafka profoundly influenced my way of thinking. Through encounters with the characters in their works, I discovered parts of myself that until then were unknown to me. Within many of us there is a Franz Kafka, someone who fears and needs love, while with all his strength he searches for his horizons of truth.

Kafka is a disconcerting writer, a unique one, whose writing does not try to involve the reader by evoking feelings. His is a pure, limpid, essential prose, apparently cold and detached, that leaves little room for the troubles of the soul. There is always a subtle reasoning. His characters move through a labyrinth of reason while waiting to meet its monsters. The unknown daimon thus takes on a thousand shapes to surprise the unsuspecting protagonist. It is the mole's mysterious enemy (1923–1924) or the neighbor on the other side of the wall (1917a); it is Odradek; or it is the insect into which Gregor Samsa finds himself transformed (1912b), or yet again the endless hierarchy of judges and officials who populate *The Trial* and *The Castle* (1922b).

My attempt to reread in a psychological key two of Franz Kafka's major works comes almost thirty years after my first reading of these novels. Each time we approach anew a text that we have loved, that has taught us something about ourselves and others, our impressions are never quite the same as before. Everything that has happened to us in the meantime, that has helped to change our interior condition, also allows us to discern aspects and meanings in the work that we missed before. Each reading of a text is always a reinvention of it. Its new images are suggested by the new horizons of our souls, by those interior spaces that have been carved out by new experiences. If our horizons have been expanded and have touched unknown lands where new worlds exist, then there is now a new flavor to this work that had attracted our curiosity when we were young and had given at least a partial reply to our perhaps too confused questions. In reality, it has always spoken the language that only now seems to us so familiar and comprehensible.

Critics have probed Kafka's work from a variety of perspectives, from the theological one explored by Brod (1937) to the psychoanalytic approach of Kaiser (1931) and Neider (1948), or to the existential one of Camus (1942) and of Gide, who in 1945 made a famous adaptation of *The Trial* for the stage, to name only a few examples. But no one has ever managed to make a definitive interpretation that exhausted the text's possibilities. A work of art contains its own reality, its intrinsic validity, which cannot be grasped or circumscribed by any one theoretical approach. In the end, every interpretation is valid and legitimate because, quite apart from the key chosen to read it or perhaps just because of the methodological choice that the interpretation makes, it reveals itself to be the secret way of bringing an author close to one's inner world. In our reading of him we imagine, in terms of our own personal categories, the human and artistic adventure of one who we believe we can assimilate through our interpretation.

My approach to Kafka's writing is void of any intention to evaluate it artistically. What interests me is the psychological aspects that emerge from these pages, to bring to light the inner drama that, possibly without the author's knowing it, is hidden behind the story he narrates. The complicated plots of *The Trial* and *The Castle* gave me the occasion to reflect on a series of themes that had more or less directly occupied Kafka in his writings. Like Dostoyevski's prose,

Kafka's is also a continuous voyage, an exploration of the human soul. It is the lacerated dream world of the soul's interior, with its desires, fears, incapacities, and paralyses.

One can read the Prague writer, then, accompanied by the sufferings and hopes of many of my patients. Thus Kafka's solitude, his need of love as well as his incapacity to abandon himself to the other, to encounter the other in a relationship, become the solitude and the fears of us all. To be aware that each of us, like Josef K., is continuously tried and found guilty before an invisible court; or, like the land surveyor K., alone and excluded, in search of a castle that will never receive him — to be aware of all this may not, certainly, reduce the extent of Kafka's suffering, but at least it may give him the posthumous comfort of a connection with others that he was not able to see during his lifetime. I believe that the most moving and sincere recognition of the writer's profound humanity is to show how close are his pain and desperate search for the truth to that of many other men and women.

One

The Parable of the Arrest

Like almost all of Kafka's works, *The Trial* is a text which challenges the reader to understand it on a level that goes beyond the simple and immediate reading. If the Prague writer's problem was in some way to approach the *truth*, that *truth* which was hidden behind the real world, he well knew the impossibility of describing it. The *truth* changes into deceit just as soon as one tries to interpret it rationally, to put it into an objective framework. No approach remains except that of the symbolic parable, metaphor, legend. Kafka's extraordinarily concrete images — as Lukăcs notes (1955–1956 pp. 89–90) — are in fact abstractions, inasmuch as the writer's *hic et nunc* has an allegorical character. The particulars described continually refer us to an ineffable transcendental dimension to which they are the key. Due to the fact that, as Nietzsche says (1881, p. 40) "words block our path," the only possible language is that of metaphor, in which reality is codified and which attracts truth and captures it by a cabalistic process (Baioni 1962, p. 20).

All of Kafka's writing proceeds through the symbolic world of parable and metaphor, from the allusions of which his stories are woven to the opposite attempt to interpret truth, to imprison it in a perfect and rational form through the purity of its syntax. It is primarily the novels that take on this double perspective, fluctuating between the symbolic value on the one hand, and on the other their need to dissolve the symbol through its interpretation and clarification. Kafka's texts are often amplified by the vortex of interpretations and comment. The variations of many stories, rather than being deeper developments, are continuing efforts to capture truth and crystallize it in form. But the interpretation tends to submerge the text, annul it, become its substitute. From this point of view, Kafka's style approaches that of the cabala. In its apparent lack of fidelity, the narrative invention fixes truth in its paradoxical form exemplified by the parable. The interpretation, that continual eviscerating return to the text, reveals its infinite potentiality (Cacciari 1985, pp. 65–66). Truth is only to be found in the multiplicity of its facets, each of which alone cannot be other than obscure and enigmatic. Perhaps it is in this symbolic density, which challenges the reader to find a sense in it, to seize it from the vortex of questions and interrogation, that the fascination of Kafka's writing lies. But the presumption of a single, unequivocal interpretation is an illusion in which reason loses its way. And the "country man" becomes a victim of this deception.

Thus, what is written is not supposed to provide answers but to arouse uneasiness, to nestle deeply into the soul and to awake it from its unawareness. Kafka's books keep faith with the proposal to disquiet, to evoke daimons buried at the core of being, to arouse doubts and questions. They challenge the reader, they nail him to his guilt, compel him to question himself, because the obscurities of the text show the soul the shadows in which it is shrouded.

If, then, it is a parable we are examining, we see its shape. *The Trial* deals with a nameless guilt, an accusation that finds no absolution. Of all Kafka's works, this is the one most closely tied to the author's sense of death, of failure.

The Trial is the parable of a failure that cannot be made good. For many years, Kafka believed that suicide was the only way out — without ever finding the courage to take that extreme step (Kafka 1902–1924, pp. 203–4). Nevertheless, he uses it as a narrative solution in *The Judgment* (Kafka 1912a), where for Josef K. the inner bankruptcy becomes a sentence of death pitilessly carried out. The assessor is killed like a dog, with only the shame surviving him.

In Kafka's case, the ruthless punishment for his inability to live was represented by tuberculosis. With lucid awareness, at the first signs of illness, he wrote to Felice Bauer in a letter of September 30 – October 1, 1917:

> For secretly I don't believe this illness to be tuberculosis, at least not primarily tuberculosis, but rather a sign of my general bankruptcy. I had thought the war could last longer, but it can't. The blood issues not from the lung, but from a decisive stab delivered by one of the

combatants . . . I will never be well again. Simply because it is not the kind of tuberculosis that can be laid in a deck chair and nursed back to health, but a weapon that continues to be of supreme necessity as long as I remain alive. (Kafka 1912–1917, pp. 545–546)

The "trial" he narrates could thus be read as a *disease,* a particular interior condition rather than an intentional act. One almost has the impression of being confronted with a pathological condition of the psyche, the signs of whose progress slowly appear on the patient's face (Neumann 1933, p. 49). Like a hidden cancer progressing in silence until the irremediable devastation it has worked on the organism reveals itself in the symptoms, so too, many of Kafka's heroes waken from this guilty unawareness when it is already too late, when the metamorphosis has already been completed, in the case of the insect/ Gregor, or when the inexorable judicial machine has already started up, as happens to the assessor K. Their only hope of salvation would be in confessing their guilt, their betrayal of themselves and of life.

In his attempt to furnish a different reading of mental suffering, Binswanger (1956, p. 12) calls it a form of "unsuccess, of a failed human existence." Heidegger (1927, p. 33) spoke of the chances in life to realize its possibilities, to seize them or to miss them.

> Dasein always understands itself in terms of its existence — in terms of a possibility of itself: to be itself or not itself . . . Only the particular Dasein decides its existence, whether it does so by taking hold or by neglecting.

Following this concept, we note that life is not only projected in a horizontal direction, in a constantly broadening perspective but, by proceeding upwards, always risks losing its way and ending up in an unsuccessful life form (Binswanger 1956, p. 17). Josef K.'s drama is that of an inner going-astray, of missing out on his own life, which is translated into the idea of his arrest.

From the very first words, the reader is confronted with the eruption of the arrest into the life of the protagonist. A characteristic of Kafka's work is that there is never any preparation for the events. The writer fixes his gaze on them when they occur like a photographer who fixes the becoming of reality with a click of the shutter.

The equation, fictional character = author, is emphasized by the choice of name: Josef, like Franz, is composed of five letters. Reading the author's diaries, we discover that already in the case of *The Judgment* Kafka (1912a) was careful to reveal his identity by constructing this code name. The single initial K. of the last name for the assessor, as well as for the land surveyor K. in *The Castle*, further underscores this identity, which was partly conscious and partly unconscious. Furthermore Kafka habitually signed many of his letters with the single initial K.

In addition to such explicit intentions, each work is always, for the writer, an interior confession, the testimony of a suffering that one attempts to confront with the written word, as if the daimon could thus be placated (Carotenuto 1982b, *passim*). One of the characteristics of *The Trial* is its entire concentration on the person of Josef K. There is not a single episode in which he is not present, not a passage dedicated to talking about other characters. All the figures revolve around the protagonist, and only in relation to him do they receive an identity. Their role and their reality is defined exclusively in terms of their relation to K. This centripetal motion in the assessor's direction indicates that he alone is the center of all that happens, as if only his presence conferred reality on the external world. Clearly, we are referring to a *psychological reality* rather than an *objective reality* that continues to exist without us and has no need of us to give it a meaning.

What makes Kafka's fiction particularly dense and at times delirious is the relationship of the characters to the external world. Kafka's universe only exists insofar as it is filtered through the fantasy, the imaginary world of those who move and act in it. Fears and desires thus become so important and all-pervading as to go beyond the private sphere of dreams, fantasies, and even nightmares and enter into the collective sphere of daily life. *The Trial* is the realization of Kafka's anguish, the concrete representation of the death sentence that his court of justice had inexorably pronounced. It seems that all the reasonings Kafka carried on inside himself were the search for an absolution that could never be granted.

It seems that what Kafka desperately sought besides communion with other beings was for him, *the excluded*, the stranger, an acceptance that would annul his guilt and allow him to stop feeling like a filthy animal rolling around in the mud, the beast in the woods, as he will later write to Milena. But exactly this feeling of being a filthy beast is what gives us the clue to deciphering the mysterious guilt of which K. is accused. In some way it also encompasses his relationship to his instincts, his sexuality. His novels always have a turbid, corrupt atmosphere through which, nevertheless, glimmers a strange, incomprehensible innocence. The two K.'s will never manage to understand the candor with which the women offer themselves to the defendants, judges, and pillars of the community, just as certainly as the villagers will never forgive Amalia, who refused to abandon herself to Eros.

If this strange universe is surprisingly similar to the world of dreams, then we may be allowed to think that all its figures do nothing but act out the raving obsessions, desires and anxieties of their author. Not only that, but the same figures seem to live in a highly rarefied reality, deformed by their own projections. Nightmares and desire alter the outlines of the external world. The relations that Kafka's heroes have with the truth of reality is in some way like Plato's myth of the cave, with the difference that the prisoners in this case do not merely see shadows on the wall of the cave from which they deduce what exists outside. One has the impression that mirrors have been applied to the walls of the cave whose curved surfaces distort everything that they reflect (Heller 1974, p. 107). The individual that Kafka's character represents knows truth only by way of the deformations produced by her individual peculiarities, or more precisely, by the peculiarities of her fantasies.

The projection of one's fantasies onto reality in such a way as to modify, almost to distort its shape is a psychological phenomenon that is part of everyone's life. The reality we experience is always subjective, altered, reshaped by our imagination. Any specific event, for example, arouses different reactions in every person because each one interprets the facts according to personal experience. To be conscious of this psychological law, according to which there is nothing truly objective in our experience, undoubtedly constitutes psychological progress. It allows us to understand how inwardness models our perception of the world and how great a part is played in our way of feeling by both our hereditary substratum and the emotional complex that forms our personality.

Therefore, if one looks at the novel from a psychological standpoint that favors the reality of the soul, to use the title of a famous book of essays by Jung (1934–1957), we immediately note how all the characters, even the apparently secondary ones, are extremely important for understanding the protagonist's personality. In fact, we can read each figure as a projection of a part of his psyche, like a series of Josef K. doubles.

The action starts off with an upheaval, the loss of certainty. The initial psychic situation is constituted by the brusque rupture of the entire complex of habits, rituals, and all the reference points around which daily life is structured. It is a crisis in the world of certainties which until that moment had sustained the protagonist's life. Every morning, in fact, a ritual took place in Josef K.'s life: the arrival of his breakfast. But one morning, unexpectedly, this reassuring event fails to happen. Inasmuch as breakfast — milk — is symbolically connected with the mother figure, the first information the author unwittingly offers us is the need to do without a vital element. All of Kafka's writings, furthermore, insist on the equation food = emotional nourishment. Along with the food, the mother figure too is missing, represented by Frau Grubach. The mother and the sense of security appear to be connected, both of them expressing the possible fulfillment of a single need. Their absence leaves the man all on his own. He has lost that inner nucleus around which his identity is structured. With the mother = food equation gone, the external world too is overturned: all the rituals that K. had created to give himself stability and continuity disappear. Thus, that condition of abandonment is again presented that we find in all of Kafka's works — an abandonment that his writings perhaps represent the desperate attempt to exorcise.

Every morning Josef K. is in the habit of ringing a bell, but that day it is not the cook Anna who answers — she who, in psychological terms, we can consider Frau Grubach's more specifically nourishment-providing aspect. A man enters the room and asks: "Did you ring?" (Kafka 1914–1915a, p. 7). From this moment the trial begins. We may be permitted to think that it is the unconscious desire for change that solicits it. Here too, as in *The Castle,* awareness begins with a *call.* In everyone's life there is a moment when an apparently external event — but which in reality is determined by a complex unconscious psychic situation — impairs the flow of daily existence. It is interesting to note that the stranger appears dressed in "travel" garb. This small detail reveals what is about to happen. The unconscious desire for change takes the form of an *interior voyage.* Every time something impairs our lives, every time we meet difficulties that cause us to abandon our habitual routine, a *trip* offers itself as a solution; because to get up and go is the only response to the monotony of a routine existence. A trip as an opening up to the unknown, to change, constitutes the reopening of a dialogue with our inner being.

But Josef K. experiences this deviation as an intrusion. This is, in fact, the psychological experience that all of us can have the moment in which, suddenly, our existence becomes blocked: what happens appears to be a distinct and damaging attack on us. It is as if an entirely new element were violently introduced into our lives with the purpose of pushing it towards the conscious search for new experiences. It seems as if we had to confront the *ineluctability* of a trip inasmuch as events themselves compel us to start out without any apparent effort on our own part.

In order for the trip to begin, an *arrest* is necessary. K. is suddenly forced to come out of the torpor he is in — the gray monotony of a reality that is by now empty of all meaning because it is worn out by routine, by pretending, by inauthenticity — and he must exchange it for a completely different reality beginning with his arrest. In the very first sentence of the book, the word *arrest* comes up.

> Someone must have been telling lies about Joseph K., for without having done anything wrong he was arrested one fine morning. (Kafka 1914–1915a, p. 7)

We are not told the reason for his arrest, which alludes metaphorically to a condition of psychological arrest. The only indication given is the possibility of calumny. One might claim that the simple fact of living implies the possibility of injuring and being injured by calumny. No one can feel exempt from the double danger of the one and the other. In Act 3, Scene 1, Hamlet says to Ophelia: ". . . be thou chaste as ice, as pure as snow, thou shalt not escape calumny" (Shakespeare 1992, p. 62). In book VII of his *Histories*, Herodotus calls calumny a horrible guilt that dirties two guilty parties: those who speak it and those who listen to it. Although it is possible to offer various explanations for the need to calumniate, surely this treacherous act arises from the need to destroy the other in order to exorcise one's own inner destruction. Calumny is to bring ruin on someone else by drawing upon one's own inner ruin. Sometimes one is only conscious of having calumniated someone after having done so: it is something that comes from an inner need which we cannot oppose. Certainly, maturity will enable us to stop an instant before we express the calumnious impulse, but no psychological integration can keep us from feeling that impulse. However high the level of our integration and our ethical standards, there will always be a destructive dimension inside us that wants to come out. So we must endeavor to confront this negative aspect by ourselves and not resort to the mediation of the other, the victim of calumny. One can live with being calumniated because it is a proof of the value of the person calumnized. Our worth is always contained in our personal autonomy, in having understood something more than others, in being a step ahead of them so that we see a wider horizon. It is the horizon of a truth incomprehensible to those incapable of risking their lives, a truth that indubitably causes one suffering.

Since our analysis of *The Trial* is in an exclusively psychological key, it is well to emphasize that everything that happens within the novel will be considered as a complex of endopsychic events relating to the protagonist. And it is in this context that calumny must be interpreted. It arises from within the Kafkian character and can be understood as the *betrayal* of self that anyone can commit who finds himself in Josef K.'s position. If it is our destiny to go on a journey—a psychological journey which impels the "pilgrim" to seek goals that have always been coveted, to search out one's deepest individuality—to refuse to go on such a journey means to "calumniate" oneself, to underestimate one's psychological resources, to feel incapable of performing the task to which our existence is *called*. This is the true "calumny" that blocks us, "arrests" us. In this case not to want to proceed does not mean simply to stay in the same place; it means to be paralyzed. We calumniate ourselves the moment we consider ourselves to be failures, the moment we give up the fight for life and despair of any favorable outcome for ourselves. To become adult means to risk failure, to risk arrest. Only if we are ready to face this fear is there any hope for growth by abandoning the infantile illusion of a life without conflict, with never a hiatus nor a retreat.

It is our failures, our blocks rather than our successes or our indubitable progress that teach us something of real value about life and about ourselves. We can well consider the possibilities of failure and psychic paralysis as the measure of our inner strength. In his spiritual testament, Kipling says to his son:

> If you can meet with Triumph and Disaster
> And treat those two impostors just the same;
> Yours is the Earth and everything that's in it,
> And — which is more — you'll be a Man, my son!
> (Kipling 1989, p. 578)

At this point it is necessary to analyze the psychological condition that caused the *arrest*. To that end the description of how K. leads his life is extremely pertinent: a tissue of habits that crystallize his work, his human relationships, his affections. All habits are actually forms of sclerosis. It is as if one considered oneself a preprogrammed computer that can in no way be modified, as if one had entrusted one's life forever to an automatic pilot. Time in this case is not the theater of our actions, it is our actions *themselves*. We are regulated, conditioned by time while our ability to *choose*, to *transgress*, to *invent* ourselves atrophies day by day, moment by moment. And this very atrophy of being is precisely the malady that afflicts Josef K.

It is not by chance that he is described by his role, his public function rather than his personal qualities. We are told nothing about him other than that he is an assessor. In Jungian terminology we could call this image a persona, which is — in the original Latin sense of the word — a mask. The archetype of the persona signifies that part of the psyche which we offer to the outside world, that social status with which the individual identifies to a greater or lesser degree and to which she thus adjusts her behavior. Josef K. is above all a persona, the mask that he dons to have relations with others. In all his life he is nothing but a caricature of a true existence, of an authentic being in the world. His contacts with other people are without depth and lacking in all spontaneity. As a rule a great part of human suffering derives from the compulsion to have strictly formal relations with others governed by rules from which no departure is allowed. If the educational process often tends to turn us into human masks who correspond perfectly to the roles we must play, it is the task of our maturing process to succeed in breaking this identification, imposed by circumstances, and to make our human presence felt. One must be capable of exposing oneself, of revealing what one really is. But all exposure is painful because inasmuch as we abolish our defenses we become vulnerable to rejection and aggression by others. Preserving ourselves from that risk, however, and accepting ritualized relationships, we end by alienating ourselves still more. The fear and the impossibility of being liberated from the dimension of the mask, the persona, isolates us all; not trusting each other, we end by banishing any kind of human solidarity.

In my personal and professional experience I have been able to ascertain that relationships marked with mistrust are the most painful, useless, and sterile of all because they prohibit the creation of a true reciprocal symmetry. These are the relationships that leave us empty, exhausted; such relationships cannot in any way nourish our souls, and impoverish them terribly instead. Unfortunately, life circumstances often involve us in relationships full of suspicion, in which we are constantly on our guard, measuring ourselves against the other, looking on that person as an adversary, an enemy who might destroy us. This is an experience of mutual fear that blocks all spontaneity, all abandon. *Arrest* is the price we pay for such relationships when they become habitual. If we accept diffidence as an existential rule, if we let ourselves be nothing more than masks, "assessors," the moment will also come for us, as for Josef K., when a bell rings to announce our arrest: neurosis will come to block our lives.

The protagonist of the novel spends his days answering calls to see the director, sitting in beer halls, indulging in mercenary sexual relations—all symptoms of the sclerosis of his personality. The life of Kafka, with its fixed rhythms, regulated by work in the insurance company, the hours spent in writing, the few relationships with friends, the occasional encounters with prostitutes—all this was perfectly suited to becoming the skeleton on which to construct his literary *fiction*. We are in the presence of an almost archetypal way of life, that of a person who has decided to sell his liberty in order to survive. It is the archetype of a human being's negative existence. I have called this interior condition *frustration from nullity* (Carotenuto, 1982a, *passim*), by which is meant that neurotic condition which develops the moment we become conscious of the futility of our actions when we direct them exclusively at maintaining an anonymous form of survival.

Josef K. is a bank employee. The bank is the extreme consequence of a system based on the monetary quantification of things that have no value in themselves but only by virtue of their power of exchange. It is easy for those who live and work in such a context to become just another object, to feel like merchandise that can be bought and sold. To become an object means, above all, to lose one's power of choice, to enter into an impersonal dimension where one loses all responsibility. The organizational structure of the bureaucratic world into which K. is assimilated, works in a way to banish individual responsibility. The greatest danger here lies in making it impossible for the individual to learn anything from his life. To survive, many of us are obliged to do work that excludes all responsibility. These are activities which, even when engaged in for decades, do not allow for learning, because they do not admit of an investment of one's creativity and responsibility. And it is in such a situation that the individual sooner or later comes to ruin and is blocked. Such a betrayal of one's "destiny" takes on the form of an *arrest* of development, as opposed to the life of vital projects that ought to characterize human life. To those who find themselves mired in such quicksands and risk sinking into inner misery, the last resort is often the analyst's office, where she seeks to renew a blocked personality and return it to its original authenticity.

Thus to be *called* in front of a court, as is Josef K., means to be made answerable for the one "mortal sin," the one "guilt" with which an individual can be stained: the betrayal of oneself, of one's own destiny. The call to personal fulfilment is the strongest inner voice that each of us is ever given to hear; but the more intense it is, the greater will be the punishment for not replying. For Josef K. the punishment will be death.

Two

The Alienation of the Marionette

Josef K. is an apparently ordinary man whose life gives no evident signs of imbalances. But it is just this banality of his life, its apparent greyness, that hides an intense inner life. Like Dostoyevski's dreamers, those personages whose lives are entirely lived on a thread of the imagination, of the inner world, K. too seems to redeem the opacity of his daily life with the imaginary sphere that gradually unwinds itself before the reader's eyes. His blindness to the real world can be compared to those bards, poets, and soothsayers of ancient Greece, from Homer to Tiresias, for whom the inability to see was precisely what intensified their inner lives. Eyes forever immersed in darkness developed an inner vision that became the custodian of memory and of prophecy. But in the case of K., the blindness will have a tragic dimension because it will render him incapable of recognizing the *sense* of what happens. The way the protagonist continually mulls over things is lacking in true contact with the unconscious. K. never learns that it is impossible for him to escape the Court because it is inside of him: K. and K. alone is the implacable judge of himself. It will be this unawareness of his own inner split that will ruin his attempts to defend himself and condemn him to death.

The novel begins with a mysterious arrest that forces K. to awake from his torpor, from the repeated betrayal of his authenticity. In his placid existence as a bank official, something has been set in motion, something that unequivocally denotes the unconscious desire for *transformation*. The physical and psychological evolution of a human being is marked by the need for continual gratification from the outside world. Nevertheless, as long as his relationship with reality ends with this kind of fulfillment, the individual doesn't even know he exists; he is passively inserted in life like a river that runs placidly within its bed to the sea. Only when there is a hitch in this process does he begin to question himself and become self-aware.

So the ringing of the bell and the arrest can be compared with the appearance of a symptom, of a deep inner malaise, that in appearing demands a process of transformation. Pain and suffering, considered in Western culture as divine punishment for the guilty act, are transformed into the most potent means the unconscious has to make itself heard at last. Like Job, the "ill" individual is obliged to ask herself the reason for what happens, obliged to take stock of her life, to scrutinize it from every angle—apropos of this, there comes to mind the long statement for his defense that K. is supposed to present to the Court. Suffering does *research* on itself. One can do nothing but shift one's view from everything that belongs to the outside world and direct it at one's inner state.

This introversion is often challenged, wrongly understood. That slowing down of activity that can sometimes verge on paralysis, has been considered the symptom of a depression from which the individual should be relieved—immediately and by any means. One forgets, however, that in this way the soul has manifested its desire to collect itself in order to revitalize itself, like the earth that remains dormant for months under a covering of snow before the next flowering. The shift of attention from the outside to the inner world is confused with a flight from reality. This is a wrong and inept perspective that seems to ignore how outside and inside are connected to each other, and that suffering arises precisely from their lack of correspondence.

Generally speaking, in human life, as Jung often emphasized, it is in youth that the individual most intensely directs his energies outwards to obtain a place in the sun, to realize more specifically social objectives such as work and family. Once these objectives are reached, there emerge instead those values that we could call "introverted," which impel the person to give particular attention to her inner world, to ask herself who she really is and what she wants from life. It is possible that the intervention of one of those precocious fractures, which we call "neurosis" or "mental illness," will oblige the individual to undertake before hand, much sooner than the age of maturity, this *interior journey* in search of herself.

The fact that Josef K. will never discover the reasons for his arrest is testimony to the fact that the desire for transformation is in reality unconscious. In contrast to K. and to any ordinary person, the creative person is equipped with a particular vision that makes it possible to see things to which other people are blind. The sensitivity of creative people, their vulnerability to penetration by the unconscious, makes it possible for them through suffering to reach a deeper understanding of the world. In this sense we can say that artists are "fortunate," not because they are spared sorrow and pain, but because they are able to give pain a universal meaning. The ordinary person is obliged to experience daily life alone, often without being able to see the connections between personal experience and the experience of millions of other people. The moment in which I, as an analyst, open a wider horizon to my patient, making his experience of life universal, I accomplish a task similar to that of the artist: in that way therapy becomes *art*. The language of myth—with which it is possible to decipher dream images, for example, overcoming their strictly individual character and inserting them into an infinitely wider context that involves all humanity—permits the expression of the archetypal basis of the psyche, the original matrix on which every artist draws.

It is noteworthy how, at the beginning of an analysis, or at particularly crucial moments, the psyche responds by drawing on an age-old wisdom. The images produced in these cases seem to come from very far off in time and have a particularly high charge of numinosity that fascinates and frightens the dreamer. The model of the *journey*, of the *path*, is one of the most common. It is usually manifested by the image of an unknown path that must be followed. Thus the psyche allows us to have an experience that belongs to humanity's past and that will also be part of our future. The famous aphorism of Terence (1986, p. 346) "Homo sum: umanum nihil a me alienum puto" (I am a man, and I consider that nothing which regards men is extraneous to me) means just exactly that what is specifically human belongs to each individual, so that the experience of others is also my own.

The unmotivated arrest of Josef K. is connected to those moments when we do not manage to understand the reasons for the suffering that grips us. These remain obscure, shrouded in mystery, not because we are not able to see them, but because it is hard to find an exhaustive rational explanation for what happens to us in life. In *Le hasard et la nécessité* of Jacques Monod, the author describes a view of life wherein a casual event turns into a necessity in the very moment in which it occurs, thus causing many consequences. To this view, which presupposes a basic lack of meaning, it is necessary to add the *search* and *understanding* of *meaning*.

Not knowing why he has been arrested throws Josef K. into that dimension of the *absurd* which is so characteristic of Kafka's writing. The absence of meaning is a highly critical experience that undermines the very roots of existence. The human being cannot survive in a dimension that lacks comprehensible connections, in which events escape all attempts at interpretation. Nevertheless, the very contradictory nature of this world in which the individual lives becomes the first cause of her searching. If truth remains unattainable, if there are as many truths as there are individuals, then each one is forced to find his own. In this search for truth, art has a role that nothing else can replace.

But the search on which the human being is forced to spend all her strength never ends with an acquisition, a final possession. She is inevitably excluded from the horizons of truth, like the country man who never succeeds in entering the edifice of the law, or like that last subject of the infinite Chinese empire who will never receive his emperor's message. And yet that search involves an entire existence, becomes its one reason for being, and ends by consuming all other activities and interests. We should not forget that the attempt to find in some way an answer absorbed Kafka so deeply that he became entirely incapable of living a normal life. We may be allowed to think that it was the misunderstanding of the goal that blocked Kafka's love life, for example. "We must not shake loose from ourselves, but consume ourselves" Kafka wrote in January 1918 (Kafka, 1954, p. 375). Kafka, in fact, ended by destroying himself like a torch that consumes itself in giving light. He had to lift the world up towards truth, purity; and this superhuman effort could leave no energy for anything else.

During the time that Kafka was writing *The Trial*, he was passing through a particularly delicate period of his life. His tormented engagement with Felice — which he felt obliged to renounce in order to remain "faithful" to literature, but more precisely because he was unable to share his life with a woman — forced Kafka to take stock of himself, to work out his need of authenticity. In a similar way, the hero of his novel finds himself pushed out of his tranquil way of life in which every moment is planned and there doesn't seem to be room for any surprises. Having to defend himself against an unspecified accusation impels him to examine his life. Up until that moment doubts and uncertainties hardly existed for Josef K. The ironclad daily routine was supposed to ward off all risks. But precisely when everything appeared to be decided and life did not seem able to diverge from the path it had been set on, the inner call breaks out in all its force and manifests itself externally in the form of an arrest. This unexpected occurrence forces him to look for a new meaning in his life, puts him directly in need of an *interpretation.*

We all know that events do not contain their meanings within themselves, do not explicate themselves, but present themselves to us as texts to be deciphered. The truth hidden within events has need of human participation, someone to experience them, in order to be revealed. Only at the moment that someone makes it his own by living it does it acquire a meaning. A truth is only real if it penetrates to the core of existence. Thus the pain of the loss of a dear one remains a distant event for us—one whose truth, whose deep meaning escapes us until it hits us directly. To hear of such an occurrence, to experience it indirectly from the mouth of a friend does not allow us to understand its psychological import at all.

Every experience is in itself enigmatic, and it is up to us to give it a meaning, to define its contours on the basis of our personal history, our humanity. Each fact is "unique" because each individual is inimitable. That is why the deepest experiences are incommunicable: the truth that one has lived through, painfully experienced and understood, is for the most part untranslatable for others. In these cases silence is the only alternative, the only possible choice, because in reality each word only betrays the truth of our experience. Thus writing in these cases becomes the only way of facing our inner truth by speaking to a secret confidant. The long statement of Dostoyevski's underground man (Dostoyevski 1864) seems to pursue this aim.

> In every man's memory there are things which he does not divulge to everyone, but really only to friends. And there are those things which he doesn't even divulge to friends, but really only to himself, and then as a secret. And, finally, there are those things which a man is afraid to

divulge even to himself, and every respectable person has accumulated quite a few of these. One might even say: the more respectable the person, the more of these he has. At any rate, not long ago I myself decided to recall various of my former adventures, which up until then I had always shirked, indeed rather nervously. Now, however, that I have not only resolved to remember them but even to note them down, I really do wish to discover: is it really possible to be absolutely open with oneself and not be frightened of the whole truth? (Dostyoevski 1864, pp. 38–39)

The truth that Dostoyevski's personage proposes to us is a truth that, by destroying illusions, blinds and stuns us, a truth that it seems cannot be contemplated for long and that can only be sought in solitude. The many levels on which it presents itself to human view make such a truth eternally enigmatic and fleeting, thus impeding any possibility that, once it has been seized and known, it can be communicated to others. This creates a certain estrangement which alienates an individual from her peers. One might simplify the problem by maintaining that on the one hand there is an individual's truth and on the other the collective truth; on one side the subject and on the other the rest of the world. Kafka always presents us with these two worlds as opposites. The individual can never identify himself on the collective level; he can only let it direct his movements like a puppet.

Each of these worlds has its own particular rules and code. In the novel, in fact, we see how K.'s language, his truth, is completely different from that of the other characters.

But the estrangement of the individual does not only occur with regard to the outside world, it also and primarily regards her alienation from her own inner truth. Unawareness of oneself reduces one to the level of a marionette, maneuvered by unknown inner contents and factors. In a brief note in his diaries of October 28, 1911, Kafka (1910–1923, p. 94) describes the image of human marionettes maneuvered by a mysterious puppeteer:

Sometimes it seems that the play is resting up in the flies, the actors have drawn down strips of it the ends of which they hold in their hands or have wound about their bodies for the play, and that only now and then a strip that is difficult to release carries an actor, to the terror of the audience, up in the air.

It is the situation that Ingmar Bergman describes in *A World of Marionettes* (1980). Peter, the hero, son of a hyperprotective mother who is married to an important couturier, ends by letting off all his aggressivity towards females by strangling a prostitute and sodomizing her post mortem. The structure of the plot shows how all the characters are nothing other than puppets. None of them seems to be the arbiter of his or her own destiny. Their direction instead is determined by obscure and unrelated unconscious motives. Their alienation from their true selves—a favorite theme of Bergman's—turns them into empty puppets.

As in Bergman's film, in Kafka's novel too, the characters, alienated from themselves, seem lost in a labyrinth of incomprehensible signs. Kafka's man is as if impaled, crucified on a spiral, a forest of signs that swirl menacingly around him, squeezing him in their inexorable grip (Fusini 1988, p. 63).

The problem of Kafka's heroes is one of finding a code. They never succeed in finding the right code for communicating with the Other, the outside world. Without this possibility of dialogue, everything becomes obscure. The question eternally remains what it was, reflecting itself as if in a house of mirrors. Kafka's world is a world without answers, where the Other continually keeps silent. The incomprehensibility of reality keeps returning him to an inner condition that constantly impresses itself on daily life to the point of distorting its shape.

Analogously, in the world of the psychotic, as Jung well knew, the signs by which one expresses oneself are apparently contradictory and enigmatic. The therapist's job is to decipher the hidden meaning, to dissolve the apparent incongruity, to break the code. This problem is characteristic not only of pathological conditions of the psyche; we all are obliged daily to confront the signs that reality presents to us. Behind the words there is often a hidden meaning that a glance, an expression of the face, can reveal. Notwithstanding the fact that our world of communication seems clearly traced out, there is always an indecipherable margin, a margin of mystery that has to do with the subjectivity of the one who is using the code. Perhaps for this very reason, in the experiences that involve us, such as love, we put more effort into throwing light on the enigma that the other, with her presence, represents for us. Every statement presents us with a puzzle of true and *false* that we can only solve by discovering the key to the interior world of the person we have before us. But if the tie with reality and the Other seems unthinkable, impossible, because there are no bridges, or if there are, they seem to collapse mysteriously as soon as one tries to cross them—as happens to Kafka and his characters—the enigma is destined to remain unsolved.

Three

Guilt and Questioning

The problem of guilt plays a central role in Kafka's works. All the writer's stories and novels are attempts to work out the question of an unknown guilt, a sin with which the subject has unknowingly stained himself like the ingenuous Karl Rossman in *Amerika* (Kafka 1912–1914), forced to leave home because he was seduced by a chambermaid. Already in the first works, such as *The Judgment* (Kafka 1912a), the reader is introduced into this world of unknown guilt, witnessing dismay at the ineluctability of the sentence, which in some cases is carried out with extreme ferociousness. Death may come rapidly as in the case of George Bendemann or Josef K., or it may on the contrary follow on a long torment as happens *In The Penal Colony* (Kafka 1914). But in any case the failing and the crime remain obscure. Their gravity plunges the subject into a deeply abject state, reducing him even to the level of an insect. In *Metamorphosis* (Kafka 1912b), in fact, secret guilt not only upsets the hero's existence but actually alters its physical form, turning him into a filthy insect. In reading Kafka's letters and diaries we get the same disturbing sensation of unworthiness, the same rejection of oneself that goes to the lengths of feeling oneself to be the most disgusting of animals. The illness of which the author writes ends by being the ontological condition par excellence.

The omnipresence of guilt, its invasion of all aspects of existence, like a cancer, is what denies Kafka's characters any kind of redemption at all. Some of the great guilt-laden characters presented by Tolstoy and Dostoyevski find the possibility of expiation in prison or Siberia. Only afterwards will come rebirth, "resurrection." But in Kafka's world, punishment for the crime committed does not lead to any transformation. As blind as the mole of one of Kafka's stories (Kafka 1923–1924), they wander through a labyrinth of many entrances but find no exits. Although the name of the crime is cut into their flesh amidst inexpressible torments (Kafka 1914), they still remain unaware. But unawareness does not spare them inner torment.

The continual mulling over the accusations made against them is not only a characteristic of Kafka's personages; Dostoyevski's underground man is also lacerated by nameless guilt:

> And the important thing is that whichever way you look at it it's always the case that I'm the first to be blamed for everything and, what is most hurtful of all, that I'm guilty without guilt, but according to the laws of nature, as they say. (Dostoyevski 1864, p. 12)

The illness of which he speaks at the beginning of his long monologue is identified with guilt, and both are nothing but tragic manifestations of conscience. This is the reason for the inexorable spreading out of angst that attacks and destroys him. This unbearable condition is what the underground man has in common with Kafka's characters.

In a note of March 16, 1922, Kafka confesses: "The attacks, my fear, rats that tear at me and whom my eyes multiply" (Kafka 1910–1923, p. 417). Guilt seems to grow huge beyond measure while an invisible enemy on the other side of the wall (Kafka 1917a) works against the protagonist, implacably repeating the death sentence with his silent presence. But what perhaps surprises the reader most is the disquieting attraction that guilt holds. The condition of being a defendant seems to have a fascination, as Leni will say, falling in love with each of them and abandoning herself to their mysterious beauty. Within the world of Kafka, falling in love with guilt takes on particular connotations which, while they smack of a religious view of life, as in Dostoyevski's case, are yet heading for a radically different outcome. In Sonya's love for Raskolnikov (Dostoyevski 1866) or in Alyosha Karamazov's solicitude for his brother Dimitri (Dostoyevski 1879–1880) we still find traces of a Christian religiosity that provides saintliness and purity to deal with guilt and degradation, to be attracted to them in order to redeem them.

A similar aspect filters slowly into the world of Kafka from mystic Hasidic sources. The Jewish Zaddikim of whom Buber tells us — and who attracted the young Kafka's interest to the point of his attempting to encounter one of them — are the heralds of a spirituality in which innocence and guilt are reintegrated, in which good and evil remain in any case manifestations of divinity. This reconciliation in which guilt is overcome because it is accepted as part of human nature, of its weakness, is missing in Kafka. His characters only bear witness to the nostalgia for a condition that they can never attain. The inner guilt which they attribute to themselves forms a closed circle, a universe that excludes any transformation. One loves one's guilt not because one accepts it, but because it allows one to justify one's way of being. With great acumen, Baioni (1962, p. 148) has noted how K.'s guilt pertains to his rupture with earthliness, with his stubborn will to avoid sinning. It is the refusal of this finite condition, the headstrong pursuit of absolute purity that imprisons Kafka's characters in their guilt and condemns them without appeal. Kafka's characters are in some way responsible for this rupture with reality. From this point of view, the "first guilty hero," the "first victim of the world's metaphysical conspiracy" (Baioni 1962, p. 33) is that supplicant we find in the "Description of a Struggle" (Kafka 1971). "The Supplicant's Story," which we find inserted in this work, is one of the earliest stories of Kafka's literary production. It contains a highly revealing dialogue:

> If there is a connection, I don't understand it. But I don't even know if there is a connection . . . How would it be if in return I were to tell you that one day everyone wanting to live will look like me — cut out of tissue paper, like silhouettes, as you pointed out — and when they walk they will be heard to rustle? Not that they will be any different from what they are now, but that is what they will look like . . . What is it that makes you all behave as though you were real? Are you trying to make me believe I'm unreal, standing here absurdly on the green pavement? You, sky, surely it's a long time since you've been real, and as for you, Ringplatz, you never have been real. (Kafka 1904–1905, pp. 38–40)

Guilt then is marked along the lines of shattered inwardness, of the impossibility of stable perception of reality. Guilt then is precisely one's "illness," the unease that slowly devours the soul.

In analysis the sense of guilt is an extremely useful clue for interpreting not only behavior, but the psychic dynamics that underlie it. It is no accident that Melanie Klein considered creativity to be the need to make reparations for the guilt of having attacked and destroyed one's inner objects. The guilt seems to become a source of energy that furthers the growth of the individual, even if at times in an unconscious manner. Feeling guilty for the mere fact of existing, oppressed by our failings, we rarely notice that a large part of our behavior is determined by an obscure sense of inadequacy for life, as Adler had realized.

Within many people's psychic structure an implacable superego is at work that forces them to compare themselves constantly with an unattainable model, with an ideal that they will never be able to resemble. The results can be different according to the individual case. It is possible that the presence of this inner image will be a spur to live life constructively. One tries to redeem one's sense of guilt for one's inadequacy by being active: the mind and the creative act permit the making of reparations. Or else this image can turn into a ruthless persecutor that produces paralysis: since no action can be up to the level of the unconscious ideal, paralysis seems to be the only solution since it avoids the comparison. Thus one remains nailed to one's destiny, crushed by the ineluctable guilt of being what one is and not what one ought to be. In this critical situation the analyst's office often becomes the place where the sense of guilt is reduced and the tension that oppresses the subject is relieved.

The problem of much psychotherapy, however, is that it deals with the sense of guilt by using an exclusively reductive approach that leads back to the event that originally produced it. This is the strategy of classical psychoanalysis. Discovering the origin of the sense of guilt is only one of the methods for dealing with it—and perhaps not the most effective. Rather than go to the root of the problem, uncovering memories lost to consciousness, the sufferer needs to face the sense of guilt, and above all, for the first time, face the law and its transgression in an adult way. The moment when the individual recognizes that she is the maker of her code of ethics, she can experience her sense of guilt in a different manner. In this case the guilt is no longer like disobedience to an external authority, but it takes on the meaning only of *the betrayal of oneself*, of one's *authenticity*.

Clearly, all of those figures in our past that have been so potently invested by the unconscious—to the point of being experienced as the incontestable judges of our comportment—in this way lose the numinous halo with which we have surrounded them. They are also deprived of their character as persecutors, and this makes reconciliation possible. In an individual crushed by the superego, the relationship with parent figures often is more or less consciously hate-filled. It is the parents who, in the process of educating, control the rise of guilt feelings. The lack of comprehension, the rigidity of the behavioral norms end by deeply wounding the child, who feels guilty and bad every time he tries to give heed to himself, to personal needs, rather than to the family's expectations. In those families where what counts is not the authenticity of and respect for the child's personality, but its adaptation to a model of behavior parents consider correct, the price the child pays besides estrangement and the creation of a false self is the birth of a devastating sense of guilt that undermines all sense of security, all inner stability—as happened to Kafka. When put into so ruthless a situation of being judged, one is always and ever guilty. The child absolutely cannot accept the idea that a parent can be unjust, and in the attempt to salvage that image on which she emotionally depends, makes herself responsible for every evil. Any cruelty of which her parents consciously or unconsciously make her the target is understood and defended by the child, not only before the outside world, but in her own judgment as well. The child prefers to take on the onus of interior isolation and a split in her sentiments rather than betray and judge her parents.

Once she is grown up she is often unable to recognize the traumas that marked her infancy. This is the reason why people who were mistreated as children often become fathers and mothers who in turn mistreat their children. The roles of victim and aggressor remain separated in the depths of the unconscious, so that the erstwhile little victim can discharge his painful past by identifying with the aggressor and acting out this psychic role. This vicious circle can only be broken when one begins to read one's own past in a different way. The moment in which one ceases to fight desperately against one's own sense of guilt, one no longer needs to discharge it onto defenseless creatures like little children. Only where such work of reconciliation can be done is it possible to offer one's children a different way of life, a different way of confronting themselves and the world (Miller 1980, *passim*). Treating children with that respect and that tolerance that used to be shown to one's parents means to lay the foundations for a better life (Miller 1980, p. 128). In this process of reappropriating one's childhood, it is important to uncover its anger and pain again. It is necessary to pass through a phase where the parent figure is experienced as negative in order to come close again to one's own feelings. To recognize the wounds one has received is a first step toward real understanding, for being able to *forgive* and to finally close the books on a past that has been secretly poisoning our lives.

From this point of view, the letter Kafka wrote to his father in 1919, without ever finding the courage to give it to him, is an important attempt to reconsider their difficult relationship. Significantly, the writer follows a series of accusations with a possible reply by his father, dictated by that same need to justify his parent's behavior that he had felt as a child.

To pass from an infantile to an adult condition means to throw off that authoritarian image that has been introduced, that awful *daimon* whose power overwhelms one, and to find within oneself the ability to establish an ethical code suitable to one's own way of being. Opposition to the parent or to his substitute thus becomes a necessary step in one's mental growth. Apropos of this, a dream of Kafka's dating back to April 19, 1916 (1910–1923, pp. 356) is of particular significance.

> A short time ago this dream: We were living on the Graben near the Café Continental. A regiment turned in from Herrengasse on its way to the railway station. My father: 'That's something to look at as long as one can'; he swings himself up on the sill (in Felix's brown bathrobe, the figure in the dream was a mixture of the two) and with outstretched arms sprawls outside on the broad, sharply sloping window ledge. I catch hold of him by the two little loops through which the cord of his bathrobe passes. Maliciously, he leans even farther out, I exert all my strength to hold him. I think how good it would be if I could fasten my feet by ropes to something solid so that my father could not pull me out. But to do that I should have to let go of my father, at least for a short time, and that's impossible. Sleep — my sleep, especially — cannot withstand all this tension and I wake up.

This dream image shows how impossible it was for the writer to detach himself from the father figure. He is forced to keep alive in himself the image that threatens to destroy him. The price he had to pay, besides the unbearable tension, was also a lack of roots in life. His inability to be an adult and a father has its source in his inability to make the necessary break with the father figure. On the contrary, Kafka seems to nourish with his very life the vampirelike image of his father that absorbs all his energy. So omnipotent and terrible a presence, with such crushing authority that generates a paralyzing sense of guilt, blocks the natural process of creating an antithesis that in adolescence generally allows for a differentiation from the father figure. In contrast to the child who needs understanding from the adult, it is important for the adolescent to have figures who will help her "fight" to the end to affirm her individuality. All those who put obstacles in her path, far from being her enemies, become the instruments of her psychological maturing. By transgressing she learns to form a relationship with guilt. What appears most important in this phase is not to demonstrate innocence, thus warding off guilt feelings, but rather the capacity to accept responsibility for one's own actions.

Analyzing Franz Kafka's dreams and comparing them with a sampling of five hundred dreams of one hundred youths between eighteen and twenty-five years of age, Hall and Lind (1970, p. 29) have shown how guilt feelings in Kafka do not appear in greater measure than in the other subjects examined, whereas they are reiterated constantly on the conscious level in his letters and diaries. More than actual feelings of guilt, shame and anxiety appear in Kafka's dreams. In only one dream of October 20, 1921 is there a specific reference to guilt.

> My brother had committed a crime, a murder, I think, I and other people were involved in the crime; punishment, solution, and salvation approached from afar, loomed up powerfully, many signs indicated their ineluctable approach; my sister, I think, kept calling out these signs as they appeared and I kept greeting them with insane exclamations, my insanity increased as they drew nearer . . . I could only have uttered brief exclamations because of the great effort it cost me to speak—I had to puff out my cheeks and at the same time contort my mouth as if I had a toothache before I could bring a word out. My feeling of happiness lay in the fact that I welcomed so freely, with such conviction and such joy, the punishment that came, a sight

that must have moved the gods, and I felt the gods' emotion almost to the point of tears. (Kafka 1910–1923, pp. 394–395)

The dreams of Kafka that have come down to us are only a small part. We do not know why he noted these rather than others, nor why he almost never stopped and tried to analyze them, although it is well known how little sympathy he had for psychology and psychoanalysis. The sensation that this dream arouses in us is the split in the protagonist. The crime is not committed by the dreamer himself, but by his brother. In that way one can partially avoid the responsibility for the crime by attributing it to the brother-Shadow. The fact, however, that he feels implicated, testifies to a vague sense of guilt for what happened. Then too, Kafka's attitude in the dream is no different from that of Josef K. who, in fact, will never feel responsible. His attitude to the Court will always be distinguished by a series of attempts to deny his guilt and reject the trial against him. Chastisement and redemption in the dream seem to be almost one and the same thing. To undergo punishment seems to be the one way to become liberated, as happens to the hero of *The Judgment* (Kafka 1912a). And yet Kafka can only confront this situation with inarticulate sounds, with crazy exclamations. The word, that word that is born of emotion and gives it expression, develops it, remains denied to him. His is always a *mute emotion.*

As commonly accepted, the concept of guilt is connected with the nonobservation of an explicit norm that the community respects. But in *The Trial* this perspective is turned around. K. is incriminated for breaking a law that is unknown. As the official of the penal colony (Kafka 1914, p. 145) will explain to the visitor: "My guiding principle is this: Guilt is never to be doubted."

In the eyes of the Court as well, guilt is indubitable inasmuch as it does not regard a single sin but is an existential condition. With a psychological intuition that makes this novel unique, Kafka transfers the reading of the guilt onto a plane that surpasses the concrete universe of the characters. In the Christian tradition, the human being is born stained with original sin. On his arrival in the world he carries with him the tragic sign of his separation from God, the sign of ancient disobedience when the first man and the first woman claimed the right to distinguish for themselves between good and evil. The original sin is witness to a fracture and an abandonment, after which the individual must construct her own existence.

The dimension in which Josef K. finds himself immersed is ambiguous in that the signs call up various possible meanings. In a world where the principle of noncontradiction has gone by the board, the logical coherence of an Aristotle has no value. Everything seems to affirm and deny itself at the same time. A is both A and not-A. The writer, with his disturbing personages, delineates a dramatic crisis of certainty that marks the Zeitgeist of the late nineteenth century.

The Court with its thousand faces reminds us of the truth in Pirandello's *Così è (se vi pare)* [*That's How It Is (If You Think So)*] (1916), where a veiled woman appears at the end of the play and the other people try to discover if she is the second wife of Signor Ponza or the first wife, daughter of Signora Frola. She tells them that she is no one in herself and only whoever they think she is.

In the same way there is, in Kafka's world, no clue, no behavior that can indicate an unequivocal truth. We could call it the *Odradek effect*. Odradek (Kafka 1971) is a strange and indefinable creature without a fixed residence. In Czech his name means "apostate." This creature, who inhabits attics, stairways, corridors, hallways, and altogether all those places of passage where his ambiguous nature finds its natural habitat, is the one to represent all the alienation and diversity that torment Kafka's characters, beings who are as indeterminate and fleeting as the world in which they live.

> At first glance it looks like a flat star-shaped spool for thread, and indeed it does seem to have thread wound upon it; to be sure, they are only old, broken-off bits of thread, knotted and tangled together, of the most varied sorts and colors. But it is not only a spool, for a small wooden crossbar sticks out of the middle of the star, and another small rod is joined to that at a right angle. By means of this latter rod on one side and one of the points of the star on the other, the whole thing can stand upright as if on two legs.
>
> One is tempted to believe that the creature once had some sort of intelligible shape and is now only a broken-down remnant. Yet this does not seem to be the case; at least there is no sign of it; nowhere is there an unfinished or unbroken surface to suggest anything of the kind; the whole thing looks senseless enough, but in its own way

perfectly finished. In any case, closer scrutiny is impossible, since Odradek is extraordinarily nimble and can never be laid hold of (Kafka 1971, p. 428).

The contradictions of Odradek are contained in this apparently rational structure from which, however, all sense has suddenly fled, disappeared. This existence on the borderline between sanity and fracture is what produces its fascination. It has a strange integrity that challenges us to discover its meaning. Odradek is the enigma that demands a solution, the eternal question that elicits an answer. But Kafka is not Oedipus. He doesn't know how to win out over the Sphinx-Odradek by solving its arcane question. Thus the power of the Odradek effect contaminates his whole life, leaving him in an absurd and contradictory sphere.

To sink into a swamp of contradiction where reason cannot guide the individual means to be deprived suddenly of the only instrument that tempts one to reply to the question of existence. It is not a question that is the same for everyone, but a specific query that every life seems to find inscribed on it as it unrolls. That particular "destiny," that "cross" which in the Christian view everyone carries or — to use Kierkegaard's metaphor (1849–1855) — that "spur," that "thorn in the flesh" that the Danish philosopher, like St. Paul, admits to having felt all his life, is for every individual a *punctum dolens* that forces one to look for a solution, an answer, to undertake the great journey into one's interior, into the depths of the soul. In psychological terms one could say that everyone is obliged to carry his own "cross" and confront a particular problem whose purpose, above and beyond the suffering it causes, seems to be that of opening up new horizons, of revealing to us who we are. It is not in its goal that this journey finds its justification and answer, but in itself. Inscribed on the temple of Apollo in Delphi are the words *gnothi sauton*, know thyself, and what they seem to open wide is the *itinerant conscience*.

For the creator of a metapsychology, working out a theory is in reality an attempt to find an answer to that essential question that her life presents her with (Carotenuto 1982b, *passim*). This reality does not seem to affect only psychologists and psychoanalysts, but any scholar who feels the obligation to reply to the mysteries of life and of the universe with a personal conception. In many of these cases the thorn has penetrated the person's flesh so deeply that it is not only impossible to extract, it is even impossible to get near it. The question has such deep and painful values that in order to give a reply one must theorize on the problem in a more general way: a direct formulation would be too overwhelming and might threaten to unhinge the mental equilibrium of the questioner. Just as the presence of a black hole cannot be directly observed without recourse to the gravitational field of this enormous and compact mass of matter (since it swallows all light rays), so too it is not possible to distinguish clearly the problem of someone who has formulated a theory; one can only sense its presence. A pansexual theory, for example, would seem to indicate an inner conflict connected to sex, of such proportions that the only way of making contact with it and confronting it is by elaborating a metapsychology.

The answers to any problem are almost infinite. Which perhaps explains the creation of new theories and their revision that marks the creative itinerary of many scholars. Every formulation represents, as it were, an approach to the goal, to the answer, to the truth.

Faced with an unknown law, Josef K. is alarmed and tries to defeat the unknown by using logic. But in the end, like the country man, he is disconcerted and blocked. He sees the light coming through the door of the Law, but the guard keeps him from entering. To K.'s attempts to understand that strange story, the priest will reply:

> The scriptures are unalterable and the comments often enough merely express the commentator's bewilderment. (Kafka 1914–1915a, p. 240)

K.'s guilt is that of surrendering to the mystery, of not knowing other approaches to it than that of rationality. Thus we can interpret his death as the impossibility of finding a *creative solution* to the question of existence.

Four

The Night of the Soul

Josef K.'s first encounter with the world of the Court is by way of the two guards who come to arrest him. Analogously, the land surveyor in *The Castle* is immediately flanked by Artur and Jeremias, the two envoys sent to him from the Castle. This kind of doubling of characters seems to repeat itself quite frequently in the work of Kafka. In *Amerika* (Kafka 1912–1914), for example, we find Robinson and Delemarche, while in *Blumfeld, an Elderly Bachelor* (Kafka 1915) two messengers appear. If we consider all these characters as Shadow figures, we could maintain that because this level is so conflict-ridden it becomes fragmented by the duplication of the figures who represent it. The identity relationship of Kafka with the two guards is underlined by the name he chose for one of them—Franz. His relationship with the Court and the Castle is endopsychic: they are parts of himself that the protagonist encounters. The confrontation takes place with an inner factor, now judgmental—as in the case of *The Trial*—now eternally rejecting, as in Kafka's last novel (Kafka 1922b).

Within Kafka's soul judges and guards infinitely repeated the accusation of guilt. Many of the letters written to Felice Bauer are dominated by an obsessive sense of guilt and unworthiness towards her, his fiancee. Any slightest detail he experienced as an unequivocal sign of his guilt. Writing and asking for replies—manifesting an insatiable lust for words—and more words that could reassure him of her affection—Kafka was convinced that he inflicted an unbearable torment on her. It got to the point where he felt responsible for her headaches, her tiredness, her agitation. And his way of loving almost resembled an obsession, a devastating disease that undermines the health of both body and soul. In a letter of November 21, 1912, about two months after their first meeting, he was already consumed by this "poison":

> But try to understand my concern for you, my terrible impatience, the torment of the one and only thought in my head, my incapacity to deal with any unrelated matter; life in the office with my eyes permanently on the door; in bed, in my mind's eye the intolerable thoughts, the sleepwalking, and the apathetic stumbling about in the streets; my heart no longer beats but is a tugging muscle, the near collapse of my writing—try to understand all this, and don't be angry (Kafka 1912–1917, pp. 51–52).

What is unbearable about human ties is that they sharpen one's sense of unworthiness, of inadequacy, sharpen the feeling of guilt for not being like everybody else, the guilt of one's *differentness*. Shortly before killing himself on March 23, 1950, Cesare Pavese noted in his diary (1952, p. 357):

> One doesn't kill oneself for love of one woman. One kills oneself because a love, any love at all, reveals us in all our nudity, misery, helplessness, nothingness.

Felice and the dream of a tranquil bourgeois existence that she seemed to represent, aroused the pitiless judge inside Kafka. Commenting on Kafka's illness, Haymann (1981, pp. 277–78) justly observes that if the tuberculosis germs were present because of a "self-destructive ovulation," they were only fertilized by the "Other," the "Judge."

The first chapters of *The Trial* are particularly rich in significant allusions. If the guards who come to arrest Josef K. seem to be an emanation of that dark night of the soul in which he is unconsciously sunk, the objects that the writer puts into the scene must serve to put this dimension into relief. It is not by accident, therefore, that the inspector, as he interrogates K., continually moves the candle and the matches that he finds on his night table. This underscores the polarity of light and shadow that surrounds the novel. The inspector even stops to count the number of matches that are in the box. Inasmuch as we have read *The Trial* in terms of an opportunity offered to the hero on his thirtieth birthday to reexamine and change his life, these matches would seem to indicate the chances offered to him. Each of them, like the candle set aside there, represents a possibility of illuminating his existence. Significantly enough, the candles in the cathedral will go out at the moment when K.'s destiny has been irredeemably determined. Continuing with the interpretation of this apparently negligible detail, we might note in the pincushion an image of the constantly wounded soul. One has the impression that Kafka continually offers us small clues that secretly amplify the meaning of the affair. His characters are surrounded by objects that express in allusive language the things that are happening.

A good detective story is structured around clues that the writer provides so that the detective can reach the solution of the case. No detail ever lacks meaning; all of them are useful for revealing the mystery. All the various Sherlock Holmeses, Poirots, Miss Marples, and Colombos base their ability as investigators on the capacity to reconstruct the subtle plot of the crime from apparently disconnected and meaningless details. Kafka's way of introducing the details of the scenes into his works is reminiscent precisely of the detective story. Robertson (1985, p. 90) calls *The Trial* a *metaphysical (or religious) crime novel* that has the Gothic novel among its antecedents. At bottom K. could be considered a detective of the absurd, whose task is to unmask God and confront him with his crime of having thrown human beings into a senseless universe. In his researches he follows the small traces left by the divinity. All the signs he finds along his road and that will allow him to discover the thread that connects these clues ought to help lead him to the solution of this enigma. If K. is in search of a meaning, it is hidden in the things that surround him: every person, every happening, and even every object possesses a tenuous spark that can illuminate his life. But his blindness keeps him from noticing this feeble light. He keeps sliding deeper into darkness and absurdity.

K.'s incapacity to understand what is happening weighs negatively on the progress of the trial. For a long time he refuses to accept his condition, clinging to the idea that it is a mistake or a joke.

> But that struck him as not being the right policy here, one could certainly regard the whole thing as a joke, a rude joke which his colleagues in the Bank had concocted for some unknown reason, perhaps because this was his thirtieth birthday, that was of course possi-

ble, perhaps he had only to laugh knowingly in these men's faces and they would laugh with him, perhaps they were merely porters from the street corner—they looked very like it—nevertheless his very first glance at the man Franz had decided him for the time being not to give away any advantage that he might possess over these people. (Kafka 1914–1915a, p. 10)

Trial is hanging over him and goes inexorably on. Those bureaucratic processes begin that will eventually crush him: the series of interrogations, of meetings with lawyers, the search for suggestions, of possible loopholes to escape judgment. Although K. seems insensible to all that is happening, it still leaves him in a state of confusion. He has trouble finding his identity papers. Rummaging around in his drawers he first finds only a cyclist's membership card and then a birth certificate. This card, along with the statement of the judge who mistakes him for a house painter, is the first sign of that process of disconfirmation that the protagonist will be obliged to undergo throughout the novel. How can the serious bank employee present himself as a cyclist to the guards that come to arrest him! All of his life seems suddenly to have been canceled; all that Josef K. can demonstrate is the fact that he was born. The threshold of his fourth decade which he passes on that very day becomes a watershed between his past and his future life. The time has come for balancing the books on his life. From this moment on he will have to give a new meaning to his life through understanding and accepting his guilt.

Indicative is a phrase spoken by the inspector at the beginning of the novel:

"I can at least give you a piece of advice; think less about us and of what is going to happen to you, think more about yourself instead" (Kafka 1914–1915a, pp. 18–19)

This suggestion is meant to provoke Josef K.'s interest in an interior dialogue. It is in a confrontation with himself that lies the key to winning his trial, even if further on it is stated that no one has ever been absolved, and in the best of cases the defendant can choose between a postponement *sine die* and an apparent absolution.

The psychological process that the arrest—or any other key event in a person's life—sets in motion has an alternating course, also marked by moments of involution. K. would have the possibility of understanding his situation by beginning to work on the changing of his personality, since he is presented with all the elements needed to shed light on it. But his behavior betrays a deep inability to accept change. The bank clerk's difficulty in understanding that he is guilty can be compared to the strong resistance of patients in analysis to facing the uncomfortable parts of their personalities, those that they have rejected. This is a common mechanism that we all frequently use to defend ourselves against bitter truths.

In reality, however, all such resistance has a reason for being. It is probable that the ego is still too weak to face a battle with those fantasies which threaten to destroy it. Every analyst knows very well that one cannot brusquely dismantle the defenses by which the ego maintains its precarious balance. First one must provide the patient with the conditions that permit the ego gradually to strengthen itself until it can support the confrontation with the part of itself which it fears. This is one of the reasons why self-analysis can only take the patient part way along the road to his inner self. To shed light on one's individuality always requires a relationship with the other, because it is only in his real presence that the deepest psychic dynamics are activated.

But for the bank clerk, the other only seems to represent a troublesome necessity. His relations with the rest of the world are lacking in warmth, in true interest, in participation. His relations with women, for instance, from Frauelein Buerstner to the washerwoman and even to Leni are purely utilitarian, just like the land surveyor's ties to Frieda, according to Gardena's accusation in *The Castle* (Kafka 1922b). K. seems to be a cold man, without feelings. It is his being closed to the world of feelings that keeps the bank clerk from having an authentic relationship with himself. In reality, he seems to have need of the other, but without wanting in the least to give up keeping his distance. The terror of intimacy is stronger than any desire for love. The incapacity to make contact with the other leads him to misconstrue the communications that are made within the relationship. This factor seems omnipresent in all of K.'s contacts with the outside world. The attitude of seduction hides the missing recognition of the other. This would explain the hero's attempt to conclude the judicial case with a handshake after it had barely begun.

"Come, gentlemen," cried K., it seemed to him for the moment as if he were responsible for all of them, "from the look of you this affair of mine seems to be settled. In my opinion the best thing now would be to bother no more about the justice or injustice of your behaviour and settle the matter amicably by shaking hands on it. If you are of the same opinion, why, then—" and he stepped over to the Inspector's table and held out his hand. The Inspector raised his eyes, bit his lips, and looked at K.'s hand stretched out to him; K. still believed he was going to close with the offer. But instead he got up, seized a hard round hat lying on Fräulein Bürstner's bed, and with both hands put it carefully on his head, as if he were trying it on for the first time. "How simple it all seems to you!" he said to K. as he did so. "You think we should settle the matter amicably, do you? No, no, that really can't be done. On the other hand I don't mean to suggest that you should give up hope. Why should you? You are only under arrest, nothing more" (Kafka 1914–1915a, pp. 20–21).

In this case K. is misconstruing the message of his arrest in thinking that reconciliation can be bought with a gesture full of feigned good-will and comprehension. His behavior recalls all of those seductive attitudes that many of us apply in our relations in order to avoid the suffering generated by a crisis. The desire of an immediate reconciliation in these cases hides the need to suppress an extremely painful, almost intolerable conflict. A true pacification implies, on the contrary, the recognition of the conflict and its causes, together with the capacity of living through it in all its intensity so as to really know it. Like K., many people seek a reconciliation even before knowing what is actually going on.

The eternal questioning that distinguishes the cases of both Josef K. and the land surveyor K., as well as of the investigating dog, would appear to be the continuous and fragmented attempt to become aware of their inner condition. Asking questions of themselves, putting themselves and the surrounding world on trial, is a process *contra naturam* that distinguishes the human being from the tranquil unconsciousness of the animal. But to find a meaning for one's own life, one's own actions; to ask oneself the reasons for things that happen, is also something that threatens the status quo, that can dismantle the inner structure of any social system based on the acquiescence of its members. When the possible reply contributes to dissolving all false illusions, it is always "subversive."

Kafka's characters seem precisely to "trip" over events. Their search for absolution and recognition will lead them from time to time to fall over a series of obstacles in such a way that their lives are changed into a constant slipping along an invisible rope that destiny extends for them.

As the trial gradually progresses, its atmosphere becomes more and more surrealistic. Despite the fact that each event corresponds to an inner logic that still connects it to reality, the features of the affair become constantly more nightmarish and hallucinatory. The reader hopes that it will turn out to be only a bad dream from which K. will awake. Instead, the events rush on until his death which, like the execution in the penal colony, presents itself as the inevitable conclusion of the affair despite its absurdity. The angst present in *The Trial* and *The Judgment*, works in which the hero dies — strange heroes, half innocent and half guilty — seem to reiterate the myth of the exile from paradise. Nothing but guilt and desperation can exist outside of an imaginary happy kingdom. And yet the tenacious search that motivates almost all of Kafka's heroes also marks their painful maturing process. It is on the level of guilt — think of Karl Rossman — that the innocence of childhood is abandoned.

Sin and transgression become the guides of conscience. However one goes about it — Kafka admonishes us — whether one chooses one's destiny or whether one is chosen by it, the human being is always guilty towards herself. It is the wound, the fracture that splits her soul, that is the sign of her guilt.

In "A Country Doctor" (Kafka 1971) the writer narrates the story of an old doctor who is called to the bedside of a young man with a horrid wound in his side. After trying to console the boy, whose case is incurable, the doctor is undressed and put forcibly into bed beside the patient. He tries to escape in the night and finds himself naked in the winter cold in a carriage pulled by phantom horses. In his house there is a successor who is robbing him and raping his housemaid. This visit has been a deception for the doctor, but once he has heard the night bell ring there is no longer any escape. In this brief story, remedy and illness are intertwined and there is no possibility of arriving at a cure. On the contrary, by answering the night call and trying to alleviate the suffering of another the doctor is drawn into inevitable ruin. The dialogue between the youth and the doctor is significant.

"A fine wound is all I brought into the world; that was my sole endowment." "My young friend," said I ". . . your wound is not so bad. Done in a tight corner with two strokes of the ax. Many a one proffers his side and can hardly hear the ax in the forest, far less that it is coming nearer to him." (Kafka 1971, p. 225)

Bemporad (1978, p. 454) has read the story as an attempt of the adult aspect of Kafka to care for and cure the traumas of infancy. But the story ends by reaffirming the doctor's impotence. This impossibility of curing the wound—which in psychological terms indicates the inability to have satisfactory adult experience—also marks the failure of the doctor, who ends by losing everything.

The capacity for self-knowledge also coagulates around the wound, which is described as swarming with worms. One can try to transform one's infirmity into an individual characteristic and construct one's entire life around it. The price one pays for the tragic equipment with which one is born is the loss of connection with the external world. From this condition, from this moment onwards the human being experiences separation and solitude, while reality becomes something disquieting. To recognize oneself in others and in things appears always more difficult. The fracture throws one into a vortex of anxiety and fears, while events, deprived of the meaning that grows out of recognition and continuity, seem mysteriously to plot against us. This paranoid dimension that runs throughout the novel and which we find in the life experiences of many artists, Kafka among them, is nothing other than the reflection of the inner persecutor.

The fear of the external world loaded with menacing fantasies is a recurring theme in Kafka's works. In "Unhappiness" (Kafka 1971), the ghost of a child materializes from the darkness in the corridor. But the hero of the story, rather than being frightened, seems to have expected this visit anxiously, to the extent of quarrelling with a neighbor for fear that he will deprive him of his ghost. The story breathes an atmosphere of anxiety, as if an unbearable weight lay on the unwary reader, who is put indirectly into contact with his own fears. One of the characteristics of Kafka's works is the negation of terror and of panic. Fear is not admitted in even the most terrifying of situations. Specters and daimons are part of daily experience; one converses with them.

Darkness is a necessary condition for the emergence of inwardness. It is no accident that Josef K., returning home from his first long day as a defendant, feels a certain anxiety on encountering the innocuous son of the concierge in the darkness of the vestibule. As he mounts the stairs, he turns once again to look at him as if to reassure himself as to his identity. In fact he even has the impression that the youth has done something bad for which he must pardon him.

It is evident that K. has projected all of his fears on the figure of the boy shrouded in shadows. The darkness allows the inner conflict to be externalized. It is the creatures born of our imagination who frighten us because we do not know how to deal with them. Fear of the darkness takes us back to our childhood. It is mostly children who are afraid of the dark. Their still undifferentiated relationship with the unconscious causes the darkness to fill up with menacing shadows for them. For that reason they need to sleep with the light on or with a familiar figure beside them, one whose affection makes them feel reassured and protected. It is not an accident that even adults — when a breach opens in their defenses against the unconscious and their sleep is tormented by fearful nightmares — urgently need, on awakening, to turn on a light, as if this simple act could magically exorcise daimons and phantoms. Darkness, which terrifies because it is filled with unknown forms, represents the night of the soul, that lower world with which we must establish a relation if it is not to destroy us with its dark power. The journey that K. undertakes when he is arrested is a descent into the abyss of his own soul. The arrest is a sinking into the absolute darkness of the unconscious. The dark night is an allusion to this abyss of the soul into which we must descend if our lives are to be capable of transformation.

This sinking into the night is an experience common to many of Kafka's characters, who find themselves in shadow and in the cold as, for example, does the land surveyor K. They are nocturnal beings who put their questions to the night, who sound the darkness in search of an answer. And it is this journey into night that gives shape to their anguish. In his diaries Kafka (1910-1923, p. 366) wrote on July 19, 1916:

> Dream and weep, poor race of man,
> the way can't be found — you have lost it.
> With 'Woe!' you greet the night,

with 'Woe!' the day.
I want nothing, save to escape
the hands that reach out for me from the depths
to draw my powerless body down to them.
I fall heavily into the waiting hands.

Words slowly spoken echoed
in the distant mountains. We listened.
Horrors of hell, veiled grimaces, alas,
they bore my body close-pressed to them.
The long procession bears the unborn along.

But on July 6, 1916 another entry echoes this invocation:

Receive me into your arms, they are depths, receive me into the
depths; if you refuse me now, then later.
Take me, take me, web of folly and pain. (Kafka 1910–1923, p. 365)

The obsession of this abyss, of this cosmic night from which the
individual tries somehow to escape, is also one of the leading themes of
the music of Mahler. In his first symphony, "The Titan," one finds the
enormous effort to liberate himself from the shadows in which he is
immersed. But death, anguish and pain recur in all the other works of
the Bohemian composer. With great acumen Charles Möller (1961,
pp. 192–195) has traced the analogy between Kafka and Mahler.

If on first analysis the deliberately impoverished vocabulary of Kafka
would appear to be very far from the exalted style of Mahler, the
composition of Kafka's phrases—long, cadenced, continually interrupted by interjections that express the writer's anguish, bringing to
life his "day dreams"—allows us to equate Kafka's and Mahler's
tempo, since in both cases the heart is squeezed in an unbearable grip.

The deep transformation of modern art is marked between Vienna
and Prague by the work of artists like Rilke, Kafka, Mahler, and
Schoenberg, to name a few, whose myths no longer tell of romantic
heroes fighting against daimonic powers, but describe the anguish
and the confusion of individuals seeking an answer. The same tremors and anguish that weigh implacably on Kafka's characters are never
resolved in Schoenberg's music in a consonant chord, as if to emphasize the endless space of the soul.

Mahler's *The Song of the Earth* (1905, p. 358) opens with the
words "Dark is life, dark is death"—strophes that are repeated in all

40

of the verses of the first song—and it concludes with an invocation to eternity, to a cosmic peace into which the solitary heart can sink. This dream of pacification becomes in Kafka a sinking into death, the desire for a tomb with its quiet and welcoming embrace, as in the tale "Dream" (1914–1915b), a fragment that was removed from *The Trial*, or as in the troubled words Frieda speaks to the land surveyor. For Kafkian man there is no possibility of escape from the absurdity and the anguish that dominate his existence. A stranger, he is condemned to wander aimlessly in a night that will never give way to dawn. Both Kafka and Mahler recount the anguish and exile of a being who is thrown into a universe which is not expecting her and which remains deaf to her questions and indifferent to her sufferings. But in the verses of Rueckert (Mahler 1905, p. 346), from which Mahler took the texts of the *Kindertotenlieder* (songs on the death of children) a tenuous hope is expressed:

> Often I think they have only gone out
> and that soon they will return home.

In Kafka even that possibility is missing, that mute prayer that one can find in Mahler even in his pain. In these lieder the suffering and torment are reabsorbed at the end in the image of a divinity, that like a mother, welcomes in his embrace the little ones who have been swept away by the tempest of death.

> In this weather, in this storm
> They rest as if with their mother;
> No storm will frighten them any more:
> The hand of God protects them.
> (Mahler 1905, p. 347)

In the world of Kafka, this hope is transformed into a sentence of exclusion without appeal. His heroes, like the land surveyor K., continue to long for a kingdom, a promised land, that they will never reach. The "soon" of Rueckert's verses becomes for Kafka a "never" (Möller 1961, p. 195). Never will K.-Kafka be accepted or received at the Castle, never will the Court absolve him, never will he enter the house of the Law, never receive the emperor's message, never will the dog be given an answer to his questions.

Five

The Return to the Mother

The darkness that K. must face is the prelude to a regressive situation. The disorientation that his arrest provokes is not long in making itself felt. The bank clerk asks for advice and reassurance from Frau Brubach. Similarly the surveyor, on arriving in the village, after having gone astray during the night, and above all after having crossed the little wooden bridge that takes him into the new village, will seek refuge in Gardena's inn, the realm of the Great Mother.

Faced with the emergence of a new inner conflict, the only valid refuge seems to be in the world of the mother. One could maintain, quite simplistically, that this is nothing but a typically infantile way of reacting since it is just children who feel the need of maternal protection so very strongly. If in infancy the relationship with the mother is necessary to the child's survival, it is important to understand the value it assumes for the adult. The moments of the return to the mother take place just as soon as life leaves the main highway and we are faced with a completely new reality. At such times, for example, we may look back on the past with nostalgia, or resign ourselves to the diminution of our will, our projects, our convictions, and cede the direction of our lives to other people. This going backwards takes the form of depression or other more serious psychic distress and constitutes a radical rejection of new forms of life in favor of something already known, already experienced. Jung (1911–1952, p. 235)—whose concept of the libido is distinctly different from Freud's—describes the "incestuous return to the mother" as an existential reaction prompted by a dangerous situation. The development of consciousness inevitably leads to the separation from the parents and, hence, to a relative detachment from the unconscious and the instincts. But nostalgia for this lost condition, which always persists within the psyche, creates a tendency to withdraw, to regress to the maternal womb every time a difficult task of adaptation is required. But to regress also means to return to a situation from which one hopes to gain strength, the nourishment necessary to face the test, to proceed along one's way. The return is a revitalizing contact with the original matrix from which a new iteration of the individual can emerge. This is the concept of regression advanced by Jung. In "Some Aspects of Modern Psychotherapy" (1930, p. 33) he in fact maintains:

> The regressive tendency only means that the patient is seeking himself in his childhood memories, sometimes for better, sometimes for worse. His development was one-sided; it left important items of character and personality behind, and thus it ended in failure. That is why he has to go back.

The tendency to regress only denotes that the patient is looking for himself in his childhood memories, which is often useful to him, but also often damaging. Up until then his development had been unilateral; essential elements of his personality had been neglected; and this was the cause of his failure. Therefore, he must return to the past.

The regression, almost paradoxically, becomes the way of fighting psychological dependence and the fear of growth. But the world of the mother also presents the danger of total engulfment in the unconscious. In *Symbols of Transformation*, Jung (1911–1952, p. 355) describes "A deadly longing for the abyss, a longing to draw in his own source, to be sucked down to the realm of the Mothers."

The problem is to maintain continuous contact with the unconscious, with the mother, without this snapping over into paralysis. As Perseus defeated the Medusa by looking at her reflection in his shield in order not to be petrified by her glance, so the human being must look at her past with the awareness that her condition has changed. To look at the trauma does not, in fact, mean to be repossessed by it. To experience the child within one, to make room for it, does not mean to *be* a child. There is the need of an adult part in us to take care of our abandoned childhood. Only by using the adult ego's strength and capacity for acceptance can one avoid being sucked back by one's daimons and end by being more and more possessed with no way of escape.

We can assume that until that moment K. had no particular intimacy with Frau Grubach, but he is forced to establish a more confidential relationship with the woman as soon as something unexpected occurs along his road. From now on he will seek the help of many feminine figures—from Frauelein Buerstner to the washerwoman to Leni, without however finding the help he needs, as also happens to K. in *The Castle*. His encounters will be marked by indifference or else resemble assaults. Thus it seems that the first psychic need is contact with the feminine. Kafka's estrangement from this factor, especially in its maternal aspect, is indicated in a few rare diary entries where he comments on the difficulty of his relationship with his mother. Very significantly, on October 24, 1911 he notes how foreign to the Jewish sensibility is the German word *Mutter*, for mother. The coldness of the word appears to him responsible for his inability to love his mother (Kafka 1910–1923, pp. 217–18).

Reading between the lines, one can notice that there is a different estrangement here that goes much deeper than any merely linguistic one. In confirmation of this hypothesis, there are other indications concerning the author such as two letters of Max Brod written to Kafka's family. Worried by the family's lack of understanding of the writer—above all the mother's, whose concern was exclusively for her son's health—Brod tried on several occasions to explain to them something about the particular nature of the young Kafka, pointing out that the sensibility of his spirit demanded a style of living different from the ordinary (Kafka 1912–1917, pp. 80–82). Two other entries in the diary allow us to glimpse his relationship with his mother. On December 5, 1913 he writes: "How furious I am with my mother! I need only begin to talk to her and I am irritated, almost scream" (Kafka 1910–1923, p. 244). And on October 18, 1916:

> Father from one side, Mother from the other, have inevitably almost broken my spirit . . . They have cheated me of what is mine and yet, without going insane, I can't revolt against the law of nature—and so hatred again and only hatred. (Kafka 1910–1923, p. 372)

What we know of the writer's childhood, of his way of speaking of his mother in his diaries, and what the letters tell of his difficult relations with women — all this can make one think of early difficulties in relation to the maternal figure, difficulties that weighed on Kafka's relation to himself and to his body.

The mother is intimacy and contact, connection and relationship. For the rest of our lives we keep the imprinting of intra-uterine life during which the fetus is wrapped in an embrace. Newborns are not the only ones to stop crying when they hear a rhythmic sound that imitates the heart beat, when they are rocked and embraced in a way similar to the oscillations they experienced in their mothers' wombs. These phenomena have a relaxing effect on us all.

A young woman only managed to calm her anguish and even more her constant fear of abandonment by tightly embracing her partner, with her face resting on his belly. Her emotional relationships were experienced under the sign of her relation with her mother. It was not just a coincidence. She was born after an extremely difficult delivery that lasted for hours during which she was in danger of dying, and for almost two months afterwards she could only get to sleep by lying on her mother's stomach. For her that warmth and that contact were the only possible guarantee of life. The woman's incessant need for contact was sharpened by the mother's coldness, her inability to show the child affection by the simple and immediate language of the body. Her unconscious choices led her to men who had the same difficulty in contact as her mother had, men who did not know how to speak the language of the body and whom she vainly tried to teach a kind of relationship unknown to them. An inner compulsion led her to repeat this frustrating experience in the hope of finally changing it. To love — as Morris emphasizes (1971, pp. 9–11) — means to touch, to have physical contact, inasmuch as this is the most basic form of communication. Only love allows us to bear and to desire the prolonged intimacy with an extraneous body, an intimacy composed of continuous kisses and interminable caresses. Being loved is experienced as an extension of ourselves. To take care of another is thus to take care of ourselves. The odors and tastes of that body not only excite us but seem to be a food which we constantly need. Significantly, one of the first signs of the end of love is the indifference, or worse, the disgust for those odors and tastes. The contact once so ardently desired now becomes unbearable.

45

In a fragment that Kafka later deleted from the manuscript, he describes K.'s intention of visiting his mother, an elderly woman who was almost entirely blind. Read from an endopsychic standpoint, the woman's advanced blindness would seem to indicate her inability to see her son's inner world. In Kafka the maternal image evokes fantasies of incomprehension.

It is a good three years since the bank clerk has seen his mother, also neglecting her birthdays. After her repeated invitations remained unanswered, she stopped writing. The response to the mother's "blindness" was to take refuge in distance. The lack of feeling perpetuated itself in a vicious circle hard to break.

The maternal aspect sets off an inner desperation that cannot be consoled and that seems to hold no true hope of salvation. On the contrary, the return to the mother evokes the fear of madness. To return to childhood means to reopen a wound that the ego never really managed to heal and against which it has strenuously built a series of defenses to avoid being destroyed by suffering.

In an article written immediately after the end of her relationship with Kafka, Milena Jesenskà (1923, p. 63) revealed her ideas about the nature of the bond between a man and a woman:

> One lives together in order to have a companion. To have someone, in the loneliness of this world, who confirms our right to life with all of our failings and errors — because what is friendship if not support of our vacillating self-confidence?. . .
>
> The greatest promise that a man and a woman can make each other is contained in the phrase that we usually tell with a smile to babies: "I shall never leave you." Is this not much more than "I will love you until death" or "I will always be faithful to you"? I shall never leave you. Everything is contained in this phrase. Respect, sincerity, the domestic hearth, fidelity, belonging, decision, friendship.

But when childhood has been marked by a subtle form of abandonment, not material but emotional, a long privation of intimacy, of contact, of real comprehension and respect for one's own being, it is hard to believe that others will not abandon us. The sphere of relationships, the sphere of the mother will always be disturbing and require defenses in order not to destroy us with their annihilating power.

Thus K.'s return to his mother will be cautious and wary. Significantly, Frau Grubach, in the excitement of the conversation, forgets to shake the hand of the bank clerk who waits in vain for this reassuring gesture. After this disappointment, which reopens old wounds, K. becomes conscious of the futility of the encounter.

> 'Will she take my hand? The Inspector wouldn't do it,' he thought, gazing at the woman with a different, a critical eye. She stood up because he had stood up, she was a little embarrassed, for she had not understood all that he had said. And because of her embarrassment she said something which she had not intended to say and which was, moreover, rather out of place. 'Don't take it so much to heart, Herr K.,' she said with tears in her voice, forgetting, naturally, to shake his hand. 'I had no idea that I was taking it to heart,' said K., suddenly tired and seeing how little it mattered whether she agreed with him or not. (Kafka 1914–1915a, p. 28)

Sometimes the pain of abandonment, betrayal, or separation can throw one into such a state of prostration that one is no longer able to live. Slowly one sinks into depression. The contact, lost or denied, leaves one without energy. It is as if one were a broken toy, an old toy that can no longer move or speak because the key to wind it up has been lost. What one feels is the futility of all attempts, of all action. The world has lost its meaning. To escape from this condition often means to take one's distance again, as happens to the hero of the novel.

K.'s reaction to the arrest recalls the words in *The Castle* where Olga describes the sad events that struck her family. The bank clerk too is convinced that if she had managed to act as if nothing had happened, she would have been able to snuff out the development of events from the start. Just as the Barnabas family would have been able to avoid being isolated by the villagers by ignoring Amalia's action, so too Josef K. would have been able to put a stop to the trial by acting indifferent to what had happened. The bank clerk's guilt seems to lie in being unprepared. In reality no really important event ever finds us prepared for it. Events take us by surprise, brusquely upsetting our quiet daily routine.

But the *sense* of many events and, above all, their potential for transforming us is contained precisely in their arriving unforeseen. It may be possible to detect a secret correspondence between external facts and our inner paths. What occurs seems to follow an invisible logic that guides our growth. Even the event that is apparently furthest away from our lives and our consciousness works to favor *transformation* in a way that escapes our immediate comprehension. Thus K.'s attempt to minimize what has happened and consider it banal is nothing but a closing of his ears to the call for metamorphosis. Not to manage to see the meaning of events and to nullify all their power to change things by recriminating against an adverse destiny, is one of the most common reactions of patients in analysis who begin to examine their histories. The resistance to accepting new ways of life makes people blind. An upheaval such as K.'s arrest can then become the means for reaching a new vision of life. What first appeared to be the tragic cause of our ruin becomes an opportunity to trigger off a profound change.

The psychological process set in motion by the arrest can be compared to the inner path that in oriental religions leads to illumination, to *satori*. This turning toward one's inner life which has the purpose of transformation, is one of the things depth psychology has in common with oriental meditation techniques. The goal toward which they both tend is to raise the psyche to a higher level. Thus the Jungian concept of the self, that transformed totality in which the conscious and the unconscious coexist in harmony, is after all not so different from that illuminated condition that the initiate must reach by practicing meditation. Fromm (Fromm, Suzuki, De Martino 1960, pp. 83–147) has put into relief the points that bring psychoanalysis close to Zen Buddhism. If awareness implies transformation and if in the act of knowing the human being changes, the revealing of the unconscious, taken to its extreme consequences, turns into a movement towards illumination. To converse with the unconscious, bring to light the kernel of one's complexes, does not only mean to make contact with one's inner *daimons*, to sink into the dark depths of the psyche, but to acquire a new existential dimension. This is a painful process that one attempts to flee by such expedients as used by K., who tries to deny that he is a defendant. But the depth of the wound and the extreme suffering of the soul force the individual to attempt the road of change. Thus the intolerable nature of one's condition is also the thing that impels one to change. In the Greek myth, Hercules becomes an immortal only after completing the twelve labors. The *test* and the *wound* needed to reach a state of illumination seem to be archetypal conditions of existence. It is not an accident that the bank clerk K.'s life only begins to take on depth after his arrest. From this moment on, like the Psyche in the story of Apuleius, he is forced to abandon his condition of ignorance. The search for the reason for his guilt, his encounter with the world of the Court, causes him to take stock of his life.

Each of us can only be hit in his weakest point. But our Achilles' heel, our wound is also what allows us to see ourselves and the rest of the world in a new way. It may be that for every person there is only one particular event capable of shaking up her "truth," of wounding and illuminating her at the same time. Nevertheless it may happen that this crucial event may not be recognized and thus one waits for it all one's life. In that case, every time anguish and pain oppress the individual, he will believe he has been hit in all its intolerability by the thing that can bring about his transformation. While to wait for this event may seem like a useless and enervating condition, on the other hand it acquires a particular value. It means, in fact, to live under tension, to consider every encounter, every fact as if it could be the decisive one. This involves a total and unceasing commitment. Life becomes enormously fatiguing, but its quality is enormously enriched by the fact that every single event is filled with meaning.

I believe human beings can be divided into two groups: the "awakened," who put before all else the search for the profound meaning of things and of deep respect for others; and those for whom success, career, riches, and power are worth more than their fellow men. The latter are in a condition that precedes the "arrest": for them no bell has rung. They continue to lead a repetitive existence: every day is the same as the one before, and they are not aware of what is happening either inside or outside themselves.

Six

The Wait in the Dark

The very first encounters with Kafka's figures reveal one of their seemingly constant characteristics: weariness. Enervated by the struggle with an invisible enemy and out to win for themselves a truth of blazing splendor but which remains forever inaccessible, these heroes slowly exhaust their strength. Even during the land surveyor's interview with Buergel, when the latter is making some important revelations, K. is overcome by tiredness and falls asleep (Kafka 1922b). In one of Kafka's various reinventions of the Prometheus myth (1918, p. 430), the titan's wound heals from tiredness, as if in the impossibility of solving the problem of the soul's pain, of healing it in some way, this failure of vital energy reappeared. In a similar way the song of Josephine (Kafka 1924) seems to fade away slowly and is finally forgotten by the mouse people.

And yet the weariness could have another meaning: along with the weakening of their strength, the defenses that allow the characters to avoid making contact with themselves might also weaken. The ever-greater fatigue that it costs the bank clerk to follow his trial could allow him to set aside his rationality and look at his situation from a new standpoint. But we know that this does not happen. Once the bank breaks down and there is nothing to contain and structure the relationship with the unconscious, the possibility of proceeding on one's way is also lost. One succumbs, one is killed by the *daimon*, one kills oneself by surrendering to external power.

The Trial is a novel of interiors: the pension where Josef K. lives, the labyrinthine world of the Court's offices, the lawyer's residence, the garret of the painter Titorelli, the bank, the cathedral. The architecture Kafka describes is certainly a description of the reality in which his hero finds himself, but it is even more the architecture of his inner world. The structures are pervaded with the same metaphorical ambiguities that emanate from the narrative — a vehicle to make concrete the dream allusions, the theatre of the absurd and the unreal in which the individual is immersed, an enigmatic space, the incarnation of bureaucratic power (Racheli 1979, pp. 21–22).

In dream symbolism, closed environments generally allude to the dreamer's psychic aspect, her inner world. We find therefore that we are dealing with an emblematic repetition of a single theme: contact with inner reality. Wherever K. turns to look he finds himself inside an edifice that often is dark and suffocating. Anything that presses obscurely on the ego, threatening to invade it, is naturally experienced as overwhelming. We will see how when making love to Frieda the land surveyor will have the impression that he cannot breathe. The misconceived emotions seem to choke him with their grip almost to the point of suffocation. It is no accident that the two figures the hero encounters in the dark of the evening are two women: Frau Grubach and Frauelein Buerstner. The first contact with a woman appears to end in frustration. K. offers his hand to his landlady, but she, in the heat of her words and her attempts to encourage him, forgets to take it. Once again K. must confront a lack of contact: the other, either deliberately, like the inspector, or accidentally, like Frau Grubach, denies the hero the gesture that is so important for him. This contact denied will turn into the almost bestial assault that K. makes on the stenographer. Even before this character arrives on the scene, Frauelein Buerstner is described as a person of little reserve who frequently changes boyfriends. At the opening of the book mention was already made of a calumny that was the cause of K.'s arrest. And now here too a calumny, a piece of gossip, is spread so that the accused cannot defend himself, cannot tell his version of the facts. Further on, in the encounter with the washerwoman, Josef K. will be warned that people are speaking ill of him. Once again privacy is violated by gossip.

Milan Kundera has noted (1986, p. 111) how the world of *The Trial* is one of *violation of solitude*. Not only is K. arrested in his bedroom, but from that moment on the protagonist's private life disappears little by little, swallowed up by the elephantine bureaucratic organization of the Court. Continually followed and interrogated, K. is forced to cope with an accusation that judges every move he makes. In a world where privacy is dissolved, the only possible dimension remaining seems to be that of calumny, of gossip. One's private life is debased by the malevolent and indiscreet eyes of others. But gossip and calumny, as Heidegger maintained (1927, pp. 211–214), are a function of our mental laziness. In the relationship with the other it is necessary to make an effort in order not to give way to an immediate and facile judgment. The fact that malicious gossip is widespread is a sign of our lack of commitment to genuine understanding. A voice heard in a corridor or on the telephone becomes a fundamental truth regarding our neighbor. To gossip maliciously, express judgment without knowing any of the facts, is an entirely spontaneous way to behave. There are people who live entirely in this manner, people embittered by life who never see the least ray of light in the landscape of existence. This makes one imagine that malicious talk is connected to an inferiority complex. Anyone who doesn't feel inferior and fights day after day to win his living space certainly has no need of gossiping maliciously, since he has been able to integrate within his personality both light and shadow.

Calumny is always connected to the misconception of the other. Immediately after this encounter when he realizes he has been calumnized, K. is mistaken for a house painter by the judge. Misconception and calumny always begin with ourselves, with our inner condition. Others judge us on the basis of the impression we offer them. To consider malicious gossip from an endopsychic viewpoint means to recognize that it is precisely we ourselves who furnish others with the terms in which they express their evaluations of us. It is Josef K. who speaks ill of himself. Not to believe in oneself is a particular condition that can be observed within certain pathological conditions such as depression where the absolute lack of self-esteem, the sense of unworthiness, can lead the individual to suicide. What Kafka writes in his diary on November 18, 1913 (1910–1923, p. 404) recalls the phrase

> "I am a sick man. . . I am a malicious man. I'm an unattractive man. I think there is something wrong with my liver. But I cannot make head or tail of my illness and I'm not absolutely certain which part of me is sick. I'm not receiving any treatment, nor have I ever done, although I do respect medicine and doctors. Besides, I'm still extremely superstitious, if only in that I respect medicine." (Dostoyevski 1991, p. 7)

with which the underground man describes himself.

To change an inner situation of desolation and death is not easy. The origin of these disturbances is always a rupture of the ego-Self axis. To have lost contact with — or still more terrible — never to have had the contact with a maternal sphere composed of love, warmth, and confidence provokes the lack of esteem, the inability to evaluate oneself correctly. One can only regain a positive attitude towards oneself by beginning to work on one's inner world, because self-esteem must pass through the knowledge of those dynamic processes responsible for this altered vision of one's being. One patient of mine who suffered from such a problem told me of having consulted the *I Ching* about it and obtained the image of the well. To reach esteem from lack of esteem one must dig deep down into oneself, draw on the necessary energy from our depths as one brings water gurgling up from the earth's bowels. By consulting the oracle she was in fact trying to consult herself, to find the key to her own malaise. And it was from the depths of her being that the answer was released.

The inability to love oneself is turned into the inability to love, to invest anyone else with a positive feeling. Corresponding to a degraded self there is inevitably a degraded Other. The feminine element that we encounter in this novel will be a guilty being that manifests its guilt through a strange glow of innocence. K. only knows women who offer themselves easily. This again is the schism of the Eros that is often present in the male imagination. Woman is experienced in the opposing forms of virgin and whore: Amalia and Olga, to mention two of the emblematic figures that personify this polarity in Kafka's world. We know that Josef K. is engaged to be married but that he has regular encounters with a prostitute. During his relationship with Felice Bauer, Kafka seems to have experienced the possibility of a sexual encounter with her as a punishment rather than as the natural culmination of their union.

Sexuality, held off and degraded, turns the human being into a beast with shameful and lascivious desires. Just because of its base character it cannot be experienced in an affective relationship but must be isolated in fleeting contact with an unknown woman. The prostitute seems to offer assurance against the danger of a tie, a relationship. An instant and violent kind of sexuality, such as occurs in Kafka's world, makes it possible to keep sentiment at a distance. If love appears as a terrible upheaval that threatens destruction to whomever falls into its vortex, sex allows for contact with Eros without one's becoming entirely trapped.

The first interviews with the feminine element come at night. There is meaning in the fact that K. waits in the dark for Frauelein Buerstner. The darkness and the waiting almost seem to be the premises for the encounter. If darkness is the realm of the imagination, the space in which fantasies take on shape, the waiting gives them time to live and multiply in the mind. It is a moment of suspension, a vacuum that the psyche peoples with its fears and desires. The event is imagined over and over again as in a film whose scenes are infinitely repeated and slightly varied with each new take. It is a time in which hope and despair alternate and cross paths and exchange their colors. One should not forget that waiting constitutes one of the recurring themes in Kafka's work.

Apropos of this, the hunter Gracchus (Kafka 1917c) comes to mind, who is condemned to drift in his boat in the lowest regions of death's realm, waiting to find peace, to finally pass on. If Kafka's other personages seem to hesitate in life, this one hesitates in death. The bank clerk and the surveyor too wait for something that never happens: absolution or recognition from the Castle. But in waiting for the impossible event they forget daily life. Thus waiting can be seen as the difficulty of living in the present, the here and now. It grows from the dissatisfaction with one's condition. It is as if the finite condition in which humanity is immersed left the individual profoundly disappointed and discontented.

All of us carry within ourselves a sense of the infinite which impels our spirits towards limitless horizons, a longing for those goals that can satisfy our hunger. But the search for the future should not make us neglect the present. Only by fulfilling our present experience can we give meaning to our search and avoid its turning into a flight.

It is no accident that analysis, as one of the possible privileged areas where the individual can interrogate himself about the meaning of his own life and direct his questions towards ever wider horizons that include all humanity, is yet rooted in the here and now. The gaze directed at the past, the nostalgia of memory, and that directed at the future, at projects, is then led back to the present. Transformation can only begin in the present moment. An ancient Zen koan (Senzaki, Reps 1957, p. 35) tells of a man fleeing from a tiger who grabs at the roots of wild vine and ends up swinging over an abyss. At the bottom of the precipice opening below him there is another tiger waiting to devour him. Meanwhile two mice begin to gnaw slowly at the vine that supports him. While in this precarious position the man notices a lovely strawberry beside him. Gripping the vine with only one hand he gathers the fruit and eats it, enjoying its flavor. The wisdom of the story, its teaching, lie in making clear the ability to grasp the moment and to enjoy it intensely.

Once he is arrested, the Josef K. affair will be marked by waiting. He will experience every encounter within this context. He will be notified of his trial, for example, a week in advance. And together with his waiting the bank clerk will have to come to grips with the unforeseen that comes up to throw his life into upheaval. Obliged to modify his programs to accommodate them to the court appointments, K. will be left alone to brood, to formulate hypotheses, to invent defense strategies. Time will acquire a particular connotation that is almost expanded by the world of the imagination which the trial opens up for him. K. now seems to live only for the event that will resolve things, that will give him back his daily life, the routine that marked his existence before his arrest. He will be waiting for salvation, but a salvation whose arrival, in truth, he despairs of. Josef K. awaits the end of the trial in order to begin to live. But a true conclusion can only come from the hero's capacity to make himself an active part of the situation. Instead, K.'s efforts are more like a futile rushing around, like those mice who are continually kept from reaching the shore and who, conquered by despair, let themselves drown. The bank clerk's twisting and turning lead to nothing, open no doors. He seems to be revolving around his own axis, his own problem. This is the anguish that is produced in reading Kafka.

But the block is actually an inner one, a *self-impeding* that precipitates the individual toward failure. K. is obsessed with his problem, but the obsession does not allow him to throw light on his inner condition. For many individuals, to gnaw at a problem is the best way to solve it. Many of the greatest scientific theories have been born from hammering away at a question, a kind of bee in one's bonnet, an obsession that tormented the scientist and gave her no peace.

But K.'s state of mind is quite something else again. He waits and thinks, but without result. His case can be compared to many patients who go into analysis. At the beginning of therapy they seem to be expecting a miraculous event that will change their lives and finally bring them happiness. "When he is able to love me as I want him to, when he takes care of me, when he really shares his life with me, I won't have any more problems"; or else "when I am transferred, when I can change my job, when I can leave the family and live by myself. . . I will finally be happy, I will feel fulfilled." These are some of the phrases one hears in analysts' offices. In all of these cases it is evident that the problem, the unconscious conflict, is being denied: being well, the mythical state of happiness, depends on some outer circumstance, a change that never affects ourselves but the others or the surrounding circumstances. In that way one lives without noticing that one is alive, deluded by a mirage, a "fata Morgana." It is the hope of a future, the nostalgia for an Eden still to come. The myth of a paradise lost is replaced by that of a golden age to be reached.

As the analysis progresses the patient begins to realize that only by changing himself will his life be changed. The analyst has the task of guiding him in this difficult search for his authentic self. During my long clinical experience I have been able to verify that the moment one begins to have faith in one's own strength, giving confidence to one's spirit, external reality really does begin to change. What is truly important is to start out on one's road of discovery, of listening to what one's inner voice is saying. In this way the individual is differently predisposed and this new aperture often makes her encounters easier.

In fables and myths when, for example, the hero begins his voyage, guardian figures appear — fairies or magical animals — who help him overcome his difficult test. To change one's attitude to the world also means to open oneself to in a new way to relationships, to be humble and available, to look at things with new eyes able to learn from experience. The neurotic is someone deaf and dumb who compulsively repeats her actions and is incapable of changing choices that have been made. What therapy "teaches" is to re-imagine events and to gather a deep new meaning from them. To do this a turning back on oneself is necessary — that sinking into one's own abyss which characterizes any voyage of initiation. To descend into the infernal regions means to follow — like Ulysses — one's own shades and hold discourse with them. All metamorphoses are prepared by retreat into a cocoon. Speaking to one's own fantasies becomes a daily occupation — the most important occupation. When one is tormented by a problem one cannot hope to resolve it by denying it. One must work on it, live with it, let oneself be approached and "burned" by its multiple facets. Then waiting really becomes the preparation to a transformation.

Darkness and waiting are the two elements that form the backdrop for the encounter with the feminine. In *The Castle*, too, K. and Frieda sit in the darkness of the deserted inn. To wait for the other while immersed in darkness seems to accentuate the imaginary character of this figure. It is an encounter with the interiorized Other, the anima image, for which K. waits. In analyzing the feminine figures in Kafka's works, Benjamin notes (1934, p. 295) their power to carry one back to "the dark womb of time," there where the coupling takes place whose unbridled lasciviousness is so hated by the celestial powers. These women evoke an instinctive, feral, animalesque dimension. They are swamp creatures, as the strange webbed hand of Leni indicates. And yet the power of their fascination, which is contained in a mysterious promise of total comprehension, makes something like divinities of them.

> To have someone possessed of such understanding, a wife perhaps, would mean to have support from every side, to have God. (Kafka 1910–1923, p. 339)

Kafka wrote in his diary on May 4, 1915. This powerful image contains all the intensity of the primal relationship. One should not forget that the woman, when she becomes an adult and forms a relationship with the man, will find herself on a level different from her original one, while for the man the relationship with the partner always evokes his fundamental love experience. Even though a woman may find maternal traits in her companion, can experience him as a "mother" and feel for him the same consuming desire that the mother figure once aroused, the man necessarily experiences a greater continuity between the figure of the mother and that of the beloved, a continuity that is underscored by her belonging to the same sex, by both of them being women.

Kafka's remark does not originate only in an idealization of the feminine, but seems to be the desperate cry of a man who wants to reexperience the same perturbing and devouring emotion that he felt in the first phase of his life. This is the experience to which Freud refers when he says that in our love relationships we always have only a surrogate. From an ethological viewpoint we could consider this experience as an imprinting that can be reactivated in all of those circumstances analogous to the one that brought it about. Clinical experience shows that the woman who excites a man's interest frequently has a face and a body similar to his mother's. In Andrej Tarkovskij's *The Mirror* (1974), the most autobiographical of the Russian director's films, which can be read as journey in remembrance, the same actress plays the part of the hero's mother and of his wife Natalya precisely in order to emphasize that imprinting guides us in the choice of a partner. The things that unconsciously attract us and make us fall in love are insignificant details for anyone watching from the outside.

The drawing near to God that the writer speaks of alludes to the inaccessibility of this guiding image: the primal experience is not to be repeated. The woman in Kafka remains an inaccessible mother, a mother whom one would want to rejoin, with whom to be fused, a mother desired and feared at once, perhaps because to abandon oneself to her love would mean to allow oneself to be destroyed again by her distance. The separation that has never been assimilated lurks in ambush as the most terrible of fantasies. The only reply, the only strategy is thus the rejection of love. This flight from a relationship is testimony to the attachment to the mother figure. If one remains entangled in the web of the primal relationship, a nonrelationship develops with regard to others because each new relationship would be a betrayal of the first fundamental experience of love.

The moment in which K. approaches Frauelein Buerstner, the configuration of the encounter itself reveals how, at bottom, he really isn't for looking for a personal relationship with her. The attitudes the bank clerk displays during their encounter, and above all the way he throws himself onto the woman, kissing her violently, do not imply any real desire for a relationship. K.'s inability to have deep contact with a woman can be referred back to the phrase the writer noted in his diary. If one carries a divine image within oneself, one cannot be unfaithful to it. To go to a prostitute once a week, as does the hero of the novel, means not to betray that primal experience since one is not committing oneself to a real relationship with a woman.

Seven

Entering the Labyrinth

Reading the affair of Josef K. in an endopsychic key allows us to focus on the psychological meaning the arrest and the trial may have for the protagonist. To have been summoned to a confrontation with himself gives him the chance to throw light on his inner condition. However, in this effort to understand, Josef K. is all alone. The figures around him are never recognized as valid interlocutors even though the bank clerk will seek outside help more than once. In reality the metaphysical nature itself of Kafka's Court and his Castle, the fact that they belong to an always-inaccessible sphere which is closed to him who continually tries to gain entrance, to be admitted—these characteristics necessarily involve a lack of interlocutors, of the Other with whom to compare oneself and, perhaps, prove one's innocence. To be able to enter into a dialectical discourse would mean to have already defined the problem, but within Kafka's world such a confrontation seems an impossibility. The Other must always remain at a distance, located beyond an ultimate boundary that one would vainly attempt to put under siege.

After the arrest has taken place, the first encounter with the Court is fixed by a mysterious telephone call during which K. is informed of the date of the first hearing. In order not to miss this summons, the bank clerk decides not to go to the meeting to which he has been invited by the assistant director of the bank where he works, an invitation that is extremely important for his career. With this decision, K. begins to give importance to the judicial affair. He begins to see things from a new psychological perspective in which social values—all the things that we could define as belonging to the dimension of the persona—are put into second place compared with inner things. K. had lived with his mask well glued to his face to the point of not being able to do without it. His relations never called on the participation of his true being, but only his way of appearing, the fiction with which he presented himself to the eyes of others. In this way, however, little by little he ended up by betraying his authenticity along with his soul. The lack of strength from which he seems to suffer comes precisely from the fact of no longer being fed by inner sources. The Trial is for him a chance to change his *modus vivendi.*

For this reason his initial difficulty in recognizing his condition as a defendant can be seen as a refusal to finally become active, to take the reins of his existence into his own hands, to open himself to change. "To become active," to question oneself on what is happening, not to allow oneself any longer to be directed by events, also means to become the witness of an existential alternative.

If the hearing means to be called to answer for one's own life, the places that K. must pass through to reach the courthouse have an extremely emblematic significance.

He had thought that the house would be recognizable even at a distance by some sign which his imagination left unspecified, or by some unusual commotion before the door. But Juliusstrasse, where the house was said to be and at whose end he stopped for a moment, displayed on both sides houses almost exactly alike, high grey tenements inhabited by poor people. This being Sunday morning, most of the windows were occupied, men in shirtsleeves were leaning there smoking or holding small children cautiously and tenderly on the window-ledges. Other windows were piled high with bedding, above which the dishevelled head of a woman would appear for a moment. People were shouting to one another across the street; one shout just above K.'s head caused great laughter. Down the whole length of the street at regular intervals, below the level of the pavement, were planted little general grocery shops, to which short flights of steps led down. Women were thronging into and out of these shops or gossiping on the steps outside. A fruit hawker who was crying his wares to people in the windows above, progressing almost as inattentively as K. himself, almost knocked K. down with his push-cart. A phonograph which had seen long service in a better quarter of the town began stridently to murder a tune. (Kafka 1914–1915a, p. 42)

Kafka describes with particular care the sites that his protagonist passes through to reach the Court. These are poor and sordid streets with which Josef K. was not at all familiar. But their desolation suggests an analogous interior condition since Kafka's architecture is a metaphor regarding the condition of the soul.

This correspondence between the world's localities and those of the soul we can also find in dreams. An emblematic motif is that of the appearance of semidestroyed houses or sunken pavements, almost as if the border between the ego and the unconscious were perilously giving way. A woman dreams, for example, of a house that had never been completed where she lived as a child. Half the floor of the room is missing and below fearful abysses populated by zombies open up. The same woman, in another phase of her analysis, when the danger of collapse has been somewhat exorcised, finds herself again in the same building that now has been completed. Collapsed walls and missing floors are also found in Kafka's dreams.

The poverty of the outskirts that K. passes through would appear to indicate that he has to have an encounter with his own Shadow before the first hearing. In a dream preceding our first session, a patient dreamed of having to bring or collect a roll of film for developing from an old man whose luxurious shop contrasted with the poverty of the neighborhood in which it was located. It is clear how this dream image alludes to a confrontation with one's own negative aspect — a negativeness which is still susceptible of being developed, of being changed into a positive.

In K.'s case, what appears before his eyes is the misery of his soul. The route followed by the bank clerk would seem to indicate that no enrichment is possible without first making contact with one's inner poverty. Such a relationship can only occur in the moment when the arrest has put into doubt K.'s identity with his persona. The confrontation with a deprived, weak, needy aspect is an obligatory moment in any analysis. The protective "container" of the analysis permits one for the first time to direct one's glance into one's abyss of emptiness and want. It is unfailingly a look cast onto one's childhood. The fact that children perturb K., that he doesn't know how to relate to them, is shown by a phrase that escapes him. On his way K. disturbs a gang of children who look at him hostilely.

"If I ever come here again," he told himself, "I must either bring sweets to cajole them with or else a stick to beat them." (Kafka 1954, p. 43)

It would seem that there is no possible way of making contact other than by seduction or violence, which are precisely the ways by which K. relates to the outside world. One must not forget, in fact, the attitude he takes to the inspector or to Frauelein Buerstner.

A phrase in a letter written to Felice November 21, 1912 is indicative of the way in which the writer related to childhood:

When children are around I prefer to close my eyes. (Kafka 1912–1917, p. 55)

Children in Kafka's writings are a presence continually noted, but always left in the background, as if dialogue with them were something impossible. One exception is little Hans Brunswick in *The Castle*, to whom the author entrusts his hero's hopes. But these child figures allude to a condition of the anima. It is when faced with the "inner child," his own child aspect, that Kafka prefers to close his eyes, as if attempting to forget the wounds and the traumas of that time long past. But the child, denied and kept at a distance, continues to work in secret, determining the way in which the adult relates to the world. The estrangement and isolation, the sense of guilt that the adult writer feels refer back to the same sensations experienced in childhood. He looks at life with the eyes of the child who feels unloved and rejected. His not wanting to see, which keeps him from being aware of the pain, invalidates the possibility of growth, of "healing."

Like the land surveyor K., the bank clerk Josef K. arrives late for the interrogation. His refusal to recognize the Court which is judging him impels the hero to keep silent and stops him from defending himself against the accusation. His first contact with the procedures of the trial, significantly, begins with a negation: the judge mistakes him for a house painter. Vainly he tries to assert his identity as a bank clerk, but this is received by those present with a big laugh. K.'s reaction is to refuse to recognize the trial. Kafka's universe is always marked with negations. His protagonists must always fight against a reality that tries to annul them. It is possible, however, to read this lack of acceptance in another key. The judge's question cracks the mask with which K. presents himself to the Court. It is his persona that is being negated. In this way there is a reinforcing of the process by which K.'s cover, his false Self, is dismantled. K. is brutally forced to face his misery, that same poverty that he was able to glimpse while passing through the outskirts of the city.

The choice of this profession is certainly not accidental. The house painter, like the washerwoman whom K. will soon encounter, has to do with cleanliness. House painter and washerwoman clean things up, bring back the whiteness to things, whether clothes or living quarters. In Christian ritual confession of guilt and absolution, the cancellation of the "stains" that the subject's behavior has thrown on his soul returns to them their immaculate splendor. The awareness of his self-betrayal should therefore cleanse the bank clerk of his guilt.

Once again in a subtle way the problem of purity returns; it obsessed Kafka throughout his life. But purity is experienced as a reality irreconcilable with evil.

Kafka the crow — in Czech *kavka* means, in fact, crow — bearing his burden of pain and guilt, seems to be in irremediable opposition to the purity of the heavens. And yet this fracture between purity and guilt seems to concern no one but the protagonist. For the others the two aspects seem to coexist. The judge, for example, reads his pornographic books and carries on a secret relationship with the washerwoman, just as the lords of the Castle seduce the village girls. The splendor of the Law shines in dark and dusty corridors.

In the novel that crowned his success, *Demian*, Hermann Hesse (1919) speaks of a gnostic divinity, Abraxas, whose task was to unify the divine and the diabolical. Good and evil are two faces of a single reality. Torn between these two opposites from his childhood, the hero Emil Sinclair searches for an inner unity. His psychic growth passes through the integration of this polarity. Only when he understands that the human being is composed of both aspects, that he cannot deny the one for the sake of the other, can he extricate himself from the destructive spiral in which he has become trapped. Thanks to his friend Demian — in whom Hesse himself saw a personification of the Self — Sinclair will learn that everyone must discover within himself his own tables of the law. This reunification of opposites that Kafka seemed to observe, fascinated, in Hasidic mysticism, remained an unrealizable dream for him. All the characters in whom the author from time to time personified himself remain stunned by that strange, and for him, impossible mixture of good and evil, of purity and guilt, of the divine and the daimonic.

After the first hearing, Josef K. is invited by a custodian to visit the chancery, the office in which all the documents are kept that are necessary for preparing the trial. The world disclosed to him here is a labyrinth.

> So the Law-Court offices were up in the attics of this tenement? That was not an arrangement likely to inspire much respect, and for an accused man it was reassuring to reckon how little money this Court could have at its disposal when it housed its offices in a part of the building where the tenants, who themselves belonged to the poorest of the poor, flung their useless lumber. (Kafka 1914–1915a, p. 69)

This labyrinthine world seems to be the realm of things set aside, the psychic space where memories and forgotten or rejected emotions are kept. The places where the destinies of the accused are decided are dark and dirty. The darkness that makes it difficult to find one's way seems to indicate the impotence of the ego. We find ourselves in an area that appears to be entirely autonomous and detached from conscious control and will power. But this rejected dimension, made up of cast-off junk, also constitutes the dynamic aspect, the power source to be tapped in order to proceed. Petroleum, the energy that our society uses in great quantities, is a product formed over thousands of years from the decomposition of living organisms. We can also view this set-aside world as the energy storehouse of the individual, which has accumulated throughout the course of our lives beginning with the earliest experiences that have put their mark on us significantly.

But to penetrate into this dark and tortuous world is not easy. It is no coincidence that on entering, K. trips over a step. From the psychological standpoint, tripping indicates the difficulty of entering a deep psychological dimension. Entering the labyrinth immediately evokes the idea of getting lost. In the Greek myth the maidens abandoned in the house built by Dedalus got lost in its windings and were devoured by the ferocious Minotaur. Only Theseus, after slaying the monstrous son of Pasiphae, managed to find his way out of the labyrinth thanks to the help of Ariadne. Descent into the labyrinth of the psyche may only be possible on the condition of finding the "thread" that allows us to come out again.

The basic questions about the meaning of life that everyone asks themselves in the crucial moments of life presuppose searching for and finding something that can direct one's progress. They represent guidance along the path of the initiate. But the labyrinth attracts and frightens us at the same time. There is the risk that we will go empty handed, that we will lose ourselves in the futilities of a sterile and repetitive existence. And this is an experience that one can have at any time in one's life. At any age one can look back and discover that one has never moved out of a circumscribed sphere. Every action, instead of signifying progress, going ahead, was instead a movement along the boundaries of an invisible circumference. It is the circle of paralysis and fear, of the inability to take one's destiny into one's own hands, to decide who to be rather than delegate this decision to others. The moment in which one manages to take hold of the thread of Ariadne, one is at last able to see a clue that was up to then invisible, a clue that contains the secret of one's own existence.

We can compare the situation to the process of individuation of which Jung speaks. Individuation means to begin seeing the world in a new way. When we have the sensation that all the problems, however difficult and serious, are our problems; when we do not desist from facing them and we are not discouraged because we feel that this is our terrain, our field of action — these are signs that we have grasped Ariadne's thread. At the beginning of adult life, it is important to understand, above all, that many of the difficulties we encounter are insurmountable only because they constrict us within a space extraneous to our nature. To ignore this truth is to risk finishing our lives trapped in unresolvable situations that have nothing to do with our authentic existential problems. Only the consciousness that the conflict is truly decisive for our lives gives us the strength to fight to resolve it.

In this day, dense with happenings, K. makes the acquaintance of another personage: the washerwoman, a woman who is generous in bestowing her body on the Court functionaries and who has been the victim of rape by a law student. In a bitter conversation the bank clerk has with the custodian, the woman's husband, the sad truth is revealed. The washerwoman is obliged to submit to the student's assaults because one day he will surely become very powerful. The custodian, in desperation, asks K. for help. Only K., because he is a defendant, can change this situation. As will happen in *The Castle*, in *The Trial*, too, the hero is considered a kind of possible savior. The hopes of the poor people depend on him, those obliged to submit to the injustices of the powerful, whether it is a question of little Pepi and her girlfriends or the custodian and his wife. It seems strange that a surveyor who is a stranger and chased away by everyone or a defendant should have this power. In reality their condition as outsiders puts them in a privileged position. Only the person who is outside the collectivity, who has perhaps nothing to lose, can fight with all his strength. From a psychological standpoint we can read the social status of the two protagonists as an image of suffering, of the isolation of the soul, that suffering and isolation that impel one to take up a search, to engage in an ultimate battle for life or death.

In a letter to Fliess, Freud (1887–1904, p. 405) confessed to his friend to have conquered depression with the help of a particular intellectual regime. The daimon that was devouring him demanded the sacrifice of all other activities. Interest in the psyche was his tyrant, but also his only possible help. In the same letter he lucidly observes: "No one can help me in the least with what oppresses me; it is my cross, I must bear it; and God knows that in adapting to it, my back has become noticeably bent" (Freud 1887–1904, p. 406).

However cruel this observation may appear, it is necessary for us to be lacerated by an inner experience in order to find the courage to come out into the open, to dare to do what earlier seemed unthinkable. It is as if inner energy were triggered by a difference of potential, and the greater this is, the greater will be our strength. It is no coincidence that the most interesting of Freud's essays are those written in his last years when cancer of the jaw was causing him intolerable suffering.

To subscribe to this thesis does not mean to ally oneself with suffering and disease to the detriment of happiness and health. But it means to ascertain a "strange" correlation, the one between suffering and creativity. It is K.'s imperceptible malaise that makes of him a man of destiny, a man with a *calling*. This calling does not in the least imply healing, but rather the capacity to live with one's own pain, to use it as a propelling force in life.

We can compare neurosis to a ship whose cargo has been badly loaded, has become untied and has shifted from the order in which it was disposed. The merchandise now moves around in the hold in a disorderly way that threatens to overturn the ship. The neurosis is a cargo that we cannot hope to unload but which we must learn to handle in the best possible way so that it does not overwhelm us with its weight. That accumulation of experiences, of rejected feelings, become destructive only so long as they are allowed to shift around as they like, only so long as they erupt destructively into our lives. The analyst's job is to "arrange" things in this inner dimension of suffering so that it can be used to enrich our lives, to make them fuller and more intense.

If K. manages to exit from the labyrinth, he will be able to show the way to all those who are in the same situation. The beauty of the accused, which is continually alluded to, is contained precisely in his searching. It is not certain that it is possible to find the thread or the one and only way of totally changing existence, but what counts is to continually search for it.

Eight

Eros and Violence

While wandering in the world of the chancery, Josef K. feels ill.
The heavy air of those dark places gives him a sense of suffocation.
He becomes dizzy and has to be supported by a girl and a man.

> He felt as if he were seasick. He felt he was on a ship rolling in heavy
> seas. It was as if the waters were dashing against the wooden walls, as if
> the roaring of breaking waves came from the end of the passage, as if
> the passage itself pitched and rolled and the waiting clients on either
> side rose and fell with it. All the more incomprehensible, therefore,
> was the composure of the girl and the man who were escorting him.
> He was delivered into their hands, if they let him go he must fall like a
> block of wood. They kept glancing around with their sharp little eyes.
> K. was aware of their regular advance without himself taking part in it,
> for he was now being almost carried from step to step. At last he
> noticed that they were talking to him, but he could not make out what
> they were saying, he heard nothing but the din that filled the whole
> place, through which a shrill unchanging note like that of a siren
> seemed to ring. (Kafka 1914–1915a, p. 83)

This disturbance makes K. feel that his body, too, is abandoning
him, that it is rebelling against him, embroiling him in another,
worse trial, inasmuch as he has managed for now to disengage himself from the first one. The body denied, uneasy vessel of all anxieties, hated still in its earthiness, seems to flee the rigid control
imposed on it, summoning the bank clerk back to a harmonious
relationship with himself through a series of somatic actions. The
vertigo that grips K. has a deep significance. The erect position
characteristic of the human being, differentiating him from the animals, almost seems to be a challenge to the law of gravity. His ability

to raise himself from the ground can be seen as an attempt to rise above the material level that yet remains his primordial form.

Just because of this capacity, humanity is condemned to live in a constant tension between two poles: on the one hand the "weight" of the sphere of instinct that drags the individual down towards animal nature, and on the other the conscience that seeks to elevate her, releasing her from the prison of the body, the body-grave of Platonic memory. It is only at the moment when this form is denied, the moment in which the spiritual dimension of conscience is chosen to the detriment of the material body, that the unity of the individual is flawed.

The vertigo expresses the crisis of the body-spirit balance. The dynamic tension between these poles has been altered by one of them prevailing. Those who suffer from vertigo appear not to have resolved the problem of human ambivalence. For these individuals the emotional sphere, the passions, push the person back toward the part denied — it is no accident that in the common phrase some people "make one's head spin." These individuals have the sensation of living on the verge of a precipice, a dark and fearful chasm that could engulf them from one moment to the next. Their lives are a desperate attempt to cling to the edge of this abyss and keep from falling into it (Masaraki, Morelli 1982, p. 5). To that end, all contacts must be avoided because any emotion could be fatal.

> He would have preferred to sit quietly until he recovered enough strength to walk away; yet the less he was bothered by these people the sooner he would recover. (Kafka 1914–1915a, p. 79)

It is the world of the Other that perturbs, that provokes the giddiness. Only the Other has the power to disturb the balance we have made for ourselves and to make us fall.

K.'s getting lost in the labyrinth of the chancery recalls a famous film of Kubrick's (1980), *The Shining*. Jack Torrence, who with his wife Wendy and small son Danny is a victim of horrible hallucinations in the empty hotel where he has secluded himself to write his book, seems to indicate this very unilateral nature of consciousness. Bent over his typewriter, Jack obsessively repeats for hours a single phrase: *"The early bird gets the worm."* What it suggests to us is an image of paralysis, an inner paralysis that makes him the victim of the unconscious. Jack, crazed, tries to kill his wife and child. In the dramatic final sequence, little Danny tries to escape from his father by running into the garden labyrinth. By the clever strategy of walking backwards he manages to cover his tracks and by using his paranormal powers succeeds in finding the exit. Lost in the labyrinth the writer freezes to death, turned to ice. The only defense the boy has is his *shining*, that clairvoyance that allows him to see beyond things and grasp what others do not perceive. Like little Hans Brunswick in *The Castle*, Danny too is the bearer of a way to salvation. Childhood, the age when contact with the emotions has not yet been lost, contains in itself a hope of survival. Danny can make contact with the unconscious without being overwhelmed as is his father. It is a new consciousness, gifted with a particular vision, the *shining*, which offers the assurance of escape from the labyrinth.

After this visit to the chancery, K. vainly attempts to make contact with Frauelein Buerstner to excuse himself for his behavior. But the woman refuses to see him and sends a friend of hers, her roommate Frauelein Montag, to the appointment with the bank clerk. The encounter is only possible through an intermediary. The situation in the novel seems in some way to draw on and allude to the Kafka's own emotional life. Very often, especially in the difficult moments of his love relationships, he had recourse to the help of a third person. During his engagement to Felice Bauer this awkward role fell to Grete Bloch. The need of enclosing himself inside a triangle to experience a love affair certainly has something to do with fear of the Other. It is as if the emotional investment was considered so dangerously destructive that the presence of a third element was required to break it up and control it.

But K.'s encounter with Frauelein Montag also gives rise to other reflections. To desire one woman and find oneself with another is the painful emotional condition of many men in whom a sort of perverse mechanism blocks the complete realization of their feelings for the beloved. It is as if every time they fall in love they discover they are unable to establish an emotional bond, whereas they can easily enter into a relationship with a woman they do not love. Brancati (1949) has described with extreme irony this split in the male animus in *Il bell'Antonio*. Antonio Magnano, a famous Don Juan, becomes impotent with Barbara, the wife he ardently loves. Opening oneself emotionally to the person one loves can, in fact, evoke castration feelings. Clearly this is not an exclusively male problem.

One of my patients carried the burden, like a painful secret, of her incapacity to unite sexuality and affection within a single relationship. Encounters with men of little significance to her, with whom she was not at all in love, allowed her to keep control of the situation and not to feel lost in the labyrinth of Eros. After about two years of analysis she was able to reunite these split feelings, and then her emotional intensity turned out to be explosive. To love meant, for her, to really live within a volcano, to be continually shaken and upset by violent eruptions of passion as desire, jealousy, and rage. The woman experienced the Other as a daimonic presence, as one who in seducing her had chained her to a yoke. On the one hand she wanted to free herself of it, but another part of her did nothing but tighten the knots. A great deal of time was needed to change this daimonic image into one with a human semblance.

The impossibility of forming a relationship is often experienced as a feeling of separation. The Other is so inaccessible that he can only be encountered through a substitute. Franz Tundra, the official who is the hero of Josef Roth's *Flight Without End* (Roth 1927, p. 263) loves his far-off fiancee in a double fashion — as a goal to be reached and as a lost possession. Past and future unite in the image of the beloved. In this way, however, one loses the present reality. Whether as a past possession or a future promise, the beloved is in any case always unreachable. The remoteness of the beloved is a constant feature in Kafka's inner experiences. It is this feeling of distance that blocks the relationship. Quoting the Talmud on November 24, 1911, Kafka writes (1910–1923, p. 268) that a man without a woman is not a human being. One who cannot love is not part of the human race, is excluded. Perhaps here lies one of the roots of the writer's sense of isolation. Continually torn between the desire for solitude and the need of communion, of the love of another being, he could not manage in any way to put his life back together. "Love is chastisement. We are punished for not managing to remain alone" (Yourcenar 1957, p. 81). Marguerite Yourcenar wrote with bitterness. But if the relationship is an essential feature of our human condition, the seed of pain is also planted there. Suffering is never connected to objects but only to people. Only others can really hurt us. "Hell is other people" says Sartre (1945, p. 165). In *Huis clos* hell is, in fact, a closed room in which a man and a woman are condemned to remain closed up together for eternity. In the game of alliances, complicity, and rivalry which is being woven, everyone becomes the other's hangman.

Only at the moments when one is in love does one really expose oneself to the risk of destruction. Abandoning oneself to another means giving her the power of life and death over one. But fear provokes violence. We want to destroy what terrifies us, what has us in its power. That may explain K.'s behavior towards Frauelein Buerstner.

If the Other is experienced as a possible enemy, a being who without any demonstrable fault is yet capable of destroying whoever comes into close contact with him, it is clear that this impossibility of contact, of intimacy, is really an inner problem. A complex psychic structure exists that makes any attempt at encounter and union impossible. Thus one can understand why the personal relationship is a prohibited and disquieting area.

The relationship with the other becomes an unbearable torture. But the images of violence which Kafka engraves on the relationship with women evoke another, more remote situation of violence — the one born in the bosom of the family, as is shown in his diary on October 18, 1916: "Because I confront my family unceasingly flailing about me in a circle with knives, as it were, in order simultaneously to injure and defend them" (Kafka 1910–1923, pp. 372–373). It is in this area of the affections that violence is born, in which Eros takes on the character of tyranny and torture. In an area deprived of warmth and welcome, tenderness and respect are extraneous sentiments.

If in Kafka's experience affection, self-interest, and desire inevitably join up with violence, it can be no surprise that Eros as described in his works is always a violent Eros whose animal nature, despised and isolated, emerges with fury. But inside an erotic relationship the propelling sadistic component is generally fused with tenderness in a way that keeps it from being transformed into an orgy of destruction.

But outside the erotic relationship, destructiveness emerges in full force. It is easy to trace this violent aspect in the writer's dreams and fantasies. The torture inflicted on the convict of *In the Penal Colony* (Kafka 1914) for its inhuman cruelty seems to have been conceived by a diabolical mind. The slowness and the brutality of it, the care with which every detail is studied to inflict the most atrocious pain on the victim in an atmosphere of gothic horror are all reminiscent of Edgar Allan Poe's (1842) famous story *The Pit and the Pendulum*.

According to Hall and Lind's analysis (1970, pp. 21–23) the writer's aggressiveness does not emerge in his dreams in a significantly greater degree than in the sample group. Arieti (1978, p. 209) reveals how the principal feature of depressed patients' dreams is a masochistic tendency. The themes of rejection and humiliation appear more frequently than scenes of anger.

Certain of Kafka's dream images strike us by their destructiveness. In a dream of July 21, 1913 (Kafka 1910–1923 p. 388), he is dragged by a rope around his neck through attics, furniture, and walls. The torture only ceases when the pieces of his horribly mutilated body drop away from the rope. Then too, everyone knows the letter to Milena (Kafka, 1920–1923, p. 204) in which there is the drawing by Kafka of a man drawn and quartered. In another dream scene of April 20, 1916 (Kafka 1910–1923, pp. 549–50), there is a battle between rival groups, at the end of which Kafka's side wins and drags the body of a captured enemy several times through an enormous stove. Sadism and masochism mix in the fury with which this destructive dimension emerges. In a letter to Milena (Kafka 1920–1923, p. 214), Kafka had confessed to not being concerned with anything but to torture and be tortured, adding as an explanation:

> The animal wrenches the whip from the master and whips itself so as to become master, and doesn't realize that it's only a phantasy caused by a new knot in the master's thong. (Kafka 1920–1923, p. 216)

For the rest, it is enough to read his letters to Felice Bauer and Milena Jesenskà to notice how this torture aspect structures the whole relationship. These biographical elements may help us to understand the whipping scene in *The Trial* at the beginning of the fourth chapter. Just as Josef K. is about to leave the office he is stopped by the sound of gasps coming from behind a closed door. It is interesting to note that the bank clerk is unaware of what goes on behind that door, which he believes to be a lumber room.

> It was, as he had correctly assumed, a lumber room. Bundles of useless old papers and empty earthenware ink-bottles lay in a tumbled heap behind the threshold. But in the room itself stood three men, stooping because of the low ceiling, by the light of a candle stuck on a bookcase. 'What are you doing here?' asked K., in a voice broken with agitation but not loud. One of the men, who was clearly in authority over the other two and took the eye first, was sheathed in a sort of dark leather garment which left his throat and good deal of his chest and the whole of his arms bare. He made no answer. But the other two cried: 'Sir! We're to be flogged because you complained about us to Examining Magistrate. (Kafka 1914–1915a, p. 94)

The opening of a door, just like the feature of the lumber room, accentuates the feeling of being in the presence of repressed contents. From the moment of the hearing and the visit to the chancery, the confrontation with the hidden part of one's soul is always more frequent and accelerated. Now the bank clerk is obliged to look at his sadomasochistic element. By keeping the door closed he had been able to brush aside his destructiveness—just as one does with a useless and forgotten object—but it was pressing to be recognized. In fact, K. was attracted by the gasps coming from that room. Jung used to say (1938–1940, p. 81) that a neurosis was a substitute for legitimate suffering. One can only be healed of the neurosis when one is able to see what lies behind it, to perceive our inner suffering, our conflicts. To open our eyes to what we have always kept hidden is not easy. It brings pain, the pain of seeing that we are different from what we have always believed, from the mask that we have always shown to others. It is from the moment when we really accept this vision that our destiny seems to change. To know oneself gives one strength to face life without any longer attributing the responsibility of one's lack of success to fate or the nastiness of the world. Neurosis substitutes for a legitimate suffering to justify us before the Court of life. However, we cannot be justified before this Court except by our way of living. The task of the analyst is thus to help the patient carry the weight of her legitimate suffering on her shoulders.

To remove an unpleasant content does not mean to make it inactive. An unconscious psychic mechanism secretly directs behavior. In the novel, the fact of having closed a door does not stop a torture scene from going on behind it. Of course being aware does not ipso facto constitute a cure even if it is an indispensable premise for it. K.

comes into contact with inner images: the whipper and the whipped. The shadow of the father hangs over this vision.

However intransigent and castrating Hermann Kafka may have been for his son, he certainly could not correspond to the sadistic image the writer carried within himself. Hence it was necessary to find a space in which this phantom could take shape. The cruel divinity of his childhood was incarnated in many of his personages, an example of which is the old commander, now dead, who has by now become a myth for all the inhabitants of the penal colony. But the contrast between the real parent and the imaginary one produces a break in the imago: on the one hand the inoffensive figure, on the other the cruel one, the sadistic bogeyman. In *The Judgment* (Kafka 1912a) or in *The Metamorphosis* (Kafka 1912b), the father is depicted as a weak and sickly man who however gains new strength from the death or the transformation of his son. It would seem that a kind of mortal duel has been going on eternally between the two of them that excludes the survival of both adversaries.

The son's victory is in reality impossible, not only because authority has been transfigured and rendered immaterial through its identification with a numinous and inaccessible power—as happens in *The Trial* or in *The Castle*—but above all because that castrating event has occurred within one's own being. K.-Kafka cannot be healed and has to die because he cannot kill the father within him. With his own life he nourishes the destructive power that devours him. Analogously, the officer of the penal colony kills himself by submitting to the same torture as the convict while the torture machine disintegrates.

The whipping scene can be read as an attack made by the father. Kaiser has noted (1931, pp. 63–65) how many of the assaults that take place in the stories are made from behind: the insect Gregor is hit in the shoulders by the apples that the father throws at him, while the convict—although his body slowly revolves—is initially placed prone in the machine whose needles slowly engrave on his back the crimes that he has covered himself with. He supposes that this is a fantasy of anal coitus performed by the father to which the son submits with masochistic pleasure. The punishment for rebellion is a martyrdom in the form of a cruelly violent anal rape. Aside from the anal fantasies, that which strikes us from behind cannot be visualized and for this very reason alludes to unconscious contents, to a problematic suppression with which one cannot manage to make contact.

A patient of mine, as a child, often dreamt that she was pursued by a man dressed in black whose face she could not see. The man brandished a shining knife in the night with which he wanted to kill her. Desperately the child tried to escape, running as fast as she could. When she was about to be overtaken she would wake up screaming. Significantly she never revealed the contents of her nightmare to the family, almost as if it was a horrible secret. Only many years later did the woman manage to see the relationship of this dream to the subtle incestuous attacks she had undergone for years in silence.

A dream of Kafka's of January 19, 1915, is extremely important for illustrating his fantasy of an attack from behind.

> A large, ancient knight's sword with a cross-shaped handle was buried to the hilt in my back, but the blade had been driven with such incredible precision between my skin and flesh that it caused no injury. Nor was there a wound at the spot on my neck where the sword had penetrated; my friends assured me that there was an opening large enough to admit the blade, but dry and showing no trace of blood. And when my friends now stood on chairs and slowly, inch by inch, drew out the sword, I did not bleed, and the opening on my neck closed until no mark was left save a scarcely discernible slit. 'Here is your sword,' laughed my friends, and gave it to me. I hefted it in my two hands; it was a spendid weapon, Crusaders might have used it.
>
> Who tolerates this gadding about of ancient knights in dreams, irresponsibly brandishing their swords, stabbing innocent sleepers who are saved from serious injury only because the weapons in all likelihood glance off living bodies, and also because there are faithful friends knocking at the door, prepared to come to their assistance? (Kafka 1910–1923, p. 327)

The crusader's sword, like the unknown assailant in my patient's dream, seems to represent the obscure danger of the Other. A persecuting animus and Shadow allude to the difficulty of relating to the unconscious. The external world in which the phantom of the Other takes shape thus becomes extremely menacing. But the weapon dreamed of by Kafka strikes us by its particular symbolism. The ancient crusaders, defenders of the Christian faith, committed all sorts of crimes at the expense of the Arab peoples: killings, rapes, and looting followed in their wake. Analogously, in the dream sequence the paladin is converted into a persecutor. By exterminating, the crusader wanted to destroy a civilization — the Islamic one — opposed to the same degree as it was unknown. In the eyes of Christians, Islam was a corrupt and idolatrous world. By worshipping a "false" god the Arabs put themselves in opposition to the Law and so had to be annihilated or converted. If we apply all of this to an intrapsychic problem, we discover a the violent suppression of an inner reality that is condemned before being known.

In Kafka's case, as in that of the young woman, we find an unknown enemy making nightly rounds in order to injure the unsuspecting dreamer. The sword that impales the back without making it bleed seems to refer to a wound that one carries within one despite having forgotten it. The danger comes from the far past here represented by the crusades. In both dreams the mysterious assailant strikes at the back as if to emphasize the lack of awareness of one's own complex. And in Kafka's case the lack of a relationship with the unconscious phantom is underscored by the absence of blood, of pain, of all those signs that can reveal the suffering of the soul through the laceration of the body.

Just as the wound will heal leaving only the smallest cut, so Josef K. will close the door on the whipping scene. Silence and repression will fall on the pain left unprobed.

Nine

The Compromise with Existence

The whipping of the guards is the first event for which K. feels himself responsible. It was his complaint that brought about that cruel punishment. The occasion has been provided for the bank clerk to become conscious of his actions at last.

A psychic structure that impels one to rationalize all life's events can sometimes induce one to externalize individual responsibility and deny it as a fact that regards one personally. But psychological development, the process of self-education, consists in assuming full responsibility for one's life. When one succeeds in opening a dialogue with the deepest psychic events, one learns that one cannot call the world to account but only oneself. Assuming responsibility is not easy and painless. K. seems to hesitate and in the end withdraws from his responsibilities. He prefers to shut his eyes to reality and close the door of the lumber room where the punishment is taking place. His only way of dealing with the situation is to attempt corruption. The bank clerk wants to pay the whipper to cease from applying the sanctions against the guards. His giving way here is particularly significant. One must not forget that he only recently had complained of the corruption of the Court. But now, to spare himself from remorse, he slides into the same behavior that he had so much condemned. The situation that Kafka describes is in the nature of a warning. One must never judge superficially in regard to problems one has never had to face, otherwise one risks behaving like Peter, who had so often proclaimed himself defender of the faith and ready to sacrifice his life for his teacher, but after the arrest of Jesus he denied him three times. It is easy to be good and just when one's life is not in danger. But it is the situations of risk that put our integrity to the test and teach us to be humble and tolerant towards others.

Many years after the end of their tumultuous relationship Jung wrote to Sabina Spielrein on September 1, 1919: "At times one must be unworthy in order to live fully" (Carotenuto 1986, p. 223). The question of unworthiness brings us back to the problem of good and evil, purity and corruption, that one can find in the works of Kafka. Within the gnostic faction that opposed orthodox Christianity in the second century, the neo-Platonic philosopher Carpocrate maintained that good and evil were only human opinions and that before his death the individual would have to experience to the end all human possibilities if he wanted to avoid returning again to the prison of the body. Only the fulfillment of every aspect, every exigency of life could ransom the soul imprisoned in the somatic world of the Demi-urge (Jung 1938–1940, p. 83). There is a popular saying that no one can ever say with certainty that he will not drink the water from the cup that is set before him. The condemnation, the violent execrating of a type of behavior, very often indicate that there is a problem of the Shadow hidden here. That which one rejects so vehemently represents a repressed aspect of one's own psyche.

The attempt at corruption pushes K. into the group of the "impure" and joins him to the corrupt world of the Court. If we read this event from a psychological standpoint, we can say that for everyone there comes a time when he is obliged to risk his reputation and to compromise himself. It may be the call of the Shadow, the need to face our obscure, our evil depths. Nevertheless this is not only something personal; it is also a collective product. In almost all cultures there is an image that comprises all evil in itself, the negative image of the world. In Christian mythology it is the devil who incarnates this aspect. He is the antagonist par excellence, the Other self to be confronted. But Lucifer, the Golem, Mr. Hyde, or the many figures of doubles that can be traced in world literature are nothing but the personifications of the ambiguities of nature, of that coexistence of good and evil, of light and shadow, of sublime goodness and ferocious cruelty that are part of the human soul as well as of the reality in which we live.

If in its subjective aspect the archetype of the Shadow can be considered the sum of everything negative that is present in the individual, in its impersonal aspect the Shadow coincides with evil as such. The metaphysical death principle that Freud conceived at the end of his life can perhaps be understood as an example of the importance of evil within psychological thought (Trevi 1975, p. 32). Evil and death intertwine to give shape to that destructive force which is part of reality. In the Hindu Trimurti, the Supreme Being is manifested with a threefold face represented by Brahma, Vishnu, and Shiva, each of which has a precise cosmic function. If Vishnu represents conservation and renewal, Shiva is instead destruction and dissolution. The balance between these two opposing principles is Brahma. Destruction and death are thus an aspect of becoming. Only from this standpoint can evil be considered a means of individuation, the instrument with which one realizes one's psychological redemption. Not by accident does Mephistopheles identify himself to Faust as

> Part of a power that would
> Alone work evil, but engenders good.
> (Goethe 1790, p. 75, vv. 1335-36)

The Shadow as evil becomes, in the individual's experience, *guilt* and *sin* which stain existence, or else that "negative destiny" too that seems to invalidate the potential for growth and change. Evil is contained in past traumas and continues to contaminate the present. In this sense a confrontation with evil, with the Shadow, is decisive for individuation. Apropos of this Jung writes in the introduction to *Psychology and Alchemy*:

> He knows that one can miss not only one's happiness but also one's final guilt, without which a man will never reach his wholeness. (Jung 1944, p. 30)

If human metaphysical negativity takes, on the personal level, the form of a negative personal destiny, like a "hereditary" stain—that which in Sanskrit is called karma—the task of the individual and his analyst is to perceive in the negative "the individuating factor of a life and raise that negativity to the dignity of one of the poles of a field of energy" (Trevi 1975, p. 34).

The moment in which the Shadow is impersonated outside of ourselves, in the reality that surrounds us, some dark thing crosses our paths throwing our "innocence" and our integrity into doubt. The dramatic quality of these experiences lies in the fact that we do not seek them — on the contrary, they take us by surprise. By observing intently we discover that we ourselves are the ones who prepare the conditions for their arising. Once one makes contact with this condition one remains "contaminated" forever. It makes no difference whether we accept or reject this proposition; a new variable has come into our lives in any case. The simple awareness of our "corruptibility" makes us realize how precarious is the linear ideal that had guided us up until then.

At times the circumstances of life can impel us to take actions that are repugnant to our egos, actions that compromise the image which had until then obtained. And yet all that is a secret *necessity*.

Martin Buber writes: "Therefore the task of a man is not to extirpate the evil instinct but to reunite it with the good one" (Buber 1952, p. 42). Only in the moment when one makes contact with one's unworthiness, one's corruption, is it possible to have full knowledge of oneself. Such knowledge is even more important for a therapist since, as Jung (1946, p. 78) well knew, "One cannot help any patient to advance further than one has advanced oneself." Anyone unfamiliar with misery, with laceration, anyone who has never been unworthy himself will hardly be able to understand the dramas her patients are going through. A famous Hasidic tale tells us:

> If you want to raise a man out of the mud and the slime, don't think that it is enough to stand above him and reach down a helpful hand. You must go right down into the mud and the slime yourself. Then grasp him with strong hands and bring him back with you into the light. (Buber, 1927, p. 419)

Those who go into therapy are generally people who never wanted to compromise themselves in life. Those who refuse to dirty their hands are generally repaid with psychic distress. This is a new way of reading neuroses. It does not imply that the cure can come from a total identification with one's Shadow. The total closure, like the indiscriminate opening, to the repressed and split-off parts of one's psyche can only perpetuate the condition of unawareness. Olga in *The Castle* and little Leni of *The Trial* are examples. The way in which they abandon themselves to the chthonic sphere, the depths of instinct, their ceding themselves to the desires of the accused and the servants, makes of them unconscious creatures who can in no way escape their destinies.

It is interesting to note how each of us has his own "whipper" and how there is a possible corrupter for each individual. It is not only that one can be wounded in one's weak points alone, but also that corruption can only take hold in the dark and unexplored zones where a reassuring moralism has chased off evil and "dirtiness." It is no coincidence that on leaving the lumber room K. will shout that they are sinking in filth, while the surveyor will make love to Frieda amidst the heaps of refuse and the puddles of beer. There is no integration between the two places.

One of the first episodes in Ingmar Bergman's *Scenes from A Marriage* (1973) is significantly entitled "The Art of Hiding the Sweepings Under the Carpet." In the beginning scenes the director shows an exemplary husband and wife watching in distress the violent quarrel between a couple who are friends of theirs. Slowly the image of the heroes' perfect menage crumbles away as betrayal and rancor show up that had been hidden behind a mask of hypocrisy. The explosive mixture of hatred that had been hatching secretly for years catches fire the day in which Marianne and Johan must sign their divorce papers. At this point one must watch a savage scene in which the reserved couple batter each other with unheard-of violence.

Everything suppressed impinges on the conscience. Both hatred and love, when they are repressed, sooner or later find a way of expressing themselves. And the more total and tenacious they have been, the more violent will be their outburst. The anchorites, for example, obsessed as they were by an ideal of purity and chastity, were constantly tormented by lascivious visions in which the "devil" repeatedly tempted them by reawakening their carnal desires.

> If I had wanted these two men to be punished, I shouldn't be trying to buy them off now. I could simply leave, shut this door after me, close my eyes and ears, and go home; but I don't want to do that, I really want to see them set free; if I had known that they would be punished or even that they could be punished, I should never have mentioned their names. For I don't in the least blame them, it is the organization that is to blame, the high officials who are to blame (Kafka 1914–1915a, p. 97).

Projecting the guilt does not help K. in his trial. Whenever evil crosses our path and, instead of accepting the whole responsibility and consciously passing through the negative sphere, we stop to point out the guilt of others, in that precise moment we cease to live. It is important to understand this mechanism if we want to avoid our lives changing into a renunciation. There is a profound difference between people who have compromised themselves and those who, on the contrary, have no knowledge of this experience. In the latter case there is a lack of the ability to understand life in its totality. One lacks the ability to find the "right word" with which to speak to others. What can anyone say who has never known the wounds that risk, that transgression, inflicts; who has never taken on the burden of his Shadow? Her words are sterile, generated by a moralizing that has no contact with life. That which I call "compromising oneself in life" happens on very subtle levels, almost as if one had established a continuous relationship with the "devil." The split between the divine and the diabolical is witness to an internal fracture of the psyche between good and evil.

This same split we find in the novels and dreams of Kafka: on the one hand there is the figure of the persecutor, and on the other that of the victim, two poles of a single reality. Kafka did not manage to understand that the hated father was in reality an inner image. To kill the persecutor is useless. The only way to destroy his power is to integrate his image. Every content, every image has, in reality, a necessary role to play within the psyche. One cannot suppress any part of it without impoverishing its inner riches. The real "murder" is accomplished by recognition, by reabsorbing into oneself the part that had been expelled. The violent and castrating father who, without any right, subjects us to his law, inasmuch as he is the only one who can receive or reject us, is not only a real figure—the parent whom we must confront in childhood—he is above all an inner image. It is this factor, cut off from the other psychic components, that is conferred with an enormous power, a power of life and death, that must be recognized.

In a story by Kafka (1920b) there appear a ruthless colonel and a mob of suppliants whose plea to him is almost always rejected. But the aspects of excluding or being excluded, like that of wounding and being wounded or of corrupting and being corrupted are in reality complementary aspects, bedfellows sheltering within one psyche.

The death of Josef K. is already foretold by his refusal to recognize the inner polarity. Faced with the guards who are beaten, he utilizes the mechanism of negation. To the servants who come running at the howls of the condemned, he will reply: "it was only a dog howling in the courtyard" (Kafka 1914–1915a, p. 98). We will find this reference to a dog at the end of the novel too: K. will be slaughtered like a dog, leaving his shame to survive him. The impossibility of recognizing and working out his guilt will push him toward a lower level, toward the unawareness of the animal. The only way of responsibly confronting life is to behave like an adult. Only in this way can we avoid being treated like animals.

The repression of guilt will make the bank clerk incapable not only of living his own truth, but also his own strength, that same strength that would make it possible for him to win his case in the trial. K.'s ego needs external supports to realize its full potential. While Leni, the washerwoman, and Fraeulein Buerstner function as substitutes for his repressed sexuality, the uncle and to a minimal degree the lawyer Huld—who was already ill when he met K.—represent the part of K. capable of opposing the Court, of attempting a defense. But the failure of the defense indicates that the road these two figures stand for is an entirely wrong one. Uncle Karl seems to be an emanation of paternal authority. In the novel he is clearly indicated as being the hero's tutor. His certain and decisive attitude contrasts with the hero's doubts. An endopsychic reading indicates that just as K.'s weakness and guilt are projected onto other figures, so is his strength.

Anyone who cannot make contact with her own helplessness and failings, also cannot fully draw on her reservoirs of vitality. In the writer's experience, his father seemed to hold all power while nothing remained for the son but weakness and the inability to live.

Contrarily, the writer remained a lost child who was ashamed of undressing in front of his father because of his skinniness; the child who was cruelly punished by being pulled from his bed and locked out on the balcony; the child in whose presence one had best close one's eyes, the child betrayed, repressed and forgotten, because he arouses discomfort and keeps one from noting one's own strength. This is the reason why he could not become a father.

As a child, precisely when one is having the most important and meaningful experiences, one often stands in a relationship of insuperable imbalance with regard to one's father. If the father figure cannot be integrated, the child will create a castrating image of him: in his experience the father will remain forever the one who is trying to destroy his individuality. Mozart, the child prodigy, grew up under severe dictates of his father; in *Don Giovanni,* a work composed a few years before his death, he created a terrific imago in the figure of the Commendatore, the stone guest, who drags the dissolute Don Giovanni down to hell with him.

In the novel, Uncle Karl is described as a busy and efficient man. With his skill, his friends, and his knowledge of life he must deal with K.'s lack of resolution, his inability to push the trial in a favorable direction. One can read these two characters as the two poles of the extrovert-introvert aspect. If the trial causes the hero to turn even more inward, in the case of the uncle the same event seems to stimulate him to even greater activism. The relationship of K. to the critical situation that has upset his existence is to be found in many patients. The analytic process itself impels one to look into oneself and not outwards. Before dealing with reality, one must come to terms with one's own fantasies so that one does not compulsively repeat those ways of being that have caused the neurosis. But in the world's opinion, K. and all those like him are losers. The one who stops to reflect, and thus does not participate with the necessary intensity in the productive effort, is a dead weight for the system.

The bank clerk and his uncle also represent two different ways of looking at life. In his way, by means of a difficult road—which not having been consciously traveled to the end will preclude final "salvation"—Josef K. is searching for his *horizons of truth.* In the face of an accusation which he does not understand and of which he will continue to proclaim his innocence, he must try to find some sense in what is happening to him. His efforts to understand, his continuous questioning, are precisely what represent the effort to reach this truth. Contrarily, the assurance of the uncle, whose only aim seems to be self-assertion, misunderstands that reality. The uncle, like the country man, will never be able to glimpse beyond the door the splendor of an ultimate dimension from which is radiated and manifested the meaning, the reply.

If we look at psychic discomfort from this perspective we discover its profound value. Those hopeless conditions into which an individual seems to have been thrown and which manifest themselves with varying degrees of symptoms—from extreme depression, for example, to total catatonia — are nothing but occasions for recovering from these abysses the necessary energy for a renewal of life.

The catatonic patient with whom Liv Ullman must deal in Ingmar Bergman's *In A Glass Darkly* (1975) is immersed in another dimension, lost in private fantasies. Jung was one of the first psychiatrists to understand that these extreme forms of detachment from the world were means by which the patient made contact with her unconscious. The moment in which one responds to one's inner *call* rather than to the demands of the collectivity, one pays an extremely high price, especially when this call bears the stigma of soul suffering. Not only does the alienation of the patient indicate a state of psychic split as much as it means in the collective mind a condition outside the norms and expectations of social behavior. The Catholic church uses the term "excommunication" — that is, the removal from the community — to indicate the exclusion of the heretic. Whatever is different excites fear. To be "different" means to pursue a direction capable of creating a crisis in the collectivity, since it invites its members to reflect on their actions and those of others and to redefine the criteria of good and evil. In a family organized for achieving success, a son who doesn't work, who drugs himself, or who in any case has different ideas, is a thorn in the flesh, a crack in the structure. His mere presence is enough to threaten the foundations of the system. When the conflict is too great and it is not possible to reabsorb the deviations of the son into the family nucleus, he is in certain cases banned. "Excommunication," to be expunged from the community, is the price paid for a search that may be conducted in a wrong way but which is not for all that less necessary and authentic.

Mutatis mutandis, this is also the condition of the creators of new systems, of scientists who succeed in formulating revolutionary theories. From Galileo to Pasteur to Freud — to mention only some of the best-known cases — the reactions of a society faced with a new view of phenomena, a view that destroys the cultural canons in force, have always been to deride and to ostracize.

The collectivity does not only try to annul the individual but also to relieve him of responsibility, as does Uncle Karl with his nephew. Every analyst knows that an extremely protective attitude to one's patient is very damaging for that person's growth. To choose for the patient by giving her advice in any circumstances whatever means to paralyze her powers of decision. It is a little like the classic situation depicted in the films of Woody Allen where the hero, immature and indecisive, always delegates to someone else — whether it is his analyst or his companion — the decisions to be made. Jung maintains (1944, p. 27–28):

> As a doctor, it is my task to help the patient to cope with life. I cannot presume to pass judgment on his final decisions, because I know from experience that coercion — be it suggestion, insinuation, or any other method of persuasion — ultimately proves to be nothing but an obstacle to the highest and most decisive experience of all, which is to be alone with his own self, or whatever else one chooses to call the objectivity of the psyche. The patient must be alone if he is to find out what it is that supports him when he can no longer support himself. Only this experience can give him an indestructible foundation.

If Josef K. represents the individual who is seeking his truth, opposing himself to the collectivity, why should the trial end with a sentence of guilty? In reality the bank clerk proceeds without seeing, deaf and dumb, because in his search he only uses his intellect, his reason. His being closed up in regard to the unconscious will prevent him from finding *his* answer, *his* truth.

Ten

Salvation in Art

Uncle Karl takes Josef K. to see Huld, the lawyer who is to take on his defense. Like all the names of Kafka's characters, this one is not accidental. In German, *Huld* means grace, benevolence, favor. The verb *huldigen*, coming from the same linguistic root, indicates rendering homage, swearing fidelity, becoming someone's vassal. Thus K. must submit to the trial in order to be pardoned. But the submission that the lawyer demands also means abdicating personal liberty and the power of decision. In this sense one can compare this figure to Dostoyevski's Grand Inquisitor in *The Brothers Karamazov* (1879–1880). The effort of his entire existence was dedicated to liberating humanity from the burden of their freedom. The dramatic dialogue between the ninety-year-old Inquisitor and Christ, who has returned to earth, reveals the contrast between two *Weltanschauungen*. Weak, incapable of using their faculties for choosing between good and evil and for being the arbiters of their own destinies, human beings, according to the old man, must be guided by a small number of the elect who take on their own shoulders the inquietude of all humanity. In exchange for complete obedience they even allow people to sin as long as the sin is committed with the consent of the authorities. In this way people will be allowed to remain in a state of happy and infantile ignorance while the elect will have taken on the curse and the misery of awareness.

> Man, so long as he remains free, has no more constant and agonizing anxiety than to find as quickly as possible someone to worship . . . I tell you man has no more agonizing anxiety than to find someone to whom he can hand over with all speed the gift of freedom with which the unhappy creature is borne. (Dostoyevski 1879–1880, pp. 297–298)

This is what the Grand Inquisitor will say to Christ. His *delirious* vision of the world on which many national leaders base their policies, promising justice, happiness, and well-being in exchange for blind obedience, is not unlike the submission exacted by the lawyer Huld from his clients. If the trial means taking stock of one's individuality, it is not possible to hope for results from a defense bought at the price of one's liberty.

Kafka seems to be expressing, as usual, a contradiction that cannot be resolved. On the one hand the narrative seems to suggest that the human being must abandon himself totally to a higher authority from which there appears to be some hope of grace and pardon; but on the other hand it is evident that this authority is, in reality, an illusion. There is nothing Huld can do. The defense—the novel tells us—is barely tolerated by the Court. The prosecution's documents remain a secret not only to the accused, but to his lawyer as well. The latter cannot be present at the hearings, which take place in closed session, and must reconstruct the proceedings from what his client tells him afterwards, thus piecing together a line of defense with great difficulty. Huld can only help K. through his personal acquaintance with judges and officials. The defense takes place in secret by practicing corruption. Thus it seems that the grace which Huld is supposed to be able to procure has no real value. He cannot really intercede to obtain pardon for his client, just as any complete and genuine absolution is revealed to be an impossibility. The trial can only be postponed or an apparent absolution can be obtained which does not mean a cancellation of the accusation: that will continue to hang over the defendant's head until a new arrest warrant is issued which will start up the entire judicial process once more. Despite that, it is explicitly stated that the defendant needs a lawyer because he cannot do without an intermediary in the Court.

The grace at Huld's disposal does not shine in a splendidly light-filled place. His house, like the Chancery, is wrapped in darkness only barely illuminated by the light of a candle that does not allow the ailing lawyer to recognize his visitors. The shadows once again appear to indicate the ego's inability to put its complexes into focus. Lack of recognition of the trial blocks any other acquisition of awareness. The naming of an intermediary, which removes the defendant from the responsibility of admitting his guilt, consigns him once again to the shadows of unconsciousness. What Huld can represent and defend is only his client's inner misery. He is, in fact, the lawyer of the poor.

We recall that on the squalid outskirts stands the building that contains the Chancery in its attic. But later we learn that there are such chanceries in almost all the attics. Kafka emphasizes the poverty and degradation in an almost obsessive manner. The lawyer's power derives from the sphere of darkness, and his is a Shadow figure. Furthermore, the sadomasochistic relationship that connects Huld and Block can only derive from the Shadow aspect that had already emerged in the whipping scene.

The self-destructive spiral into which the hero falls recalls a famous film of Joseph Losey, *The Servant* (1963) in which Tony Mountset, the weak and inept protagonist, last of the line of a noble English family, allows Barrett, his newly employed majordomo, to arrange and decide everything in his life. The young man ends up by sliding into total dependence, and Barrett takes advantage of it to destroy him psychologically. Losey shows great acumen in digging into the complementary aspect that binds the victim and his persecutor, making it a necessary and inevitable tie. The final scenes show Tony in a state of total degradation. Neither of the two can do without the other since each is the opposite of the other. So it is not by chance that the roles of dominator and dominated keep alternating until the last.

Block, too, has completely handed over his life to his defender. Although in secret he has relations with other lawyers, his attitude in regard to Huld is completely dependent. He seems to be a prototype of humanity as described by the Grand Inquisitor. The merchant has actually gone so far as to give up his work and move into the lawyer's house. The dependence of one person on another who, rightly or wrongly, can determine her destiny is a characteristic form of masochism. To remain in a situation of dependence and suffering is for some people a forgone choice inasmuch as it seems to offer the only possibility for survival in particularly difficult conditions. It is as if masochism, far from being only a destructive pathology, were a life choice because it appears to be the only condition in which it is possible to establish a relationship with the Other, however distorted and limited this may be.

The humiliations to which Block submits recall Wanda von Sacher-Masoch's description (1906, *passim*) of her relations with her husband

Leopold. The pleasure in suffering arises from the necessity of continually reproposing to the psyche a traumatic situation that occurred when one was very young, which the subject's ego has not succeeded in resolving and which must continually be relived in order to be controlled.

> The client ceased to be a client and became the Advocate's dog. If the Advocate were to order this man to crawl under the bed as if into a kennel and bark there, he would obey the order. (Kafka 1914–1915a, p. 214)

Block represents the ultimate in human degradation: the lawyer refers to him as "a miserable worm" (Kafka 1914–1915a, p. 489). We can imagine that guilt grew in him like a cancer that invades every part of the body. Besides meaning a notebook, the word *Block* in German has the figurative sense of a heavy and awkward man, a kind of bear, but also a blockage of a kind that, for example, could cause heart failure. Block seems to allude to a heaviness of being that could result in a blockage. The abdication of his liberty and power of decision, which have been totally delegated to the lawyer Huld, seems to be the result of what in technical terminology we can call "a regressive reconstruction of the personality." It is as if instead of continuing along his road of individuation, a road of becoming ever more responsible, he had returned to a condition of infantile irresponsibility. It often happens that with the feeling of not being able to proceed along one's road and to count on one's own strength, a person is pushed more or less entirely into leaning on someone, be it another person or an institution. Slowly one convinces oneself that without that tie one cannot go on living. Many couples base their relationship on this illusion. But in this case one cannot speak of love or of abandonment but only of narcissistic exploitation of the other.

In the plant and animal worlds symbiosis means a form of coexistence between two different living species that gain reciprocal advantages through a stable association. But on the human level symbiosis reveals all its regressive aspects. Not only do relationships of melding offer the highest degree of destructiveness because the other with whom one continually tries to meld is also the one who most threatens and limits one's individuality, but because when this kind of relationship is prolonged it limits all possibilities of growth.

In the experience of a young woman, her partner represented the necessary complement of her body. Not only did she find it difficult to distinguish between herself and the other—she even reached the point where she confused the odors of their bodies and felt that it was only one odor—but the least separation or threat of one made her feel she was losing the boundaries of her being. The infidelities of the man, which inserted a third element, an "extraneous body," into their fused duality, she experienced as an unbearable attack on that single body which the two of them represented.

The relationship of Block to the lawyer appears to conform to this need for fusion in which the presence of the other and the bond with him is an indispensable condition for continuing to live.

The Court that is dealing with the bank clerk's case is not the ordinary one but a higher judicial body that proceeds parallel to the first, and whose administrative offices are not in the courthouse but in the attic. On this level pardon can still be given to the defendant through the mediation of his attorney and thus through the recognition of the trial. A much more critical situation is described in *The Castle* where no pardon is possible, no absolution at all, because it is impossible to prove one's guilt as happens to the Barnabas family.

The fact that the author imagines his attorney in bed, seriously ill with heart trouble, is something that cannot go unobserved. If Huld represents the defense, this is shown from the very beginning as extremely weak. The weakness is one of the heart—the sentiments. The elderly lawyer has a relationship with Leni, a strange young creature with a webbed hand, which makes her a personification of instinct, of the chthonic world of Eros. Thus he is in contact with his animal aspect. Leni is another example of those help figures that the bank clerk encounters. She takes the case of K. to heart. In fact, Leni has a weakness for all the accused. She cannot resist their fascination and ends up falling desperately in love with them. The salvation that she proposes to the bank clerk is that of the confession, of admitting one's guilt. Just because she is an instinctive creature, Leni can be an intermediary to that inner world which K., in his rigidity, in his total adherence to the persona, has betrayed and before which he is therefore guilty.

That the woman is a personification of the unconscious is clear from the violent power of seduction she exerts on the hero. He neglects the advice of Huld in order to follow Leni, to make love to her. That cry he lets out — "now you are mine" — (Kafka 1914–1915a, p. 420) as he drags her down onto the carpet, indicates the capture of the unconscious considering that — from an endopsychic stand-point — it is the countersexual image, the anima, with which the man identifies.

Both Leni and the washerwoman have big, black eyes. This detail cannot be accidental. Kafka took great care with all details. This insistence on the glance, the eyes, surely has psychological meaning. The most intense moments in the life of a human being are registered by looks because the language of the body is the only one that never lies. The individual rediscovers the roots of relationship in this form of communication, which recalls the primal one, the one with the mother, where understanding is mute and one only draws on the syntax of the body. The glances of women are a window on his own inner aspect for the hero, a window on his anima. They appear to promise an inner knowledge mediated by the Other, a knowledge that is indispensable to K. during the course of his trial.

The lawyer and the painter Titorelli, another intermediary from whom K. gets important information, personify two opposite aspects as is evident from the fact that they live on opposite sides of town and that they reiterate that symbolism of light and darkness that encom-passes the entire novel. Huld's abode is immersed in shadows while the painter's attic is bathed in light. Huld's help is illusory, but Titorelli's information is practical and important (Robertson 1985, pp. 112–113). Titorelli seems to have an important role in the affair because he becomes a part of that group of helpers that little by little begin to form around K. (Kafka 1914–1915a, p. 458). Although the quarter in which he lives is extremely poor, it is in the opposite part of town from the outskirts that contain the chanceries. Thus the aspect personified by the painter seems to be the opposite from the one of guilt and condemnation, even if the painter, like everyone else, is part of the world of the Court.

On the house steps K. sees a child lying prone whose crying cannot be heard by anyone due to the din created by the workshop of a boiler-maker on the other side of the passage. Here we find another reference to that childhood abandonment, to the child within him that the protagonist doesn't know how to care for, but that he is compelled to encounter before having access to the level Titorelli represents. The very name of the painter, an Italian name, is connected to his work, almost as if the man could be identified with his art.

In the artist's house there is a painting of a judge, who rises menacingly from the throne on which he is seated. Among the details of the painting, the bank clerk notices the figure representing Justice. A strange kind of justice, in truth, painted with blindfolded eyes, a scale in its hands and wings on its feet, almost as if the image coincided with that of victory or, significantly, with that of the hunt. It is a justice that implacably pursues the defendant. Titorelli knows the world of the Court very well and reveals its secrets to K.

Titorelli is the man who can bring the bank clerk closest to the realm of truth that he is seeking. The detail of the brilliant light clearly is connected to the parable of the country man narrated in the next to last chapter. But if the peasant remains outside the house of the Law, whose blinding splendor he can only glimpse through a chink in the half-closed door, K. here is flooded in light. This is the sign of the transformation that has been accomplished. According to Robertson (1985, pp. 119–20), this transformation, which only involves his consciousness, cannot entirely modify K.'s relationship with reality. In fact, he immediately returns to his normal life.

To my mind, instead, it is a matter of a profound metamorphosis. It is no accident that K. can embrace everything with one glance and, freeing himself of Titorelli, the *medium* of his transformation, can proceed alone along his way. The change in his clothes, the long, black coat reminiscent of the Hasidic costume and thus of that Jewish spirituality which so attracted Kafka, is a tangible witness to the change that has taken place in the bank clerk, as if he had finally been able to reach a new existential condition, an opening to which the detail of the wide open windows alludes. One understands, therefore, why this passage was later cut from the novel. If K. was destined to be condemned—a condemnation that according to an old superstition can be read on the face of the accused, in particular by the cut of his lips—any redemption, any transformation had to be impossible.

Titorelli is connected to the possibility of salvation. The road, the *medium* of renewal in this case is that of art. For the rest, except for the episode recounted in the fragment, the painter is the only one who is able to indicate a way out for K., however partial it may be. We know how writing was to Kafka the means by which not only to justify his existence but also to open a dialogue with the inner *daimons* that otherwise would have destroyed him. Kafka aimed at molding himself with his writing; his ideal was writing performed almost unconsciously, a kind of birth, a delivery. When he ended the story *The Judgment* (Kafka 1912a) it was like a liberation, comparable to a delivery or an ejaculation.

> Only *in this way* can writing be done, only with such coherence, with such a complete opening out of the body and the soul. (Kafka 1910–1923, p. 213)

he wrote in his diary on September 23, 1912. Binder (1983, pp. 27 – 35) notes how Kafka's writing grows from the need to work on a real problem by means of a narrative in such a way that the piece of fiction modifies or replaces the actual experience. As such, Kafka's creative process has something of the visionary about it that comes from its drawing on the deepest unconscious matrix. The inner phantom asserts itself with the force that is natural to every autonomous complex.

For many artists their work represents the dimension in which they can pursue the path from inner fragmentation to reintegration. In this sense the artist is attempting to heal herself by herself, a transformation like the process of analysis, which, however, requires the collaboration of two subjects (Schillirò 1988, *passim*). But the problem raised by the presence of Titorelli is that of recuperating one's own creative potential. The creative individual is the one who succeeds in bearing up under the tensions of existence. Only creativity can allow one not to fear the condemnation eternally hanging over our heads like the sword of Damocles. Creativity represents for every individual the possibility to invent and shape his reality by obeying only his inner authenticity. Only in this way can one suspend the trial and delay a judgment that is equivalent to death. If life continually asks us to justify what we do, if all of us are always on trial, our only defense can come from nothing but our creativity. To be creative means to establish a profound harmony between the inner and the outer, between the inward dimension and the works in which it is concretely realized. Jung writes (1944, p. 25) that "every act of dawning consciousness is a creative act."

Those who manage to change the quality of their lives can only do so through creative acts. In the moments when one takes a creative approach to life, psychic energies no longer remain trapped in the condemnation—absolution dilemma, but can be led into new channels, can be utilized for proceeding along one's road of growth, of individuation.

Eleven

The Pain Denied

The episode of the cathedral foreshadows the tragic conclusion of *The Trial*. The conversation with the priest, the atmosphere in which the church is immersed, and above all the parable of the man before the law, which sums up the meaning of the novel — all of this leaves no room for hope. The condemnation that hangs inexorably over K.'s head will not be long in reaching him. The cathedral seems to be sunk in a darkness that, paradoxically, is increased rather than brightened by the light of the candles.

> K. went up to the pulpit and examined it from all sides, the carving of the stonework was delicate and thorough, the deep caverns of darkness among and behind the foliage looked as if caught and imprisoned there. (Kafka 1914–1915a, p. 227)

The aspect of darkness is emphasized by the black suits worn by the executioners and even K. himself in the execution scene. Blackness, the huge shadow that covers the chanceries, the house of Huld and the cathedral, until it engulfs the characters, is an allusion to the Shadow. It would seem that the very color the guards and the victim choose wear represents a surrender to the archetype with which they have totally identified. Incapable of holding dialogue with his own rejected aspects, the bank clerk can do nothing but allow himself to be invaded by his own destructive power and to succumb to it. If during the whipping scene K. was still able to hold off this aspect and keep it locked up in the lumber room, by now he is entirely in its power. Therefore there can no longer be any distinction between the executioner and the victim. K. is the judge and the accused, the aggressor and the aggressed, the executioner and the executed as is shown by his conviction that he must carry out the sentence on himself, stabbing himself with the knife.

In the next to last chapter several of the recurring themes in Kafka's works return: emptiness, abandonment, themes that we will find again in *The Castle*. Like the surveyor K. who gets lost in the dark winter evening and stops on a wooden bridge to look into the apparent emptiness, so Josef K. comes into contact with emptiness. The great, dark church appears empty to him. And as he advances among the pews he feels abandoned. From this condition of desolation the call arrives.

> He had almost passed the last of the pews and was emerging into the open space between himself and the doorway when he heard the priest lifting up his voice. A resonant, well-trained voice. How it rolled through the expectant Cathedral! But it was no congregation the priest was addressing, the words were unambiguous and inescapable, he was calling out: 'Joseph K.!'
>
> K. started and stared at the ground before him. For the moment he was still free, he could continue on his way and vanish through one of the small, dark, wooden doors that faced him at no great distance. It would simply indicate that he had not understood the call, or that he had understood it and did not care. But if he were to turn round he would be caught, for that would amount to an admission that he had understood it very well, that he was really the person addressed, and that he was ready to obey. (Kafka 1914–1915a, pp. 230–231)

In these few lines the entire meaning of the bank clerk's situation as well as its tragic conclusion is played out. *The Castle* takes up this narrative thread, which secretly links it to the preceding novel and which, as Baioni (1962, p. 217) has rightly suggested, can be considered the ideal conclusion of the writer's human and poetic itinerary. Through the slow weakening of the hero's strength the desperation and courage that permeate Kafka's writing appear. Death and condemnation are what await his early heroes, but a better destiny is certainly not in store for the others. The latter however appear to have more dignity and strength. Although their battle is lost from the start, they never stop fighting, never cease to hope. The emperor's message will never arrive, but the subject will stay at his window waiting for it. K. will neither be recognized nor received by the Castle authorities, but he will fight for it until the end.

Kafka is deeply conscious that the world of the Other cannot be reached in any way, that he will never be able to conjugate the *I* and the *you* into a *we,* that he will be forever precluded from the level of the two (Fusini 1988, *passim*). He knows that his inability to form ties can never be overcome in any way, just as his inner destructiveness cannot be assimilated and at least partly defused. His is so deep a despair that it cannot be consoled. And yet he seems to invite us to resist, to keep on going however deep our wounds and our inner devastation. Perhaps it is in this refusal of an easy and illusory *consolamentum* that the cathartic value of many of his writings lies.

It is clear that this last call made to Josef K., a man who to the very end has betrayed his existence, debasing it with a thousand subterfuges, can only be the call of death, which will soon inexorably arrive. Kafka's heroes, in fact, all seem to proceed inevitably to their destruction. Their strenuous efforts, their desperate searching, are nothing but a race into the arms of the "dark lady." If life is a splitting apart, a lacerating, a strenuous progress made futile by the uselessness of one's efforts, the impossibility of reaching the Other whatever form it may take — woman, supreme authority, truth — then reunion can only come in death.

Death, by dissolving the individuality of the single being, returns her to a state of fusion, transforms the individual's discontinuity of being into a continuum free of differences in which the *one* and the *other* are the same thing. The impossibility of the tie conceals — as Kafka's dreams show — a desperate desire for narcissistic fusion. That inhibition of contact, whose logical counterpart is the violent taking possession of women, creates a consuming angst. The desire to touch, to extend oneself toward the body of the other, to grasp and be grasped so that one can finally cease to plunge into a bottomless abyss — this is blocked by a powerful taboo. This is what gives every gesture its ambivalent character: the opening up, which is then immediately followed by a closing up again. The tragic metamorphosis of the real world is consummated around this phobia and the ambivalence it produces: all that was once good and desirable becomes bad and frightful. Love is changed into torment. To

Milena's bitter comment: "You do not know how to love" (Kafka 1920–1923, p. 200), Kafka can only reply:

> You can't properly understand, Milena, what it's all about, or what in part it was about. I don't even understand it myself, I just tremble under the attack, torment myself to the point of madness, but what it is and what it wants in the long run I don't know. Only what it wants at the moment: Quiet, darkness, creeping into a hiding place, this I know and must obey, I can't do otherwise. (Kafka 1920–1923, p. 200)

If a condemnation must inexorably fall on every one of Kafka's characters, because each one bears the same guilt, the manner in which it is executed will be different in each case. Revulsion and disgust will mark the end of the insect Gregor (Kafka 1912b), his abominable condition revealing the drama of his unworthiness; whereas shame will be the fate of the bank clerk. The land surveyor, since he answered the call and tried to reply to it, was to be spared an ignominious end both by the fact that the novel was left unfinished as well as by Kafka's intention according to what Brod says (Fertonani, 1979, p. 22). But for the bank clerk K., who remained blind to his guilt until the end, there can be no pity. His throat will be cut like that of any animal for slaughter.

Kafka seems once again to taste his end: he dies with the tragic conclusion of each of his works, along with each of his heroes. So there is not much difference between the execution of the bank clerk and the slowly prepared suicide of the writer who abandoned his body to the disease which was to kill him. Kafka secretly courted death, a long, accelerating seduction to possess and be possessed by his one true love.

> Once more the odious ceremonial of courtesy began, the first handed the knife across K. to the second, who handed it across K. back again to the first. K. now perceived clearly that he was supposed to seize the knife himself, as it travelled from hand to hand above him, and plunge it into his own breast. But he did not do so, he merely turned his head, which was still free to move, and gazed around him. He could not completely rise to the occasion, he could not relieve the officials of all their tasks; the responsibility for this last failure of his lay with him who had not left him the remnant of strength necessary for the deed. His glance fell on the top story of the house adjoining the quarry. With a flicker as of a light going up, the casements of a window there suddenly flew open; a human figure, faint and insub-

stantial at that distance and that height, leaned abruptly far forward and stretched both arms still farther. Who was it? A friend? A good man? Someone who sympathized? Someone who wanted to help? Was it one person only? Or were they all there? Was help at hand? Were there some arguments in his favour that had been overlooked? Of course there must be. Logic is doubless unshakable, but it cannot withstand a man who wants to go on living. Where was the Judge whom he had never seen? Where was the High Court, to which he had never penetrated? He raised his hands and spread out all his fingers.

But the hands of one of the partners were already at K.'s throat, while the other thrust the knife into his heart and turned it there twice. With failing eyes K. could still see the two of them, cheek leaning against cheek, immediately before his face, watching the final act. 'Like a dog!' he said: it was as if he meant the shame of it to outlive him.(Kafka 1914–1915a, pp. 250–251)

So horrible an end can only be the consequence of one's unworthiness. K. dies because he is incapable of living, because he doesn't know how to love, because unconsciously perhaps he feels unworthy of being loved. It is his lack of emotion that kills him. His executioners will, in fact, plunge the knife to the bottom of his heart and turn it twice. A list of the autobiographical passages in Kafka's letters and diaries where the fantasy of the knife occurs would be a long and always varied one. On November 2, 1911 he notes in his diary:

This morning, for the first time in a long time, the joy again of imagining a knife twisted in my heart. (Kafka 1910–1923, p. 101)

And a few years later, May 4, 1913:

Always the image of a pork butcher's broad knife that quickly and with mechanical regularity chops into me from the side and cuts off very thin slices which fly off almost like shavings because of the speed of the action. (Kafka 1910–1923, p. 221)

This torture constantly turned against himself derives from the Other, that other who, like a knife, digs out our hearts. If love and the sphere of the relationship are the source of this constant wounding, it seems evident that there can be no hope of salvation. That which one could hope might reintegrate his splintered inner state is the same thing which threatens to blow it up. Like Kafka, Josef K. too is a man alone who can neither know nor hope for the help of anyone. All those who try to do anything for him are attacked like

Frauelein Buerstner or treated with disdain and exploited like little Leni. That is why K. is so surprised to see the man in the window.

The motif of the window is a recurring one in Kafka's works. An old woman spies on his arrest from a window sill of the house across the way. These intrusive looks are one of the innumerable violations of his private life. The intimacy of Kafka's private world is constantly disturbed by the invasions of extraneous people who feed his persecution fantasies. We should not forget that in *The Castle* K. and Frieda make love under the obtrusive eyes of the helpers. The throwing open of windows is once again an expression of the distance separating the hero from the Other, who watches with indifference as his drama is played out. These mute, far-off faces testify to the indifference of the world to the tragedies of individuals (Basile 1982, p. 60). The open window that K. sees promises no help, induces no hope. Its only role seems to be that of inviting a chorus to witness this new tragedy in which the human being is doomed to perish because he is the iniquitous product of absurd laws, in a universe casually created as sinful (in the gnostic sense) by an inaccessible God (Basile 1982, p. 60). K.-Kafka's window thus becomes the paradigm of his relationship with otherness. The man who stretches out his hands from afar in a gesture that could or might want to save the hero stands for the impossibility of entering into a relationship of solidarity, which throughout the novel the hero has rejected, closed up as he is in proud solitude. If we interpret this situation from an endopsychic standpoint, we note how it indicates the presence of hostile forces acting within human beings and prohibiting them from making redeeming contact with the world. No one can help K. because he himself rejects all help.

In addition to the inability to love and open oneself to the Other there is the incapacity for suffering, for feeling one's own pain and learning from it to find a meaning in one's existence. K.'s drama involves all of the sentiments: for him not only emotional ties but pain too is impossible. The bank clerk's guilt is also contained in pain denied. Suffering is one of the principal ways in which one can experience one's individuality. The impossibility of entrusting one's pain to someone else is what makes the individual aware of her uniqueness. Pain and love—the two most crucial human experiences—they make the world appear completely and radically transformed. What puts itself before the eyes of a suffering person is another universe in which every sign must be given its correct meaning. Pain is, in fact, *enigma* and as such impels us to search, to question. In this sense it can be considered a royal road to self-awareness. By isolating the individual and at the same time opening him to communion with the universal, suffering lifts the veil of truth — that is to say, it puts the individual in touch with a *reality* that is not only part of his private experience but is the heritage of all men.

If K.-Kafka seems to be animated by the constant, untiring search for *the horizons of truth*, one of the roads that lead to it is suffering. But just as they do not know how to travel the road of love, Kafka's characters cannot even travel along the road of pain. They have no idea at all of what is tormenting them. They find themselves immersed in an element that they do not understand, and it is as if their feelings were always projected onto the external world. Thus the emptiness is a characteristic of the church or of the winter landscape, but never of the protagonist. To experience this dimension would mean to come into contact with loss. Pain, says Natoli (1987, p. 25), is "exposure to the radical danger of losing oneself." Pain is limitation, weakness, diminution, the foretaste of death. In the circle of solitude that it digs around the sufferer, it is reflection and slowing down. Suffering rips off the mask of efficiency and invulnerability behind which the individual hides her traumas and her wounds and binds her more closely to the true roots of her being.

Hence pain is also connection, and suffering is the sphere in which the individual returns within himself, abandoning extroversion, to look inside himself for the *truth*. The road of pain thus becomes the road of intelligence — from Latin *intelligo*, or "I gather while choosing" — "for the understanding of the world under the sign of suffering" (Natoli 1987, p. 28).

But if suffering is connection whose weight pulls us downwards and anchors us to earth, anyone afflicted with the impossibility of connecting up will not be able to experience it. For the K. of Kafka's novels, pain can in no way be recognized and absorbed into himself. It remains split off from consciousness, projected onto the other.

The split within the psyche of many people is the reason they cannot experience their emotions in any way or make contact with their rejected parts except by calling up those who personify those aspects. Thus K. expresses his violent Eros, which yet appeared in relation to Frauelein Buerstner, mostly through the animal sexuality of Leni who throws him onto the carpet shouting "you are mine"; while the land surveyor leaves to Frieda his sense of abandonment. K. experiences pain through his companion. It is Frieda who takes on the burden of all K.'s loneliness, his desperation, his sense of emptiness and abandonment.

This mechanism is very common, especially in some couples whose strong and indissoluble bond is based on their mutual personification of the other's Shadow. While one of the two slowly allows himself to be trapped in the role of the victim—painfully experiencing all the other one's sense of rejection, fears, and helplessness, the constant need of being kept in mind and loved—the other personifies the opposite pole of the rejecter, of emotional detachment, coldness, violence: the persecutor. Even if these two aspects are reversible—not by chance in another relationship or within the same one when a sudden upheaval can often bring about a change in the roles and the victim can become persecutor, the persecutor victim—there may be a certain inner predisposition, the result of traumas, of past experiences, that makes one slide more towards the one role than the other.

Kafka himself seems to have had a destructive effect on the women he loved. Notwithstanding his constant laments, his self-accusations of unworthiness, his sense of guilt, he does not seem to have been entirely aware of the suffering he inflicted on his partners. Anyone who reads the letters Milena wrote to Max Brod after the break-up of her relationship with Kafka, can note the sense of guilt and the destructiveness that he inflicted on the woman. Milena reaches the point where she wonders if she did not contribute to worsening the writer's illness. With great acumen Bemporad (1978, p. 462) speaks of the contagiousness of guilt, a contagion born of one's inability to consciously experience and work out one's Shadow side.

One should not forget apropos of this, the episode of the flogging in which K. permits others to act out his sadomasochistic side for him. The bank clerk's guilt is thus also contained in his inability to make contact with his feelings, to "suffer" his emotions to the bottom. If he were able to recognise his inner world, he would understand the reason for the trial, recognize the mysterious accusation, the "lies" that have caused his arrest. So his real guilt lies in constantly protesting his innocence.

In reading Kafka's works, we wonder where the angst, the desperation, the pain that haunt the story, are to be found in the characters themselves. The nightmare atmosphere wrought by the narrative does not seem to weigh consciously on the characters themselves. If pain cannot be experienced in the first person, if the relationship with the Other can in no way draw on awareness won through suffering, then the world can only remain deprived of meaning and definitively consigned to the domain of the absurd. And it is the absurd that confers its comical aspects on Kafka's reality. Many of the situations in Kafka do in fact recall silent movie gags. The dreamlike atmosphere, steeped in deepest angst, allows comical effects to be set off.

According to Barilli (1982, p. 121), Kafka's characters personify the conflict between the superego and the id. Therefore each of us can recognize himself in that parallelogram of forces that the author dramatizes. The clumsiness of Artur and Jeremias in *The Castle*, or the behavior of the two guards in *The Trial*, one of whom at the moment of the arrest presses his stomach against the accused Josef K., to cite only two examples, represent the safety valve by which the id circumvents the rigid obstacles posed by the superego. One laughs about something that in reality fills us with terror. But the humorous vein once again seems to take on a defensive role. It keeps us from making contact with emotion, denies us a place in which to accept and occupy ourselves with it. Such humor is a quite common mechanism. It is not unusual to come across patients who smile in a detached way while telling of events which caused them acute suffering. In their humor the pain is once again denied.

We know that in our culture pain and death are under a strong taboo. The Western world, with its myths of health, strength, indestructibility, and eternal youth propagated by the media, seems to have tried to remove everything that can remind us of the perishable, the transient. The terminally ill are often left in terrible isolation. They are the stricken that remind all the others of their mortality. Inasmuch as it restricts life, pain is *repellent* in itself and makes repellent all those who suffer it (Natoli 1987, p. 22). Job is insulted by his own friends about the sores he bears. Pain isolates us from the world and raises barriers between those who suffer it and those who do not. Thus the chorus has words of compassion for Philoctetes:

> I pity him, to think how, with no man to care for him, and seeing no companion's face, suffering, always lonely, he is vexed by fierce disease and bewildered by each want as it rises. How, how does he endure in his misery? Alas, the dark dealings of the gods! Alas, hapless races of men, whose destiny exceeds due measure! (Sophocles 1988, p. 187, vv. 169–76)

But the road that pain teaches us to follow is the one of care, without which there is no bond, no encounter. Care contains the only possible life project, the only way to defeat death.

We ask ourselves why Josef K. dies like a dog, leaving his shame to survive him. There are many possible replies. The novel delineates a dramatic, implacable triad of guilt, trial, and punishment to which the protagonist cannot oppose any valid defense. His relations with women show that he is incapable of love. In the entire work, in fact, there is never any mention of love, the one thing capable of ransoming the individual from solitude and the sense of transience. One of the characteristics peculiar to love is the sense of infinity it bestows. No one bound by love to another human being can have a feeling of termination. What she feels has to do, on the contrary, with the eternal.

The only life project capable of countering inevitable punishment is to have the courage to experience love. Salvation does not come from the confession of one's guilt and thus one's limitation, but rather from the capacity to establish a relationship based on love, because only love can suffer and accept anything. But love, if it is such, must contain the element of *welcoming*, of care. There can be no love where feelings are denied, where one has not the courage to accept existence in all its facets, where one doesn't want to recognize pain. Eros and Pathos are the two roads that lead to an understanding of life, that are a guide to *truth* by way of caring for oneself and the Other.

Twelve

From the Metaphor of the Trial to the Metaphor of the Castle

The Trial and *The Castle* delimit two different moments in Kafka's narrative work, two different dimensions of the imaginary as well as two different attitudes toward existence. The Kafka who wrote *The Trial* was a still a young man having his first important experience of love, whereas the Kafka of *The Castle* was in the last phase of his life. Almost all his experiences and decisive encounters were behind him.

After *Amerika* (Kafka 1912–1914)—or *The Dispersed*, as the author always calls the novel in his letters and diaries—his narrative perspective had already begun to take a different angle. In *Amerika* the motifs of exile, of guilt, of estrangement take their form from the concept of an evil and corrupt universe which—like the chambermaid whose seduction of Karl Rossman pushes him violently out of the uncontaminated world of childhood—conspires against the individual and makes him guilty in spite of himself.

Already here the image of an inexorable law looms over everything. Let us not forget that in the novel the Statue of Liberty, rather than holding a torch of freedom and reason in her hand, is gripping a sword. Already in *The Trial*, as in several earlier or contemporaneous stories, the problem has been shifted onto the individual.

Since Josef K. will never know what crime he has been accused of, he is obscurely responsible for what happens; in fact, it is precisely his ignorance that fatally leads him to his tragic end. We could see in this work the author's attempt to make contact in some way with his guilt, to define it, even if he will not see it clearly before his death. Josef K. is responsible for having betrayed himself, guilty of never having lived. The thirty-year-old bank clerk's futile exertions only indicate the fracture dividing humanity from the essence of *truth*, obliging us to see reality in grotesque and deceitful forms alone. Josef K. is the first of a long series of antiheroes, of exiles, whose only justification for living they base precisely on their exclusion, their diversity — sometimes extreme to the point of repugnance, as in the case of the insect Gregor (Kafka 1912b).

That sense of having no right to life which tormented the writer is personified in the emblematic form of his animals — strange creatures who, like the combined shapes in Greek mythology, are half human, half animal and experience this duplicity as another cause of their alienation. Like Odradek who, while existing, partook of no category, or like the hunter Gracchus who cannot justify his death and so is condemned to wander in a no-man's-land, the main problem of these beings is to find a *meaning* in their lives and in their deaths.

If the impossibility of finding this meaning is what causes the arrest and the death of Josef K., the same search provides the narrative structure of Kafka's last novel, *The Castle*. K.'s siege of the mysterious castle from edge of the village is a *siege on truth*, on inner truth which irremediably escapes all understanding, all efforts to possess it. It is the search for one's own soul, the search for participation in life which comes by way of an encounter with the Other.

Thirteen

The Call:
The Fascination of the Daimon

The vein of uneasiness, of searching, so characteristic of nineteenth-century fiction, runs through all of Kafka's literary production. A stranger and alone in the face of life, an orphan of that divinity who he himself has killed, shorn of reassuring certainties, fascinated and terrified at once of his inner world and of the Other, tightly enveloped in a dense net of senselessness, in the trap of the absurd, the modern man — the perfect antihero — no longer departs on impossible crusades, but sets out needing to discover a meaning to his existence. Like Ulysses, he is seeking a permanent anchorage, but without finding his Ithaca at the end of the pilgrimage.

The Castle, which can justifiably be considered the artistic summit of Kafka's works, once again deals with this anxious need of answers as exemplified in the initial motif of the journey. Unlike *The Trial,* in which the central theme is that of the arrest — which is to say, the psychic paralysis that leads to death — the leitmotif here is the call, the image of the person who breaks with the past, his or her preceding life, and sets out on a journey in the attempt to find the self, to reply to the existential questions that have always assailed him or her. To find work that gives satisfaction, a family to love and to love one, to have a house — these are, in fact, the elementary and essential concerns of life, the needs by which an individual acquires her identity, who she is in respect to herself and others. According to Kafka, it is in concrete things, in measuring oneself within daily life, within the real world, rather than in philosophical speculations, that a person can find his own identity, thus answering the questions that he has always carried within him.

The problem of defining one's own identity is connected in the novel with that of a relationship with the Other, inasmuch as establishing one's psychic limits — as the land surveyor in his job of measuring is *called upon* to do — means to exit from a relationship of the fusion type and learn to differentiate oneself, to understand where one's own person ends and that of the Other begins. Thus it is obvious that the first image Kafka offers us is of the hero immersed in shadows, lost in the unknown.

> It was late in the evening when K. arrived. The village was deep in snow. The Castle hill was hidden, veiled in mist and darkness, nor was there even a glimmer of light to show that a castle was there. On the wooden bridge leading from the main road to the village K. stood for a long time gazing into the illusory emptiness above him. (Kafka 1922b, p. 9)

Being lost is a metaphorical reference to losing all one's points of reference, the straying from the main road and setting off in an unknown direction. The psychic shadows, *the night of the soul,* indicates being blind in the sense of needing to close oneself off from the world of the visible in order to penetrate the inner world of one's fantasies. After discovering the incest and parricide with which he had stained himself, Oedipus puts out his own eyes in a gesture equivalent to symbolic castration, but also in order to remain alone with his images, the better to hold dialogue with his fantasies without being distracted by the outside world. When in old age he finally reaches Athens, accompanied by his daughters Antigone and Ismene who for years had wandered with him throughout Attica, and finds peace in the wood of Colonus, he will already be a man who has reached inner integration.

The call of the unconscious, that call which had obliged the surveyor to begin his journey, always originates in a tenebrous situation, in one of inner blindness. One feels, in fact, disoriented, confused, desperate. It is as if one were wandering quite rootlessly in a world of reality. The darkness in which K. finds himself immersed is caused by the frightful intensity that these images have reached, an intensity that keeps the light from reflecting. The chaos swallows up every ray of consciousness; not the feeblest ray of light indicates to the surveyor where the goal of his journey, the Castle, is located, and he stops on the wooden bridge hesitatingly to look into the "apparent emptiness."

A sensation of emptiness, that is, of loss and of something missing, often accompanies the shadows. There is no need for the event that triggers this psychological reaction to be objectively a tragic one. It is the meaning that we ourselves give this occurrence which makes it so, and causes our suffering. It is important, however, to emphasize how the sensation of shadows is a necessary premise if the light of a *meaning* is to begin to shine, if something with meaning is to reveal itself. A light cannot help but shine in the darkness. One could not speak of light and darkness if they were not complementary realities. The darkness that keeps us from proceeding along our way is the same that sooner or later allows a torch to shine in the distance. On an endopsychic level, that clear shimmer alludes to a new dimension that is being foretold. But to be capable of seeing it, what we have been until now must be destroyed. Destruction has to precede rebirth.

There is, however, a time lapse between the time that something in us dies and the moment when a new psychological orientation comes to light. Courage is required to bear up through the crisis, the darkness without a glimmer of light, to reply to the call of the unconscious without knowing what the outcome is going to be. The person who is able to resist the tension, to risk certainties for the sake of the uncertain, to accept an immediate death without the certainty of being reborn, is doubtlessly courageous. She knows that it is best not to resist the call of the unconscious and stay fixed in a nonlife, but to give it heed and go forward, whatever the outcome may be.

In the novel the image of shadows is immediately followed by that of emptiness. This is a theme that appears frequently in Kafka's writings as an example of his pitiful isolation. One must thus understand what it is that determines this inner experience. An example of a situation in which the sensation of emptiness always occurs is when a relationship comes to an end. Not necessarily a sentimental relationship, even if love is the bond that always best expresses what occurs in such moments. Even the end of a friendship, a job—something of particular importance in our lives and in which we have invested a great deal of psychic energy—brings on a kind of inner mourning.

If a death or another external event truncates a relationship that had existed immediately up until then, and thus produces an entirely new situation, this disappearance will bring on a sense of inner emptiness. In these moments it seems as if our bodies were held together by sheer force of gravity without anything inside to support them. We are only unsubstantial outer wrappers, moving shadows in a real world. We seem to have lost our inner core, the source of heat and energy that fed our lives. We have lost everything that counted for us. What the perception of this emptiness expresses is loss—unfortunately, a structural loss in our lives.

It is connected to another fundamental experience: that of dependence. All human life is connected to dependence, is almost woven into it, into that constant creating of it from birth until death. One cannot live without being dependent. But our psychological strength consists in an inner growth that constantly reduces our dependence. Maturity should be measured precisely according to our ability to reduce the devastating psychic consequences that often accompany this experience.

In analyzing the human social instinct, one notes how the fear of loss is one of the factors impelling individuals to aggregate. The family, before all else, is based on the need to have the emotionally most important people constantly near one. Being dependent on someone consequently implies the possibility of being controlled. Where a core of dependence is present, one can govern and control the other because its basis is the fear of loss, emotional fragility, the need of affection, of warmth, the fear of abandonment and solitude.

Nevertheless, dependence is not only a matter of emotional ties. It includes every kind of relationship. Finding a job and being inserted into a certain economic structure means being dependent. The importance of that experience comes most of all from the value of belonging that it contains. It is not easy to live knowing that one has no value for anyone, not to be in some way significant. There is no individual who can serenely pass his days feeling himself deprived of ties. Even an anchorite who goes through life in total solitude has need of a relationship with someone, in this case with God, to give her life a meaning.

From this standpoint, belonging to a context means to count for someone too. The need to be part of school of thought, a political party, to act frantically in order to be included in some list — these are all things that can be explained precisely by this need of belonging. In the moment that I feel I belong and so in some way am important, I also know that I exist. For many people, belonging seems to be the only parameter of existence.

The heroine of Agnès Varda's film *Senza tetto ne legge* (1985) rejects all ties perhaps because the experience of dependence was extremely destructive for her — getting a little bit of warmth from casual encounters from which she constantly flees or is chased away. But in the end she dies of cold on the last night of winter. Absolute independence, like absolute dependence, if such things were possible, would as extremes be equally dangerous and negative for people. To be an adult means to know how to live dependently without becoming a slave to it. What makes an apparent limitation is that it restricts the area of our freedom and makes us feel that we somehow wear a label, that we are determined by something outside of ourselves. In this way we lose the power to manage our own life and to be its arbiter.

Dependence is thus a psychological "weakness" which, while it cannot be entirely eliminated, should undoubtedly be reduced. We are born totally dependent: humans are one of those animal species whose offspring die when they were not cared for. The ability to conquer ever greater latitudes of freedom as we grow comes into conflict with our fear of loss. Unfortunately, to face this eventuality almost always means to suffer a defeat. Much of human suffering comes from having succeeded in following one's own road.

Often one looks around and discovers that a face has been forever annihilated that represented all of life for us, and we recall moments full of tenderness, in which for the first time we felt full of warmth, of inner energy, in which that awful sensation of inner emptiness seemed no longer to exist; we recall friendships, affections, loves, and we oppose our own desire to follow a different road, saying: "all right then, forget about it." All of life then is nothing but a letting things go their own way. In this way what we really neglect and lose is ourselves, the authenticity of our own sentiments, betrayed by sterile accommodations whose only point is that of avoiding pain, avoiding a loss which, however lacerating, does not last forever.

To return to that image of apparent emptiness at the beginning of the novel: in depressive states — that could be called black holes of the mind which suck up all psychic energy — the concentration of all one's libido on a particular point of suffering determines an impoverishment of the ties with the external world and results in the anguished sensation of emptiness that we all have felt at times. But the emptiness is only *apparent* and contained within the subject, since the external world obviously remains intact. What is missing is the capacity to make contact with everything, people and things, outside of ourselves. The emptiness expresses, as we have seen, a sense of loss. The origin of this sense of suffering, which is often generated by a deep, unconscious aggression against oneself, is the Self's abandonment of its inner objects. The depressive emptiness seems, in fact, to be a hard sentence inflicted by the superego on a Self that has been judged inadequate.

This experience is particularly intense in narcissistic personalities, where the normal relationship between an integrated Self and its inner objects is replaced with a "grandiose Self" and the deterioration of inner objects. The subjective experience of the emptiness can take different forms according to the structure of the personality. In depression — a psychological condition we find recurring frequently in Kafka's life — the emptiness is tinged with a strong sense of loneliness. Not only does life become entirely meaningless, but the possibility of weaving relations with others looks as if it has been lost. The outside world becomes distant and inaccessible. The capacity to desire and make projects goes by the board. It is not possible to love anyone, and, in parallel, one feels that there is no reason why one should be loved. In a passage from his diary of February 12, 1922, two years before his death, Kafka writes in great despair:

> The gesture of rejection with which I was forever met did not mean: 'I do not love you,' but: 'You cannot love me, much as you would like; you are unhappily in love with your love for me, but your love for me is not in love with you.' It is consequently incorrect to say that I have known the words, 'I love you'; I have known only the

> expectant stillness that should have been broken by my 'I love you,' that is all that I have known, nothing more. (Kafka 1910–1923, p. 413)

The damaging, the deep wounding of the Self which results from this incapacity to love, is translated into that sense of unworthiness that we constantly find among Kafka's experiences.

In schizoid personalities — which several questionable and useless posthumous diagnoses have claimed to find many traces of in Kafka — the emptiness is caused by an extremely intense splitting process that involves both the affections and the inner objects (Kernberg 1975, p. 228). It seems that the external world and the inner one, with its multiplicity of emotions, have disintegrated, leaving only empty space behind. But to notice the vacuum also opens the road to filling it anew. The pain caused by the lack of meaningful objects impels the individual to attempt a profound restructuring of his psyche.

If we interpret K.'s journey as an immersion in the *lower* world, the land of the anima, we can understand the sensation of emptiness he feels. To enter the world of the eidolons, the unsubstantial images, means to pass from the material to the psychic standpoint. The sensations of emptiness thus are caused by the passage into the rarefied world of *shadows,* with all their many metaphors (Hillman 1979, pp. 53–55).

Into this situation of emptiness and the loss of one's way among the shadows, there comes the *call* from the Castle, which obliges the surveyor to leave the place of his birth for another village. The universality of the call as a theme makes an archetype of it. In the Bible we find Abraham who, already an old man, leaves his house and goods after hearing the call of God and goes toward the unknown land that Yahweh will indicate to him. Thus too Joan of Arc and St. Paul — to mention a pair of recurring, emblematic figures in Western culture — will hear that voice which permitted them to effect such monumental changes in personal and collective history.

In all these cases the *call* is a crucial moment of life: from that moment on the subjects' continuity with their past is compromised, and instead, a passage to the unknown opens before them. It seems that at a certain time in our lives the demands for authenticity and change become so insistent that they can no longer be ignored. To listen to this inner voice means to attempt a radical transformation of oneself, of one's modus vivendi. The change we are impelled to undertake cannot be related to precisely circumscribed aspects. What is felt is only a sense of inadequacy, of the impossibility of getting satisfaction any longer from what surrounds us. It is this sense of estrangement, of the lack of correspondence between our inner needs and the things that occupy our time day after day— work, affections, social relations—that set off the irresistible impulse in us for change, which can be interpreted psychologically as an impulse towards the unconscious. From quiet, sedentary individuals, fulfilled in our daily lives, we are thus transformed into restless nomads whose life on the road is the best metaphor of the journey, the analytic path. The goal of that journey is the possibility of finding an answer to that primary question that everyone carries inside himself, the question that Blanchot (1969, p. 20) calls "the most profound question," the ultimate question whose purpose is: *the working out of an ultimate, extreme question, the question of God, of being, of the difference between the being and the condition of being.*

It is a far horizon that at times we think we can reach, but that continually eludes us. We wrongly believe that if we manage to resolve this ultimate question we will finally possess the key to our lives. In reality there is no final question because every question and all possible answers to it only send us on to another question: one ends up back where one started from.

Only the most courageous individuals are not frightened by this prospect, which is apparently lacking in solutions; only they have the courage to set out on the road. Within himself K. knows that there are no answers to his questions, but despite this knowledge he continues to search.

The novel opens on a rigidly cold winter scene, immersed in snow, a metaphor of desolation, of an inner freezing. The snow that has the landscape in its cold grip is a clear image of the solitude in which Kafka found himself after the failure of his relationship with Milena Jesenskà, whose love at first seemed to offer him the hope of a profound renewal. By means of this young woman, as is evidenced in certain of his dreams, he hoped perhaps to be able to approach his authentic Self and explore the rich and complex world of emotions from which he had always felt excluded, alienated.

But the snow does not only offer an expression of desolation. Its cold mantle in reality covers life that has gone into a sleep and is ready to be reawakened. In those very days, the writing of *The Castle* began. On January 24, 1922, Kafka noted in his diaries (1910–1923, p. 405): "My life is a hesitation before birth." If we read the snow image in the light of this assertion, we can easily imagine how it lends itself to the expression of the anxiety, the suffering, the difficulty that one feels at the moment that one has decided to leave everything, abandon all certainties, and go toward new horizons and a new life. The great journeys, for example, always involve this kind of experience. The famous explorers such as Columbus and Cook, who left the reassuring routine in their search for the new, are nothing but the externalizing of a deep psychic model. The journey, the route, the road, are the perfect expressions of those psychic models that we will always find in life, which itself, like death, is metaphorically called "a journey."

The land surveyor first halts on a bridge for a while. In a story written in 1917 and entitled *The Bridge*, Kafka imagined himself to be a bridge spanning an abyss.

> I was stiff and cold, I was a bridge, I lay over a ravine. My toes on one side, my fingers clutching the other, I had clamped myself fast into the crumbling clay . . . So I lay and waited; I could only wait. Without falling, no bridge, once spanned, can cease to be a bridge. (Kafka 1917b, p. 411)

This condition of immobile expectation was characteristic of Kafka's whole life, as his diaries attest. Significant above all for our analysis of the novel is that when an unknown person crosses the bridge in the story, his footsteps cause its wooden body a lacerating pain. And when the bridge turns toward the person crossing, it breaks apart and falls onto the sharp rocks of the torrent below. The relationship with another person who causes pain and disturbance was always considered by Kafka to be something that distracted him from his placid immobility, from this eternal, hopeless waiting, and thus brought on ruin and destruction. The bridge here alludes to the waiting condition, to the suspension between present fact and potentiality, to immediate being and to becoming. Thus one can understand how the event that can dissolve the immobility of waiting, this moment of inner paralysis, is a *relationship*, an encounter with the Other.

The motif of the bridge contains, however, another basic meaning: the anxiety of the search, the feeling of being an intermediary that runs through so much of the fiction of our century.

Our existence is such only insofar as it is a constant passage. For a human being there can be no other true life than the constant surpassing of himself. The fate of those who seek their authenticity is surrounded by doubt, by crises, by constantly putting themselves into question, risking at every moment the positions, answers, and certainties they had achieved. Anyone who is not disposed to see herself and her work as a both a dawn and a sunset at once is destined to become rigid, cut off from her inner dimension; and her word will become sterile and die, having been deprived of the sap of life. In betraying the need for transformation, that unending dying and being reborn, the individual loses the ability to communicate something, to give her soul a voice. This is why the artist as a messenger, a *medium* of the unconscious, passes his days in a borderland between life and death, lacerated by possibilities, by the thousand facets of being. Like his characters, and from them, he constantly learns new modes of confronting the world. The person who has chosen authenticity must accept acting like a *bridge,* an intermediary between the inner and the outer spheres, the perpetual transition from one state to another.

But the bridge that K. finds himself crossing at the beginning of the novel also represents, psychologically speaking, the ability to connect, to put opposing aspects in touch. For the individual to achieve a certain inner coherence and integration, he must be able to establish a relationship with those parts of his personality that have been splintered off. Emotions and events acquire interest and value only when we manage to bring them into contact with each other, to unite them. The play of meaning consists in linking one thing to another, one meaning to another, to use linguistic terminology. The illness often is nothing other than the loss of the ability to understand the symbolic language of the unconscious that substitutes one psychic element for another. Little Hans, of whom Freud speaks, is a prisoner of his phobia because he cannot understand how the image of the horse takes the place of his father. To decipher the message is the first step in escaping from the state of suffering that paralyzes our lives.

We then note how that particular event which makes us suffer refers to something entirely different which is at the root of its potency, the importance it has for us at this particular moment of our lives. To see the symbolic value of any event means that we can begin to understand it, work on it, and find new and original solutions. To become aware, for example, of how the partner that we do not manage to leave refers to an important aspect of ourselves, to our relationship with a parent figure tenderly loved in our childhood, even if we always experienced it as distant and rejecting us, means to break the chain of constant compulsion, to put our lives back into our hands, to enable us to choose new, adult, and gratifying objects for our affections.

What is really eliminated in psychic discomfort is not only the ability to understand how a certain content is replaced by another and then to make the opportune correction, but also and most of all, how to grasp and use that symbol which Trevi (1986, p. 12) calls *probletico*, which is to say *projectual*. Differently from a *sinizetico* symbol, which is a symbol understood in the Freudian sense as restoring the balance disturbed by impulses, the *probletico* symbol is not directed at the past but at the future; instead of maintaining an equilibrium it upsets one. Through this type of symbolizing, the psyche opposes the tendency to immobility that external reality is apt to exercise on the individual. It is in this symbol that the new road is contained — the project, in a word — that the unconscious has worked out. Thus what the analytic process should particularly try to do is to restore to the patient the capacity to produce transformative symbols. It is a question of being able to *re-imagine one's history.* Then the symbol functions as a bridge that connects the subject's past and future in a transformative vision that propels life forward.

For the surveyor to set out and leave his native land, he needs a letter that contains the *call* of the Castle. The invitation of destiny — one of the themes around which Kafka's work revolves — allows the hero to turn his back on certainties. All the writer's protagonists go to an appointment with destiny: the ingenuous Karl

Rossman in *Amerika* (Kafka 1912–1914) is caught up in the workings of fate when a servant girl seduces him; Josef K.'s fate is shaped when he is arrested and put on trial. For the country man, who is waiting to enter the halls of the law, fate takes the form of that admittance which is reserved for him alone but which he doesn't know how to make use of, and so he must remain forever on the outside. Kafka's tragic fables are generated, says Cantoni (1970, p. 71) in an unknown design which is often absurd. His heroes feel it as something alien, and it is far from the Greek idea of fate.

Whereas behind the *tyche* there was the order of justice guaranteed by the gods, Kafka's fate has an enigmatic and mocking aspect. What occurs is the reversal of any theological reality, of any unequivocal significance. But the destiny to which Kafka refers is to be understood as an endopsychic reality, which determines existence through the intricate tangle of the complexes. These complexes, with all the force of the images and emotions they contain, are what erupt into consciousness, demanding to be recognized. The encounter with an inner image of particular significance allows the individual to make contact with her own destiny.

When one has abandoned everything one has constructed in order to turn towards new horizons, one is giving heed to a voice that has matured within oneself. What may appear the result of fortuitous coincidence to an outside observer is instead the result of a long, hard psychological working out of one's injuries and inner problems. Only a patient return to one's images and complexes can allow one to hear the *call* and change the course of one's life. Those who have succeeded in expressing their inner life creatively have experienced this call coming from the depths of one's soul. Gauguin left his office job, his wife, his children to live in Polynesia, in that primitive, natural, uncontaminated world of which he had always dreamed and in which he was able to express all the riches of his unconscious images.

While Gauguin personifies the myth of the European who flees civilization in search of a personal paradise, Albert Schweitzer's destiny illustrates a different kind of personal realization. After having been one of Europe's greatest organists, one of the most sensitive interpreters of Bach, he decided at the age of thirty to study medicine and dedicate the rest of his life to caring for lepers in

French Equatorial Africa. In his case the *call* is expressed by a form of *pietas.*

For all of us, destiny is contained in this call, which brings us to a crossroads. On the one hand there is life, authenticity, the possibility of recognizing and respecting our deepest needs, while on the other hand there is the death of inner life, sterility, paralysis. Only those who have had the courage to make a decisive choice, abandoning an existence that had become too narrow, suffocating, and inadequate, can help others to proceed along the road of individuation. To leave the beaten paths behind and follow a new road is an act of tragic beauty in itself because the goal is never visible. What counts is the journey. Sometimes the decisions can be difficult since we are never sure that the road we take is the right one, the one for *us.* In such moments we can only count on our intuitions.

When we find ourselves in these crucial moments of life, we become sadly aware of our solitude. Not only can no one help us and tell us clearly what we ought to do but, quite the contrary, the outside world appears to hinder us. We must fight against our family, against our companion who for laziness or egoism would like to enclose us in preestablished schemes. It is not always our own fears and doubts that stop us. The hardest battle is often the one we are obliged to undertake with those around us, for whom our actions are a severe warning and a silent reproof. Our capacity for transforming ourselves, for risking everything we had constructed until then, is a secret accusation against them for the paralyzing fears that have kept them from heeding the voice of the unconscious.

The hostility, mistrust, and irony with which our efforts are greeted sometimes resemble a silent conspiracy whose purpose is to keep us from following our new choice. In responding to what we hear inside of us rather than behaving in a standard way, we are acting for the first time like *individuals* who detach themselves from the collective guidelines in order to obey their inner voice alone. From the moment of birth we are directed by others, first by the projects of our parents, then by the environment in which we live. Only when we act according to our personal choices do we become *self-directed.* In the collective imagination, this capacity for self-direction, for taking the responsibility for our own decisions, is represented by the myth of Ulysses. In the ten years of his pilgrimage he meets and loves the most beautiful creatures: nymphs, sorceresses, and mortal women. But he must always abandon them to follow his destiny, that unconscious call personified by Hermes. Ulysses is the perfect example of the man impelled by his *inner daimon,* that daimon which compels the creative individual always to follow his own road, to remain faithful to himself, despite the pain it causes him and others.

To cut ourselves off from the ones we love and turn our backs on the world we have built is a fearful thing, because our only justification is fidelity to ourselves.

This way of behaving is tantamount to *betrayal.* I betray the collectivity by turning my back on it. It is understandable then if these situations create remorse, doubts, guilt feelings. Others cannot understand or accept our actions. It is only justified in the eyes of our conscience, to which we have remained faithful by our choice.

The *call*, the obligation to take a particular direction — as in the case of K. — may also be interpreted as an invitation to death. In a famous film by Luchino Visconti, *Gruppo di famiglia in un interno* (1974), the hero tells of a mysterious tenant who settles into the apartment above. His footsteps can be heard in the silence. He appears suddenly in order to disappear with equal speed. But as the years pass his stays become longer and longer, and he ends by establishing himself permanently in the apartment. This tenant is death. In psychological terms the confrontation with death can be read as the search for a new identity. The soul, feeling the need of a transformation, which will allow it to achieve a higher degree of authenticity, experiences this kind of change as a *death.*

In transforming one's personality a part of it is killed, sacrificed, to allow for a rebirth. One must abandon everything that one possesses and has achieved, but which no longer feeds one's soul, to search out new horizons, to explore new ways of being. This challenge to the unknown implies the acceptance of situations in which, since they offer no security, death is more probable than life. We might think, for example, of the American epic of the Far West. The pioneers who left the rich, civilized East in order to push as far as California, a still unknown territory — *hic sunt leones*, as was written on maps of the ancient world — in search of fortune and riches and a new life, accepted the risk of death in their confrontations with the local populations for the sake of a possible rebirth. What is important to analyze here is the concept of the frontier. While in American history the frontier was a physical fact, in the lives of us all it is a value: it refers, that is, to an endopsychic reality.

The frontier is the place where nothing exists, where one can and must still build, but where the unknown brings with it the threat of death. To live in a frontier area means to turn one's back on a life achieved—and one must have really achieved it, otherwise the psychological value of the new lands, the frontier is nil—and to accept the possibility of death, which is to say of *crisis*, of the loss of all points of reference.

This capacity to accept possibility, change—the *call*—is a fundamental one for the analyst. I don't think one can be a good therapist, capable of helping the patient work a transformation, if one has not accepted in one's own life an unconditional opening to risk, the new, change; if one does not live permanently on a frontier. This implies the opening of a dialogue with one's inner images. This is the only way for feeling life deeply. When we find ourselves in a position of relative balance, when life runs along tranquilly without brusque upheavals, we hardly know we are alive. It is the tests we must sustain, the choices we must make, that help us to taste the full flavor of life and give the soul back its voice.

Once an airplane has finished the takeoff and is flying calmly, for example, the passengers are not even aware of any movement. But all it takes is the hitting of an air pocket for them to realize that something is wrong. In like fashion, when our life is running smoothly, neither accelerating nor stopping brusquely, we lose the *sense* of it. It is fundamental for everyone, but for an analyst above all, to feel what is happening inside herself, to expose herself constantly to encounters with the unconscious, which does not allow her the acquisition of comfortable certainties. That means, like the airplane, to constantly run into air pockets that agitate and upset one but which are the proof of progress. Only in this way is it possible to guide the patient in his difficult descent into the Underworld without his remaining a prisoner of Ade, surrounded and obsessed by shadows that he has evoked, and bringing him up again to see the stars. Every creative act, furthermore, is the result of an exposure to unconscious conflicts.

The encounter with unconscious images is the task to which K., without knowing it, will be exposed throughout his story. Unhappily, his will be an unfortunate venture that ends in failure, as almost always happens in Kafka's works. But it is life itself that often is "nefarious." Jung stated (1938–1940 p. 105), "You can say, for instance, that life is a disease with a very bad prognosis: it lingers on for years." The contemplation of this eventuality should not discourage us, however, or keep us from living it all the way to the end. For in doing this, however painfully, we will be able to give diverse meanings to what happens, discovering psychological dimensions we didn't even know existed. In order to answer the *call* we must learn to read the images that present themselves to our minds from the depths of the soul, to hold dialogue with them, and then be able to live them out.

Fourteen

The Pain of Transformation

The Castle opens with a protagonist who has lost his way and wanders in a world of shadows, accompanied by the invitation of the unconscious to compare himself with his inner images. But the *call* that comes from within raises the problem of the *answer* as soon as it is perceived. What is evoked is an impalpable and fleeting world similar to the shadows that inhabit it. Here we move in an indeterminate dimension shrouded in the mists of our unawareness. And it is precisely this indefinite quality of the thing that now opens before us, the impossibility of exactly circumscribing the goal, contrary to the clarity with which we can see the reality left behind us, that gives greater value and dignity to our actions. The entire story of the surveyor, his search, his desire to understand the world in which he finds himself living, his personal relationships, his efforts to reach the Castle — all these can be considered his *reply* to the call.

The call of the unconscious — the same heard by K — which according to Jung is primarily the prerogative of the mature in years, cannot be dated chronologically. Our lives continually pass through periods of crisis, stages of transition, in which the balance achieved up to then must be destroyed and another one created. Each new relationship, each new job, is a death and a birth at the same time. And to open oneself to the new, to change, to what at first appears unknown and confused, means to answer an inner call, to prefer the *upheaval* of an authentic choice to the stagnancy of renunciation and of accommodation. To give heed to an inner voice that impels one toward a nonhabitual dimension implies the capacity to contact the unconscious, to establish a relationship with its images. Human life, different from that of the animals, has a relationship with the *imaginary*. It is a reality that has no tangible existence, which, having no material weight, vanishes into air as soon as we try to seize it.

And yet this fantastic world obsesses us and impregnates every moment of our lives, not only in dreams, fantasies, and memories, but apparently breaking out of the very heart of reality as if to announce its imminent conversion into another dimension. The fascination of the imaginary is born from the very center of our lives, shaping itself in the form of an "elsewhere," an "out-of-this-world" that embroils us in its net and captures us (Pfeiffer 1966, p. IX). It reveals the irresistible attraction, the seduction of a dimension that eludes us, that is absent from consciousness and not reducible to it even while intensely permeating it. The eidolons that populate our world contain our past and our future inasmuch as destiny is nothing but the realization of an unconscious *image*.

All of life is a constant confrontation with our fantasies, which in manifesting themselves color the external world with meaning. Events are important to us only insofar as we project our inner world onto them. From a psychological viewpoint it is much more the inner images than external events that create our reality.

It is important to understand that the famous point of leverage, from which Archimedes claimed he could lift the world, is situated within us. That point is not outside us, nor does it involve destiny any longer. Many wrongly believe that it is enough to change external circumstances alone to achieve happiness. On the contrary—a true transformation must always take place within ourselves. A fabulous winning of the lottery will mean nothing at all if the inner condition is not changed that makes us feel poor. To be poor and a loser, if you are not living in a dramatic reality such as the Third World, often is caused by the inability to live, to let oneself go without fighting. To believe oneself to be ugly, unfortunate, helpless in the face of adversity, is often to behave as if this really were so. Life is a struggle. Those who cannot believe in their own potential, in their own abilities to overcome the obstacles with which every individual's path is strewn, have lost before beginning to fight. Heraclitus maintained:

Whoever does not hope in what cannot be hoped for will never discover it because it is closed to research and no road leads to it, because it happens. (in Colli 1980, 14, A63, p. 71)

The way in which we relate to events depends on our personal psychological experiences. Riches, to continue with the same example, are illusory realities. We believe that they can satisfy us only because we have projected onto them the power to fulfill our inner insufficiency. We should think, for example of King Midas who, believing in the panacea of riches, asked the gods to turn everything he touched into gold. But having attained this power he was condemned by his own desire to die of hunger. As the myth demonstrates, however rich and splendid external objects may be, they are certainly not able to nourish us or our souls. True riches can only be found within us, in knowing how to relate to our daimons, and thus change the situations responsible for our suffering.

To accept the confrontation with our images, to hold dialogue with the unconscious, requires a certain capacity to bear with the *tension* created between the conscious ego and the secret levels of the psyche (Neumann 1979, p. 181). The extraordinary sensitivity of artists to the imaginary and their ability to describe all the shades of the human soul is due to their condition of "permanent laceration." The artist is one who knows how to express all the multiple personalities inhabiting her soul. To write, to paint, to compose music, or any other artistic expression represent the ability to reflect the polytheistic structure of the psyche. Alongside a monotheistic conception, according to which the soul tends to an ever-greater integration represented by the archetype of the Self, it is possible to place a polycentric hypothesis. Giving a mythical background to every complex— according to which every kind of behavior is the manifestation of a "god" or a "daimon" it is possible to recognize not only the importance and the dignity of the symptom, but above all to integrate it while respecting its specific quality. To accept the multiplicity of the inner voices without trying to unify them into a single figure allows us to recognize in the process of dissolution and fragmentation a value equal to that of coagulation into a unity (Hillman 1981, pp. 12–24). A transformed personality is bound to result from the recognition of the multiple personalities that dwell within us.

To accept the possibility of a plurality of psychological dimensions, of inner focal points within us, may on the one hand give us a greater awareness of our fragmentation and perhaps sometimes a more acute suffering. What one wants to be is not clear and unambiguous but always changing, while, on the other hand, it allows for a better understanding and acceptance of ourselves. To leave room for every psychic component means to have greater tolerance even for our undesired aspects, for those which have not grown and which instead of continually progressing — in accordance with a positivistic idea of the psyche — take us back toward past conditions. The moment we encounter our own daimons, it is possible to recognize and listen to their voices. The result is an undoubted enrichment of the personality.

At this point one can see how the artistic domain to which I refer is not peculiar to those few human beings whose ability to express themselves is greater than that of most people. It is a question of the possibility of living one's life creatively, and this possibility is open to all of us — indeed, it is our task to set it as our goal. What differentiates the creative individual from others is his extraordinary aptitude for supporting the tensions provoked by his complexes. His ego, although subject to all the power of the unconscious, to its "voracity," is not crushed by it as the psychotic is, but is able to make use of symbols of the unconscious and work them into a version that is both personal and universal at the same time. The strength of the ego is not used to avoid the conflict, to defend itself, but to confront the unconscious and take its measure. In that way the injuries inflicted by the complex do not spend themselves in morbid fantasies but become the outlet for something universally significant (Neumann 1979, p. 157). This work on unconscious fantasies allows for giving a new interpretation to one's blocks, to slowly transform one's inner dimension.

> Then he went on to find quarters for the night. The inn was still awake, and although the landlord could not provide a room and was upset by such a late and unexpected arrival, he was willing to let K. sleep on a bag of straw in the parlour. K. accepted the offer. (Kafka 1922b, p. 9)

Being lost and empty is a condition that immediately calls up the need of finding a "roof," an inner point in which one can take refuge. The confrontation with inner images is always difficult, hard and sometimes painful work. One feels the need of having some support. For those who go through an experience of analysis, the therapeutic relationship, especially at crucial moments, functions as a warm and reassuring place where one can pause for a moment and call a truce with one's lacerating sufferings. But the refuge, the hostel are also and primarily endopsychic. They represent the psyche's capacity to create a containing space within itself where repressed and rejected feelings can be given some leeway. It is here that the psyche provides its own nourishment, cures its own wounds, and accepts its own illness. And such recognition is what enables one to keep the wounds from festering in isolation. The search for an inner place of refuge was predominant in Franz Kafka's life. In fact, in a letter to Max Brod, Milena will say of him: "He is without the least shelter, without any refuge" (Brod 1937, p. 259). For Kafka, who continued to wander as a *stranger* in the world, frozen by his own detachment, the only welcoming space was afforded by his writing. On December 16, 1910, in fact, we find this note in his diaries: "I won't give up the diary again. I must hold on here, it is only place I can" (Kafka 1910–1923, p. 29) For all personalities who have difficulty in relating to the outside world, in establishing emotional contact, writing offers a substitute, an opportunity for dialogue, for comparing oneself with the other even while she remains absent, distant. Those confrontations with fantasies, which the extrovert often unconsciously makes by diving directly into life, occur mainly in the imagination of the introvert.

The moment that K. accepts this confrontation by undertaking his voyage into the unconscious, all kinds of things begin happening to him. He immediately encounters two opposing aspects: the Castle and the inn. He wants to reach the Castle, be received by its lords, but he is blocked in this intent. Rather than being received at the Castle, which would be his right considering that he had been called there, he is offered a straw mat in the village inn. Being tired and in need of rest he is obliged to accept. Thus begins for the surveyor that series of exclusions, rejections, and compromises that pursue him throughout his story.

The opposite pole of the *call* is composed of exclusion and rejection, things that to one degree or another everyone is obliged to cope with from the very beginning of life. Even if no one has ever asked to be born, birth should imply the right to exist and to live in the best possible way. Reality is instead quite another thing. Taking up Kafka's parable again, if we consider the Castle to be a metaphor of that existential reality into which we have been called, we note that this dimension is always barred to us, that life is marked by a series of impediments which block our progress toward the final goal. One seeks the Castle and finds that only an inn is open. One is offered only a miserable straw mat. And if one demands better conditions, treatment more suitable to our "merits," like K., one only meets with scorn and hostility.

The psychoanalytic interpretation of a novel presupposes getting close to its elements — the characters, plot, landscape, like the parts of a dream. But a work of art has an intrinsic validity and autonomy that place it beyond any interpretation. To look for a meaning does not mean looking for an exhaustive explanation and matching up narrative elements with biographical ones. What can be traced, when one is capable of reading it, is that "secret code" (Fusini 1986, p. 165) which contains the work's inner necessity, the hidden law that has determined its birth. But what counts most, above all for a psychologist, is to be able to treat an artistic product as if it were a Rorschach test blot. I believe it is the evocative power of its images, their ability to constitute unconscious contents, which in reality establishes the validity of a work of art. It must be able to excite deep echoes, which may be different for each individual. Thus the analysis of its images becomes the pretext and the occasion for encountering an entire *lower* dimension that belongs to the darkest, deepest, and least-known part of the soul. In reading Kafka's novels — or those of any other author — we cannot be certain that the things we believe to have found in them are the things that the author, consciously or not, wanted to express.

One can try to construct a coherent interpretation so that the author himself might be able to discern a certain veracity in it. Nevertheless, the correspondences between the interpretations attributed to the single elements or the work as a whole on the one hand, and the artistic intentions of the author on the other, have little relevance. The interpretation is very often a function of the reader's psychological needs: it is his *own* fantasies, his *own* daimons that he encounters. What really counts is the possibility of carrying out a psychological task on one's self through the the stimulus of the art product.

To return to the image of the inn, we can consider this to be an extremely impoverished and modest aspect in which one can take refuge while awaiting admittance to the Castle. It is the emblem of the endopsychic reality to which one retires at the moments of greatest inner conflict and where one can find the *warmth* and the *nourishment* to survive in the battle with external reality.

Depression, the psychological condition in which all normal activities are reduced to the point of almost total arrest, is the state of a soul preparing for its own transformation. The caterpillar, in order to become a butterfly, encloses itself in a cocoon and lives in a passive, immobile condition until the metamorphosis is completed. Only then, expanding its new wings, will it be able to come out and flit among the flowers. In the same way the soul—and let us not forget that in the Greek world the word for soul was the same as for butterfly, thus revealing the deep cultural connections existing there between the two terms—needs a preparatory period of silent expectation in which to turn in on itself and concentrate on the images that populate its world. If we imagine life as a spiral in which progress is never linear but a road that also implies retrogression, the return to a preceding state, we can understand how human life is composed of constant deaths and rebirths. The passage to a new condition always implies the sacrifice of everything we have previously accomplished. The new being which we must bring to the world is born—like the Arab phoenix—from the ashes of everything we had been until that moment.

In Andrej Tarkovskij's last, very beautiful film *The Sacrifice* (1986), the hero, Alexander, can only save those he loves and the entire world from nuclear catastrophe by means of a sacrifice. Turning to that God with whom he had never before had any relations, he promises to give up all his possessions—including the house that represents his entire being—to never see his dear ones again, and even to lose his own life, so that the world will be spared and others will be able to continue living, as before. The terrible threat is exorcised through his sacrifice and the act of love that unites him to Maria—a new incarnation of the Virgin — in the generation of a new life. When the night-mare is over, he keeps his vow and sets fire to his house. But mistaken for a maniac, he is removed from his family and closed up in an insane asylum. Thus the sacrifice is fulfilled: he has renounced every-thing, even himself. Whether Alexander is a madman suffering delirium, or the one person capable of accepting the sacrifice person-ally and giving his life for others, has little relevance because it is the grandeur of what has occurred, of the visions between madness and reality that have been created, which counts.

Rebirth, the hope for a new world, thus implies the sacrifice of the old. A moment almost always arrives in life when it is necessary to burn everything that has belonged to us, everything we have loved, everything we have been, in order to make way for the new.

On deciding to begin a new analysis, a young woman who finds herself in this delicate and tormented phase of her life sees the image of a stake take shape before her. She gives form to this call of the soul in a drawing that depicts a woman in water up to her waist about to enter a cavern, supporting herself with one hand on the trunk of a tree that is also half submerged. Behind her the flames of a fire burn violently, through which she can glimpse the satyrlike figure of the man she has loved. Despite the fact that she still loves that man, she is aware that she must leave that tormented relationship behind her if she wants to come to life again. The sea cavern she is entering repre-sents her immersion in the unconscious, while the tree trunk she seizes to keep from being entirely engulfed by the waters alludes to her relationship with the analyst. A new contact with her inner dimensions is needed, a new descent into the Underworld — in the ancient world, in fact, the mythical entrance to Hades was almost always depicted as a grotto — guided by the analyst-shaman, to reemerge in a greater state of awareness. Before being able to give birth to this image, however, the woman went through a period of depression, of inner death. Detachment and sacrifice are always extremely painful because it is a part of ourselves that is being "burned."

Alexander's sacrifice is also prepared by a long period of depression during which he is detached from the world and lives closed up in the country after having abandoned the theater. Aware of belonging to a civilization in its twilight, he takes stock of himself in the search for meaning. The film — the spiritual testament of a man dying of cancer—clearly states that it is too late for the hero. The hope for rebirth, for the building of a new world, is entrusted to his son, who is still only a child. Alexander's opening monologue is a splendid presentation of the depressive anguish that precedes metamorphosis. The transformation-depression polarity was represented in the symbolism of alchemy by the attempt to transform lead into gold. Lead in alchemy is not to be interpreted literally and exclusively as a metal, but rather as a quality of consciousness that the alchemist must possess in order to complete his work of transformation. Slow and heavy, lead stands for the *heaviness* of the mind that goes through a metamorphosis by means of a depression.

Depression, sacrifice, and arrested motion are interconnected aspects of the land surveyor's story. For K. to be able to begin his quest, for him to be able to generate his new personality, he must renounce what he has been in the past. But before beginning the work of change, he must stop and regain strength and energy in the miserable inn.

The inn is the first of those maternal symbols that are strewn throughout the novel. It is a place of rest and refreshment. As also happened in *The Trial*, one of the first images in the work leads back to the problem of food, nourishment, and thus to the relationship with the female, the mother. If one of the many possible facets that can be discerned in the complex image of the Castle is that of Authority, the paternal sphere, the inn instead leads back to the maternal principle, whose primary function is precisely that of nourishment and shelter. But both these spheres are closed to the surveyor. There is no room at the inn; he can be given only provisional accommodations and will soon be chased away.

K.'s first contact with the maternal sphere is marked by *exclusion*. It is not a very hazardous interpretation to underline here the correspondence between this situation and Kafka's difficult and tormented relations with women, his inability to experience deep connections with them from whom he ultimately fled in fright. If the female is perceived as rejecting and distant, then it is terribly painful to make contact with all the aspects characterizing it.

The succession of these first images in *The Castle* induce one to formulate the hypothesis—which is furthermore supported by experience in analysis—that the first consequence of the *call*, the crossing of a bridge, in short the putting of oneself into question, is to produce a regression to the maternal sphere.

The possibility of healing one's wounds and of finding new energy seems to require a return to the first, most fundamental experience of every human being.

It is significant that even while constantly dwelling on relations with the female in his works, Kafka carefully avoids mentioning his mother in his diaries. The problem that he repeatedly brings up, on the other hand, is that of the painful relationship with his father which, in the *Letter to His Father*, becomes an implacable, relentless accusation. The heavy veil of repression falls over the mother, as if this wound were too deep, too archaic to be directly and consciously confronted.

Thus it is then that from the depths of the unconscious emerge fearful female figures like Gardena, the Terrible Great Mother. The return to the mother by way of the stop at the inn, the maternal sphere, therefore calls up the theme of the first *exclusion*. From the very start it seems that for K. there is no possibility of being taken in and nourished. The solitude and detachment that mark the hero, his great ineptitude in making deep and true contact with the people he encounters, and also with Frieda, his woman, are the sad result of exclusion. Anyone who has been rejected, injured, when he was still too vulnerable to be able to defend himself, when the lack of love caused a malaise similar to death, will later encounter strong inner resistance to entrusting and opening himself to the Other. Every intense involvement will be felt to be potentially destructive. The fear of a new rejection and exclusion will create a barrier between the Self and the external world.

To stop and seek refreshment at the inn, that is, to turn to one's own inner life, also implies stopping to reflect, putting questions to oneself, before taking up the difficult struggle to reach the goal to which one has been called. It is important to point out how this questioning arises at the moment when any sort of obstacle obliges us to deviate from our path. It is the effort to overcome suffering that makes us seek a *meaning*, something that will make what we are going through seem less absurd and accidental. Just as the blind man and the cripple continue to ask the reason for their destiny, K. too during the entire novel will do nothing but question himself and others about why he is excluded from the Castle and the impossibility of reaching it.

An obstacle creates a gap between us and life, a gap that we must try to reduce. People who are happy rarely question themselves about their condition. But whenever life, for one reason or another, seems to slip out of our hands, when it moves away from us, when its fullness is a distant memory and it is no longer possible to plunge joyfully into external events, then it is necessary to move away from the vortex and find that "magic" element that can put all the pieces of our mosaic back together. The reply would seem to be to possess that apotropaic power to ward off suffering, perhaps only for an instant, and reestablish the disturbed order with the security that it brings.

If we analyze the answers that individuals try to give themselves, we see that very often they have a common denominator: to change the hallmark of a pain that lacks all meaning and to stamp it with the seal of a uniqueness that borders on the extraordinary. Thus the pain turns into the laceration of the call. Perhaps no one is calling us. Perhaps our lives are no more useful than those of any others, but to believe that they are — even while aware that it is an illusion — helps us to bear that initial wrench, that wound that continues to sting us in secret. Thus the meaninglessness of pain is lessened by the sweet reassurance of "predestination" with its promised offer of transcendence. For the rest, we analysts can only offer the hope of transmuting the absurd into the meaningful for our patients who — with their pain, their inability to live, and their alienation — oblige us to keep our eyes fixed on what Montale has called *Il male del vivere (The Evil of Living)* (Montale 1920–1927, p. 57).

The thousand models with which we believe we understand the psyche can be considered attempts to make sense of the pain so that it seems milder, more bearable. If K. and his creator could transform their emptiness, their suffering into hope, into purpose, they would not succumb to exhaustion. Their struggle, their constant questioning would find an answer, however limited, partial, and temporary it might be. Apropos of this, there come to mind some splendid verses of Montale (1920–1927, p. 57):

> La mia vita e questo seccho pendio,
> mezzo non fine, strada aperta a sbocchi

135

di rigagnoli, lento franamento.
E' dessa, ancora, questa pianta
che nasce della devasatazione
e in faccia ha i colpi di mare ed e sospesa
fra erratiche forze di venti.
Questo pezzo di suolo non erbato
s'è spaccato perché nascesse una margherita.

My life is this dry slope,
means not end, road a ready mouth
for rivulets, slow landslide.
It is this, still, the very plant
that grows from the devastation
and in its face receives sea slaps and is suspended
between erratic blasts of wind.
This piece of grassless soil
has split open to let a daisy grow.

Let us continue to consider the problem of exclusion, which is such a central concern in the work of Kafka. We have seen that as soon as K. crosses the bridge that leads to the village—that is, the instant in which he crosses his Rubicon leaving his past life behind, he immediately has to face exclusion: the host has no rooms to let, everyone rejects him and tries to chase him away, he is offered a bed worthy of a dog. Exclusion is one of the most painful experiences of life, and inasmuch as it is unfortunately structural we meet with it from birth until death. Rejection begins very early when the child compares herself to the family. It is just the people most precious to her who are able to wound her by exclusion. Within the family circle, rejection explodes with greater violence. We reject whoever appears to us to be extraneous, different from our expectations. A parent disappointed in the personality of his child, who is unlike what he has dreamed of, often may react with terrible violence. "You are pitiable," "You are only a miserable failure" are some of the remarks which many of us— in the role of parent or child—are forced to hear. To love someone for what she is, not in the hope of a narcissistic recompense, requires notable psychological maturity. When one lacks the capacity to love and respect the other as he is because one is stuck in an infantile conception of a relationship, this latter—steeped in anger and disappointment—becomes a fight to the death.

Exclusion, then, implies a feeling of being different, of not belonging. The excluded one is the rejected and abandoned. It seems to her that she is inhabiting a kind of no-man's-land where love and understanding neither do nor can exist. There are few situations as harrowing as this. Exclusion can be the first cause of an inner paralysis through which the one who feels excluded expresses his renunciation of life. At the root of many psychological disturbances—the psychoses in particular—there is often an original situation of rejection (Benedetti 1979, pp. 83–87).

The subtle thread that connects diversity and exclusion unwinds throughout the novel. *The Castle* can be read as a constant encounter with diversity and exclusion. K. questions and seeks, following his own inner law, which cannot be assimilated into that of the village and which makes him different from all the other inhabitants. This keeping faith with his opinions and his truths is the thing that will make him forever an *outsider* and isolation his destiny.

Although the novel ends in a failure, one of its messages can be summed up in the invitation to maintain one's individuality despite any external pressures whatsoever to becoming assimilated.

In his notebooks Paul Valéry (1974, p. 207) writes:

> I have tried as much as possible to be different from others—insofar as the *others* are a type of being that one supposes to be known—who are precisely determined, thus *finite*, and whom therefore one must not repeat. One should distinguish oneself at all costs in order not to feel oneself a useless repetition, just *one more of the same*, whose existence does not result in the acquisition of anything, who only increases the number. This is the horror of being a man.

From the beginning K. knows very well—even if he won't admit it even to himself—that he is an outsider, that he will never be admitted to the Castle and belong to it. He is alone and rises above the others—whose lives flow unconsciously without questioning or torments—like the Castle tower, which might be a metaphor of the painful awareness and deep isolation of him who is in contact with his psychic world and so knows that he can only find his true reality and strength in his own inwardness.

Fifteen

The Exclusion of the Outsider

The problem of *exclusion,* which runs throughout the novel, can be considered a kind of litmus paper of the stance that K.-Kafka assumes in the confrontation with life. Up to now we have examined this condition in relation to the Other. In the first instance, when our relationship with our inner images is still only slightly developed, we can in fact believe that the rejection depends on the outside world. But, little by little, as we gain the ability to make contact with the unconscious, we understand that exclusion is not an external problem but an inner one, since what we are forced to face is our *self-exclusion.* To continue thinking that it is reality which sets us aside means to allow a paranoid attitude to prevail within us. This conviction, rather than inducing us to look, into our souls, impels us to scrutinize the signs that come from without in the desire to discover our destiny, just as ancient soothsayers observed flights of birds to predict the future.

Analysts, whose work brings them into daily contact with the inner lives of others and their secrets, know perfectly well that the beginning of a psychological transformation capable of profoundly modifying one's relationship to life is contained in the moment when one begins to integrate the Shadow.

One can in fact change one's destiny by recognizing the weak, obscure, "lower" aspects of one's personality, which we call the Shadow, of a psyche that would want to be composed exclusively of light and always victorious. From the moment we are capable of looking into our souls and discovering for the first time the things that have been rejected, refused acceptance, and our weaknesses, we can begin to take care of ourselves. If we can only learn how to look, we will see how at the center of our being there still lives the *abandoned child*. It is an aspect that is always present within us and that is not to be strictly identified with the past. The feeling of being abandoned that evokes the need of being helped and succored is not a condition which can be resolved once and for all by reaching adulthood and self-sufficiency. Alongside a fulfilled and mature personality there always remains a substratum that never develops at all, that remains forever immature, fragile, in need of care (Hillman 1971a, p. 32).

In endopsychic terms, to feel excluded means to have rejected a part of oneself that was judged inadequate. Feeling ashamed of the child, his weakness, his fears, his being too small to face life, one is ashamed of his need of love and his dependence. And not being able to nourish him, we reject him and let him die. We thus allow our sensibility and our tenderness to become sterile. By following the alienating myth of total independence, we negate our needs, and lose the childhood aspect of our minds. Along with it we lose its capacities — imagination, creativity, the recklessness of our affections. To overcome exclusion we must now effect a return to the past, to the abandoned child. We must become *nurturers* and *mothers*, learn to welcome and nourish her, accept her dependence, but avoid becoming trapped by her. If the nurturer must take care of the child without expecting anything of her, the mother, for her part, can expect the child to grow, can make room for individuality by permitting the child to fulfill her being through the mother's hopeful love. No one can hope to receive the acceptance and the love of others if he cannot feel it for himself, for his own soul. To return to the child thus means to learn to look at oneself and the world with new eyes.

Reading between the lines of hundreds of human stories, one quickly notes that not only does no one exclude us — because exclusion is something born within us — but also that the world is indifferent with regard to our lives. To be an adult means to face reality and decide what to do about it. However, when psychological suffering insinuates itself into life, sometimes undermining it like a termite, the capacity for deliberate action is damaged and blocked. Then one feels that one is not equipped for life. Silently the perverse mechanism of self-exclusion sets to work within us: we set ourselves apart, conclude that we can never overcome the obstacles in our path, decide, that is, to take a *negative* approach to reality. Of course many obiections can be made to this, but they all collapse before the observation that nothing is written anywhere, no decisions have been made, or, if they have been, they are certainly not definitive since there are no irrevocable decisions in our lives.

What has real value, what can change the game is *our* point of view, *our* attitude toward the situation. That life may then in effect win out over our intentions is not so very important. What counts is that we have made the effort, have had the courage to accept the challenge of existence day after day. Josef K., the hero of *The Trial*, does everything he can to prevent his arrest from becoming a condemnation without appeal. But he fails, and his end will be harrowing: his throat will be cut like a slaughtered animal's. The surveyor in *The Castle* will lose his battle too, since he will never be received. In these stories the only really important thing is the constancy of both personages in proceeding to the very end with the undertakings they have set for themselves.

The condition of self-exclusion — which Kafka unconsciously never stopped exercising on his life — in his novels is turned into exclusion practiced by the external world. All the characters in *The Castle* are excluded in varying degrees. They have to come to terms with an authority that rejects them and which often is shadowy and evasive in that one cannot manage to confront it directly. In the case of the Barnabas family, the ostracism that it must endure after Amalia's guilty action depends on their own inability to overcome the event, to act as if nothing had happened. The head of the family's efforts to obtain the pardon of the Authorities will come to nothing inasmuch as it is not possible to demonstrate any guilt. No official will ever agree to see him, just as Klamm will never accept a meeting with K.

From a psychological viewpoint we can see these situations as indicating the author's unconscious affirmation that no external authority is capable of canceling the rejection. The only encounter capable of healing the wound is that with one's own fantasies, within oneself. Without considering the actual traumatic experiences, and quite differently from the way things occur in childhood when one is extremely helpless, dependent, and vulnerable in relation to the external world, it is the adult herself who gives others the power to reject her. Rejection can only occur in a situation of insecurity where a deep wound undermines our sense of identity and makes us dependent on the acceptance of others. The moment in which one becomes totally dependent on acceptance by someone, one hands oneself over, helplessly vulnerable, into his power and makes a kind of divinity of him. It is as if one's mental balance no longer depended on oneself, on one's ability to change, but on the *other*, his love and his rejection. This is the dramatic situation we find described in Emily Dickinson's verses; an experience so total and obsessive as to oblige her to shut those doors to the *other* in reality which in fantasy were opened wide to him. The poet (1862a, p. 281) writes:

> And often since, In Danger,
> I count the force 'twould be
> To have a God so strong as that
> To hold my life for me
>
> Till I could take the Balance
> That tips so frequent, now,
> It takes me all the while to poise —
> And then — it doesn't stay —

We find ourselves here in a psychological situation where the borders between the Self and the Other have been abolished. To exist one must *be with and in the Other*, compose an inseparable unity with him. Once again Dickinson (1983, p. 287) describes this situation thus:

> Empty my Heart, of Thee —
> Its single Artery —
> Begin, and leave Thee out —
> Simply Extinction's Date —
>
> Much Billow hath the Sea —
> One Baltic-They —
> Subtract Thyself, in play,
> And not enough of me
> Is left — to put away —
> "Myself" meant Thee —
>
> Erase the Root — no Tree —
> Thee — then — no me —
> The Heavens stripped —
> Eternity's vast pocket, picked —

It was this deep need of the *Other,* this extreme dependence on the love and acceptance of someone else that forced the poet to spend her last years in total isolation. When the other has become *God,* one must defend oneself from his terrible power. "You are God: you could break me" confessed Marguerite Yourcenar (1957, p. 51).

The moment we put the power to accept or reject us into someone else's hands, as if our existence depended completely on her verdict, we automatically expose ourselves to rejection. Vulnerability of this kind, typical of love, can be extended, *mutatis mutandis,* to many other situations. The manager who identifies himself with his work, with the approval of his boss or his colleagues, will feel the same sense of exclusion if he should lose this esteem due, for example, to a sudden financial collapse: the world has set him aside, has excluded him. What happens in all these cases is the loss of one's own psychic center of gravity projected onto the outside world. Even though it traces its origins back to a real situation, in general very early in life, *exclusion is* always an inner experience. That which excludes us is our incapacity to face life, the fear of confronting and relating to the Other, the fear of our being different, which, instead of being recognized and lived in its creative potential, hides behind the barrier of a solitude with which we keep others away. The initial condition of being rejected thus changes into an active one of rejecting. It takes us away from a world that doesn't understand us, that doesn't love us, that can wound us.

A variant of the beginning found among Kafka's manuscripts contains a detail worthy of note. The host warns the surveyor who has just arrived not to go out onto the balcony because the supporting beam is rotten and could give way (Kafka 1922b, p. 311). From a psychological standpoint the image indicates that the relationship with the outside world is difficult, almost blocked, due to a fragile ego that cannot support the stress of emotions aroused by contact. As could happen to the beam, so too the bridge collapses when one turns to look at him who is crossing it.

If we think of another famous Kafka story, *The Burrow,* in which the mole who is the protagonist spends his entire life digging out and improving the refuge he has built for himself—a refuge that allows him to live far from the world into which he makes only the shortest excursions in search of food—we can understand how distance, the rejection of contact, can be a style of life common to all those who fear any form of relationship. To anyone who cannot raise himself above his traumas and experience a way of being together, the *other* seems to be nothing more than a curse.

When the Other is nothing but an enemy — Dickinson calls it the *Great Thief* — the only reaction can be flight, refuge in the distance. Kafka, like Emily Dickinson, reflects the dramatic condition of a creature who, being fully aware of his sense of nullity in relation to the Other's power and well knowing his own sense of emptiness, of subjection, chooses to overturn the situation by changing from the rejected to the rejecter. Once again Kafka notes on August 15, 1913: "I'll shut myself off from everyone to the point of insensibility. Make an enemy of everyone, speak to no one" (Kafka 1910–1923, p. 229).

The most extreme example of this desire for isolation is retirement into autism. The autistic child, in distancing herself from the world, from any contact that can cause her suffering, ends by regressing into a neonatal condition. In the worst cases she not only loses her facility of speech but anaesthetizes her senses, becomes blind, deaf, insensitive to pain. Thus rejection is taken to its ultimate consequences.

At the roots of the feeling of exclusion there is the incapacity to recover from an old wound, the continuing feeling of a disdain that has long ceased and which ends by perpetuating it masochistically. In his analysis of schizophrenia, Benedetti (1979, pp. 85–87) describes a *need* for rejection that compels the patient to constantly provoke this kind of reaction in the therapist. The deep sense of this "aberrant" behavior is not the person's self-destructive desire to feel confirmed in his negative identity, nor to be removed from the presence of the other, which is always charged with experiences of a conflictual nature however much the psychotic may want contact — but it is rather in his need to confront an experience that has structured his own psychological world. The new encounter with rejection in an analytic situation enables him to work it out in new terms because, however painful rejection on the part of the therapist may be, it is always less traumatic than finding oneself face to face with one's fantasies. To provoke a partial rejection in the analyst serves to "inoculate" him against the total experience of rejection, much as a vaccine would. One of the characteristics of the psychotic state is that experiences of acceptance are never strong enough to afford them complete introjection. There is nothing left for the patient to do but externalize the intrapsychic situation of rejection in such a way that it will slowly corrode the accepting attitude of the therapist. Thus it is up to the analyst to remain firm in her attitude of acceptance until she has managed to thaw the entire iceberg of inner rejection as it gradually emerges.

What we witness in these cases is a kind of challenge on the part of the patient, who continually puts our comprehension to the test and is ready at the slightest slip-up to reprove us for our inability to accept him, to support him all the way to the bitter end.

These are the objectively difficult situations that can only be resolved when the analyst has sufficiently developed her relationship with rejection and is sufficiently free from the yoke of her aggressiveness. A particularly thorough knowledge of psychological dynamics is not necessary in order to be aware of how the extreme dependence of the patient—his oral avidness which compels him to continually make demands, to think up ceaseless new situations in which to measure himself against the acceptance-rejection polarity—can provoke an aggressive reaction in the therapist and evoke the dynamics of power. Only a therapist who can allow herself to express naturally slight reactions of impatience, of rejection—without slipping into a visible negative countertransference, into a sado-masochistic spiral which, once activated is difficult to control—will be capable of allowing the patient to integrate an old trauma and induce a sphere of *self-acceptance* in his psyche.

The entire progress of *The Castle* can be summed up in K.'s attempt to penetrate it, to give siege to a mysterious reality that tries to keep him out. In order to succeed he must be able to conquer his doubts, be deeply convinced of the positive outcome of his efforts. It is his fears and hesitations, the false security with which he interrogates the villagers that undermines his success. In Andrej Tarkovskij's last film the hero is given a splendid apologue: an old Russian Orthodox monk plants a dead tree. He tells his astonished disciple to water it every day. The youth takes water to the tree at the top of the mountain every morning and returns to the monastery in the evening. One morning three years later, as he goes to water the tree as usual, he discovers that it is covered with lovely buds. Faith combined with care has wrought a miracle. If K. had deeply believed in himself then, if he had been truly capable of loving, the doors of the Castle would have been thrown open to him. But for K., as for Kafka, there can be no redemption.

If the surveyor were sure of himself he would not have to be constantly asking for information about the Castle, he would not have to consider Frieda a kind of precious hostage for obtaining an audience with Klamm. At bottom K. feels himself to be only a foreigner whom no one helps, a foreigner whom everyone continues to keep on the sidelines. Exclusion already lives within him long before it can be effected by those on the outside. In the opening variant, in fact, K. the foreigner is entertained with great respect in the "princes' chamber" whereas he had only expected "a filthy hole and dirty mat" (Kafka 1922b, p. 311). In this detail there clearly emerges the way in which it is one's inner disposition, more than the outside world, which is negative and erects the barrier of isolation. The theorists of family therapy (Watzlawick, Beavin, Jackson 1967, pp. 92–93) introduce the concept of the "self-determining prophecy" to explain how the inner attitude that guides different kinds of behavior is the factor which forges the way external events go. But the individual believes that he is reacting to attitudes rather than provoking them with his conduct. Despite his deep inner lack of confidence, the surveyor still takes the step that might turn his situation around. He has the courage to offer opposition to the villagers and to the norms of the Castle itself, accepting all the risks that this may entail. It is in this tragic, solitary struggle of his that K. approaches so many heroes of literature: Faust, Don Quixote, Ulysses — all those men who challenged a power much stronger than themselves in their search for *truth* and for an *answer* in the pursuit of an ideal.

Certainly K. does not have the nobility, the indomitable courage, the pride of these personages, because he is much closer to the man in the street than to a demigod. K. hesitates, and at times he is petty. Even garbed in the armor of detachment that should protect him from the outside world he is a man who suffers, who doesn't know how to live out his feelings. But these defects are just the sides of his character that make him likeable and make us feel close to him. It is perhaps easier to identify with Kafka's K. than with Goethe's Faust. The surveyor is a man who has abandoned his commitments to pursue his dream without having shaken off entirely the pettiness of the world to which he belonged. Cantoni (1970, pp. 42–43) considers him a kind of bourgeois Faust who doesn't dream of celestial or infernal adventures but rather desires a nice little wife, a good job, and a position in the community in which he lives. His is the clash of common sense with the mystery of existence. In this new "Divine Comedy," however, paradise and purgatory are missing. The only journey possible is the one through the circles of hell. In fact, K.'s adventures are all dreadful. At the end of his journey he will not be surrounded by flights of angels. Thus the only feature he has in common with Goethe's Faust is the conviction that only those deserve life and liberty who earn them day by day.

Every action entails certain risks; only those who renounce venturing into the world can be sheltered from the danger of the unforeseen and of failure. The moment in which one takes a certain course one cannot be sure of how the world is going to react to it and what can happen to one. To choose, therefore, is to expose oneself to *possibilities* and to risk. The Hebrew-Christian myths locate the beginning of human history in an act of transgression. Eve accepts the forbidden apple because she has *chosen* to be like God, to know good from evil, and so she exposes her destiny to uncertainty while gaining in exchange the power of decision, of choice. In that moment the world ceases to be contained in a circle of time where nothing changes and every moment is the same as every other. It plunges into linear time where each moment is different because it can be changed according to the individual will.

> It was late in the evening when K. arrived . . . the landlord could not provide a room and was upset by such a late and unexpected arrival, he was willing to let K. sleep on a bag of straw in the parlour. (Kafka 1922b, p. 9)

The opening lines of the novel insist on the factor of its being late: when K. arrives at the village it is late in the evening; the surveyor is a "tardy" guest. We know that in the first version this element was missing and instead there is another element: the "princes' chamber" in which he is to be lodged, is not yet ready when he arrives. These are two profoundly different conceptions of the situation: in the one K. is late, whereas in the other he seems to have arrived too early. Kafka then chose the version of the late arrival, which better fit into the general concept of the work. In fact all of *The Castle* is pervaded by an atmosphere of death and decline. The very name of the mysterious lord of the Castle, Count Westwest, evokes an ending. The Castle may perhaps be located in a distant border area where the sun gives up its last rays to the arriving night. In the ancient world, the entrance to Hades was thought to be located in the West. Thus K. has arrived in the world of the dead, the underworld. But what is the meaning of his being late? At this point we are obliged to recall that the novel was written in a few months, between January and September 1922 when his tuberculosis had already reached an advanced state and, above all, when his tormented relation with Milena Jesenskà had ended — events which probably led the writer to consider that he had arrived at the end of his life. *The Castle* is the chronicle of a world that is ending, of a last, failed attempt. Kafka must have had an inner feeling that death was approaching. He knew that it was *too late* to save his life, to give birth to a new world. But despite this he imagined a last possibility.

The atmosphere of desperation and angst that pervades his works and often makes them difficult to read is somewhat attenuated by this tendency towards a possible solution, by the hope of a new life. The feeling of death is contained in a slender thread that unwinds throughout his writings. Despite Max Brod's attempts at a religious interpretation and to see the Castle as the abode of the Divinity, of the Grace to which man will finally be admitted, Kafka's world is a place without hope and with room for nothing but tragic endings: Josef K. is slaughtered; the surveyor falls into an exhausted sleep; the mole is assaulted in its den by a mysterious, invisible enemy; Gregor Samsa — with a five-letter last name composed of two repeated consonants and vowels as in Kafka, in order to point out the identification of the author and the character — the traveling salesman turned into a cockroach, dies in his room after having been wounded by his own family; Georg Bendemann, hero of *The Judgment* (Kafka 1912a), throws himself off a bridge; the hunger artist dies of starvation because he cannot find the food suited to him (Kafka 1922c); the country man waits in uncertainty all his life outside the house of the law without being able to cross the threshold; the emperor's message will never reach the last subject of his empire (Kafka 1917d). The catalog could go on indefinitely. A heavy ineluctability weighs down all these figures. They are characters in a twilight world that despairs of ever seeing a new dawn.

If we compare this conception of life with that which is illustrated in Tarkovskij's last film, we can understand how the pervading despair of Kafka's world terrifies the reader while a highly dramatic work like *The Sacrifice* has, in turn, a cathartic and propulsive value. Here the experience of death is ransomed by the existence of values that go beyond the mortal existence of the individual. Alexander's sacrifice deters the catastrophe. And the film ends with the image of the child watering the tree planted by his father. The soul has succeeded in overcoming despair. Tarkovskij has been able to give a *sense* to his anguish over his imminent end. The profound religiousness transmitted by the images could not help but be triggered by an inner development capable of revealing a universe of hope even in the face of pain and death. In view of this transformation that transcends the brief span of individual life, no one could consider himself to be late.

On a psychological level, the tardiness of which Kafka speaks at the beginning of the novel indicates the inability to overcome the pain in which the soul is entangled. To feel within oneself that one has been too long in answering the call of destiny, or that, like K., one has become lost innumerable times in the snows of self-betrayal, means to throw in the towel, to be convinced that by now there is no longer any hope for salvation or betterment. K.'s condemnation is already pronounced in the first lines of *The Castle*. When the surveyor arrives at the place to which he has been called, it is too late for him. If we read the author's biography attentively, we will see how the ability to answer the call only comes at the end of his life: only then will he find the courage to leave his office, his family, and spend his last days with the woman he loves — that Dora Dymant who succeeded in overcoming Kafka's fears of the feminine.

> Some peasants were still sitting over their beer, but he did not want to talk, and after himself fetching the bag of straw from the attic, lay down beside the stove. It was a warm corner, the peasants were quiet, and letting his weary eyes stray over them he soon fell asleep. (Kafka 1922b, p. 9)

Having taken refuge, K. finds a stove by which to warm himself. Quite aside from either their aesthetic value or the reality to which they allude, the images of a novel must be considered for their evocative potential. In that way each individual, according to his cultural level, can draw on the plurality of meanings they contain. The stove stands in immediate contraposition to the snow that holds the village in its icy grip. The polarity of outside cold and inside warmth runs throughout the novel. We can advance several hypotheses. First, we can consider that Kafka wanted to emphasize that warmth can only come from inside oneself, that the inner life alone is able to furnish the emotional warmth necessary for life, while the rest of our relationships—the more exterior ones—are nothing but a long, gelid winter. All search for warmth is destined to failure if one is not able to accept what is given to one, if there is not inside one a *warm nucleus* resulting from the introjection of our love relationships. In *The Castle* warmth is connected to the home and the feminine. From relationships with women Kafka always hoped but never succeeded—except perhaps at the end of his life —in finding that source of warmth which was always lacking in his life.

The warmth of a stove comes from fire, combustion. In endopsychic terms that is reduced to two correlated processes: transformation and destruction. Every creative act, and not only in an artistic sense, is situated on the border between *life* and *death* because the production of the new involves the destruction of the old. For the stove to heat the frigid space, it must burn wood, which disappears as it is changed into energy, into heat. Just like matter, so too psychic reality is subjected to laws of transformation, which accompany all our growth. To be fertile and give birth to a new personality means, in fact, to destroy oneself inasmuch as no transformation can take place without first killing the old way of being (Spielrein 1912, p. 133). From this point of view, mental illness is nothing but the predominance of the destructive aspect of this transformation (Spielrein 1912, p. 162). It is as if the soul had been arrested at the critical moment, the moment of annihilation, without being able to define itself anew. Neurotic behavior can be considered a kind of resistance to the dynamic aspect of life, a basking in death without the ability to be reborn, to change radically what one had been. The transition to an adult condition, for example, means to detach oneself from one's parents, to turn one's back on one sphere of affections, and to open up new vistas of love. But the ability to effect that break requires the interiorizing of the preceding experience. That is, one must have brought one stage to maturity, one must have lived it totally before being able to enter the next.

Remaining longer than necessary in one stage, as in the case of individuals who continue living at home until they are forty—and Kafka is one such example—depends on the impossibility of metabolizing certain experiences and then overcoming them. Thus one can remain an eternal child, even when married, because one has not sufficiently digested one's childhood. If we did not love or were not loved within the family situation, we will inevitably have difficulty in matters of affection in other relationships where a more mature role is required of us. If no one has ever showed us what tenderness, care, and love are, these initial handicaps will continue to influence negatively our relationships and arrest our growth.

> Schwarzer hung up the receiver immediately, crying angrily: "Just what I said! Not a trace of a Land Surveyor. A common, lying tramp, and probably worse." For a moment K. thought that all of them, Schwarzer, the peasants, the landlord and the landlady, were going to fall upon him in a body, and to escape at least the first shock of their assault he crawled right underneath the blanket. (Kafka 1922b, p. 12)

Exclusion is immediately followed by negation. All future relations with the Castle will be regulated by the ambiguous game of negation and recognition of K.'s identity. In fact, the first of these two seems to be a constant in relationships within the novel. Almost all the characters have need of external confirmation to know who they are: the surveyor waits in vain for recognition of his job qualifications. On the contrary, he is offered jobs that clearly deny them: at first janitor and later stable boy. Barnabas, a messenger, has his sister sew him a uniform that looks like one for the official ushers; but the official confirmation of his job is only tolerated and it is quite possible that after many years of service, when he is already old, he will learn of the Castle's rejection of it and discover that "everything is lost and his life has been in vain" (Kafka 1922b, p. 232). The officials summon their lovers from time to time, but even here, no actual ties are created. For example, after having been thrice called, Gardena will not be invited again by Klamm and she will grow old precociously, living on memories alone.

One has the impression that everything is extremely precarious and governed by scornful and inscrutable Chance. But the impossibility of changing this external law is contained in the precarious sense of identity of the various characters. Our identity can be negated only if we ourselves allow it. No outside word can negate our individuality unless it can insinuate itself into some tiny crack in our souls. It is no accident that when two people quarrel they try to wound each other by negating each other's identity. The irate words of accusation tend to destroy the perception one has of oneself and replace every illusion with a degraded image.

This is one of the most painful psychological experiences that people can have. The need of confirmation varies in the different stages of life just as the aspects of personality do that require the recognition of others. It can happen that certain sides of one's character have greater need of confirmation by others. In such a case certain forms of negation may be more devastating than others, and lead to schizophrenia, by striking at just those areas of one's psyche that are most vulnerable (Laing 1959, p. 115). And the ways in which confirmation is effected also are different. Sometimes a smile or a caress are enough; at others verbal appreciation is desired. Each of us is dependent on the confirmation that comes from others, but if this need exceeds a certain threshold, life can become hell. Each action of ours, every way of behaving, can be undermined by a deep uncertainty that can become totally paralyzing. Here is the root of the constant hesitation that characterized Kafka's life.

Our desire for confirmation, of certainties, clashes with external reality. Little by little, as we grow, we note that such confirmations arrive late — and sometimes never come. Not only that, but the world seems to be structured in a way to negate our identity constantly.

According to transactional theory, negation of identity is one of the factors that lead to schizophrenia. The school of Palo Alto has shown how, in relationship to others, the individual not only communicates information but also exchanges definitions of the relationship and of himself. The reply of the other, in this regard, can be of three kinds: *confirmation, rejection* — which still means taking notice of the other's reality — and finally, *negation*. The message transmitted in the last case is not simply "you are behaving badly," but "you do not exist" (Watzlawick, Beavin, Jackson 1967 pp. 79–84). In that way all possible contact is interrupted. As long as the line of communication (the relationship) is not broken, but its polarity only inverted, there is still the possibility of reacting. But negation is a judgment without appeal. One is pushed into the vacuum of nonexistence.

Laing maintains that "pseudo-confirmation," or the confirmation of a false ego, is even more likely to lead to schizophrenia than negation. The typical family set-up in these cases, rather than being distinguished by evident traumas or neglect, is marked by a constant and often unconscious mutilation of the child's authentic personality on the part of the parents. The child thus finds herself in an untenable position that impels her to experience any feeling she may have as a terrible guilt (Laing 1959, p. 117).

The inability to recognize and express what one feels takes on the form of a betrayal of one's authenticity. The feelings, masked and misunderstood, cease to make sense in terms of behavior. A kind of chaos is born where the situation in which the individual is immersed loses its meaning and so he is alienated from himself and everything around him.

The moment in which we are negated, the world seems to lose its consistency. It is as if we had suddenly become invisible. In the relationship between two lovers, for example, it is much more terrible than hatred. Aggressiveness is the channel for some kind of sentiment. Energy, even if negative, passes between the two partners. But indifference implies a vacuum, the absence of any emotion. In replacing intense feeling it effects a subtle negation. "You no longer exist for me" is what one says by implication to the other. Not hatred but emotional silence is what decrees the end of a relationship. As long as there is still a current of feeling, of sentiment to hang onto, everything is still possible, any situation can still be turned around. But when the rejections accumulate, when one slowly falls out of love, the only space remaining is that of mutual negation.

From the very first lines K. knows that his confrontation with the Castle will be a battle. He is aware that it will be a strenuous fight to gain recognition for his right to live, to work, and to love within the village. As long as the surveyor opposes the rejections without letting the constant disappointments destroy him, some hope exists. But this battle exhausts him more all the time. Worn out, K. falls asleep beside the stove. He has no strength left. That first encounter has been a hard test.

It is interesting to analyze how K. reacts to negation. After the reply of the Castle that marks him as a "common vagabond" he does not protest, does not show offense, does not fight, but hides under the covers. Like animals when they are attacked, human beings can choose either to fight or flee. In these cases the sympathetic nervous system is activated, which increases the blood flow to the muscles, the lungs, the brain. The heart beats faster, and blood pressure increases to furnish the extra energy required. If the subject neither fights nor flees but withdraws into himself, the parasympathetic nervous system increases gastric activity as if the person only expected and wanted to be fed, fondled, and protected. In place of self-affirming behavior there is one of dependence. The surveyor seeks in his pallet a warm and secure womb that will keep him safe from outside attacks.

From his diaries we know that Kafka suffered from depressions that sometimes forced him to keep to his bed for entire days, incapable of doing anything. The reaction of depression means closing oneself to the world. Apathy, inactivity, staying in bed, are symptoms of discouragement, of giving in to the omnipotence of the external world, which we feel helpless to oppose. Nevertheless, every therapist knows that at bottom depression always indicates a nonrelationship with one's Shadow. What depressed people really fear is not the outside world's hostility so much as their own. They are afraid of the enormous charge of destructiveness they carry within themselves as if it were a tremendous bomb ready to go off at any moment. Withdrawing into themselves and often turning their aggressiveness against themselves, these individuals protect everything around them from the threat of destruction. What terrifies them are those dark images dwelling hidden in their souls to which the collectivity has given the name of monstrous assassin, ferocious werewolf (Raspaolo 1988, *passim*). Having repressed them for years, they no longer have any control of them. The only solution can come from a confrontation with this aspect of the personality. Anger and aggressiveness, whenever one knows how to channel them, are energies indispensable to life. Once one has become conscious of one's Mr. Hyde, Dr. Jekyll will also be free to act. A just way of asserting one's rights will replace depression or indiscriminate destruction.

After his first skirmish with the Castle, K., exhausted, falls asleep by the stove. The theme of exhaustion, the inability to live, to act, to effect creative changes in one's life is a theme frequently found in Kafka's diaries. He believed that this exhaustion was due to writing. On January 3, 1912 he noted:

> It is easy to recognize a concentration in me of all my forces on writing. When it became clear in my organism that writing was the most productive direction for my being to take, everything rushed in that direction and left empty all those abilities which were directed towards the joys of sex, eating, drinking. I atrophied in all these directions. This was necessary because the totality of my strengths was so slight that only collectively could they even half-way serve the purpose independently and consciously, it found itself. (Kafka 1910–1923, p. 163)

Writing undoubtedly constituted one of Kafka's defenses against the external world, an attempt to live through writing. Literature was an oasis in comparison to the desert of his relationships, the difficulty of getting on in the world, the fight to realize his destiny. But it was also his way of answering the *call* of the unconscious. The writer was obsessed by his fantasies, and to give them form in his characters was his only way of confronting them. Nevertheless, art cannot substitute for life, but can only be one of the ways of expressing oneself, of realizing oneself. Despite his writing, Kafka remained a prisoner of the *daimons* of solitude, of emptiness, of rejection and negation. The external experiences were not able to change this critical inner condition. In his works one can trace the constant working out of such nuclei of suffering. Destructiveness had the last word in the form of the disease that killed him. Milena had perfectly well understood the destiny of the man she loved when she wrote to Max Brod: "But Frank cannot live. Frank doesn't have the ability to live. Frank will never recover. Frank will die soon" (Brod 1937, p. 259). If Kafka had first had a love experience capable of regenerating him, if he had been able to recognize and accept it before the tuberculosis had reached its final stage, perhaps he would not have given way to negativeness. Brod (1937, p. 235) was in fact convinced that if Kafka had met Dora some time earlier his will to live would have certainly been stronger and he would have been saved.

But let us return to K.'s falling asleep. Like any image, the one of sleep also proposes different meanings that are not mutually exclusive. In the first place, falling asleep evokes the idea of detachment, of withdrawal. It is the condition of one who withdraws, who isolates herself from the external world in order to turn in on herself. It thus expresses that narcissistic closure of which the Castle is a clear metaphor. But to give in to the desire to sleep also makes us think of the desire for regression, for abandonment, that we have already found in the surveyor's reaction to the negation of his identity. K. seems to want to rediscover the warmth of the maternal womb where there is no struggle, where one is received without having to ask for it or to merit it. And finally, sleep calls up the slow slide into Hades, the underworld realm of the psyche. Just as previously becoming lost and facing the abyss, so now sleep underlines K.'s passage to a different plane of reality, to the *reality of the soul*.

To meet the crowd of figures, of fantasies, that inhabit our minds, we must temporarily close ourselves off from the world, whose hubbub could distract us from the confrontation with the unknown parts of ourselves that we pursue in dreams, fantasies, or artistic creation. Like Oedipus's blindness, the surveyor's closing of his eyes comes from the need to create a darkness around himself that will allow him to see the inner glimmer—initially tenuous—that can illuminate his life, finally giving sense to it. K.'s inactivity, his giving way to sleep is also similar to depression, when one no longer lends one's ears to the call of life and only listens to what Eduardo De Filippo in the title of one of his plays calls "The Voices from Within" (1948). Abandoning oneself to sleep also means surrendering, giving up the fight. In western films, where the enemy is always outside of one and clearly recognizable, there is a stereotype: when the place where the hero finds himself—generally a fort or a camp—is surrounded he fights to the last breath, until he and all his comrades succumb, as in the epic of the Alamo or General Custer at Little Big Horn. But in most cases, when the hero is about to be overcome, the reinforcements arrive—represented in many films by the legendary "Seventh Cavalry." Interpreted from an endopsychic viewpoint, the surrender does not refer to the enemy but to ourselves. It triggers the lack of confidence in our own capacities, the despair of being able to save ourselves. For example, it has been seen that political prisoners resist torture better than common prisoners. In Nazi concentration camps, political prisoners survived in greater numbers than others because they had an ideal to hang on to. This faith is what gave them the psychological strength to resist the oppression of their persecutors without succumbing.

If in that unequal battle with the Castle—that is, an external reality which tries to bend our souls by constantly negating us—each of us remained firm in his convictions, determined to affirm his right to exist at all costs; if he strenuously committed himself to the task of obtaining that recognition which is his right, then nothing could defeat him, nothing compel him to *surrender*. Even if we must face difficult situations — for nothing is given to us free — the certainty of being in the right, of fighting for a just cause can sustain us in the face of any adversity. I do not believe there can be any justification for avoiding the battle when its purpose is to defend the destiny to which we feel we are *called*.

The first obstacle K. will meet on the road to affirming his identity is Schwarzer, the son of the concierge. None of the names of Kafka's characters is chosen at random; they all have precise meanings. *Schwarzer* in German means someone who blackens himself. The root word *schwarz* has various meanings: it means black, dark, but also evil. *Der Schwarze* is the devil but also the chimney sweep, whereas the word *Schwarzer* means smuggler. All of these meanings indicate that we are dealing with a dark, hostile, in some way evil presence that blocks the access to the Castle. In Greek mythology there was Cerberus, the gatekeeper of Hades, whose horrible presence barred the entrance to the sacred soil of Avernus. Dante describes him as a three-headed devil who is intent, like a rabid dog, on ripping his victims to shreds. Because of the Castle's constant negation and exclusion perhaps, or because of the humiliating relations between the officials and the women of the village that make it into something like a great brothel, some critics think the Castle is to be seen as the seat of an evil power, the Evil principle itself. This, then, is why we find the "daimon" Schwarzer guarding it. It is said of him that he has an actor's face, and in Greek tragedy the actors wore masks by means of which they expressed various emotions. He seems to be an incarnation of the archetype of the persona, the mask that we all cover our faces with in order to adhere to the expectations of the collectivity.

Like the actor who plays many different roles and thus may appear to have no precise identity — almost as if it had been dissolved by his interpretations or perhaps had never existed at all — the concierge's son seems not to exist in his own right, but only as an emanation of the Authorities.

The moment in which K. affirms his identity: "I am the land surveyor whom the Count has sent for" (Kafka 1922b, p. 44), legitimizing it by a higher authority, he is rejected, negated, mistaken for a "common vagabond." The surveyor is robbed of his only possession:

his identity. In prisons, in hospitals, in all of those places where an attempt is made to activate a regressive reaction that will make it easier to control the individual, a number is substituted for the person's name. In Nazi concentration camps this number was actually tattooed on the left arm of the inmates. Deprived of their names, the prisoners were reduced to the initials K.Z.—*Konzentration Zenter* or concentration camp—followed by a serial number. The police throughout the world know that the best way of reducing a citizen's ability to oppose them is to deprive her of her identity. Here, negation reaches its apex. "You do not exist, everything that you have been no longer has any value," one tells the other.

In *The Trial*, Josef K. was mistaken for a house painter, and in *The Castle,* the hero is subjected to a greater humiliation. The house painter still has an identity conferred by his work, but the vagabond is uprooted, without past or future; his life is deprived of real features. Thus one of the other *leitmotifs* of the novel is the search for one's identity. In his fight for recognition as the Castle's surveyor, K. is trying to achieve an identity that distinguishes him from the others. He is constantly impelled by the need to be distinguished from the other inhabitants of the village. That is why he boasts of having special relations with the Castle. But it is all in vain. These relations, his being taken on in his job are sometimes confirmed and sometimes denied. He is repeatedly being told that he is no one. K. is constantly pushed back into an amorphous, anonymous mass where individual existence has no meaning. The negation of the individual, of his very right to exist, can only come from the *collectivity*, here represented by the concierge's son. It matters little that K. fails in his attempt. What really counts is the *battle* to defend his individuality.

157

Sixteen

The Utmost Challenge

The interpretation of a text requires the analysis of all the aspects that might at first sight seem to be entirely casual, because it is just in them, as in the marginal elements of a dream, that the unconscious most strongly insinuates itself. Before going on to analyze the novel, we must therefore stop a moment to consider the possible meanings of the profession that Kafka chose for his hero. Whereas *The Trial* centered on the story of a bank clerk and the entire work has the character of a defense plea before a court within himself, *The Castle* is the story of a land surveyor, one who measures the fields. The idea of measuring in both Latin and Greek lends itself to the formation of many terms. The Indo-European root *men* can be found not only, obviously, in the verb *metior*, measure, but in *men* as well, the way of feeling, thinking, and by extension the soul, the heart, the mind, the intellect. To feel and think rationally are to varying degrees forms of measurement; they imply the ability to discern the boundaries of what is happening inside of ourselves in order to put them in their proper places. The function of evaluation, which pertains to sentiments, is furthermore also recognized by Jung. As a composite of *men* there is also the verb *memini*, I remember, I think, I reflect, and *monea*, I counsel, admonish. In Greek the derivatives of *men* are: *ménos*, impetus, vital force, soul, will, the meaning of which also includes the idea of excess of measure; *mimnŕsco*, I remember; *manomai*, I rage, I go mad, I make mad; *mania*, madness, but also prophetic inspiration. These last terms are also connected to *màntis*, soothsayer; *manteùomai*, I prophesy; and *manteia*, divination. Also the verb *manthàno*, I learn, I know, I question, I understand, derives from the same root. The close correlation of these apparently unconnected words allows us to gather the plurality of metaphors contained in K.'s profession.

To measure distances, to establish borders means in endopsychic terms to be capable of evaluating one's own inner world. The function of sentiment, Jung thought, was that it allowed for understanding inner and outer reality according to the categories of pleasant and unpleasant, acceptance and rejection. Sentiment is that process by which the ego confers a certain value on a psychic content, accepting or rejecting it according to whether it is a pleasurable or painful experience. To feel is therefore a kind of judgment, different from the rational one based on thinking, inasmuch as it does not aim at establishing a conceptual connection but at accepting or rejecting the contents on a subjective basis (Jung 1921, pp. 480–81).

Paraphrasing Freud, Hillman (1971b, p. 70) maintains that "sentiment is the *royal road* of access to the unconscious." The capacity to evaluate is a process by which we come to an understanding of ourselves. By "judging" a person or a situation we can structure our psyche. Our rejection and our acceptance filter reality and establish our relationship to it. The function of sentiment is therefore a *relating* function. The capacity to confront oneself, to make contact with the unconscious, therefore depends on knowing how to receive its manifestations—states of soul, inner fantasies, external projects— and to make room for them. When this capacity is insufficient or almost totally lacking, the person is possessed and commanded by feelings she does not understand. The job of measuring which K. is called to do—but which he will never succeed in doing—is that of making contact with the unconscious, learning to recognize and experience his feelings. Such a task requires no little courage because making contact with our daimons also means facing their power and destructiveness. K. will fail in his task because he will not be able to recognize his love for Frieda, abandoning himself to it, nor make room for the rage and destructiveness that are hidden within his Soul and his hatred for the Castle, which excludes and negates him.

If isolation, solitude, the impossibility of establishing durable relationships are among the basic themes of the novel, the measuring of distances suggests other possible meanings. In the first place, it means becoming aware of one's being locked into a narcissistic condition. Recognizing the distance that separates us from others, we can attempt to reduce it. Withdrawal represents an extreme defensive measure, particularly present in schizoid personalities and schizophrenics, who find themselves in a condition of fusion that keeps them from distinctly separating themselves from the other, of being conscious of themselves as separate beings. Thus it obliges them to withdraw into isolation in order to defend whatever remains of subjectivity. What is feared is annihilation. Contact is seen as presenting the danger of penetration by the other, of falling into his power and under his complete control. Thus "freedom" can only result from becoming inaccessible. In these cases direct participation in life represents a risk of destruction. Isolation, on the contrary, seems to guarantee the integrity of the ego. Involvement with reality brings on acute angst. This may be one of the reasons why Kafka, conscious that he could only make contact with the world through his angst, said that he could not make do without it. The angst in these personalities testifies to their contact with otherness. At the bottom of the fear of the relationship is the fear of one's own destructiveness which, since it is unrecognized and repressed, appears powerful and uncontrollable. The schizoid, for example, is convinced of her destructiveness. For her, her own love and that of others are just as destructive as hatred. If being loved is dangerous, to love is just as risky. The isolation into which she withdraws is not only for her self-defense but also to avoid harming those around her. She does not believe she can fill the void she feels within herself without annihilating all that exists (Laing 1960, p. 107).

The life of the *detached* individual is dominated by the need of not being involved and influenced. To survive, he needs absolute freedom and independence; he must be totally self-sufficient. Thus all feelings threaten to demolish his ivory tower, his Castle. And if the suffering from loneliness, the cold inside him, are a torment, he nevertheless does nothing but attempt to perpetuate them while deluding himself into thinking he desires relationships. The narcissistic person seems to be telling the other by his behavior, "Love me without asking anything of me and I will be cured and will be able to love you." The myth of an unconditional love becomes his convenient alibi for his inability to enter into a relationship. But to close oneself to the world of feeling means to close oneself off from life itself. According to Horney, the most important function of neurotic detachment is to keep basic conflicts dormant (Horney 1945, p. 83).

The withdrawal is not, in fact, from the external world but from the inner one. One withdraws from one's own angst, from one's own depression, from the evil of living.

Measurement evokes the idea of *boundaries*. The inclusion of madness, passion, ardor, and volition in the same linguistic root underlines the implicit meaning of "overstepping the boundaries" that they contain. In this sense the land surveyor finds himself in an ambiguous situation: his inability to abandon himself to intoxication, to impulse, to living in "excess," above all with regard to feelings — as his relationship with Frieda indicates — is all balanced by the *arrogance* of his volition. K. is calm, he is moderate, he does not abandon himself to intoxication nor to the passion of love. Far from madness, from the Dionysian excess that reveals the contact with the god and being possessed by him — a possession that bestows prophetic power, the gift of divination and which in psychological terms indicates the bursting in of the unconscious — K. is only able to experience the excess of will in his constant sin of *hubris*. The land surveyor represents the rigidity and the one-sidedness of the ego that doesn't know how to confront the unconscious. His relationship to life is entirely rational, lacking in the visceral element. The intellect is magnified at the expense of feeling. In fact, the emotions described in the novel are always cold: the frigid air of solitude, of exclusion, and not the fiery turbulence of love and of jealousy. The reaction of the surveyor to Frieda's betrayal, for example, has nothing to do with immediacy or violence; not even on this occasion can he allow the *daimons* that dwell deep within his soul to reveal themselves. Every doubt, every hesitation is only described in its mental aspect and is minutely analyzed. The pros and cons of every situation are carefully weighed, as if K. were a "bookkeeper of the emotions." It is this coldness which all of Kafka's heroes have in common that perhaps creates obstacles to approaching his work for many readers. His characters do not favor immediate identification with themselves, but remain foreign from the start, closed in their impenetrable emotions. One has to approach them with love, see beyond their armor, to begin to feel close to them, to discover what disturbs them, to understand their fears. The foreignness gives way to sympathy, to a sense of having something in common.

The closing up to feeling that marks the surveyor's psychic world often depends on a negative mother complex. In trying to protect us from life, the mother complex also keeps us from feeling any emotions. The vice of feeling, which makes us extremely vulnerable to the external world, is transformed into a total imperturbability (Hillman 1971b, p. 121). The result must inevitably be detachment from one's own emotional world. But the negation of what one is brings with it a dangerous estrangement from oneself in which the repressed feeling seems to possess a sinister power of deflagration, as if the individual, in allowing it to express itself would, in fact, explode.

In narcissistic patients we often find this fear of feelings expressed as the idea of madness. Madness is excess, loss of equilibrium and of rational control, abandoning oneself to the power of the unconscious. The need to isolate oneself from other human beings, however, comes from fear that they, like the medieval plague-spreaders, carry contagion. The "plague" in this case is mental: opening oneself to Otherness takes on the terrifying form of an opening to madness. All contact with another person is also feared because it shows up one's essential inadequacy and obliges one to take note of and remember it. These individuals erroneously believe that the only way to cure their wounds is to forget them, to remove their gaze from them and hide their heads in the sand like ostriches. Repression and negation in reality are of little use. That sharp pain which poisons our existence continues implacably to make itself felt. And if the hope of forgetting impels the subject to look for a relationship, a superficial contact — even if in a compulsive way — the relief she gets from it is only momentary and before long, withdrawal once again takes control of her heart, leaving it cold and empty as before. It takes a long process of emotional relearning to truly fill the emotional vacuum and change one's psychological condition.

The first step in the education of feelings is to make contact with the fear of them. What one then needs is a *good mother,* understood as meaning an external figure, a real partner who allows us to express whatever is bothering our souls and, as regards the psychological capacity for *self-acceptance*, shows lively interest and prompt solicitude for all that is going on within one. Our inability to experience feelings derives, in fact, from the lack of such a "mother." For the child to be able to express his emotional world, a mother is needed who allows him to be himself for better or worse, in his most destructive rages as in his most tender affections. If this is not allowed, if the child, instead, is forced to develop a *false self* in order to keep his mother's love, then the world of feelings will remain closed to him (Miller 1979, *passim*). He will pay for this control with emptiness, depression, or total estrangement from himself while his opening of himself to the other will always be accompanied by feelings of exclusion, of rejection, of ineluctable suffering from which he will try to defend himself by putting an almost sidereal distance between himself and the Other.

Therefore measuring, taking one's distance, has to do with the fear of involvement. To allow oneself to be seized by emotion means being ready to receive everything beautiful—but also everything painful—that a relationship has to offer. If, for example, during childhood we had no "good mother" able to accept us, but a depressed mother, as adults we will not be able to reveal ourselves without fear of being crushed. A deeply traumatic experience for a child, such as the encounter with a depressed mother, makes it impossible for her to enter into a relationship. A depressed person, because of his illness, is entirely absorbed by his own problems. A mother in this condition will not be able to take care of her child. Inevitably she will be distant and inaccessible to him. The child will never receive any recognition when he shows her his feelings, as if his feelings had fallen into a void. Anger and tenderness, deprived of a response, will become extraneous to him. Very soon the child will repress the pain by deciding to keep himself closed up. Having learned it from the mother's behavior, he will choose to negate his inner life, thus perpetuating the chain of narcissistic relations. Fearing another negation, the child become adult will be terrified at the idea of revealing his feelings to feed the avid curiosity of the other. Every attempt at contact will see him automatically withdraw like a snail into shell as soon as something brushes against it. Such individuals appear to be enclosed in what Reich called the "armor of their character." They give the impression of speaking and relating only with their heads, almost as if they had no visceral aspects.

The inaccessibility of the narcissistic individual often exerts an irresistible fascination, as Freud (1914, p. 89) rightly observed. The violent desire excited by the impenetrability of the other is caused by the activation of a particular psychic need. It is the possibility of measuring oneself with the *distance* that in some cases feeds passion.

In the novel it is the Castle's impregnability that baits the trap. Just because he is rejected the surveyor is obliged to return again to the attack in the absurd hope of overcoming once and for all the Castle's defenses and penetrating it. The relations based on this secret dynamic are extremely painful. They carry an enormous destructive charge and are destined to failure unless a new element were to intervene to change the situation and permit the two partners to change these interior dynamics. Whoever has experienced, directly or indirectly, this kind of relationship knows very well that once the mists of projection which surround the other have cleared, one becomes aware that the elusive partner whom we love despite ourselves — because we are constantly compelled to measure ourselves against her distance — has nothing to give us. There is a deep fracture within her that separates her from the world of feelings and not only keeps her from recognizing and expressing her own feelings but from accepting ours in any manner. Being closed to feeling, she is not nourished by an inner life. It is an unavoidable phase in the growth of those who have gone through an analogous experience of withdrawal, to suffer the pains of relational dynamics in which they are constantly negated and annulled.

It takes considerable psychological maturity to recognize that the emotional block of the person one loves is not dictated by any conscious desire to wound but is rather the result of acute inner suffering. Only when one of the two partners manages to separate his fantasies of rejection and withdrawal from the real responses of the other will he be able to see how deep her traumas are, how much pain, mistrust, and fear are still alive in within her. This awareness cancels out the sensation of betrayal, of rejection, and leaves room for an understanding full of tenderness. The violence of desire and passion that had previously characterized the relationship change at this point into an *acceptance* without demands, an acceptance that no longer depends on the claim to change the partner.

The subtle trap in such relations consists, in fact, in the illusion that by adapting one's partner to one's own idea of love one can finally achieve happiness. The problems of the relationship replace one's personal problems: one desires to change the other because one is unable to change oneself. The moment one gets out of this destructive spiral, becoming aware of one's own conflicts, it is possible to direct one's attention to more mature relations. Sometimes the opening to change of one of the two partners implies the end of the relationship, as one becomes aware that love is not possible because there is no common way of looking at and relating to emotional life. In some cases then the relationship can change into a deep and true friendship.

The idea of knowledge is also connected to the idea of measuring, as the Greek verb *manthano* suggests. Knowledge is a kind of measuring that implies being able to distinguish the limits of what is before us. But *manthano* also means to question. Knowledge presents itself to us as a kind of *challenge*, a going beyond the bounds of the known. The incessant asking for explanations that marks K.'s way of relating to the new world he has entered is entirely compatible with his job as a surveyor. All of K.'s behavior constitutes a challenge. He never passively accepts the law and the regulations that constantly block his path. He insists on understanding. Opposition is implicit in his questioning. This continuous effort to not let himself be absorbed into the collectivity and to escape from an unconscious adherence to life makes the surveyor a modern hero. The sympathy we feel for this personage, despite his undoubted limitations, is based on just this fight for greater knowledge. K. seizes our sympathy. He moves us because he stands for each of us; he personifies the courage and passion of all those who fight unceasingly for an objective that they will never achieve but which they cannot renounce. Like the land surveyor, many of us have a Castle in our lives, which attracts us with its siren song and ends by taking possession of and perhaps destroying our entire lives.

Measuring is then a challenge: to measure ourselves, in the common phrase, means to enter into contest with reality, to confront it. Measuring can be thought of as an attempt to know the distance that separates us from our desired objectives. Whenever a desire takes a strong hold on our minds it becomes an *absolute* with which we must establish a relationship. Every desire is in reality a Castle that calls us and which we must manage to reach. From a dynamic point of view, what we always feel is a kind of inner urgency that gives us no peace, that obliges us to act, to move toward our goal.

The need of people to measure themselves with things, to understand them, evokes what for the Greeks was the sin of sins: hubris. Volition and knowledge are a kind of arrogance, haughtiness, an open challenge to the gods. In German the word *vermessen*, to measure, from which is derived *Landvermesser*, land surveyor, has connotations of *Vermessenheit*, presumption or audacity, similar in meaning to the Greek hubris. In the reflexive form, *sich vermessen*, it means to commit an act of pride, to have the audacity to do something, but also to take the wrong measurements, to apply the wrong measure.

According to many critics, K.'s actions symbolize the effort to measure the distance between himself and the Truth, the Absolute. With his rationality he is attempting to impose a logical order on the absurdity and injustice of the laws of the Castle. K. puts trust in his reason, in the power of his ego, and thus commits the sin of pride. The whole of *The Castle* revolves around challenge and struggle. But these can be interpreted in many different ways. Kafka's cultural formation was influenced by Kierkegaard, and in particular by *Fear and Trembling*. The theme of the relationship with the divinity, the Absolute, is primary in Kafka's writings, but deprived of its explicitly religious connotations and turned into the relationship with the Authority. The episode of Amalia has been compared by many to the sacrifice of Isaac that so greatly occupied the Danish philosopher. In contrast to the capacity to accept the will of God, to that *amor fati* which permeates, for example, the works of Marguerite Yourcenar, Kafka always offers rebellion, no matter if it is destined to failure.

Greek culture, in particular the tragedies of Aeschylus and Sophocles, is deeply religious. However obscure and inscrutable the decisions of the divinity may be, however capricious the gods that dwell on Olympus, soaring above them all is *Dike*, Justice. In a world that believes in a higher order, that follows its own path of justice — often incomprehensible in the immediate course of events — it is still possible to abandon oneself to the wisdom of the gods.

But the world of Kafka is the kingdom of the Absurd, of Chance, that no hope and no explanation can redeem. Thus Kafka's heroes can only fight, can only raise their fists to the gods even if the gesture is like that of a pygmy defying a giant. Rebellion has its importance and its necessity at certain moments in life. But beyond a certain point, one must have the capacity to yea-say one's destiny because things are full of hidden and obscure meanings. One must love what happens in order not to be carried off by events, like an incautious swimmer who goes against the current. Only in this acceptance, in this deep love, will life finally reveal its hidden meanings. Everything that before appeared to destroy us — pain, loss, rejection, separation — becomes the secret spur, the thorn in the flesh that awakens us from our sleep and directs us along the path of growth.

Nevertheless, at the start, this condition cannot help but open a deep wound in the soul of a man, divided as he is between the desire to understand and change his destiny and at the same time the knowledge of the ineluctability of many events. Only acceptance can allow us to modify the destructiveness of what occurs. Faced with a person in the final stages of cancer or AIDS, for example, we clash with the impossibility of intervening in a death sentence. In this case inner peace is generated by the *acceptance* of the sense, the still inscrutable secret value of one's pain. For this reason Paracelsus (1922–1935, p. 199) was able to say: "Every disease is a purifying fire."

To that Oedipus who searches, questions, and finds a terrible truth that causes him to put out his own eyes because of the oppressive guilt with which he has unwittingly stained himself, there is opposed another Oedipus, an old man who has finally found peace and can thus be received by the gods as he disappears into the woods of Colonus. Oedipus is precisely the symbol of the *tragedy of knowing*. A kind of necessity is contained in knowing. Once one has set out on the road of knowing, all the world and its manifestations seem to take shape, condensing by means of the thirst for truth alone. No halfway measures are possible, and knowledge becomes the only measure of reality (Untersteiner 1974, p.186).

The person who sees beyond appearances, whose knowledge becomes a lucid vigilance over her actions, over the consequences of his actions, cannot help but be constantly tormented since the burden she carries is extremely heavy. She directs her glance far beyond the point that others watch in their daily lives. And if the impulse to know and understand, to progress always further in her discoveries imposes itself implacably on her life, she often must pay a high price for it. The fearfulness of knowing appeared clear to Oppenheimer. When in 1944, in the New Mexico desert, the scientist saw the experimental explosion of the first atomic bomb, seeing a white light more violent than that of the noonday sun illuminate every object, in the face of this terrifying power he could not help but recite a passage from the Bhagavad Gita (XI, 12, p. 273): "If the light of a thousand suns were to blaze forth all at once in the sky, that might resemble the splendour of that exalted Being."

His culture allowed him to see what would be the consequences of the splitting of the atom. And it is another, modern example of the sin of hubris if then atomic energy, from the bomb to nuclear power plants, subsequently were turned against humanity.

The terribly high price that knowledge has always exacted is represented in many myths: Prometheus was chained to the Scythian crags and condemned to having an eagle every night devour his liver, in which it seems the Titan's arrogance was contained. Among many peoples, in fact, this organ is considered to be the seat of courage and daring. Ulysses was overwhelmed by a tremendous vortex when he had passed the Columns of Hercules, the far end of the earth, and was in sight of Purgatory. And each of us pays a higher or lower price on his path of growth. Knowledge always demands a burnt sacrifice. Daring and the arrogance of knowing subsequently must be paid for with the humility of acceptance. The man whose knowledge has made him rise highest must be able to kneel before the obscure wisdom of life. If his knowledge is not to become sterile through pride and presumption, he must not only overstep the bounds, but he must also know how to accept it. Challenge and acceptance, hubris and *amor fati* are then not opposing and mutually exclusive attitudes, but complementary postures of the soul.

Knowing also means being able to take one's own measure and that of others. The path of individuation ought to bring the human being to a point where his knowledge of life is so deep that the world becomes almost *transparent*. This crystalline quality that reality and the Other take on, and which makes it impossible for one to be deceived by false attitudes and tricks of appearance, is a heavy weight to bear. The moment in which words have lost their camouflage, when their masks have fallen and we manage to perceive the essence behind the sounds, living becomes difficult. As Freud maintained (1929), humanity, especially in a stage of not very advanced development, has need of illusions. To be able to look into the depths of the souls of those around us also means to see all human misery, destructiveness, pettiness, and to have the Shadow always before one's eyes. It means noting the false friendships, that perhaps our partner continues living with us only out of self-interest, or that our children are only waiting for us to weaken in order to destroy us. Daily life becomes a tragedy. One way of surviving may be to pretend to see nothing in order to avoid being plunged into despair and depression.

It is never the little things that cause us suffering and malaise. Pain is generated by a deep knowledge of life. Great strength of soul is needed to overcome the discouragement that invades us when we are able to see beyond appearances. Because analytic training tends toward the acquisition of this kind of knowledge, it often happens that analysts are more pessimistic than other people. Jaspers (1959, p. 870) maintained in this regard that analysis can produce two different results: either one becomes skeptical and no longer believes in anything, as if one's glance remained fixed on the negative things alone that dwell in the human soul, or else one overcomes one's bitterness and reaches a philosophical level, a human way of considering the world. Together with the shadow one will also see the light.

If it is true that human beings are petty, egoistical, and violent, it is also true that many of them are able to make the gift of disinterested love and to spend their lives trying to improve themselves and those around them. When one conquers the pain that a true vision of reality can inflict, one is also able to lay hold of the positive things. Love contains a very potent energy for transformation, but in order for it to enter our souls we must throw the doors wide open. It is inner disposition that can modify our reality. As long as we remain prisoners of our negative judgments, however well-founded they may be, there is no way we can sweeten the bitterness of our suffering. Only when our eyes are ready to see some light and our spirit accepts the warmth of a ray of love and tenderness can anything change inside of us.

Sometimes it takes years for the miracle to occur. But if those who are close to us are able to wait patiently for the ice in our hearts to thaw, sooner or later they will be rewarded by seeing our face brighten and soften. It is never too late to close the books on a painful past of abandonment and injuries and return to hope and, above all, to learn to love. Andersen's *The Snow Queen* (1990) tells the story of girl who goes in search of a childhood friend who has been kidnapped by the cruel queen of the snows. Little Gerda overcomes every sort of obstacle and test to reach the queen's palace at the North Pole. Here she discovers her friend Kay turned to ice. Cold and impassive, he no longer recognizes his old friend. But the burning tears she sheds on his breast thaw the ice covering his heart, freeing him from the fragment of diabolical mirror by which the queen kept him under her spell. Kay too begins to cry and becomes aware of the cold and emptiness around him. Gerda's love, tenacity, and patience have worked the miracle.

> And Gerda kissed his cheeks, and they became blooming; she kissed his eyes, and they shone like her own; she kissed his hands and feet, and he became well and merry. (Andersen 1990, p. 339)

The evil circle of a negative mother complex, the soul's imprisonment in the net of an interior mother like the cold and distant snow queen, can be broken by the tender and disinterested love of another being who does not allow herself to be defeated by the difficulties of the task. The image of Gerda and Kay also appears in the dream of a thirty-year-old woman. After a furious fight with her lover that threw her into a terrible depression, reactivating her fantasies of abandonment and rejection, the woman reported this dream to me:

> I am an unmarried mother. I have a seven- or eight-year-old child. I learn that he has been invited to lunch at the home of the man I love. I am afraid for him, but since no one knows that he is my child, my man's family treats him with affection. I am hungry too. Waiting in the living room for my son to finish eating, I nibble at a little book that contains Andersen's *The Snow Queen*. Seeing me eat the book, my man offers me a sandwich. We quarrel again because his wife has thrown the sandwich at me with rancor. Finally realizing that I am justified in resenting this behavior, he takes my side. We both burst into tears and embrace tightly.

In elaborating this, the woman tells me the Andersen fairy tale, alternatively identifying herself and her man with the figure of little frozen-hearted Kay. To break the spell that makes her seal off her emotions and keep them frozen under ice, means for her to find a Gerda and be emotionally nourished. In endopsychic terms this figure represents the recuperating of her own feminine aspect, of her own capacity to take care of her wounds, to accept pain without denying it anymore. Only if one stops despising one's inferiority can one begin to hold dialogue with the "abandoned child," thus permitting her to grow and to see one's own ability to love develop together with her. It is no accident that in the dream there is a child which the woman takes care of with love.

There is a point within us where, once it has been passed, we can close the books on a past of death, rejection, and inadequacies and begin to feel the love that surrounds us. If during our whole lives we have never been capable of feeling fulfilled by our emotional relationships, if in some way the void was always within us, if our relations with others were a constant demanding — like perennially hungry children — what we suddenly experience is a sensation of inner warmth and fullness, as if the soul had suddenly turned a dark corner and saw a chink of light. Naturally that does not mean that solitude and emptiness have been forever banished from our lives — they are part of the human condition — but that these psychological states are deprived of the tragic amplification that distinguished them until now. The relationship with Frieda seems to promise just such a thaw in K.'s soul. We should not forget that K.'s love for the barmaid reflects the relationship of Kafka and Milena Jesenskà.

After the tormented story with Felice Bauer, Kafka found in the Prague journalist the warm and passionate companion who would have been able to teach him tenderness and love. She was the first woman who was interested in Kafka's world, who shared his love of literature and who was able to appreciate the talent of the man she loved. The encounter with Milena was Kafka's first venture into the erotic world. Milena, in fact, seemed to contain in her body the mysterious secrets of Eros, and the key to life, growth, and individuation.

K. falls in love with Frieda in his way because he believes that this relationship can open the doors of the Castle to him. He has felt intuitively that love is the only way of breaking through his narcissistic wall. The inability to abandon himself to feeling, the excessive evaluation of his rationality will bring about the failure of the land surveyor. When Frieda abandons him, K., without a lodging any longer and now an incorrigible outsider, will give way to his exhaustion. Without a woman who can put him in contact with his unconscious, he will no longer be able to reply to the *call*.

The relationship with one's own inwardness determines the measure of one's ability to give. Inaccessible, evasive people who are incapable of giving any part of themselves to the other or opening

171

themselves to feeling are the same ones who have an inner fracture that separates them from their emotions. What all Kafka's characters have in common is the *inability to love*. This handicap generates a kind of rigidness in them. Joseph K. of *The Trial* and K. of *The Castle* believe that they can overcome all obstacles with their intelligence and their rationality. This is where they sin from hubris. Their unilateral form of awareness deprives them of that mental flexibility necessary for glimpsing new solutions. This can only be generated by a deep relationship with inwardness.

The question of mental flexibility takes us back to a theme implicit in the idea of measure or of limits: the borderline situation. Beyond all precisely pathological features, the mind can always find itself in a borderline situation. In the Greek world Hermes was the god of the roads. His monuments, the herms, were columns in the form of phalluses, which were used as road signs. From a psychological point of view, Hermes marks the limits, the *borderlines*, of our inner frontiers, of the territories beyond which the foreign, the alien begins (Lopez-Pedraza 1977, p. 3).

What is indicated as a hermetic capacity is, therefore, the capacity of the psyche to move from one border to another, to live in constant change. As the messenger of the gods, Hermes was continually in transit from one place to another. He seems to have had no fixed residence, no center. The psyche rediscovers Hermes when it is able to connect up its complexes, to move from one image to another, thus continually transferring psychic energy. In every analysis the myth of Hermes will inevitably take form. Significantly, Hillman defines the analyst as a *mercurial prostitute*.

The land surveyor's task can be seen as the duty to measure the limits of the psyche by moving from one extreme to another. The demand of change is one of endopsychic mobility to which he, however, will not be able to reply. It will be the rigidity of his ego, his intellectualism, that paralyzes him and determines the negative result of his mission. But there is another element that must be kept in mind because it is a determining factor. Hermes and his sons, Pan and Priapus, are phallic divinities whose symbolism contains precise instructions. Sexuality marks the road of life like a milestone. The erotic imagination marks the border between the inner and the outer, between the fantasy and its realization. And sexuality in *The Castle* plays a decisive role. K.'s relationship with Frieda, the interest that Olga and Pepi show for the officials of the Castle, are played out erotically. Behind every figure there is an erotic history: for Gisa the village schoolmistress, for the son of the concierge, for Gardena, and even for the mysterious woman who is the mother of little Hans Brunswick and also belongs to the Castle. We will see how the so-called *call* — that is, the sudden summons by means of which the officials exercised a strange right over the women, a little like *jus prima noctis* — structures the entire novel. If sexuality has this central role, and on the psychic level the erotic imagination is one of the ways for venturing into the labyrinth of the soul, its extraneousness to the surveyor will be one of the keys for explaining the failure of K.-Kafka.

Seventeen

The Illness of Identity

We have considered *The Castle* as a *call* to the search for identity. By means of the normal goals that each human being pursues during the course of life—work, place in the community, the ability to form and maintain emotional relations—our hero K. tries to understand who he is with regard to himself and others. He struggles to achieve an identity. The consciousness of this man, who like his author we can imagine to have reached the halfway mark of his life, is still extremely precarious and uncertain. We can compare him to other famous characters such as Zenone, the hero of Marguerite Yourcenar's *L'oeuvre au noir* (1968) and Herman Hesse's Siddhartha (1922).

Zenone, "the adventurer of knowledge," abandons the University of Leuwen, turning his back on a career as a prelate in order to discover his still-unknown authentic personality. He explains to his astonished cousin:

> ". . . Someone awaits me elsewhere. I'm
> going to him." And he resumed his pace.
> Henry Maximilian, astonished, asked,
> "Who? That old man, the Prior of
> Leon?"
> Zeno turned around, then replied,
> "*Hic Zeno*. Myself."
> (Yourcenar 1968, p. 12)

And just as K. leaves the high road and takes the wooden bridge that leads to the village, Zenone too, having arrived at the symbolic crossroads of his life, will not choose the high road, but a small path, a shortcut. Zenone and Siddhartha will face a thousand vicissitudes, will seek their true natures through ever-new ways of being. Siddhartha, the son of the Brahman, will become an ascetic among ascetics, a merchant among merchants and a boatman on the river. All of his searching for himself will also be searching for meaning, for the absolute, for an answer. From asceticism to love, from the pleasures of the senses to total renunciation, Siddhartha will travel all the roads because the soul needs to explore all of its possibilities before settling on the most congenial one.

The land surveyor experiences the search for himself as a confrontation with the Castle. He arrives "late" for this appointment with destiny. On an endopsychic level the delay is a result of inner conflict. To face the unknown always provokes fears and uncertainties that can express themselves as apathy and lack of enthusiasm for what needs to be done. The goal seems hardly to be important. In the end that snowy landscape, in which K. gets lost several times before reaching the village, can also be interpreted as the inner cold, the lack of interest and commitment to our objectives that delays our progress even if not blocking it completely. We can get lost whenever we lose sight of the grand design of a vast project, even though we may realize that we are playing a role — and only seemingly a small, secondary role — in it. Our habit of constantly dividing and cutting up events keeps us from seeing the connections between them, the slender threads that bind one action, one life, to another.

A prisoner of his uncertainty and blindness, the individual forgets how important is his contribution to the construction of the completed work. The basic idea of Jung's essay *An Answer to Job* (1952) is that God has need of humanity. The conclusion reached by this audacious and deeply felt analysis of the relationship between Job and Yahweh is that the divinity needs people in order to become conscious of himself. The biblical God seems to possess no form of self-reflection and so no self-perception. He can only know he exists by having at his disposal an object that recognises him. In this manner Job is elevated to an almost divine role in contraposition to God, as God's conscience. Even leaving Jung's thesis aside, one must remember that Western mystics have always attributed an important role to humans. Though we are nothing in comparison to God's omnipotence, the human being is considered the indispensable tool that allows God to realize his designs. Deprived of humanity's sometimes unconscious participation, the divine projects would have the impalpable consistency of dreams.

Each of us has a task no one else can perform. Without our participation even the lives of others would be mutilated, like a mosaic from which a stone has been removed. In an old Frank Capra film, *It's a Wonderful Life*, George, the hero, is about to kill himself from discouragement. He asks the angel, who has come to dissuade him from this act, for the gift of never having been born. Thus he has the possibility of seeing what would have become of his dear ones and his town without him. In this way he discovers that his wife would have remained an old maid passing sad days as a librarian, whereas his uncle, whom he wasn't able to save from a terrible mistake, is an old madman who has lived for twenty years in an institute for the criminally insane. And his hometown itself, without the village he built for the poor, has become the fief of an unscrupulous banker.

To recognize the necessity of everyone's life is a fundamental moment in psychological growth. He who does not manage to discern the sacredness, the uniqueness of each individual life, will not be able to love and respect either himself or others. Like one of many other tragic marionettes being pulled by the strings of Chance, he will live in an alienated world on which nothing and no one can bestow a meaning.

All of us know we live in a mass world where the collectivity constantly tries to crush the individual and diminish her value. Kafka was the forerunner of this theme and depicted how the individual loses his way in the contemporary world. The very fact of Kafka being a Jew deprived him of roots. Living on the verge of two worlds, the German and the Czech one — in neither of which, despite the father's efforts, the Kafka family ever managed to become entirely integrated — Franz was even deprived of his Jewish identity because he was educated outside the scheme of his culture. The strength of the Jews for thousands of years was due to the compactness of their culture which, despite the diaspora, had maintained its traditions intact everywhere and anywhere in the world. This extreme condition made of the Jew the strongest and the weakest depository of the sense of identity. Strongest because the Jewish faith never lost its characteristics, and weakest because these always kept them separate from the local populations. The myth of the wandering Jew is that of the *outsider*, one who roams the earth without ever being able to have an established dwelling anywhere.

Exclusion, rejection, and negation, themes that run through Kafka's works, are also the legacy of a centuries-old experience. But in Kafka these cease to be the sad trappings of a single people and broaden to become the symbol of the human condition in general. One peculiarity of Franz Kafka's work is the way it revolves around the great themes of Jewish thought—exile, sin, expiation—without his depicting the condition of a single Jew, without the word *Jew* ever appearing in his writings (Robert 1979, p. 5).

Within Kafka's works we can discern that "illness of identity" as it was defined by Robert (1979, p. 27), which is manifested in the progressive loss of the heroes' names. It is no accident that last names are increasingly replaced by the roles the persons play or by indications of the animal species to which they belong. Thus we find the officer and the condemned man in *The Penal Colony*, the messenger in *An Imperial Message*, the dog in *Investigations of a Dog*, the monkey in *A Report to an Academy*. Or else we witness the progressive deterioration of the identity of the heroes of the three novels: from Karl Rossman of *Amerika*, who can still recognize himself as belonging to a specific family, we proceed to Josef K. of *The Trial* whose first name is still intact, the oldest bulwark of identity and the most intimate hallmark of the ego since it is connected to the sphere of the affections. Complete erosion finally arrives in *The Castle,* where the name of the protagonist, a land surveyor, has been reduced to a single timid initial. With the passing of the years, Kafka's inner crisis worsens and he progressively loses hope in the possibility of a recovery that would furnish him with a more stable and clear identity. So the author's personages become increasingly evasive, disquieting, and indefinable, almost frozen in a border zone, an intermediary stage between "a man and an object, between the unnamed and the animal" (Robert 1979, p. 7).

It is interesting to see how this interdiction of a name strikes only the protagonist and not other figures, who continue to display their integration in the community, their strong ties to the milieu, by means of a secure and specific family denomination. The interdiction of the name has always been a feature of the Jewish religion. The name of God was sacred and thus unpronounceable, but it was just this prohibition that gave the pious Jew his sense of identity. In Kafka's world—which is living through the last phase of the diaspora, the prelude to the holocaust which will annihilate six million Jews—the prohibition will include the human as well as the divine; everything is embodied in silence, in clandestinity. Humanity is an impotent witness of its own annihilation.

In arriving late at his appointment with destiny, K. is also trying to flee from his own fantasies, since destiny is nothing but the actuation, the encounter with an inner image. In this regard, Jung wrote (1951, p. 71): "When an inner factor does not become conscious, it produces itself externally in the form of destiny." Unfortunately—or perhaps luckily, since otherwise our mental development would be arrested—it is not possible to avoid obstacles, to reject this confrontation with the unconscious, with our *daimons*, because the obstacle, the fantasy, is *inside* of us. Pirandello's Mattia Pascal (1904), who thinks he can escape from himself by making others believe he is dead, will always find himself implacably faced with his inner images. Every new life and every new love will be in reality impossible because everything is likely to betray him. Thus he will be forced to return to his home town and live with his past, with his condition as "defunct," the expression of his alienation.

The vicissitudes of K. take on tragic values just because he does not know how to give them a meaning, how to incorporate them in some coherent existential progress. For the surveyor they remain exclusively impediments, ancillary events that only make him waste time rather than facilitate his task. Since the way each of us relates to things reveals our personalities, the nonacceptance of suffering as an integral part of psychic development is a clear sign of K.'s immaturity. Unable to assume responsibilities, to love a woman without constantly demanding that she be a mother to him, he has a baby's concept of life as a font of continual gratifications. These, on the contrary, are only a small part of it and must be won with great exertion inasmuch as the world does not offer them spontaneously. Only the efforts of the individual, the development of her inner world, can transform suffering and allow her to find room for satisfaction and fulfillment. From certain aspects, K. is a personification of the *puer aeternus*.

The problem of becoming human, both on the individual and on the collective level, can be seen within the archetype of the Senex-Puer. Whereas the Senex represents reflection, order, structure, accomplishment, the capacity for knowing that forms the ego, the reply to it, the Puer expresses in turn the dynamic seed, the original spark of spirit, impulse, searching, exploration. When the psyche disowns its complexity and chooses the unilateral road of identification with only one aspect of the archetype, it arrests its own development. Anyone who has lost the Senex aspect of the mind will find himself unable to relate to the world with any ability to reflect. Unable to put its searching in order, to find a meaning in its actions, the Puer acts without managing to connect its behavior with the demands of the anima (Hillman 1967, *passim*). In

K. we find the negative polarity of both the Senex and the Puer aeternus. His emotional immaturity, his impatience, his inability to give a meaning to his acts and connect them to his deepest inner needs, all pertain to the Puer, while his coldness and distance are typical of the Senex. The surveyor is *he who measures* by profession. K. evaluates, calculates every decision and action. He is the prisoner of reflection which, since it is done without true awareness of the soul, becomes a sterile cage for any true *dynamis*. He is frozen by a saturnine cold in which depression, "the black bile of melancholy," coagulates. He cannot relate to sexuality and the feminine. Saturn is, in fact, associated with widowhood and the lack of children. Like Cronus, he devours his children as soon as they are born, destroying, that is, all potential for change. The impossibility of relating to Frieda, and so to his anima, will block all hope for the surveyor to understand his own complexes. Far from being a road to illumination of his inner world as in the tantric tradition, Eros will be for him the venturing into a foreign land whose air suffocates and stuns.

The obstacles that K. finds along his path are connected to the fact that the journey he has begun—a metaphor of an opening to mystery and the unknown—requires a break with his past. We can understand the surveyor's difficulties and fears by putting ourselves in the shoes of an immigrant who leaves a place he knows and loves to go a new part of the world where he has no roots, where no memory can give him a sense of continuity. Inner strength depends upon our history, our past, whose points of reference constitute a kind of mental map by which we can orient ourselves. The loss of these fixed points, of these milestones which are our memories, unleashes a panic like that of a traveler who has become lost in an unknown district. The new landscape that opens before our eyes at the moment that we break with the past is not located on this mental map. We no longer have categories within which to classify events and situations. This is frightening. To open up to the unknown means opening up to the daimon of possibility. This is the only way to live in a world in which you must be able—like a snake—to change your skin constantly, to undergo an evolution of identity or else to succumb, to be killed by the void, the sense of futility, the betrayal of oneself. In confronting one's fears that impel one toward a new reality, there are contained the creative possibilities of life. From a world of rigid necessity in which everything is taken for granted, we pass into a sphere of absolute possibility in which the ability is required to read and interpret events rapidly without being able to count on any outside reference, on any known canon drawn from our past.

For the entire length of the novel, K. will search for recognition. If we connect this problem in the novel with the personal ones of its author, we recall how Kafka searched desperately for the love and acceptance of his father, who persisted in not understanding this son, so different from the one he had dreamed of and had expected. The *Letter to His Father* is not only an accusation, it is also, and most of all, an implicit and painful plea for recognition.

In the feeling of his son, Hermann Kafka has the numinous character of a god. The description that Kafka draws of his father recalls the image of the Jewish God. Yahweh—primarily as he appears in the Book of Job —is gripped by terrible rages, his judgment indiscriminate, his immorality absolute because he himself is not able to keep faith with the Law he has decreed for men. The God of Job is a divinity full of contradictions, who exercises indiscriminate power and destroys Job because of the bet he has made with Satan. A God like that cannot arouse love but only terror. Faced with such unpredictable violence, the soul steps back appalled. Whatever he does, man is always guilty. It is impossible for him to feel deserving of divine love. All that is left to humanity is its *inadequacy* and its *guilt*.

> If I sin, you watch me,
> and do not acquit me of my
> iniquity.
> If I am wicked, woe to me!
> If I am righteous, I cannot lift
> up my head,
> for I am filled with disgrace
> and look upon my affliction.
>
> (Job 10: 14–15)

Job will exclaim, destroyed by suffering. Although Job calls God "father," nothing in the relationship suggests the idea of love or parental understanding. Job, who still continues to confide in God, appealing to his sense of justice, knows that he can be annihilated by him at any instant, just as his family and his herds have been. In his eyes the divinity is a terrifying power. In his analysis of the phenomenology of the sacred, Rudolf Otto (1936, p. 26, passim) considers the *tremendum* one of the distinctive signs of the experience of the divine. A "shiver" is the response of the soul when it feels the roots of its being vibrate mysteriously. What one experiences is a sense of one's nullity and the shattering of one's being in the face of the terrifying reality. The *tremendum* springs from the absolute inaccessibility of the divine, from its power, from its majesty. When terror grips the soul, the individual can be completely paralyzed.

Interpreting religious experience in a psychological key, Jung compared the *numinous*, which the religious person feels in regard to the divinity, to the terror and dismay that overcomes the subject faced with the power of the archetype. The sense of nullity that Kafka feels with regard to his father—and that in his novels will be the constant reaction of his characters when faced with the Authorities—can be likened to the annihilation the ego feels when the unconscious erupts. When inner images are not recognized and no dialogue is held with them, they acquire a terrifying supernatural character that is almost daimonic. The duality of nullity-omnipotence is the translation of a condition of deep asymmetry, of the lack of synchronization between two realities, two beings. The Other can assume this form of absolute power by virtue of being distant, far from any category by which he can be understood, and so brought close, assimilated. The moment in which the other is made into an insoluble enigma one consecrates him as "god" (Barthes 1977, p. 134).

When it is impossible to reduce the mystery of the one who we have before us to a predictable behavioral scheme, we feel ourselves to be completely in her power. With regard to his father, Kafka—like K. before the functionaries of the Caste—felt his own *inadequacy*. This extremely painful kind of psychological experience is particularly evident in narcissistic personalities. From a dynamic point of view, we can consider such a perception to be the result of a conflict between the ego and the ego ideal, which in the narcissistic individual takes on gigantic proportions. Incapable of living up to the ever-greater demands of the ideal, the ego is crushed and plunges into depression. Such a sense of inadequacy can only derive from a highly unstable self-esteem. The precarious sense of identity—one of the novel's leitmotifs—has connotations with Kafka's psychic reality and emerges frequently between the lines of his letters and diaries. At the source of this psychic condition there is often a repeated traumatic experience that goes back to the earliest objective relations, as if the child had only experienced rejection and exclusion in contact with the mother.

The feeling of inadequacy that K.-Kafka experiences in regard to the Authorities-father perhaps has its source in the pain and frustration of the family's inability to accept and love him. Faced with the lack of love, we feel ourselves *inadequate*. The indifference and coldness of the Other end by making us feel somehow guilty, as if not being loved were the result of a personal defect. K.-Kafka imagines that some recognition from the outside would be enough to heal his wounds, to wipe out his feeling of being worth little or nothing. In reality, as we will see, this decisive recognition awaited by the suveyor will never be forthcoming, because it cannot come from the outside. Only if K. were entirely convinced of being a land surveyor could he recieve confirmation and ratification from the Castle. Inasmuch as he was capable of self-recognition, he could be accepted.

In remembering how he related to life in school, Kafka (1919, p. 44) emphasizes, in a way emblematic for understanding his personality, that in every subject and every examination he was convinced that he would be failed.

From this interiorizing of disdain, we are only a step away from the identification with the cockroach that occurs in *The Metamorphosis* (Kafka 1912b). The cockroach is the tragic symbol of rejection, of feeling unworthy, inferior, repulsive to the point of being forever unloveable. In the story the death of the protagonist comes as a great relief to the whole family, for whom Gregor by then was only a source of shame and distress. The detail of the maid who sweeps out the remains of the gigantic and monstrous insect can be connected to a bitter memory that the writer (Kafka 1920–1923, p. 28) confides to Milena regarding his childhood: the attempt of his sisters to throw him into the river.

> Sensible or intuitive children tried to push me over without any partic-
> ular reason, perhaps because *they considered me superfluous.*

The English psychoanalyst Martin (1959, pp. 65–71) compares the writer's feelings of inadequacy with those of several of his patients, who suffered from the same imaginary identification with a cockroach, and maintains that the feeling of not being loved is decisive for associating one's own image with that of an insect. Incapable of forming an entirely independent evaluation of themselves, the individuals also manifest an extreme vulnerability to the judgments of others. Any criticism immediately takes on enormous proportions because the source of their self-esteem lies in the approval of those around them. They appear to be incapable of unhooking their present perceptions of themselves from the rejections they were subjected to in childhood.

The only recourse left for a child who is extremely vulnerable emotionally and dependent on parental affection is to repress all criticism, all inner opposition together with the feelings of hatred these would arouse and convince himself that he is the repugnant one who is unworthy of love. In this way he preserves the parental figure, which is his only point of reference at that early age. But Kafka remained a prisoner of that perverse mechanism that at one time had helped him to survive. His perennial feelings of guilt in reality were an attempt to protect the introjected parental image. Even though he managed to attack his father in that letter which he never found the courage to let him read, the writer continued to live all his adult relations under the sign of that same infantile dynamic of unworthiness and to extend it to his fictional creations.

From a psychological viewpoint we must note how insecurity and the feeling that one is somehow a "mistake," are conditions that most easily predispose the individual to defeat and operate in life in such a way as to bring about the very things that one fears. A person with an "ugly duckling" complex inevitably acts in a way to make herself disagreeable to everyone. Her gestures will be awkward and graceless, thus attracting the ostracism of those she lives among just as happens in the Andersen fable.

A clear example of this dynamic is found in the sphere of love. Freud (1914, p. 89) called attention to how one's idea of one's inadequacy for love because of real or imagined physical or mental disturbances acts in a negative way on everyone's self-image and ends by hiding one's charm. A person's *inner negativeness* discourages those around him, thus provoking exclusion. That reinforces the person's anxiety in a pitiful vicious circle that is hard to break until one learns to see oneself in a new way.

Many patients who enter analysis and are deficient in self-esteem need to regain confidence in themselves, to learn to see themselves in a new way. That is to say they must regain love for their own individuality. Thus they often are fascinated by the analyst's self-recognition and confirmation. Anyone capable of radiating outward her self-recognition appears to be gifted with a charm, a particular "beauty" for which we use the Greek word, *charisma*. To rediscover within oneself one's psychic center of gravity means to attain a power that he never knew existed.

This means to be capable of managing one's life by oneself and assuming one's responsibilities for better or for worse. One gradually becomes more impervious—and thus less vulnerable—to both criticism and approval. The moment in which one confronts the world, one must be able to remain firm on one's positions, on one's acquisitions, without allowing oneself to be nullified by possible criticisms of one's actions or ideas. The "truth," that is to say the psychological meaning of our actions, is contained within ourselves. This means we must be able to put ourselves into question continually without losing faith in our possibilities, in that cluster of contradictions which is our soul.

Criticisms are useful for our growth only when we do not allow ourselves to be destroyed by them. If we look behind us, we can see how often our difficulties in taking action were caused by accusations from without, which crushed us by their negativeness. We remained as if petrified, frozen, paralyzed by a negating opposition without being able to offer our view of things in contraposition. The confrontation with the Other is at the same time *contraposition and acceptance* of her viewpoint. Inner firmness should not be confused with a narcissistic inflation into the belief that one is the only depository of absolute truth—our own—among many. To find the courage to carry forward a *modus vivendi*, a *Weltanschauung*, makes it possible for us to be humble toward others. Psychological strength is never the annihilation of one's fellows but being open to others' truths.

Eighteen

The Faces of the Mystery

To start out toward the Castle, to reach it, and, above all to manage to be received by its officials, is a task bristling with difficulties for K. Each time he feels sure of soon winning out, someone intervenes to dampen his hopes. We can use this constant alternation of failures and successes as a metaphor of the spiral-like process typical of the psychic function and which is particularly visible in the world of dreams. Those who pay particular attention to the workings of the unconscious know very well that a dream which clearly indicates the realization of a more elevated state of consciousness can immediately be followed by disquieting images, messengers of a new regression and vice versa. It often happens that painful external events are accompanied by reassuring dreams while, contrarily, happy events generate anguishing dreams. Jung is known to have spoken of this as a compensating function of the dream, which makes the attitude neglected by the ego emerge.

The Jungian model of the psyche is constructed on polarity: the conscious-unconscious division that has a compensatory relationship. The psychic attitudes (introversion-extroversion) and the four psychological functions (thought, intuition, sentiment, sensation) are described in polar pairs. Recurrent themes of Jungian thought are polar (within the dynamics of coupling): logos–eros, individual–collective, power–love, ego–shadow, masculine–feminine. Polarity, for which the Swiss psychiatrist showed an extraordinary interest, is an important key for explaining the psyche's alternation of contrasting aspects, given the fact that it must be experienced in its totality.

An emblematic case can be found in the dreams of a woman who is particularly sensitive to attitudes of acceptance–rejection. The critical moments in her emotional attachment, when she believes that the relationship has by now reached its end, are often underscored by dreams of reconciliation, whereas periods of happiness, when she feels she is loved and accepted, can evoke in her old fantasies of exclusion. Since the relationship she is involved in has been marked by a continuous and very destabilizing swing from acceptance to rejection and back, it is quite normal if she does not manage to feel entirely at ease. But the emergence of this latter polarity immediately accompanied by a profound change in her way of relating to the world, almost as if she had developed a second personality experienced as "psychotic," suggests another possible hypothesis.

The psyche has need of living with and relating to its fractures, its failures, its sick parts. The growth of pride of the ego which, after a long period of stability comes to believe that it has killed its disturbing alter ego, generates the reappearance of the latter with greater force.

An old American film, *The Forbidden Planet* by Fred Wilcox (1950), tells of a group of galactic explorers who land on a far planet in order to bring back to earth the survivors of a previous expedition. They discover that the only ones left are a Dr. Morbius and his daughter. A new series of mysterious deaths among the crew, who are attacked by a monster of gigantic size, brings the truth to light. It was the scientist himself who destroyed his rescuers. Thanks to a particular experiment he practiced on himself using a machine that was left over from the ancient civilisation of the Krell, which had disappeared suddenly, Morbius was able to expand the powers of his mind. Besides greater knowledge and intellectual capacity, he developed too the possibilities of expressing his unconscious contents. When he was angry or hated someone, these feelings that were repressed by his conscious mind were unleashed and took the from of a gigantic primordial animal. The only thing that could stop the monsters of the id would be the death of the scientist. He drops dead when, having realized the truth, he orders the monster generated by his mind to stop in order to save his daughter.

A Jungian reading of this film would immediately underscore how the light, the power that the conscious has reached, is directly proportional to the Shadow, the power of the unconscious. Thus an ego that is particularly evolved and refined from the rational, intellectual point of view, can hide a fragile and infantile emotivity, so split and so little structured as to be at the edge of the psychotic, incapable of experiencing emotions without being overwhelmed. And since psychic growth cannot consist of the impossible repression of the unconscious or its reduction to consciousness — as would suggest the Freudian motto *where the id was there shall be the ego* — but of the attempt to relate these two components to each other, a psyche that removes a part of itself is doomed to be invaded by the rejected part. Thus each time that our dreamer believes she has conquered "the madness," it promptly appears in her behavior, upsetting her relations.

We can see how in the same night the woman generates totally different dream images that balance each other. In the initial sequence of the first dream appears a nude boy rejected by his mother. The dreamer tries in vain to convince her to take care of her boy and for that purpose shows her the brilliant essay the boy has written on the localization of the emotions in the brain. In the following scene the woman herself decides to take care of him and become his true mother, overcoming her fears of not being able to feed and dress him because she — who has not noticed that she is sufficiently clothed in a bathrobe — believes herself to be nude. This dream, which appears to indicate the capacity of the psyche to take care of its infantile aspects and "raise" them, is followed by another, very dramatic dream. The woman, in fact, dreams that she has been split into two identical people, one of whom is mad. But she cannot determine which is herself and which the mad woman because they constantly exchange clothes. The dreamer would like to exclude the other, remove her, chase her away forever, but the latter insinuates herself into her life and ruins everything she does.

Both these dreams are the reply of the unconscious to a particularly emotional moment in her relationship with her man; fearing rejection, she feels extremely vulnerable and experiences this painful sensation as the outbreak of madness. The specter of madness is the antithesis of the myth of a totally rounded kind of mental health, an ideal that wants to hide and suppress all those mental aspects considered weak, inferior, and nonadaptive. Madness is tied to the outbreak of emotion, which having never been lived, has acquired a sinister explosive power. Behind madness, understood as an inner discomfort becoming chronic, the psyche expresses its need of being recognized and accepted in all its facets. Only total acceptance, the willingness to love our sick sides even in their possibilities of becoming chronic, can transform a dimension that was considered immutable. As soon as the dreamer is capable of holding dialogue with her "mad" side, ceasing to ignore and be ashamed of it, it will stop erupting into her life to sabotage it, as is shown by the answer the woman receives from the "madwoman" when she begins talking to her through the method of active imagination.

To love one's sick side, accepting it as it is, requires great strength, because we all desire to close our eyes to our failures, our wounds, and hope to heal them magically.

The problems of polarity and of the split have a central role in *The Castle*, where the various characters seem to be doubles of the hero, magical incarnations of his inner images. Thus the two helpers represent K.'s infantile aspect, while Frieda, Pepi, Olga, Amalia, Gardena are clear representations of the diverse aspects of the feminine archetype. The incapacity of the surveyor to speak with his sides will increase their power and the disturbance they cause. Jeremias and Artur, for example, appear at the least opportune moments, creating problems for K. rather than helping him. As in the dreams mentioned above, in the case of K.-Kafka too, the nonrelationship with the unconscious makes an enemy of it, a foreign otherness that is fearful.

K.'s progress toward the Castle not only demands that he be able to live up to the alternations of success and failure, but obliges him to descend to compromises. Just for the sake of staying near the Castle, K. talks to the villagers, comes to terms with them, reluctantly accepting certain compromises. Thrown out by Gardena, he accepts the job of caretaker in order to make ends meet. This withdrawal to a temporary position allows the hero to catch his breath before taking up the fight again for recognition by the authorities.

But the compromise should be read in endopsychic terms. Daily life often obliges us to come to terms. All of us, as soon as we leave the child's world of illusions and easy conquests and enter the adult world, become aware of the great gap between our dreams and the real conditions of life. To reach the objective, the established goal, means to run a course filled with many detours. Each partial change of direction represents, at bottom, a compromise, the concession to life of something we would never have wanted to give it, but which we are forced to renounce simply in order to survive. Sometimes we are obliged to lock away a precious dream because life imposes that sacrifice on us.

A moralistic interpretation of these episodes serves little purpose. The natural world teaches us, in fact, that compromise is a function of survival. The story of evolution on earth shows that those organisms survive which best succeed in adapting themselves to the environment, shaping their bodies to the changing conditions of life. This natural law is also valid on the psychic level. We have learned a strategy of survival when we acquire the inner elasticity to surmount obstacles without crashing directly and violently into them. To learn to *survive* does not mean to betray oneself. The reed which bends in the wind does not deviate from its nature, but resists the hurricane much better than the great oak whose rigidity risks its uprooting.

When one accepts the need of following secondary routes to reach the goal, one can begin to see the obstacles one finds along the way in a new light. It is then that one understands how the obstacle, apparently created by the outer world, is actually *inside* of us. This changed vision allows us to converse with the obstacle, to relate to it and little by little to smooth and level it. The obstacle that forces us to slow down our march and perhaps to halt can be the occasion for taking stock of ourselves. Only a superficial attitude toward life can delude us into thinking that the world is against us and is blocking our way; in reality it is *we* who are fighting against *ourselves*. Just as soon as we succeed in seeing our difficulties and relating to them in a new way, the inner transformation that comes about cancels the negative and destructive character of the situation. The events follow their course, but we know how to interact in a different way with our destiny.

As K. was going out he noticed a dark portrait in a dim frame on the wall. He had already observed it from his couch by the stove, but from that distance he had not been able to distinguish any details and had thought that it was only a plain back to the frame. But it was a picture after all, as now appeared, the bust portrait of a man about fifty. His head was sunk so low upon his breast that his eyes were scarcely visible, and the weight of the high, heavy forehead and the strong hooked nose seemed to have borne the head down. Because of this pose the man's full beard was pressed in at the chin and spread out farther down. His left hand was buried in his luxuriant hair, but seemed incapable of supporting the head. 'Who is that?' asked K., 'the

Count?' He was standing before the portrait and did not look round at the landlord. 'No,' said the latter, 'the Castellan.' (Kafka 1922b, p. 14)

In the contemplation of the picture, the surveyor comes into contact for the first time with the *mystery*. Although it soon turns out that the portrait is of the gatekeeper, what counts is that K. believes it to be the count, of whom nothing is told in the novel. His figure may represent the allegory of the Unknowable, of the Enigma, of that Truth, that ultimate knowledge which K. makes vain efforts to reach. Thus it is perfectly natural that it appears to him to be an empty frame: the mystery cannot be represented. This obscure personage who inhabits the most secret rooms of the Castle is put into connection with Eros in its most disturbing and negative form as an aspect of the obscene. When K. asks the schoolteacher if he knows the count, the latter will answer him in French, the language which more than any other is associated with things licentious: "Please remember that there are innocent children present" (Kafka 1922b, p. 16). The Castle seems to be the site of immorality, of vice, where the officials use the village women for their pleasure. It represents the most unbridled instinct, pure sexual pleasure cut off from all forms of affection or love, sex with no connection to a relationship, with no tie to deepen it and give it meaning in continuity, in duration. If all that appears perfectly normal in the eyes of the villagers, to the point that to refuse an obscene invitation from an official—as Amalia does—is considered a horribly guilty and shameful thing, for K. it will be a motive for execration and condemnation. The erotic was experienced by Kafka as something anguishing and guilt-ridden. The world of desire, of sexuality, was for him a nocturnal and infernal realm, a chthonic and mysterious abyss that excited horror and attraction at once. To enter there, to venture in, meant to lose oneself, one's liberty, and abandon oneself to a deceitful and tormenting power. In the same period that saw the writing of *The Castle*, January 18, 1922, Kafka (1910–1923, p. 400) noted in his diary:

Sex keeps gnawing at me, hounds me day and night, I should have to conquer fear and shame and probably sorrow too to satisfy it; yet on the other hand I am certain that I should at once take advantage, with no feeling of fear or sorrow or shame, of the first opportunity to present itself quickly, close at hand, and willingly.

Here we see delineated that compulsiveness of gratification which we find in many of his characters and which seems to dominate the sexual relations described in the novel. The villagers with their acceptance of the customs of the Castle manifest, at bottom, a greater understanding of sexuality. They are in some way aware that it is an ambiguous sphere in which the *sublime* is united with the base, in which violence and domination take the place of tenderness and respect.

In ancient Greece it was Pan who represented the joining of the sexual instinct with aggressiveness. And Pan, with his pursuit of nymphs and his rapes, personified an aspect of the psyche. His half-human and half-goat body alluded to the union of the human with the animal side. Pan was, therefore, accepted and honored in the pantheon of divinities. But when Western culture lost its connection with the body, with the physical, Pan's numinous quality changed into a sinister, diabolical power. The devil, the prince of evil, also became the image of Eros repressed. In the Hebrew myth, Lilith, Adam's first wife, abandoned her man because he refused to concede an equal role to her and wouldn't let her lay on top of him. She then was turned into a horrible daimon that strangled babies and seduced men in their sleep, pushing them toward madness.

In the same way, K.-Kafka's repressed sexuality ceases to be a creative, propelling force and is transformed into a mental obsession, imprisoned by that coercive force. Incapable of grasping the mystery of the Castle, whose sexual aspect assumes the value of a test of initiation, a surrender to the power of the *daimon*—reawakening its kundalini as in tantric rites—the surveyor can do nothing but take a moralistic attitude toward the eruption of the Dionysian or else lose himself in its labyrinth like an unwary traveler who ventures into unknown woods at night. The sexuality that K. thinks he knows is lacking in fantasy. There is no room in it for any erotic imagination. In the village, contrarily, the multiformity of this sphere is recognized. As Lopez-Pedraza (1977, p. 67) emphasizes, sexuality is a complex sphere with extremely variegated forms that include the participation of all the gods. A monotheistic sexuality could not be other than idealized. Deprived of its multiple images, its polymorphous quality, it is extremely impoverished.

But let us return to the portrait. K. doesn't know who lives within the Castle walls and can only see a portrait, an enigmatic image. The lineaments of the man on whom his destiny is supposed to depend are obscure, elusive, wrapped in mystery. The obscurity of the mystery that K. is trying to unveil is the human condition itself. The confrontation with an enigma constitutes a *topos* of which the most famous example is Oedipus. The mythical sovereign of Thebes personifies the man that who has found his essence in rationality, in the power of the intellect. He battled with the mystery and defeated it with the use of logic. But the mystery enters his life again in the form of a destiny that cannot be avoided. Like Oedipus, K. too believes he must test himself against the *enigma* using his rational faculties. Therefore he questions, hypothesizes, and asks again: ought he to build a coherent picture of events by grasping that lead which will allow him to win the game and bend events to his will? Like his Greek counterpart, the surveyor is forced to come to terms with the *inscrutable*. At bottom, K.'s desire to decipher that image can be understood as the need to have points of reference. K. doesn't know how to live in uncertainty, in the realm of possibilities.

The need for security is to be found at the root of all religions. Dogmas and metaphysical constructions indubitably fascinate the human soul because they try to provide an answer to fundamental questions and save the individual from the chaos of the doubts and perplexities that torment him. They furnish a simple and incontestable key to the interpretation of existence, thus helping to counter the unease of those who have surrendered in dismay to the difficulties of grasping the ultimate meaning of life.

If the count's portrait is supposed to represent — in the same way as many events — a kind of signal, of information, it is perfectly logical that its outlines should be indeterminate. The indications that life offers us are always extremely ambiguous. It is up to us to decipher them. This capacity is inscribed in our inwardness, allowing us to attribute a meaning to the things that happen. The external world is indifferent to its own possible meanings. In Rorschach tests, for example, the blots that are showed to the patient do not in themselves have any meaning, do not represent anything in particular, and yet she sees a thousand things in them: objects, animals, mythical monsters, people, human organs, thus projecting onto the indeterminate blots all the fantasies that populate her unconscious. Thus the blot becomes the image of a psychic condition. It is not by chance that one will see different things in them at different times, because the psyche is constantly changing. Often in life the unknown, which irresistibly attracts our desire to know, takes on in time new enigmatic appearances. The same problem, the same enigmas, present themselves anew under different forms. One repeatedly returns to the same problems but each time with a new and deeper understanding.

The episode of the count's portrait reveals the uselessness of attempting to interpret events literally. The signs that life offers us must be respected in their ambiguity, because it is not possible to translate these indications into incontrovertible answers. If we translate the myth of Faust into everyday terms, we see how he who sells his soul to the devil to gain knowledge expresses an analogy to the fear of life and its becoming. For this character the longing for knowledge indicates the attempt to know everything in advance, perhaps in order to forestall the consequences of his errors.

This same desire impels some of us to seek comfort from the fear of tomorrow by consulting astrologers and fortune tellers. Even the most skeptical person has a hard time resisting the promise of knowing in advance what is in store for him, because to glimpse such a possibility sets off deep dynamics. One finds oneself at a kind of crossroads: on the one hand there is the feeling of knowing nothing of what life has in store for us, and on the other, the desire and hope that our destiny might be revealed to us. People fear the future, the unforeseeable that escapes our control and makes us feel helpless and impotent with regard to what destiny will bring. In reality we only mistake our ignorance for the obscurity of tomorrow. To become aware of oneself, of the deepest and most secret part of one's being, certainly does not mean that one can control life and bend it as one pleases, because there is always an imponderable *quid*; but self-awareness surely allows one a greater mastery of so-called "destiny." The pact with the devil is then the bartering of our souls in exchange for a promise of absolute knowledge. Instead, knowledge demands consciousness of the relativity of what one knows, to understand that the sense of what happens to us may not be immediately clear to us and that to acquire a preview of events does not get us away from our *karma*. At the age of eighty-five, Jung wrote in his memoirs (1961, p. 358):

> I have no judgment about myself and my life. There is nothing I am quite sure about. I have no definite convictions—not about anything, really. I know only that I was born and exist, and it seems to me that I have been carried along. I exist on the foundation of something I do not know. In spite of all uncertains, I feel a solidity underlying all existence and continuity in my mode of being.

To live accepting the uncertainties of tomorrow means learning to welcome *inquietude* as the faithful companion of one's life. In the form of a parable, Lessing (1968) expresses in a poetic tone this way of relating to life. The poet says that if God presented himself to humanity with his fists closed, telling us that the right hand contains all the truth and the left only the restless search for the truth and asking us to choose, we would choose the latter. Truth and certainty are only consonant with the divine. Only by living in disquiet is it possible for the human being to not betray the meaning of life (Lessing 1968, p. 27).

Inquietude is for all of us an irreplaceable stimulus to knowledge, to creativity. The unquiet individual is never content with the certainties he has acquired, never satisfied with what he has been able to realize, since every work, once it has been produced, becomes an element of the past in his search. He cannot help but impel himself toward what he does not yet know and has not yet realized. It is this continuous search, this thirst which nourishes his creativity. Nietzsche maintained (1876–1878, p. 325):

> That restlessness of the soul, which I curse, is perhaps the very condition that urges me to produce. Those pious souls who yearn for perfect tranquillity eradicate their own best activities.

Inquietude obliges people to find ever new forms to express their inner worlds. Painting his *Les demoiselles d'Avignon* in 1907, Picasso abandoned the traditional canons of figurative art, breaking with centuries of painting in which the effigy was the only way of expressing reality. With this work he opened a revolutionary conception of art, whose guiding principle becomes the artist's way of being and feeling. He shows that reality is not that which we think we are grasping with our senses, because these too can "see" an apparently implausible world. The splitting up of figures which then are shown in various different aspects is also the representation of several truths equally valid and coexistent among themselves, of which none is truer than the others.

The same inquietude compelled Schoenberg to "invent" a new kind of music very different from the melodic and veristic tradition that had dominated up to then. With the dodecaphonic experiment the "tuneful" musical motif goes by the board. There is no longer a ritornello that can be easily kept in the memory and so permit an almost automatic repetition of the sounds heard.

Inquietude is witness to an inner vitality and thus to the existence of an energy that moves from one pole of the mind to another. The opposite of this state is what in physics is called *entropy*: that condition of tranquility in which the homeostasis that has been reached indicates the end of an imbalance, of a tension between extremes which is responsible for the movement of energy. Each time a large amount of energy is present in a certain zone and very little in the neighboring one, the energy tends to move from one zone to the other until an equilibrium is reached. Contrast, difference, tension — these are what distinguish existence in its becoming.

Returning to our hero, we can suppose that if from the beginning he had had the coordinates, the precise information that would allow him to enter the Castle, his adventure would have quickly ended and so too his researches, the intimate dynamics of his existence. Instead, the land surveyor is obliged to fight to the end and maintain his vitality intact. In a famous bon mot the humorist Marcello Marchesi (1975, p. 115) affirmed:

What matters is that when death comes it finds us alive.

Despite the accumulation of weariness that makes him fall asleep from time to time and culminates in the final sleep, K. continues with his attempts, his interrogations, impelled by his inquietude.

After passing the night in the inn, K. sets out for the Castle the next morning.

Now, he could see the Castle above him clearly defined in the glittering air, its outline made still more definite by the moulding of snow covering in a thin layer. There seemed to be much less snow up there on the hill than down in the village . . . Here the heavy snowdrifts reached right up to the cottage windows and began again on the low roof, but up on the hill everything soared light and free into the air, or at least so it appeared from down below.

On the whole this distant prospect of the Castle satisfied K.'s expectations. It was neither an old stronghold nor a new mansion, but a rambling pile consisting of innumerable small buildings closely packed together and of one or two storeys; if K. had not known that it was a castle he might have taken it for a little town. There was only one tower as far as he could see, whether it belonged to a dwelling-house or a church he could not determine. Swarms of crows were circling round it. (Kafka, 1922b, p. 15)

Once more we find the details of the winter landscape characterized by ice and snow that serve as the background for the whole novel. On its appearance the Castle manages to synthesize the condition of the protagonist. If the mysterious and inaccessible abode of the count is the allegory of proud isolation, of the narcissistic withdrawal in which he has always locked himself—and of which Amalia is the perfect personification; if the Castle is the concrete representation of that ideal of purity, of the surmounting of all limits which was Kafka's predominant concern and to which he desperately tried to make his life conform, then it is natural that it should be situated beyond the site of frozen solitude. The achievement of detachment, of an absolute aloofness from the sentiments, ought to assure the individual of an imperturbable condition in which she finds herself "free and light." For he who feels himself afflicted by the need of and dependence on others and thus looks up "from below," from his condition of need, at the impossible sphere of self-sufficiency, the latter will appear to be that happy condition capable of liberating him from the anxiety, terror, and suffering which is part of daily experience.

Narcissus blissfully contemplated his own image, which contained his whole world, and in the vain effort to reach it did not notice that he was slowly slipping into the lake where he would only embrace his death. The ideal of the narcissist is to perfect her condition of detachment and self-sufficiency. She apparently thinks that love could save her from her desperate solitude, from the cold that freezes her soul, and is convinced that it is only the lacerating lack of the Other that pains and confuses her. But this search for the Other is in reality a total rejection of the relationship. At bottom her request for love is a challenge thrown at the Other. Secretly his moves and gestures are measured to discover if he is really capable of melting the ice that covers her heart, or if instead, once again the soul will remain impassive to every caress.

> How many times these low feet staggered
> Only the soldered mouth can tell
> Try — can you stir the awful rivet
> Try — can you lift the hasps of steel!
> (Dickinson 1955, p. 88)

The narcissist does not make efforts to overcome his inability to love. He waits for the other to fail, for his weariness or betrayal to reinforce his conviction that in reality there is no other way to survive except by suppressing need and privation. In this way he ends by perpetuating the alienation and the isolation from which he would like to flee and plunges deeper into the abyss and the cold. The bliss of self-sufficiency is only a phantom, as is also indicated by what K. sees on approaching the Castle.

> But on approaching it he was disappointed in the Castle; it was after all only a wretched-looking town, a huddle of village houses, whose sole merit, if any, lay in being built of stone, but the plaster had long since flaked off and the stone seemed to be crumbling away. (Kafka, 1922b, p. 15)

Continuing with our interpretation, we can affirm that as we approach our condition of isolation, of aloofness, and examine it with pitiless eyes, we bring to light all its misery. This proud isolation turns out to be a hodgepodge of awkward efforts in which the wounds of the soul, far from being healed, are still bleeding. Everything that has been done to distance one from the world, from the suffering that taking stock of one's conflicts procures, crumbles into dust. The hard and unfeeling facade that we have used to protect our fragility, that being always and everywhere vulnerable to life and relationships, will not stand up to a close analysis or a close look (Schillirò 1989, p. 155). The moment in which — due to distraction or perhaps the imperious need to let ourselves go just for once — we allow someone to approach our Castle, or we approach them (in the course of therapy or a love affair), lo and behold all the cracks in it!

In Kafka's description a flock of black crows was swarming around the structure. Crows and ravens, the black birds which in many cultures are considered to be auguries of misfortune, are connected with the lower realms. In Egyptian mythology the raven was a theriomorphic incarnation of Nekhbet, one of the oldest mother goddesses who in her positive aspect watches over the dead, but in her negative one feeds, just like the raven, on cadavers. In the Germanic world the Valkyries, whose task was to select during battle the heroes to be transported to Valhalla, are equated with ravens.

According to Neumann (1956, p. 167) we are dealing here with the sombre and mortal aspect of the feminine, which is felt to be alluring and voracious at the same time. In the relationship that K. tries to establish with Frieda, fear and mistrust are in fact visible. Rather than being interested in an emotional relationship with the woman, the land surveyor wants to use this bond as a passkey to the Castle. But the negativeness with which he looks at the feminine world works against him. The more the feminine unconscious is feared and held off, the more it threatens to crush him with its power, as happens in the case of Gardena. All of K.'s relationships are lacking in feeling. In the novel the reason seems to be the extreme prostration of the protagonist.

> He felt irresistibly drawn to seek out new acquaintances, but each new acquaintance only seemed to increase his weariness. (Kafka 1922b, p. 17)

If this access to the depths of the psyche is precluded by the difficulty of experiencing feelings, the individual's inner growth is mutilated. A refined and complex rationality may develop — such as Kafka's — but the inner sphere will remain mute. Even dreams will be incomprehensible messages since the key to their interpretation is not at hand. Cutting oneself off from the sphere of emotions, one keeps the ego from speaking with the unconscious. The difficulties that many patients experience at the beginning of an analysis are due to their fear of their emotions. Having built a dike against them, they are afraid of being overwhelmed by the ocean of feeling that has been artificially restrained. When one is only prepared to see life from a rational standpoint, letting oneself go and evaluating it from an emotional point of view means moving on terra incognita. To make that possible, an education in feeling is first necessary.

Let us think, for example, of those relationships of couples where one of the partners—whom we could call "the silent one"—only speaks of superficial things and carefully avoids all conversations that might brush up against the meaning of the relationship. In this case we are dealing with a problematic subject who has scant relations with her feelings. To speak of the relationship means to speak of emotions. For someone who is not trained to it this situation can be an indescribable torment, like throwing oneself into the voracious jaws of a shark. A notable effort is required to overcome this condition, which threatens to destroy both the individual and her relationships.

A particularly good example is offered by a short story of Dostoyevski, *The Timid One* (1876). A newly wed husband challenges his young wife by presenting himself as an enigma to her and at the same time depriving her of the means to solve the mystery. Their relationship is based on the total silence of the man, which the wife is supposed to overcome by maintaining an equal silence. Paradoxically, the woman kills herself when the husband, shaken by her illness, decides to break down the wall of silence that has separated them by showing her all his love.

The atmosphere of silence, of non-communication, also characterizes K.'s relationship with Frieda. The surveyor asks his woman to understand his silences, his movements, and the emotions within him, without asking questions, without using words. The young woman is asked to demonstrate a total capacity to accept the attitudes of K. without any regard for her own needs, her own desires. It will be the impossibility of making room for both of them to express themselves freely that will oblige Frieda to leave the surveyor. K.'s inability to make contact with his own inwardness will compel him to avoid all feelings and experience them only through his lover. This a quite common situation, in which the other becomes necessary because he allows one to approach one's own inwardness in an indirect manner.

By analyzing relationships of this kind, we see that they hide a precise and secret need whose origins go back to the primal relation. Since it is not possible to approach feeling directly because of its extraneousness, the partner must take on the burden of the other's feelings, accepting them in toto. She is asked, that is, to take on the role of mother, providing for our privations and making up for a past of suffering and frustration with her love.

Nevertheless, since often the secret bond of these relations is the reciprocal need of total acceptance, it is indispensable for maintaining the relationship that each should concede to the other the same degree of acceptance. The goal is to learn day after day to experience the emotions and to put them into words. However, when a total block exists in one of the two, when all attempts of the one to open a small breach in the other's wall of silence fail, all development is cut off. The partner we have called "the silent one," impelled by his own needs to a total and intuitive understanding, not mediated by any verbal code, seems to fear that words with their burning power will manage to crystallize the image of his emotional incapacity. But without words, without a confrontation with feelings, no development is possible.

The other face of acceptance is that of inaccessibility, of aloofness. Where no living space is shared, the condition of a momentary acceptance, the fruit of an intuition capable of reading the secret in the other's heart, can change just as quickly into aloofness and isolation. For lack of a common emotional basis reciprocally expressed, any feeling can be interpreted in a different manner according to mood, to the play of projection, often causing misunderstandings. To be in this position may preclude any positive outcome.

Since it does not seem possible to get out of a hidden-communication relationship, that is, to confront directly the implications of the communal interaction, the only way out is flight, abandonment—as in the case of Frieda—or death—as in the case of the timid one. Only the capacity of one of the partners to understand this subtle and often destructive game can overturn the situation and get it away from its compulsive progress. The awareness of one partner can also resolve the problem for the other. It is not a question of brutally bringing a truth to light and violating the secret that the other is keeping concealed with all her might, but to modify attitudes little by little. Being able to accept and respect the fears of the other may allow his heart to thaw and open. And, furthermore, to take loving care of the other's wounds means learning to cure one's own. In the attempt to heal him we also heal ourselves.

The destructiveness, the terrifying quality of the feminine and thus of the unconscious and of feelings, symbolized by the black ravens that swarm around the Castle, can be mitigated by the opposite aspect of fertility and of transformation that these animals represent. In Scandinavian mythology, the two ravens perched on Odin's throne represent the creative principle. Several Native American groups also see the raven as a primordial hero and demiurge who generates the dynamic and organizational element in the world, spreading civilization (Chevalier, Gheerbrant 1969, p. 328). This bird is, in fact, an extremely complex symbol. In many fables it appears as the theriomorphic figure of the devil, thus suggesting a connection to the Shadow.

What we are concerned about making evident is that the chthonic dimension, in emerging and pressing on consciousness to be recognized and integrated, also becomes—as Jung maintains with regard to the devil (1925b, p. 300)—a *principium individuationis*. The raven represents the voluntary isolation of one who has decided to live on a higher level, to soar exclusively in a spiritual dimension. And it brings with it a message of hope. The cry that according to Suetonius the bird constantly emits is *cras, cras*, that is, "tomorrow, tomorrow" (Chevalier, Gheerbrant 1969, p. 329). Together with the call of the Castle, the ravens are the expression of the deep need of renewal that K.-Kafka must have felt within himself.

The bird's black color is also that of melancholy. This connection between the black raven and melancholy is found in alchemy. The *nigredo* phase, corresponding in psychology to the relationship with the Shadow, which is initially manifested by depression, is in fact symbolized by the raven (Sharp 1980, p. 48). In Kafka's diaries (1910–1923, p. 393) on October 17, 1921, we can read an extremely significant passage.

> I don't believe people exist whose inner plight resembles mine; still, it is possible for me to imagine such people—but that the secret raven forever flaps about their heads as it does about mine, even to imagine that is impossible.

The black ravens that fly around the head of the writer as well as around the Castle, are also an image of that malaise, that angst, that suffering that squeezes the soul as in a vise, making it impossible to live, to enjoy, to love as one would like. The subsequent picture of the Castle that Kafka gives us seems to reinforce this experience of despair.

> Was uniformly round, part of it graciously mantled with ivy . . . a somewhat maniacal glitter, and glitter, and topped by what looked like an attic, with battlements that were irregular, broken, fumbling, as if designed by trembling or careless hand of a child, clearly outlined against the blue. It was as if a melancholy-mad tenant who ought to have been kept locked in the topmost chamber of his house had burst through the roof and lifted himself up to the gaze of the world. (Kafka 1922b, pp. 15–16)

The figure of the sombre inhabitant evokes the sensation of an anguish that has broken through the narcissistic repression of feelings and, instead of remaining hidden in the depths of the soul where it cannot be seen or heard, shows itself to the world. Baudelaire's verses come to mind (1861, p. 141):

> When, like a lid, the low and the heavy sky
> Weighs on the spirits burdened with long care,
> And when, as far mortal eye can see,
> in sheds a darkness sadder than nights are;
>
> When earth is changed into a prison cell,
> Where, in the damp and dark, with timid wing
> Hope, like a bat, goes beating at the wall,
> Striking its head on ceiling mouldering;
>
> When rain spread out its never-ending trails
> And imitates the bars of prison vast,
> and spiders, silent and detestable,
> Crowd in, our minds with webs to overcast,
>
> Some bells blurts out in the fury, suddenly,
> And hurl a roar most terrible to heaven,
> Like spirits lost for eternity
> Who start, most obstinately, to complain.

And, without drums or music, funerals
File past, in slow procession, in my soul;
Hope weeps, defeated; Pain, tyrannical,
Atrocious, plants its black flag on my skull.

This first contact of K.'s with the Castle does not change his condition. He gets to know its inaccessibility concretely. K. does not manage to near the construction because he does not know how to reach his inner world and sink into the "snow."

> For the street he was in, the main street of the village, did not lead up to the Castle hill, it only made towards it and then, as if deliberately, turned aside, and though it did not lead away from the Castle it got no nearer to it either. At every turn K. expected the road to double back to the Castle, and only because of this expectation did he go on; he was flatly unwilling, tired as he was, to leave the street, and he was also amazed at the length of the village, which seemed to have no end; again and again the same little houses, and frost-bound window-panes and snow and the entire absence of human beings. (Kafka 1922b, p. 17)

For a detached personality the beginning of every relationship seems to promise the long-awaited remedy for her inner coldness. But once again, the inability to let herself go and stop being afraid for once makes her miss the chance to repossess her own being and her denied feelings. When we have the impression that we are approaching our narcissistic ivory tower to explore it, get to know it, and so opening the doors to the encounter with another human being, in reality we are going away from it. The limbo in which, exhausted, we desperately wander, incessantly and futilely searching, cannot be composed of anything but "ice-encrusted windows" — like our own hearts — and "snow and the absence of human beings."

After having torn himself away from that road which kept him a prisoner, terribly fatigued by the effort he had just made, the surveyor seeks shelter in a peasant's hut. There he is received in a large, half-dark room immersed in thick smoke where two men are having a bath while a woman, a little way off, nurses an infant as other children surround her. On arriving in the village K., who had become lost in the rigidly cold winter evening, had been saved by the warmth of the inn. In this scene too he finds shelter from the snow and from his futile wandering, by being received in a house whose every detail underlines the connection with the maternal sphere.

The only remedy for renewing the correct functioning of the emotions is the return to the primal relationship, to those emotional depths where feelings have become blocked. In this backward journey we rediscover all of our vulnerability. Deprived of the steel armor that we have constructed—whose elements are called solitude and aloofness—we once again become as defenseless as children. And it is at this point, as all those who have experienced a dramatic regression during analysis well know, that we are immersed and almost drowned in the unexplored vastness of the chaos of feelings. To go through this psychic development of ours once again means putting ourselves contact with the darkest passions, the wildest desires, the devastating rages, and the tormenting desire to be caressed, fed, protected. The encounter excites horror, despair, and suicidal impulses. But it is the only way to be what one is and not what one ought to be.

In a famous play of Pirandello, *As You Desire Me* (1930), the heroine, a dancer in a Berlin night club, exploits her remarkable resemblance to the wife, Lucia, of the Count Bruno Pieri, to take her place. At the beginning the woman, who has lost her memory, only tries to escape from misery and a destructive relationship. But slowly she begins to believe more and more in the comedy she is playing. She changes her way of dressing and of speaking to change herself into a different person. In fact, in the meantime she has fallen in love with the count and is prepared to go to all lengths in order not to lose him. She knows that she cannot be loved for herself but only for her perfect resemblance to the other woman. In the final scene, in which she tries to clear up who she really is, the woman will tell Bruno that she only wants to be "as you desire me" (Pirandello 1930, p. 972).

The betrayal of sentiments always comes about through being different. It is as if some ruthless monster within us threatened to devour us every time we dared to be our authentic selves. What we feel, if compared to an inner, tyrannical, and inhuman ideal, is always inadequate and misplaced, because our entire way of being is a "mistake." Thus our love is excessive, our tenderness a weakness, our anger too violent. In reality what we are lacking is a love capable of accepting us entirely. All educative efforts have tried to alienate us from ourselves and have modeled our faces into a mask in which the true shape of our souls is hidden, disguised, distorted. The richness and protean character of our individuality have been leveled into a stereotyped expression that has reduced us to cold people, whose only preoccupation is that of being accepted by those around us.

The ability to express what we feel, to really be ourselves, demands a deep degree of self-acceptance. To give value to one's light side as well as one's shadow, one must love oneself, and this is only possible if one was loved at one time. If, on the contrary, our life was marked by early and repeated experiences of rejection, each act of ours, each feeling represents a "guilt." Our very existence is a witness to our guilt in which there is no room either for redemption or for pardon.

Kafka knew this guilt throughout his life and transferred it to his characters. Amalia and K. in *The Castle* are incarnations of a hopeless guilt. He who finds himself in this painful condition believes that to deserve to live, to be accepted by others and his superhuman ideal of the ego, he has to be perfect. No dangerous emotional surrender is allowed. By prohibiting all contact with himself and his feelings, he condemns himself to an inner death, he kills himself slowly while fooling himself into thinking he is still alive.

The bathing and nursing scene seems, after the preceding images of confusion and despair, to open the door to hope. To regain this maternal aspect, understood as the inner capacity for self-acceptance and self-nourishment, is the road to self-healing. In all cultures the bath is associated with the idea of purification and renewal. The Catholic ritual of baptism, which originally saw the neophyte immersed in a consecrated font, symbolizes the wiping out, the washing away of original sin and the ensuing rebirth to a new life and a new condition of the soul. We can hypothesize that for Kafka the relationship with Milena was the occasion, miraculous and fearful at the same time, for rebirth, if he was able to write to her (1920–1923, p. 71):

> For me, you see, what's happening is something prodigious. My world is tumbling down, my world is building itself up . . . The tumbling I don't deplore, it was in the process of tumbling, but what I do deplore is the building up of it. I deplore my lack of strength, deplore the being born, deplore the light of the sun.

In fact, the rebirth can only occur by way of the unconscious waters of feeling. In alchemical texts the process of transformation begins with immersion in a font, the symbol of plunging back into the original condition. The *vas hermeticum* was also called the uterus. Jung (1946, p. 251) compares the immersion in the font to a kind of night sea voyage, to a descent into the unconscious. But the image of the bath also evokes an idea of communication, of intimate and all-enveloping contact, similar to that within the uterus. It is, however, a significant fact that in the tub, "as big as two beds," there are two men. A relation with the feminine so personal, deep, and total as takes place during a bath, where one is obliged to be completely nude before the other person, was ruled out for Kafka. For many years it was only in the relationship with Max Brod that he was able to be himself. Throughout his life, notwithstanding his letters, he continued to defend himself from complete intimacy with women, surrounding himself with his solitude like an impassable barrier of high-tension barbed wire.

Nineteen

The Other as the Mirror of the Self

When he leaves the peasant's cabin, K. once more finds himself immersed in snow and darkness. As he tries to pick up the road to the Castle again, the surveyor meets two figures who will play an important part in the novel.

> From the direction of the Castle came two young men of medium height, both very slim, in tight-fitting clothes, and like each other in their features. Although their skin was a dusky brown the blackness of their little pointed beards was actually striking by contrast. Considering the state of the road, they were walking at a great pace, their slim legs keeping time . . . K. . . . he felt a strong desire to accompany them, not that he expected much from their acquaintance, but they were obviously good and jolly companions. (Kafka 1922b, pp. 20–21)

From the very first description of them, the resemblance between K.-Kafka and those who will become his helpers is evident. Thin and dark like the writer, they resemble him mostly for their long legs, which he frequently cites in his diaries as being his distinctive feature and which he transfers to many of his characters. But at this first encounter, the two do not appear to pay much attention to the surveyor and thus his desire for company is frustrated. K. has to exert himself quite a little to convince the cart driver Gerstaecker to accompany him with his sled to the inn. Only when they are near the tavern does the surveyor notice that night has fallen, whereas according to his calculations two hours had scarcely passed.

In the period when Kafka lived, the clocks of Bohemia were not synchronized. Time seemed confused, and only the cannon shot off from St. Mary's by the official of the imperial time-keeper allowed the citizens of Prague to regulate their clocks according to the official hour. Curiously, even today the clocks in the Jewish quarter of Prague do not all indicate the same time. It seems to be impossible to make inner time coincide with external time, the same impossibility we find in Kafka's works. The time of the soul, the succession of inner events, has a different rhythm than that of reality and they can never coincide. This phenomenon accentuates the outsider condition of the Kafkian individual, lost in space as he is in time.

The temporal aspect carries great weight within the narrative structure of *The Castle*. The entire story takes place within a few days. In the strange contracting and dilating movement of time, an essential point of reference is the darkness. After the promise of renewal that the bath scene represents and the mysterious figure of the woman nursing a baby, K.'s soul seems to plunge back into the depression to which the darkness alludes. The mysterious, enveloping shadows summon the soul to those of its depths where the light of consciousness has never penetrated. In this new condition of disorientation, the surveyor sees his helpers for the first time. Immersed in shadow the two figures personify an unconscious *daimon*.

In the technique of psychodrama, some members of the group can be called on to play the role of the *auxiliary* ego of the protagonist of the session. By representing his inner images, they allow him to see himself and his way of behaving as in a mirror. Similarly, Artur and Jeremias's presence ought to allow K. to become aware of several aspects of his psyche that he was ignorant of. The helpers represent its *Puer side*, bringing to light an infantile and irresponsible K. for whom life seems to be only a continuous game. Good for nothing, always ready to joke around, with no desire to work, they are the unconscious counterparts of an extremely serious man who only lives for his work, who is a prisoner of his worries, who has forgotten how to laugh. One of the characteristics of psychic uneasiness is the loss of a sense of humor. Anyone who lies prostrate in a depressed condition thinks he is at the center of a terrible tragedy. Reality is tinged in black; there is room for nothing else but pain. To know how to laugh at one's ills, to discover the comic side, even the grotesque and paradoxical side of a painful situation, requires the ability to suspend for a moment the identification of the ego with the suffering one feels. To distance oneself from a situation that one experiences as a catastrophe allows one to revitalize its dramatic quality, thus supplying the basis for a new vision of what is happening. It is the first step in analyzing oneself with new eyes.

The two helpers remind K. of life's aspects as a game, which he seems to have forgotten. And it is this possibility that gives the encounter its relevance. The meaningfulness of a relationship with another human being is revealed in its allowing us to win back, thanks to him, that which we do not know about ourselves. This is why Jung (1946, p. 318) was able to write: "We meet ourselves time and again in a thousand disguises on the path of life." The Other whom we meet is our destiny. The fascination with which it captures us is nothing but the spell of an unconscious inner image of ours. Thus a one-sided relationship is begun based on need, which can only be modified when we succeed in realizing that inner destiny that the other represents.

Artur and Jeremias are described as being so similar to each other that the surveyor cannot manage to tell them apart.

> 'You're a difficult problem,' said K., comparing them, as he had already done several times. 'How am I to know one of you from the other? The only difference between you is your names, otherwise you're as like as . . .' He stopped, and then went on involuntarily, 'You're as like as two snakes.' They smiled. 'People usually manage to distinguish us quite well,' they said in self-justification. 'I am sure they do,' said K., 'I was a witness of that myself, but I can only see with my own eyes, and with them I can't distinguish you. So I shall treat you as if you were one man and call you both Arthur, that's one of your names, yours, isn't it?' he asked one of them. 'No,' said the man, 'I'm Jeremiah.' 'It doesn't matter,' said K. 'I'll call you both Arthur. If I tell Arthur to go anywhere you must both do it, that has the great disadvantage for me of preventing me from employing you on separate jobs, but the advantage that you will both be equally responsible for anything I tell you to do. How you divide the work between you doesn't matter to me, only you're not to excuse yourselves by blaming each other, for me you're only one man.' (Kafka 1922b, pp. 24–25)

So much alike as to be mistaken for each other, as if they were two twins, the helpers seem to be the doubling of a single image, almost as if Kafka had wanted — perhaps quite unconsciously — to represent the split in his soul that was capable of infinitely duplicating, cloning its faces. The total resemblance that Artur and Jeremias share immediately suggests the theme of the double, which is so frequent in literature. To find yourself face to face with another who is absolutely the same as you is perturbing.

The doubling of the ego is the result of an inner split. The double always represents an unconscious, neglected aspect that one becomes aware of through the encounter with another self and whose obsessive presence is like a kind of persecution. From Baldovino, the hero of Rye's film *Der Student von Prag* (1913), to the monk Medardo of Hoffmann's *The Devil's Elixir* (1815), to Goljadkin in Feodor Dostoyevski's *The Double* (1846), we are dealing with another being perceived as different from oneself and at the same time identical. A constant factor in all stories containing the theme of the double is that the latter makes its appearance precisely when the desire for a change is manifested and almost always connected to a love relationship. Baldovino tries to escape from his miserable and dissolute existence thanks to the love of the Princess Schwarzenberg, whereas Goljadkin wants to become part of the family of his patron by marrying his daughter.

Rank (1914, p. 13) has interpreted the double as the manifestation of narcissism. As a personification of narcissistic love, the double becomes a rival of sexual love. Originating as a defense against a feared event, this motive reappears in superstition as a messenger of death. In fact, the subject finds herself in a condition of fusion and symbiosis, which makes her experience every change as a threat of death. The double, who in many cases impels the protagonist to suicide, always appears at the moment when the latter is trying to form a relationship. In *The Student of Prague,* all the encounters of Baldovino with the young princess are disturbed by the appearance of his alter ego. In *The Castle* too, the helpers turn up at every intimate encounter between K. and Frieda. The narcissistic ego of the surveyor and the student breaks in dramatically when the two figures try to break out of their armor and form a relationship.

The lascivious and infantile behavior of Artur and Jeremias lets us suppose that they represent K.-Kafka's Shadow, that repressed part of one which is unknown to consciousness because it is considered unbearable. Who, in fact, are these two infantile, lying, lazy, and muddled creatures, if not a part of the writer himself, whose psyche splits into a thousand different characters in order to be caught in all its possible aspects? The double of Goljadkin is described as being a scoundrel, a lackey, a vacillator, a wag, a buffoon, a scamp, in contrast to the hero who is timid and reserved, incapable of winning the interest of others. Just as Jeremias in *The Castle* takes Frieda away from K., so too Dostoyevski's double wins the love of the beautiful Klara Olsufievna, while the real Goljadkin is taken away to the insane asylum. Not capable of experiencing an adult love, which he leaves to his alter ego, he is a victim of his own narcissism.

This inability to construct an adult love relationship produces a laceration within the personality. The conflict between the narcissistic part, which refuses to change and open itself up to the Other, and the more mature nucleus of the personality, which is trying to escape from its neurotic block and overcome the symbiotic state, generates an alter ego whose role is to remind the individual of his repressions. The double is the visualization of a crisis situation that is the prelude to an inevitable change.

It is no accident that this motif often presents itself within the analytic situation. We saw before how in the dream of a woman there appeared another self who bore the signs of madness. The latter personified the frightened part of the patient that was changing. This dream was preceded about a year before by a drawing that showed two identical women who seemed to mirror and almost to enter into each other. The image of the double was bound to a deep change in the structure of the woman, who was trying to escape from her narcissistic shell and open up to a mature relationship. In the imaginary conversation which the girl began with the other, the "crazy" one, the latter declared that she wanted to destroy her, accusing her of not knowing how to love.

But the double also has a positive value, because its appearance offers a concrete possibility of another way of being in the world. By means of this fantasy the patient dramatizes the existing conflict between her fusional and splintered parts, on the one hand, and the better integrated and structured ones on the other, with the purpose of favoring a possible acceptance of her identity (Funari 1986, p. 39).

The benevolent aspect of the double appears in a novel by Joseph Conrad, *The Secret Sharer* (1912), where the relationship with the other self does not necessarily end tragically. A young captain, the hero of the novel, about to set sail for the first time with his ship, discovers a man in the water who will, from that moment on, share his cabin secretly with him. The first officer, Leggatt, unlike the

captain, has already had the experience of resolving navigation problems and managed to save his ship from going down, even if he had
to relieve the captain of his command in order to execute his maneuver. The relationship between the two men becomes more and more
intimate, but in the end Leggatt goes away, while the captain, in
order to help him return ashore, will guide the ship landwards in the
dark and avoid hitting the rocks.

A psychological reading of the work will point out how in the novel
the misunderstood parts of the psyche, which are projected outward
become integrated within the self and thus produce a new, more
mature personality.

At K.'s first encounter with Artur and Jeremias he doesn't recognize them.

> 'What?' said K., 'are you my old assistants whom I told to follow me
> and whom I am expecting?' They answered in the affirmative. 'That's
> good,' observed K. after a short pause. 'I'm glad you've come.' 'Well,'
> he said, after another pause, 'you've come very late, you're very slack.'
> 'It was a long way to come,' said one of them. 'A long way?' repeated
> K., 'but I met you just now coming from the Castle.' 'Yes,' said they
> without further explanation. 'Where is the apparatus?' asked K. 'We
> haven't any,' said they. 'The apparatus I gave you?' said K. 'We haven't
> any,' they reiterated. 'Oh, you are fine fellows!' said K., 'do you know
> anything about surveying?' 'No,' said they. 'But if you are my old
> assistants you must know something about it,' said K. They made no
> reply. 'Well, come in,' said K., pushing them before him into the
> house. (Kafka 1922b, p. 24)

Although Jeremias and Artur are his old helpers, K. doesn't recognize them. Nevertheless, in considering them old acquaintances, the
surveyor shows that they are still part of his personality. As manifestations of the Shadow the two have been expelled from his consciousness and thus appear "extraneous." The helpers display the "lower"
aspects of K.'s personality, one of whose elements is that immediate
and unconscious eroticism he experienced with Frieda and which was
catalyzed by their silent presence. The barefaced lasciviousness of
Artur and Jeremias alludes to a sensuality that one strongly desires to
display but which is repugnant to an inflexible superego. The severe
judgment he makes on them does not keep the surveyor from need-

ing their help. He will say of them that they are as alike as two serpents, displaying again the sexual metaphor hidden in these figures.

If the erotic sphere is a sore spot for K.-Kafka, if he excludes from it the playful aspect, the infantile and tender qualities, precisely that must be the point of departure for any process of renewal. The biblical animal is not only a symbol of the lascivious, of evil, of the dark, insinuating instincts, but it is also a symbol of transformation because of its ability to shed its skin. There can only be room for change where a wound or a lacuna makes us more vulnerable, where the incompleteness of the ego calls for a new psychic set-up. With their names, Jeremias and Artur seem to furnish the coordinates for such a change.

In the Scriptures, the prophet Jeremiah is he who warns the Jewish people of their imminent deportation to Babylonia because God is disdainful of the moral degradation and idolatry into which Israel has fallen. Like Job, Jeremiah has known the lacerating relationship with the divinity. Like Job, he has found himself immersed in pain, in a suffering without justification. His cry is generated by the sense of the absurd, the incomprehensible position into which God himself has thrown him. He will say in his celebrated Lamentations (3:1–13):

> I am one who has seen affliction
> under the rod of God's wrath;
> he has driven and brought me
> into darkness without any light;
> against me alone he turns his
> hand,
> again and again, all day long.
>
> He has made my flesh and my
> skin waste away,
> and broken my bones;
> he has besieged and enveloped me
> with bitterness and tribulation;
> he has made me sit in darkness
> like the dead of long ago.
>
> He has walled me about so that I
> cannot escape;
> he has put heavy chains on me;
> though I call and cry for help,

> he shuts out my prayer;
> he has blocked my ways with
>   hewn stones,
> he has made my paths crooked.
>
> He is a bear lying in wait for me,
>   a lion in hiding;
> he led me off my way and tore
>   me to pieces;
> he has made me desolate;
> he bent his bow and set me
>   as a mark for his arrow.
>
> He shot into my vitals
> the arrows of his quiver;

The reference to Jeremiah seems to allude to that desperate cry against a life crushed and tormented by the inscrutable decisions of an implacable and mysterious Being, a cry that pervades all the works of Kafka.

In his essay on Kafka, Canetti (1969, p. 139) notes that the indulgence in lamentations was a distinctive feature of his. The letters to Felice Bauer, particularly in the first period of their engagement, are thick with discontent, with the feeling of always being inadequate and in every way, different from others, and therefore difficult to accept, to tolerate, to love. Diversity, individual uniqueness seem to have been experienced by Kafka as a sort of wound, an incurable injury, which might also make one recall the words of Jeremiah (30:12-13):

> Your hurt is incurable,
> your wound is grievous.
> There is no one to uphold your cause,
> no medicine for your wound,
> no healing for you.

The wound, an allegory of the guilt of being alive, is a point in common between Josef K. of *The Trial* and the land surveyor of *The Castle*. Like Kafka, they are guilty for their particular psychological aspect, which makes them incapable of loving, which orients them toward solitude and distance rather than toward relationships and contact. In their souls nests the blind mole of which the author writes in one of his stories.

Jeremiah represents the pain of living, the desperation of one who is immersed in unawareness and finds life absurd, incomprehensible. Like a terrified child crying in the darkness, asking his mother to speak to him — since the voice is in that moment the only bridge by which he can feel connected to life and to a relationship which sustains him — Jeremiah laments and invokes God so that he might speak and reassure him. The Lamentations are not yet questions but pleas for help. In a question a rational working out of the problem is implicit; the ego opposes itself to the absurd with a request, its attempt to understand. The lament, instead, is acceptance, surrender in the face of the inexplicable. It is the feeling that one's rational faculties are of no use since the mystery is too thick to be analyzed by the mind. The lamentation declares the absence of an instrument by which to interpret reality. But what one does not understand automatically becomes unjust, cruel, and a persecution.

Jeremias is accompanied by another helper, Artur. To explain this choice of a name we must refer to the Breton legend of the Knights of the Round Table. Just as the prophet Jeremiah alludes to a state of paralysis, a passive submission to one's destiny, so Arthur evokes an image of power. If the first example personifies the tendency of the soul to come to a halt, to turn in on itself — perhaps to better understand what it is happening to it — the second personifies the desire to act, to intervene and actively modify the event. We are dealing with the two opposite poles of a single reality, inasmuch as the soul, in its progress towards individuation, has need of both these aspects. K. is obliged to confront two diverse but complementary ways of relating to the world: *activity* and *passivity*.

There is an interesting detail in the Arthur legend. Having defeated Lancelot, who had won away from him the love of the beautiful Queen Guinivere — just as Jeremias took Frieda away from the land surveyor — the fatally wounded Arthur is buried by the fairies in the lake of Avalon. But as every Englishman knows, if the country were threatened and invaded by enemies, the mythical king would awake from his centuries-long sleep along with his knights and return to defend England. Arthur would seem to represent a hidden force that can be reactivated in a moment of extreme peril. The helper Artur's name seems to recall this possibility of not succumbing to events, the hope of recuperating the forgotten energy.

In neuroses, as in other forms of psychic discomfort, the capacity of not giving in is lost, the ability to see beyond the immediate difficulties. The neurotic remains trapped in the apparent absurdity of what is happening to her. She continues to look for guilty parties, for the causes that can explain the ills of her existence; she wants justifications that will absolve her of her paralysis. She has the sensation that the world is always stronger than she is, and she gives up the fight. Not only has she lost the sense that suffering and pain are part of life, but she is not even capable of understanding it. A prisoner of her infantilism, her potential for change is enveloped in a lethal cocoon. She is the victim of an illusion. She thinks that life should proceed in an orderly way without jamming, halting, without meeting obstacles. Every obstacle seems to her to be a terrible injustice. Lost in sterile recriminations, she ends up by agreeing with her negative destiny and renounces all action to alter it.

Artur, contrarily, represents the one who awakens from sleep, escapes from paralysis and depression and decides to take hold of the reins of his life. For that to be possible, one must direct one's attention to one's inner sphere. Imagination contains the possibilities of conceiving various solutions. In neuroses the ability to make plans is neglected or lost. The inner world seems to exist only in its obsessive-compulsive aspect. Fantasies are nightmares to be fled from and not precious indications of the needs of the soul. For such people analysis is a way of relearning how to plan by conceding an adequate hearing to the voice of the unconscious. That same event that a little earlier was experienced as a terrible injustice, can now reveal its necessity. To overcome a neurotic block means to reacquire the ability to look ahead, to read one's own history in a new way and to reimagine oneself.

By believing in one's own strength, one opens the road to change. Favorable postoperative progress depends, for example, on the will to recover, on actively helping, with one's hopeful fantasies, the organism's process of recovery.

Unfortunately, education does not always help to develop this capacity; on the contrary, often enough it suffocates it. In many families, every time the child tries to see the world in a different way from the adults he is negated. This constant erosion of his potentialities prepares the ground on which his neurosis will germinate. As an adult he will have a hard time imagining himself in a positive way; he will always see only his weak sides, his negative aspects. The analyst often is the first person ever disposed to believe in him, to give him confidence. The operative optimism of the therapist, who constantly bets on her patient's possibilities for recovery without ever surrendering, is the most effective of medicines.

Artur personifies a heroic dimension of the psyche, too. To reacquire one's capacity for making projects implies being capable of facing whatever dangers or obstacles can present themselves. Only the acceptance of risk, without trying to cheat in life, allows us truly to draw on our energies buried at the bottom of the "lake" of the unconscious.

In all mythologies the rediscovery of a treasure is preceded by a fight with a dragon. The terrible monster, ready to devour us, is not found on the outside but within our souls. It can assume the form of our parents if, during childhood, these played a castrating role. The ferocious creature who was generated by the fears, the prohibitions, the lack of self-confidence, and the sense of inner paralysis, becomes a psychic component with whom the individual must constantly come to terms.

The mistake of a bad psychoanalysis is to think that it is enough to know the causes of an illness in order to eliminate it. On the contrary, the change is due to a slow and patient digging at the things that have happened, returning to them a thousand times, and becoming able, little by little, to look ahead, because whoever stops to stare back at his past runs the risk of Lot's wife of turning into a pillar of salt.

In his essay on the alchemical psychology of salt, Hillman (1982, pp. 141–43) compares the trauma to a salt mine, a place where through the crystallization of the event held in memory, the individual can begin to reflect on his own nature, recognizing himself in his specific character. The soul has the need of returning to its wounds, to keep licking them in order to obtain this "salt," that is to say, the crystallization of the event experienced.

Salt is one of the most precious substances of the organism, without which there can be no life. To return to the crucial event means, then, to go back in order to discover the precious thing we need. The danger is that a fixation will occur. We tend to become fixed on what was done to us and on who did it. In its crystalline structure, salt also includes fixation, immutability. In the Hebrew myth, Lot's wife stops to look back because she is worried about the fate of her children. She lingers too long on the past and so loses her mobility. The soul, however, needs to look back without losing its ability to look forward.

In *The Castle* the retrieval of the imagination and its ability to plan passes through the hero's relationship with his helpers. At the end of the novel we learn that it was the Castle itself that sent these strange characters to K. to distract him and to help lighten his task. That comic aspect of theirs, their ineffectualness, would seem to indicate that the land surveyor must acquire the sense of life as a game. A child discovers a new world as he plays. Simulating allows him — like an actor — to take on various roles, to bring to life and to know all the aspects of his psyche. In fact, the infantile sphere is also the mental condition of illusion, of hope, of growth. To keep the child alive within one means to be ever ready for change, open to new possibilities; it means to succeed in enjoying oneself, to be enthusiastic even about little things, to look at the world with an inexhaustible desire to go forward. To retrieve the child is to retrieve joy, pleasure, diversion. According to Huizinga (1946, *passim*), all cultural expressions can be read as game forms. Only a terrible misunderstanding of our culture makes it identify maturity with the abandoning of the infantile aspect that is an essential element of life.

Deprived of her infantile ego, which has been denied and relegated to the furthest recesses of the psyche, the individual also loses her vitality, the source of inner riches. People who are immersed in desperation and obsessively pursued by their inner fantasies often lose their pleasure in play for the sake of an illusory and serious "happiness." Where everything is serious and tragic, there is no room for laughter and frivolity. It would seem that one's road must be determined by a rigid law of productivity, according to which the result is more important than life itself. This betrayal constantly perpetrated on childhood sooner or later turns against the subject himself, who has neglected an essential part of his soul. In the clinical history of these people we will often read of children who were required to be adults, strong and mature. Anything like a tantrum or a whim dictated by the only fundamental right of childhood, which is to find living space and to express itself in the moment when it is experienced, is negated, disdainfully repressed in the name of a more proper seriousness.

The child is told to use her head, to understand the needs of the adults and behave. From these same case histories we learn how the impossibility of living out one's fragility, one's inconsistency, of being "crazy" and "wild" later is transformed into the fear of living. Paralysis, neurotic or psychotic blocks, through the pressing symptoms that threaten social adaptation, being "up to par," being "normal," reveal the desperate need of authenticity. To misunderstand an aspect of the psyche causes a critical split within it. Then it can happen that the dark side we have repressed takes possession of us. The individual identifies himself with his shadow, just as happens in an Andersen fairy tale (1990, pp. 161–71), *The Shadow,* which tells of a philosopher whose timidity, whose fear of living, makes him employ his shadow to discover who is living in the house across the street where he has seen a wonderful maiden. The next morning he notices that he has no shadow. He will meet it again years later completely transformed and dressed like a man. It took advantage of the opportunity to gain an independent existence.

During the intervening years it had succeeded in mastering the world's whole culture by living in the house of poetry. Noticing how poor and naked it was, it had procured great riches by practicing every form of deceit—as a shadow it was able to see all the evils of men without being seen. By blackmail it thus acquired fame, money, and power.

But on seeing its old master, it took pity on the miserable state to which he was reduced and, with a tone of disdainful superiority, offered to serve him as a shadow and to follow in his footsteps. The man, tired, ill, and desperate, accepted after a moment's hesitation. But the philosopher threatens to reveal everything when his old shadow becomes a friend of the king and is about to marry his daughter, who has fallen hopelessly in love with such a learned man. The shadow anticipates his move and rushes to tell the king that his crazed shadow thinks it is a man and asserts that he, the future son-in-law of the king, is only a shadow. The philosopher naturally is arrested and decapitated while the shadow marries the princess.

As in Andersen's tale, where the dark, irresponsible, and egoistical side, represented by the shadow, wins out over the serious and balanced philosopher, so too in Kafka's novel the repression of the infantile aspect will contribute to K.'s downfall. By choosing to live with Jeremias, her old childhood friend, Frieda demonstrates that a relationship needs that tenderness and light-heartedness which the surveyor has renounced.

Twenty

The Affliction of Questioning

In endopsychic terms, the surveyor's inability to recognize the two helpers seems to indicate a difficulty of the ego in making contact with his unconscious fantasies. K. doesn't manage to put these inner images into focus. Their lack of differentiation makes any comparison impossible. So they end by operating outside the control of the conscious mind. The independence of the image, which is the basis of a complex, always is a source of psychic unease. The unconscious becomes an enemy that threatens to destroy, to submerge the ego. The individual no longer acts but is acted on, the victim of himself and his unawareness. In this split condition, K. tries to make contact with the Castle.

> The receiver gave out a buzz of a kind that K. had never before heard on a telephone. It was like the hum of countless children's voices—but yet not a hum, the echo rather of voices singing at an infinite distance—blended by sheer impossibility into one high but resonant sound which vibrated on the ear as if it were trying to penetrate beyond mere hearing. (Kafka 1922b, p. 26)

The telephone call with its mysterious noise, reiterates yet again a call from the unconscious speaking with the voice of childhood. It is the child within that asks to be heard, not by the ear but more deeply by the soul.

Continuing the game of masquerades, of pretending that represses the inner need of authenticity, K. begins the telephone conversation pretending to be one of his helpers. With the landslide of questions and answers K. hardly manages to keep up the fictitious identity he is using and ends by no longer knowing who he is, expecting the voice on the other end to clear up the riddle of his true identity.

Much like the episode in the first chapter, here too the hero's precarious sense of his identity is underlined. He must depend on a confirmation, an external recognition to know himself. It would seem that K.-Kafka lacks an inner mirror that lets him see his face. Since the image of oneself depends on the complex game that is played in infancy through relations with others, the constant repetition of negating experiences creates a dramatic crisis for the sense of one's identity. This problem is particularly in evidence in narcissistic personalities. In them it reveals the tragic loss of their authentic selves. Their extreme vulnerability to their environment shows how these subjects identify themselves with the results of their endeavors. Failure in any field is for them an incontrovertible proof of their nullity.

The concept of identity is generated and structured by the stability-change polarity. The awareness of self is bound, above all, to the beginning of life, to stability, that is to say to the presence and the permanence of constant points of reference, of a nucleus that binds all the changes that occur in the course of time to both the subject's relation with herself and with others (Green 1977, p. 79). Such a condition depends on the primal relationship with the mother, whose principal function in the original phase of life — where there is not yet any distinction between subject and object — is that of "reflecting." Winnicott (1971, p. 189) calls the mother's face the *precursor of the mirror*. Being reflected is a fundamental need of the child from birth and comparable to the need of a primary object, to the need of company, which, as ethological studies have shown, are independent of the need for food (Rollmann-Branch 1960). It is an experience that includes touch, smell, and other primal sensations more than visual perception. Through such *media* and the way they interact, the child begins to become aware of the lineaments of his image. This *primal identity* (Liechtestein 1964, p. 52), which is different from the subsequent sense of identity, can be considered a psychic organizer similar to those described by Spitz. Since it is formed at a time when there is no clear distinction between subject and object, its constitution and its reinforcement have the character of a *duplication* (Fiumara, Caporali, Zanasi 1983, p. 57).

Because the process of reflecting occurs in a nonverbal sphere, the body has a guiding role as the go-between, the channel, through which the *primary identity* is constructed. In the contact between two bodies, the child discovers herself and the other. In this exchange of messages, of sensations, the little person first feels herself recognized and loved. Caresses and attention have a fundamental role in the first years of life. When they are missing or given in a perfunctory way, when the real presence of the other, the mother, is denied, it will be very hard for the child to be aware of her bodily being. She will move in the real world as if disembodied.

Kafka's relationship with his body was very difficult. We know very little about his first years of life, but the birth of two other children when little Franz was two and four years old respectively, allows us to suppose that his childhood was not only troubled by the normal experiences of losing his mother's attentions, but also by an atmosphere of desperation and sadness due to mourning for these children. One can suppose that the body contact between mother and child was reduced to automatic care, lacking in a positive cathexis. His subsequent relations with women, the problems with his body, and not least his difficulties in taking food and the constant fantasies of fasting, would seem to support this thesis.

A woman's ability to take loving care of the body of her child essentially depends on the attitude she has toward her own body. Until the positions taken by the feminists, the education of women was dominated by the repression of sexuality. In making love the woman was not supposed to feel any pleasure. Pleasure was something reserved for the man. Husbands, in fact, did not concern themselves at all with the sensations of their wives. In the large majority of cases, sexual relations and maternity were perceived by women as social and biological obligations to be fulfilled with sacrifice and suffering. For this reason intimacy with one's own body, with that of one's partner, and subsequently with one's children, reflected an absolute lack of relationship with corporeality. A woman who does not accept or feel love and trust for her own body certainly cannot permit her child to create a satisfactory bodily identity. For example, if she feels shame and fear for the sexual sensations experienced during nursing, she will try to keep the child at a distance.

The repulsion she feels for her genital zones she will also inevitably transmit in her contact with these parts of her child. The child, who cannot understand the mother's fear of intimacy, will experience her embarrassment as a total rejection. He will develop a sense of shame and fear for his own corporeality and intimacy analogous to his mother's (Leonelli 1987, pp. 101–102).

The sense of identity is, first of all, awareness of one's own body. The body is the medium by which the soul manifests itself. It is something more than a mere container — it is pulsating matter whose presence and transformations influence our minds.

My experience as an analyst has allowed me to ascertain how disturbances in the image of the self are inevitably reflected in the entire sense of identity. In the case of a patient of mine a childhood malformation had weighed on her for years and caused a total estrangement from her body. At the time she arrived in my office, her esthetic problem had been resolved years ago and yet she continued to feel that her body was unacceptable. She confessed to me that she felt like a shadow, completely disembodied. For a long time she had to hide behind a mask of indifference for her body, which allowed her to overcome the sense of annihilating impotence in the face of the pity and disdain that she noticed in others. Even her mother had unconsciously rejected the child, whose appearance was hardly in agreement with her desires.

The only physical contact she had known in childhood was with her mother's companion. A navy officer, he was often obliged to be from home for long periods. He had always had a very ambivalent attitude toward the child, with alternations of violent anger in which he beat her hard and moments of seductive tenderness. Probably without being aware of it he had turned the child's body into an "erotic toy." For years this man and a friend of his had secretly caressed the little girl's private parts before the eyes of all the rest of the family, who seemed to notice nothing. With her body petrified by unconscious agitation and the fear that she would be given the entire blame for what had happened, my patient submitted in silence to these "attentions." It impelled her, however, to consider the body a "danger" from which she had to protect herself. Whether rejected, denied, or manipulated, the body was in any case an uncomfortable and disquieting presence that seemed to preclude any real experience of acceptance and love.

This had damaged her sense of her identity and made her very insecure. The girl never seemed to know who she was, as if she entirely lacked an inner image with which to compare herself, or as if this image was so painful for her that it was best to ignore it.

The affection that I showed her, my care, understanding, and proximity managed to give her back the desire to live and to escape from the secret hell in which she had been living. The young woman gradually began to be aware that she had a body and to stop being afraid of her desire for men. At first she substituted her past indifference with a reactive erotic cathexis; then she slowly managed to acquire consciousness of her body and to familiarize herself with the sensations that it felt. To know that she was a body and not only a mind gave her back her self-confidence and helped her to face the world with greater security. Finally, she managed to perceive her identity, to recognize herself. Looking at me with eyes full of gratitude and happy astonishment, she told me often that *she was becoming flesh*.

The lack of a satisfactory relationship with one's body not only precludes the sense of identity, but compromises all emotional life as in Kafka's case. The story of the hunger artist who dies of starvation because he hasn't found the food he likes contains precisely this impossibility of loving oneself, recognizing both the needs of the body and those of the soul. All problems of nourishment, from extreme anorexia to bulimia, reveal the incapacity to take care of the corporeal self in a stable manner, which is mortified, starved, or, contrarily, stuffed with food. In both cases care is lacking, the love of one's body, which is made to pay for the guilt of once not having been adequately loved.

Not only should the mother permit the child, with her affection, to invest his corporeal self with libido, but also recognize it and its needs as different from those of the soul. It is important that, being mirrored in his mother's eyes, the child should see reflected there his own feelings and expectations and not those of others. That would otherwise mean making narcissistic use of the child who would be obliged to play the role that the mother's needs impose (Miller 1979, *passim*). On the contrary, it is his own human uniqueness that must be transmitted with love and care to the child. When this does not occur, when the child can only discern in the mother's face her own desires and fears, he will remain without a mirror for the rest of his life and will continue to search for one in vain.

Lacking this mirror, which allows him to distinguish and recognize his own needs, his own desires, the complex and subtle world of feelings, the individual will not be capable of understanding who he is or what he wants. His destiny will then be to seek constantly, impelled by a dramatic compulsion to repeat symbiotic relations in which the presence of the other will be for him a condition of his identity, of self-awareness. In that way the road to independence and individuation will be blocked.

This is precisely the situation we witness in K.'s case. He is always waiting for an external confirmation that will put an end to his terrible insecurity. Frieda, the Castle and its officials, Gardena, and all the other characters must function as the mirror of which K., like the author of the novel, was perhaps deprived. Since the land surveyor pursues something that must spring from within in him, his search is doomed to failure and he will obtain nothing but negation. Wandering in the nebulous vacuum of his nonidentity, K. will continue, in fact, to negate himself.

Only the perception of one's own identity can bestow the fullness of being, only this permits one to bestow meaning and value on oneself, thus changing the course of one's existence. From the moment in which the mirror is possessed inwardly, human relations can change profoundly. The other can cease to be a reflecting surface, the mere support of our narcissistic lacunae, to become an identity that encounters our own.

In the case I previously mentioned, the acquisition of the sense of identity was due to my functioning as a mirror for my patient. Having regressed to the phase of the primal relationship, the woman had to find again in the analytic relationship that climate of affection, understanding, and trust which she had never had. Only in this way, by reliving the very first years of her life in a climate of acceptance very much different from her childhood, was she able to restructure her primal identity, which her mother ought to have allowed her to form.

But the theme of the search for identity goes beyond the individual sphere to become a problem of our times. The pole around which the angst of nineteenth-century people condensed, it is a widely spread literary motif. The turbulence of our century is also the malaise of entire generations who have been alienated from themselves.

It is enough to consider the emblematic protagonist of Pirandello's *Uno, nessuno e centomila* (1926). Ever since his wife made him notice the imperfection of his nose, Vitangelo Moscarda has become aware that he is not at all like he had thought of himself as being, but is impersonating an evasive, changing reality that is reflected in the eyes of others. He is at one and the same time "one person, nobody and a hundred thousand": a hundred thousand for others and nobody for himself. The problem of identity in this case is connected to the question of changing. Is it possible to speak of a static and unequivocal identity, or is it truer, rather, to consider the possibility of a dynamic and multiform identity?

This would mean not only accepting the idea of metamorphosis, but above all accepting coexistence with a thousand selves living within oneself, either all at once or in succession. We can consider identity as a theoretical concept that, like many others, has a certain practical utility for explaining several phenomena, without having a real existence.

The changeableness of the ego — its possibilities for being different, for taking on a thousand personalities, in reality as in dreams and fantasies, would make it perhaps more useful to postulate *nonidentity* rather than identity as a point of departure. The possibility of changing one's visage, one's identity, not only in the "realm of physical phenomena" but also in that of "mental and rhetorical phenomena" as Lai says (1988, *passim*) cannot be simply closed up in a cage of a single and unvarying identity within a single universe. The analyst finds herself constantly involved in this dilemma. The patient who questions himself about himself, about his relationships, about the meaning of his life, turns to the analyst precisely to bring about a change. Often, however, the demand for consistency, confusing identity with identicalness, becomes the attempt to escape from change, to escape from life. The therapeutic action of the analyst ought then to aim at making the patient accept the coexistence of various identities in "various worlds."

K.'s desire to establish contact with the Castle is refused yet again.

> K. was listening to the new note, and almost missed the question: "What is it you want?" He felt like laying down the receiver. He had ceased to expect anything from conversation. But being pressed, he replied quickly: "When can my master come to the Castle?" "Never," was the answer. "Very well," said K., and hung the receiver up. (Kafka 1922b, p. 27)

The reply K. receives totally contradicts his *call*. He is the surveyor who has been called to the Castle, but when he tries to make contact with the one who has employed him he is told that he can "never" be received. The episode of the telephone call smacks of the absurd. This experience, which all of Kafka's characters have to face, comes from the impossibility of their having complete control over the surrounding reality. It eludes them continually, causing anxiety and apprehension. The laws that govern it are unknown and inscrutable.

Such a hallucinatory vision recalls surrealist and metaphysical paintings. In many of De Chirico's paintings—think only of *L'enigma dell'ora* (1912), *Le muse inquietanti* (1916), or the famous series of the *Piazze d'Italia* already in his mind in 1910—time is suspended, becoming heavy and immovable. The forms, deprived of their life substance as in the mannequins of *Ettore e Andromaca* (1917), are located in an empty, uninhabitable place whose rational geometry, paradoxically challenging the logical principle itself, opens like a door on the absurd and the incongruous. Certainties dissolve while all things appear to exist in an unrelated condition, a condition of impossibility—not unlike that described by Kafka's person praying. Art then seems to find its justification in the proclamation of an apparently simple enigma that is, however, in reality inexplicable. It becomes a speculation on the nullity of being (Argan 1970, pp. 594–95).

Kafka's antiheroes resemble remarkably the mannequins that populate De Chirico's pictures. Unconscious marionettes, they degrade and nullify their humanity through the identification not with an inanimate object—the marionette—but with animals considered repugnant: moles, mice, cockroaches. Evasive in their metaphorical multivalence, they themselves are the carriers of absurdity, the incongruity of existence. Half human and half animal, the ambiguity of such characters proposes one of the *leitmotifs* of Kafka's works: that constant indeterminacy which makes all reality elusive, the acquisition of any identity impossible. Everything that occurs is always changing its appearance, and reality transforms itself unexpectedly into its opposite just when one thinks one has understood and grasped it. And that is when the angst begins.

Our brains are not built for receiving contradictory messages. When that happens, the ego goes into crisis and experiences something truly terrible. The absurd and the incongruous paralyze us.

The individual has need of finding herself in a linear situation where every stimulus is accompanied by an appropriate response. But reality is often different, and sooner or later we all must make the acquaintance of the absurd. Kafka describes with great subtlety and wealth of detail the condition of a human being who is suddenly thrown into a world that contradicts all his expectations. The same reality whose call he hears is also the one that denies his existence, that answers "never" to his requests. The Castle, understood as the repository of the ultimate reality, of that meaning, of that truth which humans seek to grasp, throws its challenge in everyone's face by its refusal. Kafka's realism, his apparent rationality, become a trap with which the absurd breaks into the rational world. Behind the apparently ordered vision of things there hides a total panic: the terror of him who finds himself immersed in a nightmare.

Kafka's personage is like the sleeper in Fuseli's *The Nightmare*, painted in 1781, confronted with daytime creatures who are transformed into terrifying nocturnal monsters of ambiguous shape. Thus the reality of the Castle is at times innocuous and commonplace, and at others dangerously sinister. Nevertheless, it is just in nightmares that the doors of mystery open up. The absurd and the disquieting sphere of madness contained in his hallucinatory vision become the revelation of a deep truth that can be read from different standpoints. It is born from the knowledge of the hiatus that exists between humanity and the world, from the observation of nature's indifference that seems to follow a law which evades all possibility of human determination and control. It is the sense of our impotence in the face of a reigning reality.

In Greek tragedy, the fate that hovers above the hero, crushing him for a crime for which he is not directly and consciously responsible, still leaves room for catharsis, as in *Oedipus at Colonus* (Sophocles 1988). But in Kafka's works, as in the existential philosophy of Sartre or Camus, there is no possibility of any redemption at all. Humans—who, once aware of the absurd experience it as suffering, have a commitment to live not the best of it but the greatest possible part of it—can do nothing but challenge, confront, fight it.

This *modus vivendi* can have no other characteristic than inquietude and angst. These are generated by the loss of all points of reference, by one's alienation from oneself. *Comprehend* means being able to grasp reality, make it one's own, impress one's mark on it. But *comprehension* takes place by going through a relationship, through the presence of the other. Only a world empty of love takes on a full load of absurdity. The child learns to understand reality by means of her relationship with the mother. It is this contact which gives a meaning to things. From a psychological standpoint, therefore, the absurd is connected with the problem of abandonment and rejection. In fact, the absurd is created by human questioning and the unreasonable silence of the world (Camus 1942, p. 56).

The moment in which the individual stops to reflect on himself and his condition, the "question" is formulated in his mind. He asks himself the reason for his particular destiny, why he was born poor or rich, ugly or beautiful, why his life is full of bitterness, why he has one psychological formation rather than another. A very young patient of mine, who began precociously to meditate on such themes, called this formula of hers the "original question." But the world replies to this question only with an "unreasonable silence." The paradox lies in the fact that the one who asks is aware of the necessity of her question. Thus her pain is all the more acute, since she feels abandoned, betrayed in what she considers to be an inalienable right. People are left alone with their doubts and their questions, to receive a "never" without appeal for an answer. There is nothing left for a person to do but to accept the challenge of the absurd, whose victim he has become, and seek to discover by himself a meaning in the things that happen. This is the moment when one understands that the answer can never come from the outside, from the world — indifferent as it is to human life, to its anxieties — but only from oneself, from one's own inwardness. All of life is nothing but the search for an answer to that "original question" that assails and disturbs us, that makes us restless but which also impels us to go ahead, not to stop, because the road is long and we are only at its beginning.

If the Castle represents the answer, it is right that K. should never be admitted, because no answer can ever be other than partial. In this novel where nothing reaches a conclusion and everything begins all over again in an eternal game of infinite contradictions, Kafka expresses the adventure of humans in search of themselves. Like Dostoyevski or Kierkegaard, Kafka ends by embracing that same absurd divinity who is devouring him. And his message, apparently so full of discomfort, instead holds out a secret thread of hope that one can grasp. The "never" that the individual — like K. — gets for an answer has the purpose of referring her back to herself.

We believe, with a conviction typical of childhood, that we must always have someone to protect us, to tell us what to do, someone who does our thinking for us and directs our actions. To be adult means to decide alone what is good and what is bad, discovering independently the answers to our questions. For as long as we make strenuous exertions in search of a Castle that will guide and defend us, we are destined to be rejected. And it is now that loneliness, never entirely accepted, appears frightful to us. The cry of Christ on the cross — "Why have you abandoned me?" — is the cry of us all. It conceals the desire of a welcome that the world cannot give us, and for that reason the sky seems frighteningly empty to us.

The moment when we put our question we are obliged to confront total solitude, with no one around to furnish a response. This is because any human being we meet along our road is only able to make us a gift of his small part of the truth, the one he has arrived at during the entire arc of his existence. Others can give us warmth and affection, they can share our sorrows and our joys, but they cannot find in our place the meaning that we seek. The absence of another who guides and protects us may lead to despair, paralysis, a total rejection of life, or it can, on the contrary, lead us to gather all our courage and accept the challenge of life.

The moment in which we accept this challenge, *our being in the world really* becomes a personal victory, a reality that has no points of reference other than our inner nature. If external supports neither do nor can exist, life must be won moment by moment, putting all of our potential to the test. The possibility of rejection — the "never" of the Castle — awaits the individual only when she expects a reply from the outside to her personal question. The protection so hard-won becomes in this case self-protection and is the condition for inner development, for always greater growth and enrichment. Those who have experienced the silence of the world and have succeeded in evolving toward psychological independence are the ones who can stand up to the difficulties of life. They have begun to formulate a personal reply to the "original question." And this is a job that takes up our entire lives. The reply is a phrase without end, except with our deaths, but it is enriched little by little as we grow older. Every new experience is another piece to add to our mosaic.

We can compare this human condition to a river that does not flow to the sea in a straight line, but with deviations and bends through which it finds its direction. And for each of us there is a precise itinerary, different for every individual. Useless, then, to look around and seek in the lives of others the direction for one's own, because every model is always mistaken, given the singularity of human beings. The road depends on an infinite series of variables: one's family, one's country of origin, one's sex, and the experiences we have gone through, which combine in a unique way.

The betrayal of this uniqueness in order to conform to a collective scheme may appear to facilitate our search, but in reality it inevitably leads us to the loss of ourselves and to the discovery only of false and useless answers. The choice of authenticity, the respect of our unique lives, always involves committing a certain number of errors. To live in this way is certainly more uncertain and risky, but it allows us to savor more completely the flavor of life. In one of the last reflections contained in his autobiography, Jung (1961, p. 358) wrote:

> The world into which we are born is brutal and cruel, and at the same time of divine beauty. Which element we think outweighs the other, whether meaninglessness or meaning, is a matter of temperament. If meaninglessnesss were absolutely preponderant, the meaningfulness of life would vanish to an increasing degree with each step in our development. But that is — or seems to me — not the case. Probably, as in all metaphysical questions, both are true: life is — or has — meaning and meaninglessness. I cherish the anxious hope that meaning will preponderate and win the battle.

From a psychological point of view the "original question," before being a metaphysical demand, the desire of an ultimate reality, the sense of a rational justification of one's existence, is a demand for love in the very first moments of life. The silence of the world in this phase is only the absence of the other, first of the mother and then of other significant figures. Abandonment and rejection are experienced with unbearable pain, like a sort of progressive dissolution of one's being. The unspeakable suffering of the soul is often followed by the "disintegration" of the body, which allows itself to die. In this way one wants to annul, reduce to impotence and silence that howling demon who rips with his horrible claws the bowels in which he has nested.

One of my patients used to describe this condition with an extremely evocative expression: "liquid pain," a pain, that is, which expands throughout one's entire being and invades it totally. When the psyche has been repeatedly marked by an early experience of abandonment and rejection, the absence of the other becomes a constant condition, a wound that cannot heal, which is manifested by the inability to love and to perceive the love around oneself. Kafka will note in his diaries (1910–1923, pp. 420–421):

> He feels more deserted with a second person than when alone. If he is together with someone, this second person reaches out for him and he is helplessly delivered into his hand. If he is alone, all mankind reaches out for him — but the innumerable outstretched *arms* become entangled with one another and no one reaches to him.

Only a single unbearable silence, deprived of all hope, echoes the thirst for love. Then the world loses its meaning. The distortion of reality we find in Kafka's works, which becomes ever more inexplicable, ever more terribly hallucinatory in its absurdity, is the realm of emptiness where the nightmare of absence deforms every possible kind of existence. At bottom, there is an unuttered cry to be heard in the resigned acceptance with which the heroes of *The Trial* or *The Judgment* go to meet their destined deaths. It is like *The Cry* represented in Edvard Munch's painting (1893), where a man's howl becomes an undulating reverberation of sound waves that deform the entire landscape. The disintegration of the soul, dissolved by the insupportable weight of solitude, becomes the disintegration of reality itself.

Abandonment, once it has been inflicted, installs itself permanently in the psyche, producing a particular psychological condition that no current gratification seems able to modify, to heal in any complete way. What one feels in abandonment is a lack of meaning. Meaning is orientation, is direction in the world, is the fullness of life offered by the introjection of a love experience. Abandonment soon is transformed into a self-abandonment and a self-rejection, which constitute the tragic state in which the depressed individual is immersed.

Apropos of this, one cannot help thinking of one of Samuel Beckett's most famous plays, *Waiting for Godot* (1952). The reality that the Irish playwright depicts is a meaningless wasteland. Vladimir and Estragon, the two protagonists, seem to have no consciousness of themselves. They spend their time in a park waiting for Godot, who would be able to offer them food and a roof as if he were the Savior who had been prophesied. Prisoners of their immobility, the two vagabonds have lost the possibility of altering the course of their lives. They have to make a strenuous effort of memory even to recall their happiness or unhappiness. Even their idea of committing suicide is absurd: rather than an extreme and desperate gesture, it seems to be a passing thought with no more value than any other diversion for overcoming the monotony of the present. Throughout the play there seems to reign the atmosphere of the myth of Sisyphus. This hero, who chained death and dared to return to life, was condemned by the gods to push a heavy mass uphill which, as soon as it reached the top, rolled back down, condemning Sisyphus to repeat the senseless labor.

In such a world any action whatever seems futile. And yet in Camus's words, who more than anyone else recounted the absurd in his works, wafts the consciousness and the value of the challenge. In commenting on Sisyphus' destiny (1942, pp. 119–21) there is in Camus's words the same deep respect for the human being that we find in Pascal's thought. Humanity may be perhaps of little account, the reality in which we live may be contradictory and ambiguous, but we still always have the option of action, of thought, of self-awareness. The only vain thing is despair. Meaning is contained within us, and it is up to us to use our capacity to descend into the depths of our inwardness and retrieve it.

To accept the challenge of the absurd means being able to accept one's condition of abandonment, one's solitude, as an existential fact that cannot be changed, and to take this condition of checkmate as a point of departure from which to construct our lives.

In the titanic battle that the individual takes up against the world, aware of being alone in her fight, she gives her own meaning to things, becomes the only interpreter of her reality, even while knowing that at bottom there is only the absurd, the incomprehensible, the ungraspable. In the lucid swinging between the will to fill the world with herself, to become the only measure of her life, and the awareness that she can never completely succeed, she lays herself and her life on the line. There is no solution, but only a probability. The reply to the absurd can only be the acceptance of the risk of living.

Twenty-one

The Realm of the Word

After the curt reply with which K. has been denied entry to the Castle, it once again shows its contradictory face in a letter K. receives in which Klamm, the inaccessible head of Section X, acknowledges his appointment as land surveyor. Rather than read it at once, K. stops to observe the messenger who, at that moment, appears more important to him than the missive itself. And here another character, Barnabas, enters the scene.

> There was a great resemblance between this new-comer and the assistants, he was slim like them and the same tightfitting garments, had the same suppleness and agility, and yet he was quite different. How much K. would have preferred him as an assistant! He reminded K. a little of the girl with the infant whom he had seen at the tanner's. He was clothed nearly all in white, not silk, of course; he was in winter clothes like all the others, but the material he was wearing had the softness and dignity of silk. His face was clear and frank, his eyes larger than ordinary. His smile was unusually joyous; he drew his hand over his face as if to conceal the smile, but in vain. 'Who are you?' asked K. 'My name is Barnabas,' said he, 'I am a messenger.' His lips were strong and yet gentle as he spoke. (Kafka 1922b, p. 27)

In the mirror game that goes on in the novel, another reflected image of the surveyor is projected externally. The messenger is is one of the unconscious *daimons* with whom he has to converse.

The identity relationship between the surveyor and the messenger is underlined by their social roles as well. Both K. and Barnabas are outsiders, excluded. Both have a desperate need of official recognition that will never be granted. They spend their lives, therefore, studying ways of obtaining the status they aspire to. But their days fade away in a continuous state of exasperation that borders on obsession. Every detail, every least action or phrase that has anything to do with the Castle or with their condition, is analyzed, dissected, broken up into microelements in search of a meaning, of the hoped-for key. If failure seems to discourage them for a moment, immediately afterwards obstinacy wins out and they return to excogitating new solutions, new possible ways of getting the Castle to recognize them — Barnabas as an official messenger and K. as a land surveyor.

Reading Kafka's description of this new personage, there takes shape before our eyes a fragile-looking youth, an ephebus who in some way resembles the author himself. Barnabas also seems to personify a female aspect of Kafka's psychology, as is pointed out by the resemblance of the messenger to the nursing woman. As always, K. turns to the inner world in the hope of finding help.

Recourse to a female figure is a theme common to all fables and mythologies. In fables, the hero, who has to complete a difficult mission, at the crucial moment of his undertaking often sees a fairy appear who reveals to him what he has to do to pass the test. If we think about this imaginary situation, we will understand that the importance of the feminine is contained in its close connection with Eros.

Theseus must make contact with his feminine side and connect up to it by the famous thread when he ventures into the labyrinth of his soul, encountering his animal side, his instinctive nature as represented by the half-animal, half-human, child-devouring Minotaur. In a similar way, K., on his way to the Castle, must relate to his unconscious feminine counterpart, his anima. All attempts whatsoever to explore our psyches demand that we entrust ourselves to Eros and to the feminine. In the sphere of analysis, for example, the work that the individual does on himself requires the ability of the analyst and the patient to listen to the voice of the feminine. Any analyst who has not developed this side of himself will have great difficulty in his work because the world of emotion and sentiments will be foreign and closed to him.

Barnabas represents the messenger of the anima. Recourse to the feminine is a constant factor in Kafka's works. In *The Trial* and *The Castle,* the female figures have a particular function: they are the intermediaries between the hero and the authorities, the world of the father. But the women also seem to have a particular knowledge that makes them superior to the men. Especially in the latter novel the men appear as faded stand-ins. It is the women — Gardena, the mayor's wife and Gisa, the schoolmistress — who by virtue of their relationship with the Castle's officials have every right to direct the life of the village. Their power comes to them from Eros. Differently from their companions, the village women have a deep relationship with this world. They are rooted in instinct whose call is represented by the summons from the officials.

Since in Kafka's world the relations with the feminine are always difficult, these must be mediated by an androgynous figure, in this case, Barnabas. The decisive encounter with Frieda is prepared by the messenger's arrival on the scene. Barnabas' relation to the erotic is a double one. As the brother of Amalia, he is connected to the rejection, the negation of sexuality, while as the brother of Olga, who prostitutes herself to cancel out her sister's guilt, he also has ties to the unconditional surrender to the power of Eros with the immediate and unconscious satisfaction of desire. From this figure, which is on a familiar footing with both extremes, K. hopes to get help, to receive an indication of how to reach the Castle and to penetrate into the narcissistic matrix of its inaccessibility, its closure to otherness.

And yet Barnabas is very far from representing this possibility of salvation. In reality he is a weak and infantile creature who lives in a state of perpetual illusion, since his messages have no value. His condition and his role are the result of that climate of ambiguity, of appearance, that makes up the dominant atmosphere within *The Castle*, where everything is true and false at once, where there are no certainties and the only law appears to be that of the absurd. Barnabas is also the messenger of appearance, of illusion, as indicated by his ethereal aspect and his false uniform, which is like that of the officials but which was sewn by his sisters.

This curious "angel," then, also has another function. Behind his sweet and reassuring features his disquieting condition of outsider lies hidden. His presence opens to K. the sphere of guilt, of the excluded, the realm of doubt and of solitude. Barnabas' infantile ostentation and uncertainties make him the incarnation of the suffering and tormented way the Jewish writer made his way in the world. But if, on the one hand, the youth's activities result only in uncertainty, anxiety, and despair, on the other hand his role as messenger embodies the value of the word and of memory.

In primitive societies that have no writing, the cultural heritage is transmitted orally down through generations. The word is the first code by which humanity learned to fix its experiences. Language is the bridge between the inner and outer worlds. It connects the inwardness of the soul to outward behavior. The moment in which feeling and emotion externalize themselves in words, awareness and reflection unite with them. The word pertains to Apollo who, in the guise of Phoebus, is the bringer of light. The word has the task of illuminating the dark depths of the psyche. Language is in fact the vehicle by which the complex analytical ritual is celebrated. Analysis cures by means of the word.

The pact that analyst and patient stipulate at their first encounter is to communicate exclusively through language. They force themselves to translate the sphere of Eros into that of Logos. But this attempt is not always successful because the word is situated on the borderline of the sayable and the unsayable. And in the unsayable, in the primitive reality of the body, in the carnal aspect of emotions, the word sinks into silence. Then it presents itself as a challenge. The desire to interpret, to give voice to the soul is a fight, a road to awareness that knows many halting places, many flights. As long as we remain enclosed in the nonverbal world, what we feel is destined to silence, to the impossibility of being transmitted to those with whom we do not share gestures and caresses. The immediate transmission that two bodies can establish between themselves will always be lacking in reflection and awareness, which are the prerogatives of the word. The relationship therefore is a harmonic union of gestures and words, of shared bodily experiences and words.

There is another divinity connected with the word: Hermes, the god of thieves, the swindler, the messenger of the gods and the guide of souls on the journey to Hades. The word is, in fact, ambiguous, obscure, enigmatic, hermetic, because it forces itself to connect two realities, two different worlds. In taking on substance, in being pronounced, it delineates itself as a route, often uncertain and troubled, from the Underworld to Olympus.

Words and writing have to do with inwardness. They represent the attempt to give form to human suffering, to reply to the questions that life itself poses in every instant. In language the individual tries to face up to the anguish, the sadness for finiteness, the malaise of living.

In Kafka's life the written word assumed a primary role. It was the living space of his liberty, his authenticity, from which he expected to receive help, perhaps some comfort for his difficult existential condition.

In the novel, Barnabas, whose name in Hebrew means "son of comfort," represents this possibility of relief and support that the word offers. This is why the surveyor at once receives him like a kind of savior and from the very beginning shows him his almost unlimited faith and esteem. In binding himself to the messenger, K. knows that he is binding himself to communication. If "narcissism" is his illness—the impossibility of opening himself to others, of loving, of having a deep relationship with someone else—Barnabas personifies the effort to overcome this closure, to break down inaccessibility by means of the word. We know, however, that his messages are worthless. Not being rooted in feeling, in sentiments, and lacking contact with this primordial sphere, the word loses its meaning. Being sterile, it is doomed to failure.

The help that K. receives from the Castle through the messenger is tied to the two characteristics that Barnabas personifies: the word and sentiment. It is as if the surveyor had been sent a precise message: "If you want to enter the Castle, if you want to open your narcissistic fortress to the Other, you must learn to establish a relationship with these two spheres." The word to which the surveyor must have recourse cannot be an empty rationalization; it must be rooted, on the contrary, in feeling and contain sentiments.

My work as an analyst always brings me into contact with people in deep suffering to whom I can offer no help by repeating banal, detached, and apparently consolatory phrases. If I am to bring about a change and illuminate the shadows in which my patients are submerged, my words must come from my involvement, my participation: they must, that is, be marked by Eros. We all immediately notice when the things we say are received by our listener with indifference, or at best, a tepid interest. And if, in that moment, we are opening our souls, the coldness of the other can be more paralyzing than rejection. The scarce interest that our words arouse is the worst kind of negation because it makes our effort at communication futile and ridiculous.

When such a situation takes place in analysis the result is even more disastrous because the indifference of the analyst can plunge the patient into the deepest chagrin. The most brilliant of interpretations is useless if it is lacking in feeling. In fact, one is incapable of entering the other's psychological field if one does not use one's own soul as a working tool. Only involvement and solidarity can give the word a curative power.

In the face of K.'s confusion and solitude, Barnabas intervenes with the word. The word has the capacity to transform desperate situations as well as, on the contrary, to throw the other into misery. To have a therapeutic value it must be "right," that is to say, it must communicate a message that can reach the depths of the soul.

Mallarmé made a fundamental distinction between the *raw word* and the *essential word*. Whereas the former refers to the reality of things, describing and representing it, the second removes it to a distance and makes it disappear. The essential word is allusive, evocative. It is the site of revelations (Blanchot 1955, pp. 25–26). The capacity to intuit and pronounce this essential word allows for keeping a difficult situation under control and for arresting a depressive tendency that could end in suicide.

The messages in *The Castle* are always lacking in feeling. Messages of rejection and negation, they are announcements of death and not of new life.

The grinding down of K. and his slow submission to the power of the Castle are determined by the lack of support from feeling. Since only his rational side nourishes him, K. doesn't have the key with which to unlock the gates of the Castle. Psychological development requires both elements. When one of the two predominates over the other, the total structure is damaged and the individual is destined to failure.

Twenty-two

A Look at Death

K. interprets the letter Barnabas delivers to him as the sign of recognition from the Castle that he was looking for. It is the tangible proof of his being taken on. And yet not one line of it mentions the position that the surveyor has been given. It only states that K. has been employed in the service of the count. But who is this mysterious lord whose name Westwest, only rarely mentioned, is connected to the idea of sunset and death? What is the employment in question? If the Castle is a metaphor of narcissistic closure, of extreme distance from the world and from people, its lord can only be death, the symbol of distance and absolute inaccessibility.

The Castle represents a mysterious and constantly elusive reality that prevents anyone from penetrating to its essence. Because the narcissistic individual does not manage to get out of herself and open her soul to others, all possibilities of relationship are closed to her. Her extreme psychological weakness obliges her to use all her energy to survive. The effort of fulfilling the normal tasks of daily life absorbs her energy so totally that none is left to employ in relationships with others. But in the myth of Narcissus this self-absorption ended with a sliding into death. The youth was so fascinated by his reflection that he did not notice himself slipping into the lake. Analyzing the myth, we understand how this total closure to the other must inevitably end in death. The Castle as the fortress of renounced communication, as a locking up in oneself, can only be an abode of death.

For the rest, several other details underline the Castle's relationship with death: the spectral silence of the place, Klamm's black jacket, the tolling of the bell, which seems to announce the fulfillment of a last desire. Without knowing it, K. is in the service of death; that is who has employed him. The surveyor's efforts are an unconscious movement toward the end of life. The exhaustion that takes ever greater hold of the protagonist, even making him fall asleep while Buergel is revealing important things to him, is nothing but a slow sinking into a sleep from which there is no reawakening. The call of the Castle is the call of death.

Especially when one is young and full of vitality, it is hard to comprehend that life is nothing but a journey toward its inevitable end. Often young people feel themselves to be like perennially rising stars, as if, having reached its zenith, this sun would never set again. But reality is quite another thing, because what goes up must come down. To be aware of one's own life means to be able to face the idea of one's death, calculating its possible presence in all our actions. The recognition of this appointment does not mean to stop making one's plans or to compromise the desire to live, since life is never savored as completely as when one is conscious of its eventual end. Only those who know they are not immortal can give every action its just measure, can raise themselves above the petty and ephemeral problems that constantly worry so many people. It is in the contemplation of death that the spirit recognizes the value of love, of friendship, and of solidarity among people, and that it considers the vanity of exertions for power and money. The consciousness of death makes us choose to be rather than to appear. Each time any of us has witnessed the death of a loved one, or merely trembled for their life, or has himself been on the point of death, time and things have lost that glaze of the quotidian which often hides their sense. These are the moments when one sees life with different eyes and when we become aware of how stupid were our quarrels, for example, and of how we made ourselves and those around us unhappy.

Once the fear has passed, we sometimes forget these insights and life flows back into its usual channels. Again we become unconscious of its deep value and its dignity. In a few cases, however, the experience of death cuts deep into the soul so that we neither can nor want to forget what has happened. Like K., one has looked beyond the wall and the view has profoundly modified life, providing comfort and reassurance in difficult situations.

The encounter with death and its call has been a widely treated theme. In Ingmar Bergman's *The Seventh Seal* (1956), this call takes the form of a chess game that a knight plays with death. The desire to escape from the fearful adversary also appears in a famous oriental fairy tale. It tells of a soldier who, having encountered the "black lady" and believing that she had made him a threatening gesture, pleads with the king to give him his fastest horse on which to flee as far as possible. Galloping desperately without rest he reaches Samarkand. Meanwhile the king summons Death to his palace and reproves her for having frightened one of his best men. Astonished, Death tells him that her gesture was not one of menace but of surprise at seeing the soldier in the market with whom she had an appointment on the morrow in Samarkand. The frenetic ride of the soldier was nothing but a precipitous rush into the arms of death.

The mysterious seduction that death exercises on humankind is accomplished by way of the complicity of secret and indecipherable signs that capture and fascinate us (Baudrillard 1979, p. 102). The goal of K.'s breathless search, of his useless effort to find an unequivocal meaning in what happens to him and what is said to him, is hidden in this fascination. The ambiguity of the signs the Castle sends him draws him more and more into its trap, forcing him to proceed toward this dark goal. The rush toward the Castle, the abode of death, appears to be the restless search for the extreme limit, the absolute.

People seek the *truth*, but they can find it only in death. The final, unequivocal meaning that is drawn from life's mutability, from its incessant rhythm of transformation, coincides with the stasis, with the end. The constant questioning, which can never be satisfied by partial—and therefore illusory—answers, is an implacable proceeding towards the end, the final threshold. It is as if all existence were playing out a strange game, that of opening a series of doors, one after the other, which follow each other like Chinese boxes. At the end there is the abyss, the extreme limit, where emptiness and fullness, beginning and end, absence and presence coincide. The fascination and the irresistible seduction lie in throwing open the door that opens on the abyss, on the mystery, thus challenging the impossible. This hypothesis helps us to explain the mysterious scene in the cemetery which Kafka puts at the end of the second chapter.

Walking side by side with Barnabas, K. is seized by a childhood memory. Alongside the church in his village there was a cemetery surrounded by a high wall that only a few boys managed to climb over.

> It was not curiosity which had urged them on. The graveyard had been no mystery to them. They had often entered it through a small wicket-gate, it was only the smooth high wall that they had wanted to conquer. (Kafka 1922b, p. 34)

One has to ask what the meaning is of this "high, smooth wall" surrounding the cemetery. In one of his famous poems, Eugenio Montale (1920–1927, p. 30) compares life to walking close alongside a wall.

> Lazying pale and thoughtful at noon
> along a scorching orchard-wall,
> listening amid the thorns and the scrubs
> to the crackles of blackbirds, to the rustles of snakes.

Montale's wall can be connected to the one mentioned by Kafka. In both cases there is a distinct separation between humanity and the ultimate reality, whose secret is defended by an insurmountable barrier. The sharp broken glass on top of the wall cuts the flesh of whoever tries to scale it, just as their questions stick in the souls of those who interrogate life. Montale doesn't say what there is on the other side of the wall, but in any case human life seems marked by this separation.

The cemetery wall clearly represents a passing place. On the psychological level the experience of the wall, a boundary to be passed, is a constant factor of existence. But the boundaries that mark the life of one individual have no universal validity. Everyone must discover which boundaries to respect and which to violate, according to personal nature and experience. Facing the protagonist are many doors, but only one of them is the right one which, when opened, will provide access to the world she is searching for. To open a door or to scale a wall means to be capable of violating a prohibition that relegates us to a state of unconscious life and to accepting the responsibility for our transgression. Consciousness is already a transgression because it marks the exit point of the unconscious, undifferentiated matrix for the sake of moving in a universe where every decision is legitimated only by the inner life of the individual.

Consequently, violation of the limits requires reflection. An indiscriminate transgression is without value because it is the fruit of ignorance. The boundary to be passed, the door to be opened, take on a distinctly individual meaning. One person might trace back this point of passage to having left his parents' home while still young and choosing to live alone; for another it could be marriage or else the separation from a partner she no longer loves; for yet another, lastly, the boundary could be leaving a well-paid job which, however, does not offer any authentic self-realization. Everyone must seek this door without taking into consideration any external factors. In this sense to open the door or scale the wall means to look death in the face because it implies a passage, a ripping of the fabric of life, which profoundly marks the psyche.

The appearance of death in the dreams of a patient often means that the soul is taking leave, is dying to its old, habitual condition in order to enter a new state of consciousness. In the most problematic phase of his analysis, a patient of mine often dreamt, with great anxiety, of meeting death or of dying. At times he saw himself falling into an abyss and experienced this as a kind of death despite the fact that he always mysteriously saved himself in the end. In another dream sequence, a woman dueled with Death in my office, crossing her own sword with the long, fearful scythe of her opponent. The soul needs the experience of death in order to proceed on its road of individuation. This experience, however, is valueless if it is not followed by an analysis of what one feels. To understand the dynamics of one's actions is of little use if that understanding is not accompanied by a transformation of one's being.

Whether considered from a religious standpoint as the passage to another level of existence, or from a lay approach as the end of life — a conviction that can perhaps impel one to make the best use of the one chance we have — death in any case is a *memento homo*. It is as an ultimate experience that it has its value. For each of us, sooner or later, the moment arrives when we have to look this reality in the eye, possibly when scaling a cemetery wall as does the land surveyor. Everyone has ultimate experiences. These are extremely difficult situations which can literally break a life, but which, if they are overcome, fortify it. Those who choose to live within tranquil boundaries, where there are no shocks, where they need not confront crises or death, are destined not to evolve, to live without awareness in flat, anonymous greyness. But the individual who decides to live the extremes, to run risks, to face death, makes a life choice.

The cemetery symbolizes the other reality, that world of the dead on which the living sometimes look in terror, and at other times with the desire for pacification as a sign of reconciliation with our origins. The cemetery and the dead, from an endopsychic standpoint, can be considered as parts of the self which, despite their belonging to the past, must always be kept in present consideration and given the tribute of recognition and remembrance.

The theme of death, the attraction to the cemetery and to horror which are connected to this sphere, are an integral part of a long period of Western culture extending from Romanticism to Decadence. One needs to trace this vein in order to understand the role that the cemetery and death can have in the work of a writer as near to us as Kafka. In the period of *Sturm und Drang,* death was seen as a safe refuge. In the string quartet *Death and the Maiden*, which Schubert wrote in 1824, for example, the maiden's terror is assuaged by the lullaby of death.

But the embrace of death as consolation acquires a character of deep unease in the twentieth century. In a famous picture of Egon Schiele's, *Death and the Woman* (1915), the woman grips her companion in a desperate embrace, while the latter violently grabs her hair and pushes his mouth against her head as if wanting to suck out all its vital sap. The attraction-repulsion relationship is here mixed up with the eternal Eros-Thanatos conflict, which also incessantly runs through the work of Edvard Munch. Our culture projects the image of death onto the feminine in such sinister figures as Baudelaire's and Munch's woman-vampire, or all the *femmes fatales* — from Carmen to Marguerite Gautier — whose love brings death to themselves or to those who love them. The fascination with the theme of death soon ends by turning into an obsession.

Death as an illness of the body, invaded and decomposed by an invisible enemy, is equated with the passion of someone beloved enveloping the lover, depriving him of reason and leading him to an inevitable end. Love and death, the erotic as dissolution, are *leitmotivs* of the culture of the past two centuries. From D'Annunzio to Bataille, love is seen to be the rupture of individuality that returns a being to the primordial state of continuity, of fusion and appearing, as such, something like death. One cannot help but think of the series of Munch's preparatory studies for *The Kiss*. In the painting of 1897, as in the woodcuts and etchings that repeat the same theme obsessively from 1895 to 1902, one observes the dissolving of the faces of the lovers, who kiss each other as if they were interpenetrating and their two individualities melting together. The image does not transmit a feeling of serene fulfilment but a subtle shiver, which becomes ever more strongly and totally agitating. Death, the "black lady," takes on the form of the Other, as if the relationship inevitably brought on destruction.

But if death is the dominating theme of a great part of our culture, we must still discover what role it plays in the work of Kafka. The first thing we note is that in many of his works death is presented in a muted tone. At the moment of their end, Kafka concedes his heroes only a few words. This would seem to contradict the concern with death that often appears in the pages of his diary. In a reflection dated December 13, 1914, he writes:

> On the way home told Max that I shall lie very contentedly on my deathbed, provided the pain isn't too great. I forgot — and later purposely omitted — to add that the best things I have written have their basis in this capacity of mine to meet death with contentment. All these fine and very convincing passages always deal with the fact that someone is dying, that it is hard for him to do, that it seems unjust to him, or at least harsh, and the reader is moved by this, or at least he should be. But for me, who believe that I shall be able to lie contentedly on my deathbed, such scenes are secretly a game; indeed, in the death enacted I rejoice in my own death, hence calculatingly exploit the attention that the reader concentrates on death, have a much clearer understanding of it than he, of whom I suppose that he will loudly lament on his deathbed, and for these reasons my lament is as perfect as can be, nor does it suddenly break off, as is likely to be the case with a real lament, but dies beautifully and purely away. (Kafka 1910–1923, p. 321)

Kafka's writing seems to find one of its justifications in the need of establishing a relationship, familiarizing himself with death. Through his characters he fixes his gaze on the abyss that swallows up all creatures; he imagines the extreme moment so that he may die content, lucidly, without lamenting.

The scene that Kafka inserts into *The Castle* sums up his need of a relationship with death, of dominion over it. In fact, the surveyor recalls that one morning he finally managed to scale that wall very easily, precisely at a point where others had failed. And K. had planted a flag there to commemorate his success.

> He stuck the flag in, it flew in the wind, he looked down and round about him, over his shoulder, too, at the crosses mouldering in the ground, nobody was greater than he at that place and that moment . . . The sense of that triumph had seemed to him then a victory for life, which was not altogether foolish, for now so many years later on the arm of Barnabas in the snowy night the memory of it came to succour him. (Kafka 1922b, p. 34)

The victory that K. wins is a victory over death. By surmounting the wall and planting the flag he managed to throw an investigating glance over that mysterious realm that evades all rational understanding. If Sisyphus had succeeded in chaining it, K. had looked it in the eye without retreating, without becoming petrified. The consciousness of having violated that unknown boundary, of having for a fleeting moment neared the final essence and fixed it from above with his eye, was a source of security that helped to surmount the difficult tests of life. It is the strength of him who knows, who has seen and is able to utilize his knowledge.

For two successive days, July 28 and 29, 1918, Kafka (1910–1923, p. 295) jots down the same thought almost obsessively:

> *I am more and more unable to think, to observe, to determine the truth of things, to remember, to speak, to share an experience; I am more and more unable even in the office.* If I can't take refuge in some work, I am lost. Is my knowledge of this as clear as the thing itself? I shun people not because I want to live quietly, but rather because I want to die quietly.

And on the next day he writes again:

> Began things that went wrong. But I will not give up in spite of insomnia, headaches, a general incapacity. I've summoned up my last resources to this end. I made the remark that "I don't avoid people in order to live quietly, but rather in order to be able to die quietly." But now I will defend myself. (Kafka 1910–1923, 298)

Having lost the hope of being able to change his destiny, his relationship to life, Kafka appears to feel the need of finding in death the inner peace that he vainly sought in life. If life has been mainly a failure, death must offer itself as a compensation. To die content means here to underline his discontent with life: it is the bitter declaration that his relationship with life is irremediably broken. Kafka knows that in some sense he is already dead. His condition as a stranger, an exile within his country and his family are already a declaration of death. In a letter to Brod of July 5, 1922, he will say again: "The writer has a terrible fear of death because he has not yet lived" (Kafka 1902–1924, p. 458). But this exclusion from the normal possibilities of life does not guarantee him the mastery of the extreme moment. So he has to conquer death as does K. by scaling the wall of the cemetery.

Blanchot (1952, p. 104) considers the writer to be an individual whose peculiar power derives from having an anticipated relationship with death. Art is always a relationship with death. The relationship of literature with death is undeniable. In the act of naming any reality whatsoever, the word does indeed deliver its essence to us, but only after having deprived it of its carnal existence. What appears in the image that the word delivers is the absence of being, "its nullity, that which is left when it has lost its being" (Blanchot 1947, p. 28). In order to pronounce the name of any object at all, it is necessary to take away its reality, its materialness, annihilating it in a sound, an image, from which its true being is absent. Thus language is generated by the annihilation of things. We can only capture them by destroying them and resuscitating them in words. If common language seems to consider somewhat distractedly this power of destruction it possesses—since, in the moment when the term is completely identified with the thing named, the latter is totally revived—literary language, for its part, maintains a margin of ambiguity, a not-total coinciding between the word and the object it designates, thus opening up infinite possibilities of meaning.

Kafka was perfectly aware of this margin of uncertainty, of the literary word's elusive quality. His writings are perhaps one of the most exhaustive examples of it. Kafka's words never offer us a definitive reality: they constantly evoke and allude to it, but then seem to turn in an opposite direction, representing only the impossibility of an unequivocal meaning. The character dies and is reborn a thousand times, and each time is the incarnation of another possibility of being.

Both the look at death and the letter from Klamm — another occasion in which the choice is offered between being and appearing — make K. confront his solitude. In his autobiographical memoir, Jung (1961, p. 356) noted:

> Loneliness does not come from having no people about one, but from being unable to communicate the things that seem important to oneself, or from holding certain views which others find inadmissible. . . . If a man knows more than others, he becomes lonely.

K.'s solitude comes from his being different from the villagers, from maintaining his independent judgment in all situations. He will be the only one to consider Amalia's presumed guilt to be absurd and to condemn Sortini's actions instead. His ideas, even his way of proceeding to obtain an audience with Klamm, differ enormously from the ideas of the villagers. Even Frieda, his woman, will not manage to understand him. For her, too, K. will remain a stranger. But it is just this radical diversity of his that will make him, in the eyes of the women from Frieda to Pepi, a sort of liberator, a savior. Freedom can only come from the consciousness of our individuality. Because the surveyor disengages himself from an acquiescent acceptance of the laws of the Castle, which he continues to contest by opposing them with his implacable logic, he is the only one who can liberate the women from their servitude to the Castle and give them back their independence.

The solitude that K. imposes on himself by choosing to be rather than to appear is the same that afflicts all those who have undertaken this difficult road. Solitude means awareness of one's uniqueness; it means always finding oneself alone with one's choices. In the face of the infinite possibilities open to humanity, we are often overcome with anxiety. We know that every new action can involve being lacerated and breaking with what has been until then. The awareness of one's freedom and independence with respect to the collective canons of behavior generates fear. No one can advise us or indicate the right road because the choice can only come from our own souls. Whoever desires to remain faithful to herself knows that she has no real or absolute imperative that determines her path, that directs her decision among "the possibilities." Each person is, in this case, alone with the power of choice, but is also aware that every choice, once taken, must be annihilated, surpassed, and that as an individual he must always project himself beyond himself, because his freedom—as Sartre suggests (1943, p. 586)—condemns and obliges him at every moment to invent himself. In the face of the terror that grips him, one can try to flee from himself, desiring for a moment to abdicate this liberty. Nevertheless, he remains conscious of the fact that his existence is only a constant attempt to transcend himself in search of his essence, which can never be reached, thus confirming the human fate of incompleteness.

Twenty-three

Eros Unaware

Kafka's personages, who are generally designated according to their occupations, are so totally wrapped up in their jobs that their humanity is to some degree crippled. Already in *The Trial* the guards, the inspector, the washerwoman—to cite only a few examples—are formed entirely around the work they do. The crisis of identity that afflicts Kafka's protagonists reaches its culmination in the land surveyor K. A foreigner without a country and above all without a job—since the title of land surveyor is continually denied him—he has no definite identity, unlike the other characters in the novel. K. seems to be one of destiny's jokes, the absurd hoax of a cruel divinity.

The abstractness of Kafka's figures has often led critics to consider them solely as the function of an idea, whereas it might instead be more opportune to note how this indefiniteness, which turns them into allegories, is derived from their total absorption in their projects and their occupations. It almost seems that winning a trial or obtaining a residence permit doesn't leave time for developing individual characteristics or letting them emerge completely (Arendt 1944a, p. 96).

Notwithstanding all this, one has the impression that the characters in *The Castle* are psychologically more fulfilled than those in *The Trial* or the stories, which seem like simple profiles, sketches rather than real people. Kafka shows us their desires, their anguish, their fears. If Barnabas seems directed in all his actions by an infantile desire for recognition not unlike the land surveyor's, Frieda is a woman in love who only seems to long to be near her man, while Amalia is closed up in her sad narcissism. All of these figures take on an emblematic value because they personify a certain way of being and relating to life. The "miracle" of *The Castle* of which Morpurgo-Tagliabue speaks (1983, p. 33) consists precisely in having maintained in the characters of the novel "the concreteness of natural people while raising them to the level of living symbols." The men and women that one encounters in the work are endowed with the touching vitality of real beings without blemishing that dreamlike atmosphere that makes emblems of them.

The enlarged capacity for psychological introspection along with his great mastery of the allegorical form seems to mark the maturity of this Bohemian writer. The Kafka who writes this last novel is a man already near the end of his life with two failed love affairs in his past. Thanks to his relationship with Milena he was able to make a secret descent into the labyrinth of Eros. The letters he wrote to the young woman, unlike those addressed to Felice, are full of tenderness and passion, as if for the first time the writer succeeded in giving vent to his feelings. The figures he drew in the writings of this last period cannot help but reflect that descent into the sphere of the soul. Their greater psychological substance goes hand in hand with an evolution in Kafka's style.

A statistical analysis (Olivieri 1969, pp. 376–81) of his works shows that his syntax develops from paratactical constructions characterized by brief, concise phrases of ten to fourteen words, to hypotactical constructions containing twenty-four words. The choice of words changes as well. If Kafka's style always remains anchored to common language, much closer to a juridical vocabulary than to a poetic one, and with a preference for concrete rather than abstract words, in the last period we find a greater number of "highly conceptualized," more "recherché" words. *The Castle* can be given a place in the middle period of Kafka's production, because its syntactical constructions already show greater extension, passing gradually from parataxis to hypotaxis.

Another characteristic of this work is the great number of female figures who play more decisive roles than in his other works. The women enter on the scene only after the some of the principal male figures have appeared. Except for a brief reference to the hostess of the bridge inn and the mysterious of appearance of the young woman nursing a baby, all of the figures sketched up to then were men. But the encounter with Barnabas opens the way to the appearance of the first women. From this moment K. will make the acquaintance of the feminine personified in all its possible forms: the sister, the Great Mother, the lover. This consideration might induce us to imagine that an androgynous figure would be needed, situated almost on the border between the masculine and the feminine, in order for K. to encounter women and relate to them. The messenger would have the function of mediating the entrance of the feminine. But for K., the feminine-anima also means a relationship with Eros, with feeling.

The description Kafka gives of Olga and Amalia at the end of the second chapter once again underlines the similarity.

> The yellow-haired sisters, very like each other and very like Barnabas, but with harder features than their brother, great strapping wenches, hovered round their parents and waited for some word of greeting from K. But he could not utter it. He had been persuaded that in this village everybody meant something to him, and indeed he was not mistaken, it was only for these people here that he could feel not the slightest interest. If he had been fit to struggle back to the inn alone he would have left at once. (Kafka 1922b, p. 36)

Kafka continues his mirror trick: the helpers resemble each other and their aspect is no different from that of Barnabas, whose sisters are almost identical to each other. One seems to see the same figure duplicated to infinity. But in this case the physical characteristics usually attributed to the two sexes are interchanged: while Barnabas has a sweet and feminine appearance, his sisters' features are harder and more marked. The psychological features also followed the same law of inversion with respect to the collective stereotype: the men childish and indecisive, the women strong and sure of themselves. Kafka appears to experience his feminine side in an ambiguous manner, so that the sensitivity of his soul, in contrast to the crudeness of his father, can only be depicted in the androgynous face of an ephebus. Feminine psychology, composed of tenderness, of the capacity to grasp the soul's subtle nuances, of intuition and sensibility, can find no abode in a male body. Virility is coarse, heavy, corpulent, inconsiderate, insensitive like Klamm's. Femininity in a man seems almost to be a quality out of place, which only has the right to be manifested in androgynous creatures on the borderline between the two sexes. And the slender body of the writer, in the same way as those of the helpers or the messenger, had to lend itself unconsciously to the personification of the feminine just because of its ephebuslike quality.

Now one must point out a detail that may appear secondary but which will reveal itself in fact to be most useful for understanding K.-Kafka's relationship with the feminine. The women expect the surveyor to give them some greeting, but he remains speechless in front of them. The same incapacity to speak also characterizes his relationship with Frieda. Both K. and his creator are solitary types who live more in their dreams, in their inner world than in the real world, for which they possess no adequate language. The surveyor with his continuous pondering over his thoughts, over the possible stratagems that will help him gain entrance to the Castle, reminds one of many Dostoyevskian characters. The hero of *The White Nights* (Dostoyevski 1848, pp. 12–14), for example, describes himself thus to the person who has just saved himself from being attacked by an elderly man.

Lost in their fantasizing, the figures from Dostoyevski's underground seem to be suspended in a limbo populated by inner images. But such images, deprived of a deep relationship with the soul, with life, become pure abstractions that only increase the alienation of the individual and his precipitation into an absurd, unreal universe (Bucelli, Fiorentino 1988, p. 51). If many of Dostoyevski's characters seem to live on their dreams alone, those of Kafka act, or try to act, even though their actions—accompanied by a constant inner activity that is bent on analyzing each situation in all its possible aspects—reveal themselves to be equally vain.

Kafka's whole narrative set-up can be considered an opening on the fantastic, on the dream world, like the business of the traveling salesman who turns into a cockroach or the ape who tries to humanize himself (Kafka 1971). Kafka cannot do otherwise but dream of all his experiences. The writer is always a dreamer, of whom one can say with Calderon de la Barca (1983) that "life is a dream." He does nothing but constantly transform the quotidian into a magic and secret world. Thus the dark corridors of the insurance company where Kafka worked are turned into the corridors of the chancery, into the labyrinthine world of the thousand doors described in *The Trial*, while the Castle of the knight Von Doubek zu Wossek—around which had been constructed a small village administered with great severity by the nobleman and where the Kafka family had its origins—found its mirror image in the disquieting construction around which the entire story of *The Castle* revolves.

If life is a dream, if what really is important is this secret activity of the soul which nests in the imagination, it is almost impossible to translate its delicate and protean nuances into the analytical precision of the logos. In fact, Kafka's correspondence with the women he loved is marked by a deep suffering: writing, like speaking, is tremendously difficult for him, because his inner world does not admit of being contained in words. "Sometimes" he admitted to his sister Ottla in May 1920, "one becomes incapable of writing" (Kafka 1909–1924, p. 125). Perhaps he was referring to the letters to Milena and to the insomnia they caused him. Feelings, sentiments, everything that belongs to the soul and the nocturnal world, is untranslatable for him.

K. believes that his silence originates in the indifference of those around him without being aware that he doesn't know how to speak to a woman. From a psychological standpoint, that is, he doesn't possess any *medium* for relating to his anima aspect. His lack of relationship with feeling keeps him from unlocking the door to the feminine sphere. It is worth noting that *Das Schloss,* the German title for *The Castle*, means not only castle, but lock. Kafka, then, doesn't possess the right "key" for unlocking the feminine. If we let pass the obvious sexual metaphor that this consideration evokes, we will be able to interpret this image instead as a clear figure to represent the difficulty of making contact with the unconscious feminine aspect.

The presumed indifference masks a vast and complex problem. We have seen before how narcissistic and schizoid personalities are marked by a great need to distance themselves. One becomes indifferent to the world because one cannot bear its emotional impact. K. is interested in others only when they can in some way facilitate his approach to the Castle. The indifference of the surveyor toward the world, an indifference that allows him to isolate and protect himself from it, recalls a passage in Jung's memoirs (1961, p. 357) in which the Swiss psychiatrist lucidly—and perhaps with a touch of bitterness—analyzes the way in which he had constructed his human relationships all his life.

> For some people I was continually present and close to them so long as they were related to my inner world; but then it might happen that I was no longer with them, because there was nothing left which would link me to them. I had to learn painfully that people continued to exist when they had nothing more to say to me. Many excited in me a feeling of living humanity, but only when they appeared within the magic circle of psychology; next moment, when the spotlight cast its beam elsewhere, there was nothing to be seen. I was able to become intensely interested in many people; but as soon as I had seen through them, the magic was gone. In this way I made many enemies.

Interest in others is directed exclusively toward the possibility of discovering roads of access to the soul, to penetrate its labyrinths so as to know and describe them. One is fascinated and captured only by the "dream like inner life." For an introverted person—and Jung as well as Kafka, despite the great differences between them, were certainly introverts—what has the greatest weight and value is the inner sphere. External reality takes on meaning and importance in the degree to which one can establish points of contact between the two worlds. Relations with all other human beings are interesting only when they can offer room and stimulus for one's own dream world. In introverted personalities a relationship is only possible when the subject can identify and recognize himself in the object of his interest.

Once this tenuous thread is broken, the other seems to disappear, swallowed up by one's indifference. The stereotype of the philosopher can be applied to many introverts: the man who, always absorbed in his thoughts, walks along without seeing anyone, living with his head in the clouds, detached from the world, like the Socrates of Aristophanes' comedy (1985), who dominates everyone with his basket suspended from the ceiling. They appear not to notice anything; they pass through reality like shadows without being in any way touched or involved in what goes on around them. They are entirely absorbed by their inner world alone until a mysterious thread of similarity binds them to another individual.

Jung notes that he learned with difficulty that others continued to exist even after he lost interest in them. Indifference is a defense. To forget the existence of another person, canceling her presence in our inner world, is often a way to negate, to forget the feelings that link us to her. It is surprising to note how indifference in some people can be so much stronger than other feelings as to conquer even hatred.

The psychological mechanism in these cases is used to dam up an invasion of too-intense feelings: thus, for example, rancor or the pain of having been abandoned are annulled by the absence of any reaction whatever.

This is the strategy for surviving that is used by several of my patients. In the case of a girl, for example, who hides a violent emotionalism behind a veil of calm and rationality, the end of a relationship is a point of no return, as if from that moment on the other ceased to exist. Each time that a love or a friendship reached this shadow zone in her, the person involved was plunged immediately into oblivion. The pain of having been wronged, in her opinion, for having suffered a gratuitous offense or abandonment, is canceled out by indifference. Emotional distance reinforces a person's defenses and isolates him from feelings. It is not by chance that the sensation of being wrapped in a "cloud," and thus separated from the outside world, occurs in my patient precisely when an intense emotion has made her feel extremely vulnerable. The cloud is the need for detachment from the world and from feelings, which can thus be catalyzed. It means she has regained her indifference.

K. too appears to use indifference to protect himself from the world precisely because he has no relationship with his emotions and is not able to control the intensity of feeling that may be manifested. The origin of that "defect of feeling" called indifference is often an excess of passion, a too-intense way of experiencing one's feelings. In a short novella by Marcel Proust written in his youth entitled *L'indifferente* (1896), a very beautiful woman, who has always been used to receiving homage and the immediate attentions of men, falls desperately in love with Lepre just because he is cold towards her. Astonished by his distant attitude she is convinced that he is trying to hide his tender feelings for her, perhaps because he is timid or frightened. Madelaine forces herself to believe that Lepre's indifference is only feigned and that it is necessary to encourage him, because it is certainly impossible that such an insignificant man as he can resist the fascination of one of Paris's great beauties. In this way she is not aware that she is falling into a trap prepared by her own hands and falling prey to a violent infatuation. For Madelaine, indifference only means not knowing how to show one's passion. In his introduction to the story, Giorgio Agamben (1976, pp. 14–15) notes how the function of indifference in the system of passions is opposed to and symmetrical to that of love. It shows itself as the prevailing of the symbol over its significance, of the code over the message.

In psychological terms we can translate this interpretation of the phenomenon into the prevailing of the defense over the affect: the walls of the container are excessively dilated, almost made elastic, so that no contents, which is to say no feelings, can ever fill them completely and spill over to the outside. The ego is almost made id-proof even if the repressed unconscious contents find other ways of expressing themselves—for example, in somatic forms. All the physical disturbances of which Kafka speaks in his diaries and letters—palpitations, stabbing heart pains, headaches, up to the onset of tuberculosis—can be considered attempts of the unconscious to find a channel to the outside. The unconscious does not recognize any separation between body and feelings, making use of either to express itself.

Indicative is the fact that K. feels indifferent when he first makes contact with the feminine in the form of Olga. Apparently contradictory descriptions are given of her: "Then Olga, the gentler of the sisters, got up, without a trace of maidenly embarrassment" (Kafka 1922b, p. 37). The surveyor calls her "a big baby" (Kafka 1922b, p. 69). This gentle and kind girl who takes care of the surveyor and tries to explain the laws of the Castle to him, brings to mind in some way Kafka's younger sister Ottla. In contrast to his other correspondence, the letters to Ottla reveal an unknown Kafka: a man who joins a great tenderness to his sensitivity and introversion and who seems in certain ways less fearful. With Ottla Kafka complains very little, minimizing the pains and discomfort that the progress of his illness began to produce.

Ottla is a little mother who looks after him, cleans the room he has rented, brings him his meals, and has the fire going for him on his return from the office. It is no accident that Kafka calls only her and Milena "mamma." If Julia Loewy was an absent mother, Ottla must have represented "caring" for Franz, the capacity for a loving presence beside someone. Without her Kafka felt lost. When Ottla could no longer go to him because she had been transferred to the Zuerau farm to manage it, Kafka felt disoriented.

In the Olga of the novel we find the image of the feminine, a serene kind of femininity, not at all disquieting—on the contrary, reassuring. Olga signifies that sweetness, that welcoming and understanding which, when they are not experienced within a sexual relationship, lack the nocturnal, chthonic character of Eros that the writer feared. It is not the surveyor to whom the girl is sexually tied—and so he has no reason to fear her—but the lackeys of the Castle. Olga's Dionysian side does not seem to soil in any way her virginal aspect precisely because she is an unconscious "child" who plays with sex without knowing what she is doing.

Olga calls to mind Jeanne, the heroine of *Last Tango in Paris* (1972). Bernardo Bertolucci's much-discussed film can also be read as an introduction to Eros. The stranger the girl meets in the empty apartment is something different from her fiance Tom, a weak fellow only interested in cinema. The stranger seems to represent for her an encounter with an extremely turbulent and violent animus image. As a good middle-class girl who is about to get married without ever having really lived, Jeanne suddenly and brusquely becomes a woman by means of the sexual rituals that she and her older partner celebrate. In a key scene of the film, they make love while playing at Red Riding Hood and the Big Bad Wolf. For Jeanne sex is a prohibited game, an unknown sphere, which she explores with avid curiosity. Her participation and involvement make Jeanne lose her psychological virginity and finally fall in love with the stranger who is her partner in sex. But in Olga's case her virginity undergoes no change. The sister of Barnabas continues to play with sex without ever becoming aware of her experience. There is nothing erotic in her sexuality. Whereas the sexual instinct can become immediately activated, eroticism, which belongs to the world of the imagination, requires a psychic as well as a physical involvement. But Olga makes love with the lackeys only in order to pay off Amalia's guilt. There is no participation in her. Her body and her soul are shut to Eros' power of transformation.

If we compare the virginal shyness that plays over Olga's face on K.'s visit to the Dionysian dance the villagers draw her into, this unconscious aspect of her behavior emerges even more clearly.

> But the peasants would not let her go; they made up a dance in which she was the central figure, they circled round her yelling all together and every now and then one of them left the ring, seized Olga firmly round the waist and whirled her round and round; more raucous, until

they were insensibly blended into one continuous howl. Olga, who had begun laughingly by trying to break out of the ring, was now merely reeling with flying hair from one man to the other. (Kafka 1922b, p. 43)

Little Olga seems to us to be an absolutely unconscious creature. Baioni (1962, p. 265) saw in her "the dedication and sacrifice of the soul to the forces of the irrational." Overwhelmed by the instincts, she does not manage to establish a relationship with them. As for all other instinctive needs, to live out one's sexuality in an adult and conscious way, one must have the capacity to defer satisfaction and find the best way of obtaining it. The relationship between the ego and the unconscious tends precisely toward achieving that goal. In the course of development the human being should be able gradually to enter into contact with those forces that are capable of destroying her so that instead of being possessed by them she is the one to control and direct them. To grow means also to know how to enjoy sexual gratification without being ruled by it. When, on the contrary, it is instinct that takes over, a destructive dynamic is set up.

The compulsive hunger of the sufferer from bulimia forces him to gorge on food constantly. In this case it is not a question of a physical need, but a psychological one. Desideria, the heroine of Alberto Moravia's novel *La vita interiore* (1978) for example, lets out her rancor toward her mother by eating. In the same way the compulsive need for sex, cut off from a conscious awareness, reveals an inner problem. A psychic aspect is activated that is destructive because it has no connections with consciousness.

The unconsciousness of Olga makes of her a projection of Kafka himself, of his relationship with Eros. The heedless and frivolous girl seems to be the only way Kafka can find for relating to the depths of the soul. For this reason Olga can be of no help whatever to the surveyor. Because of the unawareness with which he lives out his relationships, she cannot open up the world of the relationship to him. Olga and Amalia are two complementary figures, the two faces of a single being. By giving form to two divergent types of femininity, the virgin and the prostitute, both can be seen as images of the impossibility of making true contact with the erotic. The virginal timidity of the former foreshadows the virginity of the latter. Amalia personifies total closure to sexuality, Olga an indiscriminate and unconscious opening to it. In the one there is a hypertrophy of consciousness, in the other of unconsciousness.

Kafka was obsessed by an ascetic ideal, by purity, by chastity while feeling oppressed, almost persecuted by the flesh, by sex, which was a continual source of fear and uneasiness for him. His long engagement to Felice was for a long time consummated almost exclusively through letters aside from a few brief encounters. Only toward the end of their engagement, in July 1916, did Kafka spend ten days alone with his fiance at Marienbad, noting immediately in his diaries (1910–1923, p. 365):

> I have never yet been intimate with a woman apart from that time in Zuckmantel. And then again with the Swiss girl in Riva. The first was a woman, and I was ignorant; the second a child, and I was utterly confused.

Since Kafka's first sexual experiences were mainly obtained in brothels—which then frequently recur in his dreams—Olga in a certain sense synthesizes all the prostitutes he encountered, those women with whom it was possible to experience sex without any kind of tie or responsibility—one need only think of the writer's constant fear of marriage. The erotic dimension personified by the girl has no aspect of continuity, no future. It is sex without aftermath, with no consequences in the sphere of feeling. Perhaps this was Kafka's great dream: to enjoy the instinct in its immediacy with that infantile innocence and irresponsibility that pertain to all myths of Eden. Kafka was terrified by the capacity of the instinct to possess one, to bind, to impose its demand for satisfaction forcefully, bending freedom and choice to its will. But what he feared more than anything else was the relationship, the tie to another person, unaware that only in continuity and duration can sex be a way of growth.

Olga introduces that instant sexuality which is peculiar to the Castle. All the amorous relations between the officials and the women of the village are concluded quickly without there being room for tenderness or eroticism. The partner's body is never enjoyed in its entirety but only rapidly. In the letter Sortini sends to Amalia he commands her to come to him at once since he must depart in half an hour. The official seems almost annoyed that the girl's visit has excited his sexual desire so strongly as to upset his plans. Amalia must, therefore, offer "sexual services" that will put back in order the equilibrium she has upset. This way of going about sex leaves no room for psychic development. It is no accident if the women of the village are all immersed in a state of deep unconsciousness.

The passing from one partner to another, as does Olga, blocks any acquisition of consciousness. Forced relationships with so many men may have the purpose of avoiding an encounter with one's own image of the animus. Olga also brings to mind Sabina, the protagonist of a novel by Anais Nin, *A Spy in the House of Love* (1959), who spends her life going from one lover to another in the search for a freedom without bonds. Rather than knowing love, she spies on it as if through a keyhole. The complete lack of truth, of authenticity in her life, leads her to ask help late at night of a stranger, an inquisitor, whose questions oblige her to look into herself. Sabina desires relief from her sense of guilt, that terrible feeling of being a prisoner which paradoxically results from her absolute freedom. She is, in fact, a prisoner of her compulsion to repeat. Incapable of confronting her animus, Sabina constantly flees from it, thus strengthening the passion that enslaves her. The inquisitor, in whom we can discern a higher level of consciousness, in whom Eros is finally experienced in a responsible way, tells her she will be free only when she is able to love.

Both the adventuress Sabina and Olga are eternal maidens behind whom perhaps are only hiding wounded women who have been made fearful of men by a bad relationship with the father figure (Schierse-Leonard 1982, *passim*). Very often, under the guise of a secure and uninhibited woman, there is concealed a fragile creature who, through the disdainful use of her body, seeks that warmth and that tenderness of which her childhood was deprived.

If *The Castle* is in some way the realm of the father, since Authority reigns there, its fearsome power always looming over everything, in reality this paternal figure is distant, absent, locked up in its inaccessible fortress. There is no possibility of encounter or dialogue with this father. Even Frieda and those village women, who have somehow approached the officials cum fathers through "incestuous" relations with them, have submitted to the relationship in silence, which is to say unconsciously.

Olga, profoundly immersed in unconsciousness, has no choice but to encounter the male in a coerced manner until a true, conscious relationship succeeds in waking her from her sleep. This perhaps is the reason why the land surveyor is considered a "savior" by the village women. K., with his excessively developed rationality, represents an encounter with conscience. All the girls, from Olga to Pepi, are secretly in love with him since only he can bring them out of their psychic lethargy.

In certain respects Olga and the other women all resemble Psyche as depicted in Apuleius' version of the myth (1982). As maiden cum anima, they too make love in the dark, but with the difference that they never turn on the light and remain prisoners of their unconsciousness. The initial phase of the Greek myth, as taken up by the writer of Madaura, where Eros asks Psyche to make love with him in darkness and silence, without ever asking him anything, takes us back to a primitive phase of human development where there was as yet no relationship and what impelled a man toward a woman was only a sexual impulse spontaneously experienced. In the fable Psyche, egged on by her sisters, cannot resist her curiosity to see her lover by the light of a candle. Eros'awakening and his abandonment of Psyche begins a series of misadventures that end with the reconciliation of the two lovers and the birth of a beautiful daughter whose name, significantly, is Pleasure.

The pain and despair with which Psyche must pay for her desire to know her lover would seem to indicate that the richness of a relationship can only be gained by the slow and painful working out of the emerging sentiments. Day after day a relationship deepens and acquires value. It is hard to say if it is possible to experience Eros only in a spontaneous way. Certainly one must be free to experience it in this primitive way as well, but to stop there would be to limit our inner development. We would lose all the richness and poetry of the love relationship. It is no accident if social development has impelled people to weave a fabric of relationships based no longer on transitoriness but on continuity. An exclusively physical level is replaced by a psychological one in which the love object fulfils something missing in us, a psychological need.

The myth of the androgyne (Plato 1982, pp. 165–67) is generated by the experience of the complementary psychology between two beings. The search for one's soul mate, the missing half, and, once having found it not being able to do without it, alludes to a psychological meaning the beloved has for the lover. The encounter with the

Other, who gives form to an inner aspect of ours that can only be activated and recognized within a concrete relationship, occurs in a moment when we are ready for an encounter with this part of ourselves. The meaningfulness of an encounter is always contained in the correspondence between the beloved and the inner image. This correspondence is never static but changes every time we fall in love again. The partners that destiny seems to place along our road are, in reality, the result of our psychological growth. It is as if having discovered this inner image we then became capable of discovering it on the outside, embodied in a particular person.

It is difficult to say if the encounter we are speaking of is a unique one or whether there is a different relation that corresponds to each phase of our lives. The capacity for transformation of each individual is such that her growth allows for the focusing of different characteristics and aspects. In a certain period of our lives we can be convinced that our partner is truly the missing half because he or she was capable of putting into focus those aspects of ourselves that our development up to that point had made emerge. Nevertheless, progress along our inner road may activate other parts, other buried potentialities. This then is when the image of the Other changes and we have need of seeking a new partner. Perhaps one of the tragic elements of our emotional ties are their fragility in that it is hard for them to pronounce the word "forever." Although being in love involves the "eternalizing" of the sentiment, it can rarely escape from the deep sense of its precariousness.

The relationship of K. to Frieda will, in fact, follow this development. Whereas an initial attraction will unite them, causing the one to find himself in the other and to abandon his previous existence for the sake of the lover, it will later turn out to be the difference in their desires, their *Weltanschauung*, that determines the end of their love.

Twenty-four

The Encounter with the Other

Frieda's entrance on the scene marks an important turning point in the affairs of the land surveyor.

> The beer was drawn off by a young girl called Frieda. An unobtrusive little girl with fair hair, sad eyes, and hollow cheeks, with a striking look of conscious superiority. As soon as her eye met K's it seemed to him that her look decided something concerning himself, something which he had not known to exist, but which her look assured him did exist. He kept on studying her from the side. (Kafka 1922b, p. 40)

For K. Frieda represents the possibility of the encounter with the Other, with the part entirely unknown and opposite to consciousness. Through her the surveyor had made contact with the feminine in a different way than he had with Olga. The unawareness of Barnabas' sister, her uncontrolled instinct, was in endopsychic terms a level of the anima with which it is impossible to form a relationship. Frieda, instead, is a much more developed feminine image. She is a decisive woman who knows what she wants, who makes choices, who is capable of risking everything she has once she falls in love. Frieda is the only personage in *The Castle* who knows how to love. She is a passionate woman, capable of devotion, capable of abandon. She will stay near to K. and support him in his fight to be received by Klamm. She will support him in silence, asking nothing, until the distance of the man she loves will make her love impossible, empty it of meaning. Only when Frieda comes to feel abandoned, when she realizes that a lack of communication has raised an insuperable barrier between her and the surveyor, will she decide to leave him.

And as Frieda takes on shape in the pages of the novel, we cannot help but think of another woman, equally passionate, who put her mark on Kafka's life: Milena Jesenskà. A woman of Prague, daughter of a dentist famous for his many duels and many lovers, Milena had inherited from her father her pride and willpower. Her name, translated into German, means "lover" or "beloved." It can be considered a kind of predestination, because Milena loved intensely all her life long. She was very young when she met Ernst Pollak, a man ten years her senior, who fascinated her with his exquisite intelligence and his air of sage detachment from all human foibles. Pollak introduced her to the Prague intelligentsia and presented her to a group of writers — Werfel and Kafka among them — who used to meet in one of the city's cafés. Notwithstanding her father's opposition, Milena tied herself to Pollak, almost drowning him in her love. Her passionate way of loving, her complete dedication to her partner, Kafka later transposed to the character of Frieda.

In her biography of her mother, Jana Cerna (1985, p. 29) reveals how Milena's tie to Pollak was based on her desire to share every experience with him, a desire which Frieda too will delude herself into thinking can be a basis for her relationship with K.

For Pollak's sake Milena faced an abortion and also attempted suicide. In desperation her father had her locked up in an asylum for the mentally ill from which she nevertheless managed to get out and meet her lover. In the end Dr. Jesenskà had to agree to their marriage. But marriage proved fatal to their relationship. Once she moved to Vienna with her husband, Milena had to come to terms with the economic difficulties that seemed to leave Pollak untouched, who was only interested in his intellectual meetings with his friends. Milena pawned all her belongings to provide for the house and to be able to continue giving gifts to the man she loved with her whole being — gifts which he considered only the whims and caprices of a rather infantile wife.

To earn the money necessary to survive, the girl was obliged to give Czech language lessons and work as a porter at the train station. Ernst meanwhile grew tired of his marriage. He was always surrounded by beautiful women with whom Milena could not compete, ravaged as were her looks by fatigue. Justifying himself by his philosophy and women's emancipation, the husband ended by imposing on her his repeated infidelities and establishing a sort of *ménage a trois* by bringing his mistress into the house. Despite being very jealous, Milena put up with everything because she was still in love with him.

That slow psychological torture eroded her soul and plunged her into despair. But this was precisely the time when she began her writing — at first only with translations and short articles — and got to know Kafka more intimately, whose work she had begun to translate into Czech. The meeting with Kafka at first only resulted in making her marriage more tolerable, and then by giving her back her security, liberated her from the isolation in which she had lived during those last years.

The writer's love for her also caused Ernst Pollak to renew his interest in his wife. Milena wasn't yet able to choose between the two men. She continued this new relationship without breaking up her marriage, something which made Kafka, who was really in love for the first time, suffer intensely. Nevertheless, the two were able to show themselves freely as they really were since they did not have to confront their love with the realities of a life in common.

The love of Kafka and Milena was characterized by authenticity and reciprocal acceptance. They each supported the other. And for a while the writer seemed to have signed a truce with his anguished feeling of solitude. But they were too different for their relationship to be able to work: to the hesitations of Franz, his fear of marriage and a relationship, always oppressed by a sense of guilt for everything he did or thought, Milena's courage and vitality was the opposite pole. In love the young woman knew no half measures. She gave herself completely, ready to risk her whole life like a gambler.

But to understand what Milena meant to Kafka one has to read one of his dreams:

> Last night I dreamt about you. What happened in detail I can hardly remember, all I know is that we kept merging into one another, I was you, you were me. Finally you somehow caught fire. Remembering that one extinguishes fire with clothing, I took an old coat and beat you with it. But again the transmutations began and it went so far that you were no longer even there, instead it was I who was on fire and was also I who beat the fire with the coat. But the beating didn't help and it only confirmed my old fear that such things can't extinguish a fire. In the meantime, however, the fire brigade arrived and somehow you were saved. But you were different from before, spectral, as though drawn with chalk against the dark, and you fell, lifeless or perhaps having been saved, into my arms. But here too the uncertainty of transmutability entered, perhaps it was I who fell into someone's arms. (Kafka 1920–1923, p. 207)

The process of transformation that is activated by the relationship with another was experienced by Kafka as destruction. In all cultures fire is considered an element of purification and metamorphosis: burning modifies matter, making it change from one form to another. But it is also an element that warms, and where there is warmth there is life. Love really can change a person, but it has to burn long and deeply for that to happen. Then the soul is renewed.

Kafka was afraid of just this new birth, which must have appeared to him as a loss of identity. The contact and temporary fusion with the beloved, which one experiences on the physical level during orgasm and on the psychological level when the lovers are at the most intense level of communication, assumes for a fragile ego a terrifying character of dissolution, seems a nebulous and disturbing chaos. In the dream we see how the writer makes haste to put out the fire with an old suit, which in psychological terms means putting on his old personality again. This dream, generated when the relationship with Milena was entering a crisis, foretold the end of their connection. In the confused finale, in which one doesn't manage to understand who is saved, the therapeutic value of love is nullified by the sequence in which Milena appears in a spectral form, "a chalk design in the dark."

There was nothing left for Kafka but to succumb to his self-destructive tendencies. The last possibility of renewal, of salvation having failed, there was no way in which the soul could express its disquiet except by fleeing deeper and deeper into disease.

But let us return to the Frieda of the novel. The first description Kafka gives of her is that of a barmaid. Her encounter with K. first occurs in the Herrenhof (Lordhotel), and the two make love for the first time sprawled on the floor "among the small puddles of beer" (Kafka 1922b, p. 45). In Kafka's imagination beer is always part of the father's world, and Frieda represents the key that will open it because of her relationship with Klamm. It is the drink of virility, of that adult sphere from which Kafka felt excluded. Sex and marriage like alcoholic beverages are the prerogatives of the father that K.-Kafka can only occasionally seize. The abstemious Franz, during the last months of his life, confided to Dora his desire to drink beer with his father. Only after being able to live with a woman, to be a companion to her, would he feel himself to be in some way his father's peer and share with him the habits and privileges of being an adult.

For its disinhibiting effect, alcohol has to do with transgression. And the love of the "little blonde" has all the flavor of transgression, underlined by the peculiar circumstances of their encounter as well as the ensuing disapproval of the villagers, especially of Gardena, Klamm's ex-lover and Frieda's "little mommy" (Kafka 1922b, p. 87). This transgression takes on many meanings. First of all it can be connected with the incest taboo. Kafka lived his erotic life with a great feeling of guilt because it seemed to him something he had stolen from his father.

The Oedipus fantasy constantly insinuated itself between the writer and his partners. "Do you want to take me away from Klamm, perhaps?" Frieda will ask the surveyor diffidently, hearing him reply: "You've seen through me. . . that's exactly my real secret intention." Taking a woman away from someone is an oft-occurring theme in Kafka's works, where sex always has something to do with rape, with a violation that aims at breaking the Oedipus triangle and taking possession of the father's woman. In *The Trial,* too, Josef K. wants to take the washerwoman away from the student and, above all, from the judge who is courting her.

Among the Hottentots the passing from puberty to adulthood is marked by an initiation rite in which the youth must take his own mother sexually. By making her become his woman, he puts himself on her level. The incestuous relationship contains the possibility of growth (Jacobi 1959, pp. 90–92). One appropriates the sexuality of the parent in order to draw on the very source of vital energy. If incest is symbolically comparable to a new birth, the incestuous character of the relationship between K. and Frieda ought to allow the surveyor to be radically transformed. Like Milena, Frieda is the mother cum lover who guards within her body all the secrets of the erotic together with the key to growth and individuation.

The young woman is also profoundly changed by the encounter with K. Despite her relationship with Klamm, she still has strong ties to the maternal sphere personified in the novel by Gardena. The violence of the passion that binds her to K. makes of her a new Kore. As in the mythical case of Persephone being carried off by Hades, the feelings that suddenly assail the woman push her into the chthonic depths of passion.

The theme of sexual kidnapping occurs frequently in the collective imagination for which the famous rape of the Sabines is example enough. On the psychological level this represents being violently torn away from a primordial condition that one needs to abandon in order to proceed towards individuation. A new psychological situation which is initially felt to be strange and painful — such as falling in love — can be that moment of rupture which convulses our lives and marks them with a decisive new departure.

On her first appearance Frieda is described as "an insignificant little blonde."

> Her low-cut cream-colored blouse which sat oddly on her poor thin body . . . Her hands were small and delicate, but they could quite as well have been called weak and characterless. (Kafka 1922b, pp. 41–42)

This insistence on Frieda's insignificant appearance seems to be a defense to hold in check and reduce the importance she assumes for the land surveyor right from the start. K. is convinced that the girl has great power, great influence, that she knows what he is so anxiously seeking. From a psychological point of view, no one is entirely insignificant, because it is the way in which one experiences another person that determines his significance and importance. K. is seduced by something, by a particular charm that this slender creature emanates. The perception of beauty does not arise from conformity to a collective canon, but from the attribution of meaning to a body, a face, onto which we project our inner contents. This is what makes the other unique, irreplaceable, and allows that person to capture us.

With regard to the surveyor's attitude, it is not necessary for us to establish whether the girl is objectively beautiful, since it is much more important to understand how, in the dialectic of a relationship, the image of the other suddenly seems beautiful, capable of cutting deeply into our soul and almost opening a wound in it. The meaning of the beloved person has its origins in the imprinting we receive in the course of our lives. The details that attract us — a certain cut of the eyes or the mouth, a type of hair, the shape of the hands, a certain kind of build — have in the far past had a decisive importance in our lives, even if they now seem to be forgotten. The unconscious stores up these experiences and turns them into a conditioning that emerges at the opportune moment. When we look at someone and are transfixed by their image, it is our inner disposition which is struck, almost as if we were "programmed" to react only to that precise stimulus. With fetishists, for example, the object that excites erotic interest is almost never objectively fascinating: that certain garment or part of the body owes its ensnaring power to an inner disposition or matrix which it activates.

If I am *"touched"* it means that I "recognize."

Plato (1966, XVd, p. 1268) grasped one characteristic of psychic functioning when he affirmed in *Menon* that knowledge is the recognition of something preexisting within us. A *coup de foudre* is only the recognition in the other of all the data composing our inner image. This is what happens to the protagonists of Goethe's *The Elective Affinities* (1809). The love of Edward and Ottilia on the one hand, and Charlotte and the captain on the other, which destroys the marriage of Edward and Charlotte and creates two new couples, is justified in the theory of the affinities of chemical substances which Goethe sets as a motto at the beginning of his novel:

> We say there is an affinity between those substances which, on making contact, immediately interpenetrate and influence each other reciprocally. In the case of alkalies and salts which, even though opposites, or perhaps just because they are opposites, seek each other and join together with the utmost vigor, modifying each other and forming a new body, this affinity is evident . . . One has to see with one's own eyes these substances in action, apparently inert and nevertheless always intimately ready, and observe with participation the way they seek, attract, absorb, devour and consume each other, and then their re-emergence from the most intimate conjunction as changed, new, unexpected forms. (Goethe 1809, pp. 35–39)

Love here is born from the recognition of a secret affinity, from a complementary quality that makes a single being of the two lovers. The impulsive Edward discovers his other half in the timid and patient Ottilia. He is conquered, believes himself to be overwhelmed, almost possessed, by love for the girl. In reality, as with all lovers, he is fascinated only by his anima image which he projects onto her. "We looked into each other's eyes: I only saw myself, she herself alone" (Lec 1957, p. 19). Fortunately the fact of knowing these psychological mechanisms does not prevent one from falling in love. Knowing that the visage that has ravished me is a materializing of the image I carry within me, that the other is re-created in my imagination—and perhaps does not even exist as I see them—does not soften the violence of the emotion; on the contrary, the lover is ready to defy the world and his own convictions just to keep faith with what he feels.

A patient of mine, who for some time has been in the grip of a turbulent love affair, describes the first encounter with the beloved man in terms of a recognition. The first time she saw him talking in a group of people, the girl suddenly felt her heart begin to race. Listening to his voice, looking at his face, she felt she already knew him, almost as if he came from her past. It was most of all his way of using his hands that struck her: in those hands was contained the woman's whole history, as if they had touched and caressed her an endless number of times. At first she didn't realize she had been struck by lightning; she was only disturbed by what she had felt and tried to minimize it by frequenting other people. But as time passed these first feelings of hers grew stronger, forcing her to try to see him constantly, even using banal pretexts, until the full force of her feelings exploded. When she happened to be making love with another man, although she desired the physical relationship with her partner, she had for a moment to hide her tears when she felt stabbing pains in her heart. She had become aware that her thoughts and feelings were far from the present occasion, were with that man whom she had only known for a short time.

For a long time, on every occasion when she made love with someone, she had the feeling that she was betraying the other, whose image she continued to carry inside her. No physical sensation ever managed to be complete, to involve her totally, because a part of her was not present but was dreaming of the other man. Only once she managed to realize her desire for him did she feel complete and a sense of belonging. Despite the conflicts in the relationship she established with this man, the woman is aware that only with him can she make contact with her animus image.

But what is the mysterious fascination that Frieda exerts over K.? What part of himself does the surveyor see in her? "There was a certain mirth and freedom about her" (Kafka 1922b, p. 45). With the compelling force of her sexuality, the girl represents that obscure world of instinct so much feared by K.-Kafka and which in her appears to be free of conflict and illuminated by Dionysian energy. For K., whom we have seen prostrate in the winter ice of his solitude, Frieda represents a return to life, the possibility of rebirth, renewed contact with his own emotional roots. This is what bewitches K. and is why he finds her "beautiful."

The relationship with the Other allows us to draw on an energy unknown before and which can finally be reappropriated. It cannot but lead to total transformation. One often happens to see people who are rapidly and radically transformed by the birth of feelings of love. Their physical aspect changes in the way they move, the way they dress: a new light radiates from their whole being.

To understand when it is that one comes to an experience of this kind, one can consider the relationship one has with the body of the beloved as a sort of love thermometer. Not being able to kiss the other or to perform acts of deep and total intimacy, for example, are the signs of a limited involvement. In these cases there can be affection or sexual desire, but not love.

In German the name Frieda means "peace." K. expects from the barmaid, in fact, a pacification of his inner life. With her he hopes to make a new family. Frieda is intended to be his secure passport to the Castle. Instead, the woman seems to bring disorder into his life. K. is upset by this: with her he will experience love and the violence of desire up to the point of the bitterness of betrayal and abandonment. Only with Frieda does K. experience and learn about the unknown aspects of his being. This is the reason why she is a *perturbing* image. The scenes in which the two lovers unite in making love all have an atmosphere of agitation. Frieda opens wide the door of the erotic realm to K.

For this reason some commentators have been inclined to see a "man-eater" in this slender blonde, one of those creatures whose perverse and mysterious fascination traps the other sex, defenseless before her fearful, sinister power. Literature is full of such figures: demonic and ruthless women like the Carmen of Merimée and Bizet or Wedekind's Lulu; vampirish creatures like those drawn in the poems of Baudelaire, or the disquieting Madonnas of Edvard Munch. They insinuate themselves into the lives of the lover-victim, annihilating him.

An attentive analysis of these negative images of the feminine shows the deep fear that they conceal which men often feel for their women companions; and how it is deeper and more intense the more intelligent and emancipated the men are. The old image of the "toothed vagina" perpetrated by the phallic and castrating mother lives again in a changed form in the modern-day masculine fear of woman, who remains a disquieting figure in the imagination. Among many peoples the women live in separate tents from the men, while in Arabia they go around thickly veiled. In London there even exists an Arab sect whose women are obliged to live wearing masks. In the West the evolution of mores has mitigated the upsetting reaction that the sight of women and the daily contact with them inspires in men, and which comes to the surface again through the sudden aggressive explosions that reveal the fear generated by the relationship. In counterpoise to the image of the castrating female there is the one of the male rapist, which in women expresses the same fear of the other. What is disturbing in this is not then the male or the female per se but rather the other per se, the diverse, that which cannot be reduced and "domesticated" to a similarity. This is the disrupting experience that K. must confront in order to set off the process of rebirth.

Twenty-five

The *Deus Absconditus*

The beauty which with Frieda captures K. springs not only from the surveyor's projection of his anima image, but also from the woman's psychological freedom. Frieda is an independent creature who enjoys the respect of the villagers. Even if her authority seems to come from her relationship with Klamm, the powerful and elusive chief of Section X, the girl has a strength and a moral superiority that no other village woman except Amalia seems to possess. Both of them know the drama and privilege of *choosing*, and this kind of freedom is what confers beauty and energy on them. Frieda accepts the call of Klamm; she does not submit to it like the others, because she loves him. When she leaves him to go and live with K., she does it not so much because of the impulse that pushed her into the surveyor's arms, as because of the specific desire to make a new life for herself, to find the emotional security that she has not had before. Frieda wants to be the companion who can share everything with her man, and not the occasional lover who is only allowed to share the brief moments of a sexual encounter. It will be K.'s emotional absence and distance that will later push her into the arms of Jeremias.

The young barmaid has the courage to defy the opinions of the villagers in order to keep faith with herself, to live her life in the most complete authenticity and autonomy. A person capable of shaping external reality according to her inner categories, bending destiny to her choices, is someone who develops a great fascination, because her liberty and strength capture above all those who, like K., appear to be hesitant and tormented by doubts. This fascination acts in silence, without fuss, by the force of its example.

Frieda, like Milena, represents the capacity to choose one's own destiny to the very end. The two women are both endowed with that pinch of audacity and "craziness" that makes them different from others and impels them to act only according to their inner impulses and not on the basis of collective norms. In the eyes of the world, both Frieda, who leaves the powerful Klamm to take up with a stranger, a jobless, homeless foreigner, and Milena, who works as a baggage porter at the station in order to live with the man she loves, are "crazy." This kind of folly cannot help but perturb. In the verses of Emily Dickinson (1870, p. 209):

> Much Madness is divinest Sense —
> To a discerning Eye —
> Much Sense — the starkest Madness —
> 'Tis the Majority
> In this, as All, prevail —
> Assent — and you are sane —
> Demur — you're straightway dangerous —
> And handled with a Chain

Differently from the empty puppets, those robot individuals all alike who live anonymous lives without room for their subjectivity, these two women have made their authenticity into the one valid law. By displaying such behavior, they constitute a mute reproof to all those who base their psychological strength on the approval of others.

To choose one's existence is the only way of truly realizing one's being. When one analyzes certain people's destinies that seemingly are determined by outside forces, one notes how in reality they are the result of inner ones. Only by taking the reins of one's life into one's own hands and directing its course day by day can the individual totally live her life. But the egocentric will to choose one's own future must not blind one to the undoubted objective limitations of such a choice. One cannot help but bend before the impossible. A wise person knows how to accept the intervention of the imponderable without losing faith in himself, without letting a defeat make him renounce future battles. In reality the truly impossible goals are very few. An education that teaches one a conception of life as a sequence of events to be borne without any chance of forging one's destiny is a swindle. Only by hoping for the impossible can this sooner or later be realized.

Human life is in fact the outcome of one's dreams, one's aspirations; and the more abject these are, the more conformist, the greyer and poorer one's future will be. Many individuals who consider themselves to be unfortunate are really only conditioned by the pettiness of their horizons. If they widened these, their lives would change instantly. We are what we think, what we desire, and only by aiming high can we grow. Life is the project of living in one way rather than another. Human existence acquires meaning only in the strenuous effort to completely realize our most authentic and profound natures, fighting the external world as well as those sides of ourselves which oppose that goal.

Ernst Bernhard (1969, pp. 20–30), in taking up again the old Aristotelian concept of the entelechy, considered the whole phenomenal world, from the inorganic and animal level up to man, to be the realization of order of an entelechy. The very etymology of the word, composed of *échein*, to have, *en*, in, and *télos*, fulfillment, indicates something that carries its goal within itself: the meaning of life and its development are contained in itself. The realization of the entelechy is the realization of the divine within us. In this sense the projects of humanity cannot help but tend towards a transformation that will allow us to reach a higher level of existence.

In the beer hall K., with the complicity of Frieda, has the opportunity to see Klamm by watching through a keyhole.

> The little hole had obviously been bored for spying through, and commanded almost the whole of the neighbouring room. At a desk in the middle of the room in a comfortable arm-chair sat Herr Klamm, his face brilliantly lit up by an incandescent lamp which hung low before his. His face was still smooth, but his cheeks were already somewhat flabby with age. His black moustache had long points, his eyes were hidden behind glittering pince-nez that sat awry. If he had been planted squarely before his desk K. would only have seen his profile, but since he was turned directly towards K. his whole face was visible. His left elbow lay on the desk, his right hand, in which was a Virginia cigar, rested on his knee. A beer-glass was standing on the desk, but there was a rim round the desk which prevented K. from seeing whether any papers were lying on it; he had the idea, however, that there were none. (Kafka 1922b, p. 41)

This will be the only occasion on which K. manages to get a look at Klamm. It is fairly indicative that this glimpse was obtained through a keyhole. If Klamm represents Authority, Power, and the paternal factor, it is natural that he should keep his distance, be unknowable. In Kafka's works Power and the Law are always situated on a level of reality beyond the reach of human beings. Within the tortuous labyrinths where both Josef K. and the land surveyor get lost, they suddenly find themselves in contact with a *deus absconditus*. The "divine" of which Citati (1987) speaks in his interpretation of Kafka's works can be understood as the making absolute of otherness, and placing it in a sphere that transcends the individual. Just because the subject is closed up in his narcissism, because he is incapable of a relationship, the other appears as the most remote and absent of divinities, who govern the world from their insurmountable distance.

Like Klamm, all the servants of the Law have this slippery and contradictory quality: they too, like the "divinity" they represent, are elusive, protean, not to be laid hold of. Klamm is a Proteus in constant transformation, so that no one can say they have ever really seen his face. The vision of the divine that K. would like to have revealed to him does not in fact take place; he is only shown a meaningless appearance. The indiscreet look that K. throws on the official reveals nothing of his secret.

Not only the officials but also their decrees remain unknown: K. will never succeed in seeing the documents that regard him. In the novel, everything that is decided concerning the life of the individual remains unknowable, strictly wrapped in mystery. Already in *The Trial*, the washerwoman explained to Josef K. that justice is always administered in such a way that the defendants are ignorant of the laws (Kafka 1914–1915a, p. 562). The splendor of the Law is changed into thick darkness when it descends to the level of the human world (Citati 1987, p. 131). It would seem that the *Deus ignotus* can only reveal himself through shadows, ambiguity, mystery. K. seeks a clear and unequivocal answer, but instead he finds himself having to deal with a multiplicity of meanings. The god who reigns over *The Trial* and *The Castle* is a divinity who unites opposites within himself: truthful and deceitful at once, just and unjust, ruthless and merciful. "Two ideas that exclude each other can be equally necessary for him, because [necessity] is the category closest to the sacred" (Citati 1987, p. 131).

The world of *The Castle* is wrapped in the same inscrutability, this last novel being the ideal continuation of the preceding one, many of whose themes it brings to fulfillment. If Josef K.'s sentence is pronounced without his being able to be present, the decisions regarding the surveyor are also made without his knowledge. K. will claim the right to decide about his own life, but this right will never be recognized. The impossibility of being present at one's own trial, like not being able to be received by the officials indicates, on a psychological level, the unconsciousness of the protagonist, who doesn't know how or doesn't want to establish a relation with his inner regulating factor, which in Freudian terms is called the superego.

The nonrelated state between the ego and the other psychic structures causes these inner forces to secretly direct human beings. One can only have an uncertain, fragmentary vision of them, as if one spied them through a keyhole. The outlet remains closed because fears and defenses prevent us from opening it. A wall has been erected, a castle, between the mask and the true face, between that which the subject believes herself to be and what she really is.

In his inaccessibility, Klamm evokes the remote distance that separates the dying emperor from the least of his subjects to whom he has directed his message (Kafka 1971). The remoteness of the "god" is the distance from the unconscious, the separation of the psyche from its deepest and most archaic parts. This progressive estrangement from itself is the result of a slow erosion of the soul due to a continuous hardening. K. in reality is deaf to the voice of the soul. He himself is responsible for his alienation because he is incapable of recognizing the voice from within.

In the world of Kafka, alienation is accepted as something natural. The crisis of middle-European culture and the decline of science as an objective fact cause the decline of the objectification of the human being. From Roth to Musil to Kafka, the new problem generated is that of a life without norms, because these lie in a universe that can be known. What comes from this is the impossibility of realizing oneself in a stable way outside the context of social commitment (Morpurgo-Tagliabue 1983, p. 22). In the world delineated in the nineteenth-century novel, such as Dostoyevski's for example, there is still a struggle between good and evil; one can be an atheist like Ivan Karamazov or deeply religious like Alyosha. But after Nietzsche there is no longer room for these values: God is dead, morality is relative, and the "Over-man," as Vattimo (1979, p. 283) translates the German *Uebermensch*, is beyond good and evil. All of this ought to lead us to direct our lives independently, without leaning on transcendental principles. On the contrary, this new existential condition turns into the failure of humanity, stunned by vertiginous freedom, which ends by paralyzing all decisions.

The new heroes are the rootless, the isolated, even though they apparently have a role. Morpurgo-Tagliabue (1983, p. 19) calls *The Castle*, *The Trial*, and *The Metamorphosis* "nightmares of solitude without an awakening." The surveyor K., homeless and jobless, is almost as excluded as Roth's holy drinker (1939), the drunkard who lives on the margins of society and must entrust himself to fortune, to "miracles."

The regulation of which the individual is deprived is identical with the official who personifies it. Klamm is the Law, just as his father Hermann was for Kafka many years earlier. It is the relationship with his father that gave the writer that feeling of paralysis with regard to his life and his destiny, together with a crushing sense of nameless guilt. The portrait Kafka draws of Klamm is remarkably close to his image of his father. Klamm is described as fat and heavy. This physical appearance is already in sharp contrast to the protagonist's. Authority has an elephantine bulk that corresponds to its strength, whereas the human being can only be slender and weak like the child Franz. Kafka dwelled almost obsessively in his diaries and letters on his skinniness — a clear metaphor of his helplessness in the face of life.

The body's extension in space is, in this case, directly proportional to its relation with physicalness. The fat Klamm is connected to instinct, carnality, to that world in which Kafka moves uneasily, like a foreigner. For K., as for his helpers and all those creatures of Kafka's who are ill at ease in reality, the body seems to be nothing but an encumbrance. The principal ambition of Artur and Jeremias, for example, is to occupy as little space as possible. This makes incomplete creatures of them, who are still in a nebulous state, who do not belong definitely to any sphere even if they are not totally extraneous (Benjamin 1934, p. 281).

This lust for invisibility — which marks so many of Kafka's characters who thus give shape to a secret desire of his — seems to relate to the difficulty in eating (also found in Kafka), which impels the victim of anorexia to reduce the physical space she occupies in the world. The ideal of being thin, behind which is always concealed a rejection of one's body and one's sexuality, represents the claim of an absolute independence and self-sufficiency that "spiritualization" seems to promise. While everything material — food, flesh, body — is equivalent to need, the spirit appears to soar without chains. From this conviction comes the need of those repeated attempts to shed one's flesh by refusing food. But what one is really rejecting is not nourishment so much as its emotional implications.

It is no accident if Kafka (1902–1924, p. 335) writes in a letter to Brod at the end of January 1921 that he connects the impossibility of eating to that of taking a wife. In these problems we find again the deep suffering connected to a lack of love. The inability to control the original object of one's love, its being absent, the infant's impossibility of defending itself somehow from being abandoned, causes the refusal of anything that implies a tie, because dependence seems to conceal a mortal threat within itself. In anorexia this rejection is already deeply rooted and becomes always stronger. The "body-skeleton-rejection" is in fact something that belongs entirely to oneself. Outside factors cannot modify or manage it or invade it by means of food. Its unattractiveness also frees it from love, puts it beyond all emotional dependence. In this reduction of one's physical space, one actuates the strongest and most extreme defiance to all forms of power (Ganzerli, Sasso 1979, pp. 71–73).

All the cultural attributes of virility surround Klamm: cigars, beer. He seems to represent the pleasures of the flesh. He is the *Satyr god*. And like the fat Klamm, the other officials too are "gods of undifferentiated vitality" that "supervise the most full-bodied, violent and bloody human reality — a mass of flesh that desires and lusts" (Citati 1987, p. 240). For the ascetic Kafka, tormented by desire like a secret and shameful guilt, a carnal aspect so brutally revealed and practiced could only be something incredibly distant.

Klamm's kind of eroticism is a spontaneous sexuality and thus free of all reflection as of guilt, an Eros that recalls Brunelda in *Amerika* (Kafka 1912–1914). Brunelda is the picture of degradation. She hardly seems human, but a soft animal of enormous weight: whale or elephant, she represents a nightmare of fatness and its lasciviousness.

Brunelda without doubt refers to a voracious image of the feminine, a cannibalistic aspect. We know how the compulsive gorging on food conceals the attempt to annul the trauma of loss (Massa 1989, p. 108). This is certainly an opposite way to the one used by Kafka, who proffers rejection to the angst of separation and of the void, a rejection that includes food as well as ties. In the labyrinthine house of Brunelda as in the realm of Klamm, the erotic can only be obscene, violent, consist of domination. But in the poetics of Kafka, this abjectness of sexuality is slowly made sacred. In *The Trial* sex is still a disquieting fact, a sign of the corruption of the judges which, however, cannot be verified, as is shown by the irate reaction of the priest to Josef K.'s disdain; but in *The Castle* it becomes incorporated into the divine plan, in the recondite designs of the mysterious Count Westwest. Kafka seems to celebrate the apotheosis of that dark desire which had always troubled him, compelling him to call himself a "woodland beast . . . lying in a filthy pit" (Kafka 1920–1923, p. 198). In this way his violent and spontaneous sexuality that had so often occupied his dreams is almost justified by being located outside the realm of the human.

Klamm is a sort of modern Eros, without whom no union can be consummated (Robert 1963, p. 199). In German the noun *Klamm* means a gorge, a craggy place, a cleft in the mountains, and as an adjective it means restriction but also the body's becoming sluggish from cold. *Klammer* means a hook or a parenthesis. In all the words coming from this stem, therefore, there are two opposite meanings: union and separation, inclusion and exclusion. Klamm, like the capricious Cupid, is he who binds and loosens ties. If he stands for the complex world of the erotic, he cannot help but be a "cleft" and a "hook," because love decomposes and recomposes. The idea of Eros as an inaccessible place, craggy and impassable is perfectly consistent with the events of Kafka's life. Love for him, even more than for others, was something turbulent. It was a rupture with daily affairs — to the degree of keeping him awake at night — with points of reference, in order to venture into the unknown. K. must be content with watching through the keyhole, since he has no conscious relationship with this sphere. He can only look the "god" in the face when he is asleep, that is, at those moments when the passions have been calmed. The reawakening of the instinct implies a convulsion, an emotional storm that impedes a clear view of reality.

Another episode underlines the association of Klamm and Eros. When Frieda wants to chase the servants out of the inn because they have become too impudent, she will raise the lash to them and cry: "In the name of Klamm into the stall with you, into the stall, all of you!" (Kafka 1922b, p. 44). At the sound of these words, becoming aware that the woman is serious, the servants are overcome by a terror that K. finds incomprehensible and retreat toward the stables. Klamm, then, is the daimon who presides over the dark forces of life, over the chthonic depths of the soul represented by the servants, that is, those whose social status is "low." As Klamm's lover, Frieda is in contact with instinct. She can accept, even though unwillingly — one should not forget that she often vainly asked Klamm to leave his servants at home — contact with the "lower" aspects of sexuality. The servants are the symbol of the part of Eros that borders on the bestial and the perverse. In the rites dedicated to Dionysus, the Maenads were possessed by the god, went into a frenzy, and were capable of doing anything. It was in this state of furor that the Bacchantes ripped up Pentheus, taking him for a lion (Euripides 1982), or Penthesilea cut Achilles to pieces in the drama of Kleist (1808). Dionysus takes his adepts to the extremes: madness and destruction, the shadow side of sexuality.

As a surveyor, whose duty is to measure borders, K. is obliged to remain always within fixed boundaries. The sexuality that K. will get to know with all the violence of his desire, opens on the disquieting realm of folly and transgression. It is the world Bataille describes, in which the erotic means excess, darkness, laceration.

Frieda's appearance thus opens to K. the ambivalence of Eros. By way of the barmaid, the surveyor will become acquainted with the multiple dimensions of love. The world of desire will appear in its polarity of violence and tenderness.

> She was seeking and he was seeking, they raged and contorted their faces and bored their heads into each embrace and their tossing limbs did not avail to make them forget, but only reminded them of what they sought; like dogs desperately tearing up the ground they tore at each other's bodies, and often, helplessly baffled, in a final effort to attain happiness they nuzzled and tongued each other's face. Sheer weariness stilled them at last and brought them gratitude to each other. (Kafka 1922b, p. 49)

Violence is an aspect often found in the phenomenology of the erotic. But aggressiveness, the need to take possession of and to be possessed by the other, converge and amalgamate with the aspect of tenderness, thus producing strange, disquieting fusions. In the more exaggerated objectifications, in the total transgression of every taboo, a chink is opened on the darkest depths of our inner world. To desperately, furiously seek a body, is to seek one's own soul, that part of ourselves which we do not know and which is pressing to be brought to light.

In the erotic ritual, the psyche loses its innocence, and from its depths the Shadow begins to stand out ever more clearly. In the body which one appropriates and allows to take possession of oneself, the revelation of the flesh is mixed with that of the soul.

All of that, however, has need of reciprocity. Abandonment and possession are two equally necessary and complementary aspects for the soul to know and express itself in its entirety. The violence of the lovers is also the frenetic search for fusion, the attempt to overcome the fragmentariness of individuality and dissolve it in continuity. The violence of the bite, for example, recalls, in its cannibalistic voracity, the desire to nourish oneself with the other and incorporate her definitively within oneself. It is the need of knowing, familiarizing oneself with an initially extraneous body. We should not forget that it is the mouth the infant first uses to get to know the world around it. By bringing objects to its lips, biting them, tasting them, it recognizes their form and dimensions. By "nourishing" oneself with the body of the beloved, the lover overcomes the danger of abandonment, annexing the other to himself.

Nevertheless, the disturbing side of erotic violence is hidden in the secret desire to destroy the other, whose fascination has been able to bind the lover's ego and take away its defenses. The birth of every love opens a fearsome breach in the individual's narcissism. The subject is obliged to come out of her omnipotent self-sufficiency and admit her shortcomings, limitations, and needs. When the lover tries to destroy the other, she is also attempting to delude herself with the idea that she can do without him. Freud already understood the subtle interplay between tender and violent love when he spoke of a life instinct and a death instinct.

The child who observes the sexual relationship of her parents only grasps its violent aspect (Freud 1908, pp. 220–221). From this comes the traumatic power of what Freud called the *"primary scene."* The lover, feeling himself gripped by a "ferocius raptus," notes that there is a force within him compelling him to violence. If violence stands for *alteration*, tenderness is continuity. Love is made up of a continuous alteration of balance and imbalance: tenderness reconstitutes the being that the violence of passion upset; but it is this very serenity regained that opens the way for a new commotion. If one of these components is lacking, the relationship cannot work. A relationship in which only the tender aspect is present can certainly be prolonged in time, but it remains limited. If the lover is involved, as is K., his involvement inevitably tends to change the other, making him desire a kind of possession that borders on destruction.

In the encounter with Frieda, the controlled character of K. seems to come into contact with the no-holds-barred character of the amorous sphere. His behavior, marked by sudden advances and brusque retreats into his solitude, his inaccessibility, is in contrast to the total closure of Amalia, who Mittner (1960, p. 1185) called a "Kafka of the feminine sex." Behind her disdainful reaction to Sortini's call, it is easy to note her fear of a violent and spontaneous sexuality that assails her with a force she is unequipped to dominate. Rationalization and prejudice intervene to cover and remove that which gushes from the depths. Frieda, on the other hand, does not retreat in fright from the return of repressed contents that emerge from the lower world. She can control her "lower" aspects because she is familiar with them. She chases them into the "stables" while awaiting the moment in which she can activate them. A short while later, in fact, she will abandon herself in the arms of the land surveyor. It is this deep relationship of hers with instinct that makes her so indispensable to K. that he thinks of proposing a kind of alliance to her.

> Your eyes — don't laugh at me, Fraulein Frieda — speak to me far more of conquests past. But the opposition one meets in the world is great, and becomes greater the higher one aims, and it's no disgrace to accept the help of a man who's fighting his way up too, even though he's a small and uninfluential man. (Kafka 1922b, p. 42)

This declaration of K.'s contains the deep meaning of his relationship with Frieda. The feminine world appeared to the writer in many ways as a refuge, a support in this fight against an Authority — represented by the father figure — which he experienced as incomprehensible and cruel. Women for him were mediators, life-savers, as his mother had once been.

What the surveyor proposes is not so much an ordinary joining of forces as a kind of symbiosis. If Frieda represents his anima image, then she is indispensable for continuation of his fight. His relations with the Castle consist of something more than a recognition of his professional position there: they are his battle for existence.

Twenty-six

The Amorous Possession

Klamm, K., and Jeremias, the three men with whom Frieda successively forms a relation, represent three various aspects of her animus image. In personifying very different emotional needs, they mark the development of her relationship with the male. The Satyr god Klamm is the manifestation of a numinous male image with which it is very difficult to establish a relationship. One can allow such an image to possess one by obeying its call. But it is important to recognize the deep significance that the image of the Satyr conveys in feminine inwardness.

In Greek mythology Pan personified the union of sensuality with irrational violence, the disquieting chthonic aspect of Eros in which the sex act borders on rape. The appearance of the masculine in this guise forces us to consider that there may be a very deficient contact with the opposite kind of sexuality. The violence with which Pan takes possession of the nymphs expresses the need of an encounter with the dark side of one's sexuality. Pan's sexual violence, like the call of Klamm, is nothing but the craving and the search for a contact which, just because it is feared, cannot be achieved in any other way. The Satyr Klamm is the image of violent possession.

The encounter with this dark and turbulent aspect is what D. H. Lawrence described in his most famous novel, *Lady Chatterley's Lover* (1928). To fall in love with one's own gamekeeper, to make love in a hut in the woods, evokes an archaic and primitive aspect of Eros with which Frieda is able to make contact thanks to her relationship with Klamm first and then K.

To explain the influence and the fascination that the officials exercise on the women of the Castle, we might refer to another famous example. In Elia Kazan's film version of Tennessee Williams' A *Streetcar Named Desire* (1959), the fragile Blanche Dubois, who lives in a refined and elegant imaginary world, is secretly attracted by her brother-in-law Stanley Kowalski, a crude and violent man. In a famous scene, there is a significant conversation between the two sisters in which Blanche continually calls her sister's attention to Stanley's brutal behavior. She calls him an animal, a gorilla, "the last living troglodyte." At this moment Stanley enters bathed in sweat and machine oil. He pulls his wife to him, irremediably spoiling the tender, spiritual fabric, woven of music and poetry, with which Blanche conceals her explosive sexuality. From this moment on Blanche slides inexorably into the feeling that overwhelms her and which she tries to ward off even while playing a subtle game of seduction with Stanley. When, abandoning all loyalty to her sister, Blanche makes love with him, her fragile body cannot stand up to the eruption of Eros. The streetcar named Desire had taken her to where she is afraid and ashamed to stay. Giving in to the impulse marks her destruction. Unable to bear the sense of guilt and live her passion to the full, she winds up in a mental hospital. In this case, too, it is the chthonic, animal aspect of Eros which seduces. Love is made in silence, violence and frenzy, as if one's own life depended on the possession of the other's body.

The passion that binds an individual to the other causes her to be experienced as a daimon, a supernatural being, whose power seems to drag the lover away from reality. In myths and fairy tales this situation presents itself when the beloved is a spirit or a divinity. Harding (1932, p. 52) calls this the *lover-shadow*. In the dreams of one patient, her unconscious presented the love relationship she was going through as making love with the devil. In one dream sequence the woman felt herself seized from behind by a dark figure who possessed her and whose features were now those of her lover, now those of the devil.

Christian iconography has superimposed on the satyr, the half-man, half-beast, the figure of the devil, who is the cultural precipitate of a negative vision of the body and of sexuality. The fracture in the worlds of nature, instinct, and culture reveals itself in our alienation from our own bodies, the rejection of the things of the senses, of that sphere which Westerners feel limits or possesses them.

But the devil also represents the impossibility of having a gradu-ated and differentiated relationship with Eros. As an endopsychic reality, he personifies another sphere, a different way of moving in the world, which precisely because of its foreign character is perceived as a menace (Sassone 1988, p. 50). Repressed desire assumes the disturbing features of the principle of evil which, as the Prince of Shadows, expresses the psyche's unconsciousness.

Forms of hysteria were once taken to be cases of diabolic posses-sion. The conception of sexuality as a reality that invades the organ-ism and subjects it to its malignant will, can be rediscovered in tarantism. In the Italian south, those—women primarily—who have been bitten by the "tarantula" abandon themselves to wild convul-sions that imitate the sexual act and the orgasmic discharge. The ritual is an outlet for a psychic disorder that would not find forms of expression other than the codified ones. Sexuality is experienced as an invasion, a poisoning, and an illness, rather than being recognized as the activation of our most primitive impulse. De Martino (1961, pp. 62–63) compares the victims of tarantism to the Maenads. It is indicative that tarantism is cured by an exorcism that utilizes music, dance, and colors. The mystic-ritual symbolism of tarantism simu-lates the poisoning syndrome of latrodectism, which is the poisoning from the bite of an arachnid.

The unifying principle of this myth, widespread throughout the Italian south, is the idea of the spider that bites and undermines the victim with his bite. Analogous to the cases of diabolic possession, the victims of the tarantula also manifest disturbances caused by an external enemy. To kill the spider that has taken possession of its victim's body, to make it "burst," the victim has to imitate the spi-der's dance, the tarantella. One must dance with the spider, identify with it, but all the while managing to impose one's own rhythm on it. This is the only way to tire it out and crush it violently under one's feet that trample the ground in the frenetic tarantella rhythm. Liber-ation comes by way of identification, the individual thus finding his resemblance with the thing that is dominating him and making him a slave.

As in homoeopathic therapy, the cure consists in administering the toxic substance in constantly diminishing quantities—*similia simili-bus curentur*—so in the exorcisms for tarantism, the "patient" is obliged to make contact with the characteristics of the spider. In fact, in the course of this identification one sees the patient converse out loud with the spider, submit to its orders, impose his own commands on it, make a pact with the animal, negotiating the beginning and the length of the seizure as well as the dance service to be offered.

The mythic-ritualistic horizon of the tarantula's victim allows for the evocation and resolution of an unconscious conflict that "bites" his conscience so as to reintegrate the victim into the group. By way of the motif of the bite, which injects a poison into the veins that will last for the victim's whole life and can be transmitted to his descendants, a possible cyclic return of the repression is controlled. The individual's crisis finds a mythic space that mitigates its antisocial nature. The fearful violence of the affect is controlled by a container, which allows it a disguised expression. In human evolution, instinct is the most primitive aspect of a being, but one the individual cannot ignore. To misunderstand this part of oneself means sooner or later to fall victim to it, to be overwhelmed as happens to the tarantula's victim or to Blanche.

As soon as one experiences the other as lover/shadow, what counts is not the effective reality of the beloved person but the image that is projected onto him. The process of the imaginary re-creation of the partner is so strong that if you ask a person in love to describe the beloved physically, the resulting portrait will often be very far from reality. Not only the psychological traits of the beloved will be falsified by the emotional investment, but the perception of her form will also be totally transformed. We are dealing with a situation in which the actual individuality of the other only exists insofar as it is capable of activating a powerful inner world.

It is in these states of possession that we become aware of the power of the imagination. Every gesture of the beloved, for example, is constantly reinterpreted on the basis of our own unconscious aspects. The other becomes a window that opens onto our own soul. Because of its violent impact, this experience is felt to be destructive, a suppression of the boundaries of an individuality that is absorbed by those of the other. Insofar as it is a relationship with the daimon, love, both for mystics as well as for lovers, is the annihilation, the dissolution of the Other, of the creature in the "divinity." Thus Gialâl ad-Dîn Rûmî (1980, p. 111), one of the most famous of Sufi mystics, describes his experience:

In You the soul is dissolved, with You it is mixed:
That is why I caress life, only because it holds your odor!

If in the West this deep connection between the erotic experience of the lover and that of the mystic is limited to the realm of imagination — it is enough to remember the famous visions of Teresa d'Avila — in the tantric tradition it is also accompanied by the union of the bodies. The path of eroticism is one of the ways to spiritual growth. The kundalini, the vital energy that in the guise of a serpent lies head down within our bodies, is awakened during the ritual relationship. Rising through all the chakras of the body, this creative energy, the Shakti — which is the feminine principle in tantric thought — can rejoin Shiva, her husband. In this way the individual unites with the divine.

Klamm is the one who tears Frieda away from her feminine universe. For the women of the Castle he represents the "bursting in of that patriarchal Uroboro" that Neumann (1956, p. 70) considers a psychological stage of feminine development. In fact, Klamm is surrounded by mystery. No one knows what he really looks like, no one — not even Frieda who is his lover — has ever spoken to him. Love, if one can speak of love, is not generated by the relationship, by recognition, but by possession on the part of one's own inner reality. Sometimes the same situation arises in the transference during analysis, or in all those forms of love — as in mystic states — in which projection has great force, in that the object of love, be it the analyst, the god or the goddess, remains unknown in his human reality. In fact, the more the relationship is impersonal or nonexistent, the more the unconscious projections will be able to emerge. What the woman feels is subjection by an unknown entity, which appears numinous.

Love cum possession, capable of completely revolutionizing our lives, is a recurrent theme in our culture in which, because of the break with the world of instinct, this kind of relationship with Eros is the only one possible. Entering into contact with this daimonic part of the soul is the only chance we have of controlling the situation even partially. A film by François Truffaut, *L'histoire d'Adèle H.* tells the life story of Victor Hugo's daughter as related in her diaries. In love with the officer who had seduced her, the girl cannot resign herself to the end of their relationship despite all his rejections. She follows him around the world, persecuting him with her love. Pretending to be pregnant, she sabotages the lieutenant's engagement to a rich girl. Pinson, made desperate by the behavior of his ex-lover, attempts to flee by getting himself transferred to the Barbados Islands. But Adele, as much in love as ever, breaks definitively with her family, who implore her to return home, and follows him. The flow of pictures shows us a woman whose mind progressively deteriorates in following the inner image that has possessed her soul. Destroyed by a miserable existence, her mind ever more darkened by shadows, Adele collapses. Sent back to her country, she is confined in a mental clinic where she will live the rest of her life completely mad.

In *Phaedrus* (1973, pp. 261–62) Plato identifies four types of madness: the mantic kind, the madness of the mystic initiation to the rites of Dionysus, the poet's madness, and the lover's. In all these aspects madness is always the invasion by a divinity. To remain fixed in a state where love is experienced as possession very often causes the destruction of the individual's traits, almost as if they were absorbed by the personality of the beloved. One shapes one's being according to the latter's conscious or unconscious demands. Dedication to the beloved is total. One annuls oneself completely in service to the other, since the boundaries between one's own individuality and that of the beloved are not well established. It is as if in doing something for the beloved, one really did it for oneself. In this case one can only approach one's own inner being through the *medium* of the other. This state of amorous "folly," in which one is deprived of one's freedom of behavior, is what the so-called wild analyses take advantage of. The regressed patient, who sees her divine savior in the analyst, is ready to do anything to please the "god" upon whom her life depends. It would seem that she can only continue to exist by nullifying herself. But the intensity of this feeling in some cases also triggers the mechanism that permits the individual to escape from so annihilating an experience. One grows by passing through a phase of total subjection that recalls the primal relationship.

After having passed through a phase of love cum possession, such as her relationship with Klamm seems to have been, Frieda can begin to recognize and differentiate herself. And it is at this point, seeing how unsatisfactory her relationship is, that she throws herself into the surveyor's arms. This new relationship is very different from the other. K. is no "boss." His appearance is perfectly visible to all. He is not a god, but a man. He feels tiredness, disappointment, doubt. He is frightened, insecure. He is neither great nor powerful. His actions are continuously wrong. But he is a foreigner. Frieda's binding herself to a foreigner implies, in psychological terms, the impossibility of recognizing the animus image as part of herself. The masculine element in this phase is extraneous because it speaks a language which is not one's own, which limits or excludes mutual understanding.

By falling in love with the land surveyor—who remains distant and inaccessible—Frieda comes into conflict with a particular aspect of the relationship: incomprehension. The evasiveness of the other throws its shadow over the possibility of approaching and understanding him. It seems that he can never be entirely possessed or understood. The inner world of the lover cannot entirely recognize itself in that of the beloved.

Paradoxically, the more incomprehensible and inaccessible the other appears, the more he fascinates the lover and traps her in his net. What attracts us, then, is the obstacle, the insuperable difficulty. The effort to capture the beloved, which is the measure of one's own attractiveness, becomes a challenge. The relationship is not experienced as an encounter but as a constant struggle. And it is the struggle which attracts rather than the fruits of victory. If, in fact, one finally succeeded in understanding the foreigner, in translating her enigma into the commonplace, she would be deprived of all power to interest us.

We have here a tragic and masochistic way of experiencing the love relationship. All energy, all attention here is devoted not to the final relationship, which is, once the game of seduction is over, the confrontation of the imaginary with the reality, but to the "trip," the chase, the seduction. As raising the stakes nails the gambler to the roulette table, so the lover in these cases is fascinated only by the inaccessibility of the one he loves. In fact, it would seem that from one moment to the next this distance could be ultimately reduced and the two personalities made to coincide. But this moment is a vanishing horizon. What really attracts is not the challenge to the other, but the challenge to ourselves. We can imagine that the individual is feeling the irrepressible need of testing his own capacities — he must constantly prove that he is up to the task he has set himself, that he is worthy of love. He must prove his ability to seduce. This narcissistic game in which all Don Juans, all Carmens lose themselves, can become a mortal trap that precludes all possibility of growth.

The inability to share their lives, to invent an idiom that they both speak, will irreparably damage the relationship between K. and Frieda. The woman will leave him for Jeremias, her childhood friend. One could think that she has finally reached the necessary maturity for recognizing the masculine element as a part of herself, as something that belongs to her past. Jeremias is a figure in whom the infantile is mixed with the erotic, revealed in his impudent lasciviousness. He indicates the reconnection of Eros with his infantile component as well as the emergence of an amorous aspect in which tenderness predominates over violence.

Twenty-seven

Jacob's Stigma

Despite his desire to be recognized and received by the Castle, to conform to the norms that regulate village life, the foreigner K. represents a disturbing element for the village. His inability to understand the local laws and customs is a barrier to communication between him and the other inhabitants. To their minds he is another species and someone to be careful of. The greatest of their cruelties to him is to make him constantly doubt and despair of his own existence. Since he does not belong either to the village or the Castle it is impossible to classify him: so he is nobody. He is constantly reproached with being superfluous, just as Kafka felt himself to be throughout his life.

And yet K.'s aspirations are modest, the goals he pursues are such as ought to be the natural right of any human being. Hannah Arendt (1944b, p. 78) called the surveyor a man of good will, who only asks for justice, but who is not prepared to settle for anything less. He doesn't want to accept the right to live, love, and work as a concession from the Castle, as if it were a gift of alms from a divinity whose laws furthermore were absurd and unjust. That is why he continues to fight to have his requests granted as an expression of his rights. Because of this lucid awareness which prohibits him, despite his own desire, from being like everyone else, he represents the individual in conflict with the collective. Each of his acts proclaims the supremacy of the individual over the law. In a perfectly regulated world, transgression becomes the worst of sins. To the Pharisee who was outraged because he healed a paralytic on the Sabbath, Christ replied: "The Sabbath was created for man, not man for the Sabbath" (Mark 11:27).

One of the surveyor's first acts is a deliberate transgression: by taking Frieda for his lover he launches his challenge to the Castle, because to his mind precisely this gesture ought to win him Klamm's recognition. To enter the Castle he does not follow the traditional route; he even refuses to reply to Momus' interrogation. K. wants to encounter the divinity, to challenge him as an equal. In this fight he will be seconded by Frieda, the only village woman other than Amalia who dares to transgress. By hiding K. under the bar and passing the night there with him, she comes into conflict with the collectivity as represented by the host.

> It bothers me not to know for certain that he's gone. Not only because of Herr Klamm, but because of the rule of the house. And the rule applies to you, Fräulen Frieda, just as much as to me. (Kafka 1922b, p. 45)

The etymology of the word *transgression*—from the Latin *transgredior*—implies a passage, a going beyond an established limit which until that moment was considered impassable. Thus transgressing means leaving behind everything known and familiar—and for that reason reassuring—to invade the unknown. Breaking away from every Eden, from every warm womb is an act of hubris. Progress and knowledge are often paid for with pain. The destiny of those who place themselves above the law, beyond good and evil, who seek the horizons of truth, can only be loneliness. She who believes in herself and the possibility of being the architect of her own existence is at bottom a dreamer. Driven by her daimon, she pursues her truth, her ideal knowledge, respecting only one law: her authenticity. A choice such as this always generates incomprehension and loneliness, because such a personal life-style does not easily find friends. To live authentically is a creative act, and creativity is always a transgression. It is looking where others have never looked and discovering connections that evade common sense. One stands looking by oneself at a new world, as did Galileo, for example. Anyone who dares to live his life on a borderland and continually passes the frontier is in reality possessed by a daimon that no one and nothing can stop. Jung noted in his memoirs (1961, p. 357):

> A creative person has a little power over his own life. He is not free. He is captive and driven by his daimon . . . There is something heart-rending about that. And I myself am the victim; I *cannot* stay . . . Perhaps I might say: I need people to a higher degree than others, and at the same time much less. When the daimon is at work, one achieves moderation.

His independence makes the transgressor a menace to the collectivity, which does not want to be disturbed in its placid, immobile unawareness. His life becomes an irritating testimony to an unacceptable *modus vivendi* in a mass world. Therefore he is considered an irresponsible madman. But true transgression is never a blind adventure, the giving in to an impulse. Rather it is a laceration, a conscious choice. It is not blind obedience to an impulse, but the attempt to discover one's own nature. This perhaps is truer than ever in analysis. Every real therapist knows that she is alone with her patient, because all the theories are worth little in the face of the uniqueness of the other, who will not allow himself to be reduced to any "manual of healing."

Often the most important turning points take place in a way that no one has codified. Since the analytic situation requires one to respond with one's own authenticity to the authenticity of the other, in some cases it is necessary to abandon all points of reference and take new roads, with all the risks such a decision contains, in order to open up an existence blocked by the masks the collectivity has imposed. It is the doubts, the fears, the hesitations, the inner lacerations that distinguish the true analyst from the so-called "healer." The latter has found in the theorizing about transgression at all costs, a comfortable refuge for her neurotic incapacity to live and relate to others. Lacerations can only be borne on the condition that one becomes aware of one's own actions.

A famous gnostic saying from the *Codex Bezae Cantabrigensis* (Erbetta 1982, p. 88) admonishes: "Man, if you know what you are doing, you are happy! But if you do not know, you are cursed and a transgressor of the law." Those who pass the border of transgression always bear the mark of this experience. They carry with them their "secret guilt." At bottom, the fight for life, for a life that has the mark of one's individuality burned into it, is in itself a transgression. We fight against something that is infinitely greater and more powerful than ourselves, and we always bear the scar, as in the myth of Jacob told in Genesis (32: 23–32) — to which Ceronetti's poetic translation gives new life.

> And that night he arose
> Taking his two wives and two slave women
> Taking his eleven children
> And passes the wadi of Iabbòq
> Taking them with him he brings them over the shore
> All his household will pass it with him.
>
> And Jacob was alone
>
> And a Man gripped and twisted him
> Until the dawn came up
> But beat him he could not he saw
> So let loose a blow to the hollow of his groin
> From the blow to his groin
> And Jacob's strength to fight left him
> Let me go the dawn's come up he says
> And the Other no if first you do not bend
> Your knee I will not let you go
> Then asks him what is your name?
> He says it's Jacob
> You shall no longer be *Ia'aqob* he tells him
> You shall no longer be the Usurper
> You shall be *Isra-'El* the Victor
> Because you are he who fights with God
> And among men the Invincible
> And Jacob asked him
> Tell me now your name he says
> The Other asks do you want my name to be yours?
> And in that moment with grace was pervaded
> Jacob called that place
> With the name Penuel *God is revealed*
> For having looked God in the face
> And come away from it alive
>
> He was a blazing sun
> When he walked beyond Penuel
> But he was weak and limped.

The weariness of K. and of Kafka himself, the pain and fatigue with which they move, almost limp through life, is the sign, the deep scar that the fight for existence has marked on their souls. Jacob's stigma is what every transgressor has burned into his flesh (Freschi 1984, p. 93). Frieda's decision to hide K., a decision that goes against the villagers' habits of behavior, against their rigid observance of the norms, comes from the need to recognize and accept a male in a deeply humanized way and not as a daimon or lover-shadow. To base a relationship on acceptance ought to imply the sharing of a life together.

Many relationships, even though protracted for many years, remain fixed on a level of estrangement. The estrangement of the souls is echoed in that of the bodies. Once pleasure has gone, the body that one had caressed and kissed suddenly loses its meaning. One cannot touch it any longer because the satisfaction of desire has removed it to a distance. The emergence of Eros has for a moment turned it into a "simultaneous translator" that makes two very different languages comprehensible: the male and the female. In this case intimacy is limited to the moment of sexual pleasure without the fusion that was experienced being able to make the lovers come close and create a stable, reciprocal acceptance.

Each time a relationship is damaged and breaks there is the loss of the ability—or perhaps there had never been—of being close and living within each other. All possibility for transformation is connected to letting the other person become an inner psychological reality, become the Other. The "encounters" that take place in estrangement, limited to physical satisfaction, are not destined to make much difference to those who experience them, to leave any marks on their souls. In taking in K., Frieda guessed the importance for her of this man, "small and without authority" (Kafka 1922b, p. 42), and so she throws herself unhesitatingly into his arms.

> Frieda had turned out the electric light and was under the counter beside K. 'My darling! My darling!' she whispered, but she did not touch him. As if swooning with love she lay on her back and stretched out her arms; time must have seemed endless to her in the prospect of her happiness, and she sighed rather than sang some little song or other. Then as K. still lay absorbed in thought, she started up and began to tug at him like a child: 'Come on, it's too close down here,' and they embraced each other, her little body burned in K.'s hands, in

a state of consciousness which K. tried again and again but in vain to master as they rolled a little way, landing with a thud on Klamm's door, where they lay among the small puddles of beer and refuse gathered on the floor. (Kafka 1922b, p. 45)

In this case too, Kafka underlines the temporal aspect. The sense of eternal time is an experience peculiar to love. In Japanese Buddhism there are two expressions, *nin* and *ten*, to indicate the forms of happy life. *Nin* is the time of tranquil daily life. One day of *nin* corresponds to a year without serenity; *ten,* on the other hand, is emotional time, the time of love, and one day of it equals ten thousand years of ordinary time (Alberoni 1979, p. 15). For the happy lover time has stopped. The intensity being experienced is such as to make one wish there would be no sequel. It is as if having reached the apex of sensation, everything that follows must necessarily be decline, the slow slipping into the flatness of the quotidian.

This scene, which contains the meaning of the relationship and its future development, displays the enormous difference in the attitudes of the two protagonists. Frieda's eroticism is all abandon.

Tenderness is not detached from her sensuality. There is no trace of fear in her giving of herself to her lover. Sex is familiar and reassuring for her, as if the relationship with the god had really opened the erotic world to her. But what the encounter between the two lovers reveals is above all the contrast of participation and distance, a contrast which is at the bottom of the whole relationship. The psychological attitude of K.-Kafka is narcisisstically closed. He is holed up in the fortress, the castle, of his isolation, which guards him against possible injury that may come from without.

The hero's awful solitude is proportional to his desire for contact, for relationship. The other face of absolute separation is, in fact, fusion. Anyone who has suffered the pangs of abandonment, the emotional remoteness of the beloved figures, without managing to work it out, is obsessed by an ideal of total union with the other. The partner's right to a life of his own, the right to distance himself, go unrecognized, because such a rupture of the umbilical cord would amount to certain death. Each new encounter, each new relationship seems to carry within itself the hope that this magical situation will be realized. The enthusiasm with which projects are made, with which the heart opens itself to hope again is ineluctably followed by disappointment. And it is a new wound inflicted on the soul.

The relationship with Milena was for Kafka like a return to primal narcissism. His greatest happiness lay in the possibility of losing his own self in hers (Bohme 1977, p. 87). This desire to return to a phase of fusion with the love object in an atmosphere of suspended time emerges from many passages in his letters.

Already during his relationship with Felice, Kafka wrote (1910–1923, p. 435): "I have lost myself in F." This breaking out of one's shell, which is part of the experience of losing oneself in the beloved, is described in the novel with extreme violence. Frieda seems to have become the tool with which to try to break into *her own* castle. Through the violence of Eros, the psyche, which before was totally locked within its boundaries, loses its impenetrability.

This violent feeling is often accompanied by a violence of expression that at times is greater in proportion to the need of force if the desire to give oneself to the other is to make headway and break down the resistance of its own fears and defenses. Violence in these cases allows the situation to be unblocked, just as when one takes someone by the shoulders and shakes him energetically in order to wake him from sleep. One of the treatments for autistic children, for example, consists in holding the child in one's arms and squeezing it hard, paying no attention to its scream, so as to provoke a crisis that can revive its contact with the outside world.

In the same way the violence of the lover, which keeps the other from escaping from her embrace, often works to free emotion. It is as if feeling one's body in the throes of violent pleasure were the only thing that could allow one to abandon oneself to what one is experiencing.

Such is the attempt to bring about fusion with the loved one. It seems to impose itself with particular need in relationships, such as K.'s and Frieda's, where there is a lack of harmony between the two partners, a structural difference so strong that, initially at least, there is no other way of overcoming the incompatibility. The encounter with the other in itself often produces a paralyzing fear. For a man there is nothing so remote, so alien to himself as the feminine, just as for the woman the masculine is an obscure and disquieting dimension. Seen from this point of view, the choice of homosexuality is the attempt to defend oneself from that panic of upheaval which opening up the other involves.

One way of reducing the sidereal distance would seem to be the violent objectification of the beloved, especially when that form of anxiety, of timidity, which is a structural part of every relationship, has turned into armor. To be able to abandon oneself to a violent form of appropriation by the lover, presupposes in the love object, in fact, an awareness of his own necessity, the knowledge that the other cannot do without him. It is this awareness that is his guarantee against the danger of violence turning into total destructiveness. The beloved allows the lover to feed on him, since he knows that this is the only way in which the other can experience the most complete closeness and intimacy. It does not matter if in these cases it is only a particularity of the other's body or a certain way of making love — apparently insignificant particulars, which nevertheless contain the entire past experience of the lover — that trigger off this necessity-objectification level, because what counts is the possibility of finally overcoming the fear of the encounter, the fear of what is different from oneself.

One of the measures for evaluating the relationship of a couple in crisis is to establish how necessary each of them is to the other. For as long as a relationship lasts, the mutual effort of each partner is directed at making himself more and more necessary to the loved one, acting like a drug which built-up tolerance forces one to use in ever-greater doses. As the relationship intensifies, the other one also becomes more and more necessary. It is wrong to imagine that psychological maturity coincides with having no need for anyone, because that deep need which impels us to seek the other is also that which, by keeping us in a state of perpetual tension, of constant search, allows us to remain young physically and mentally. The other always corresponds to a horizon of a different life that opens to us in all its novelty, thus helping us to avoid becoming crystallized in old models of life.

But the moment in which, overcoming our fears, we surrender ourselves to love, we also resign ourselves to living like disarmed prophets. Prophets inasmuch as we can clearly see what we have before us, intuit both that boundless happiness, that sense of immortality and infinity, that unceasing palpitation of the heart gratified by the presence of the beloved that the new relationship seems to promise, as well as seeing the inevitable laceration, the annihilation and suffering, with which we will be obliged to pay for our ecstasy. This is precisely the thing that disarms our clairvoyance since we are vulnerable to any violence, any attack on the part of our beloved. Having abandoned all defenses, having put ourselves in the hands of the other, hoping in a boundless welcome, is also the thing that has made us extremely vulnerable.

Even if the meaning of the relationship between K. and Frieda depends on their attempt to make themselves mutually necessary to each other, the varying success of this effort is due to the particular way in which the two protagonists of the novel experience love. Frieda's participation clashes with the land surveyor's detachment. After having made love to Frieda, and while he is leaving the inn with her and the helpers, he remarks to himself that if he were alone he would have walked faster (Kafka 1922b, p. 80). Love would almost seem to imply for him a kind of slowing down, an obstacle in his ability to move around in the world. Whereas K. experiences love intermittently just because he perceives it as representing an obstacle, for Frieda Eros is of a continuous nature. Her feelings for the land surveyor permeate all aspects of her life. Her way of living the relationship is not split into differences between the before and the after, and intimacy is not merely sexual for her: it is participation, nearness, the presence of the other in every moment and situation of life.

For K., on the contrary, the relationship has very well-defined limits: love, sexual and emotional encounters have limits that do not invade the work and social spheres. In an individual like K., who has made solitude into his *modus vivendi,* discontinuity spreads fearfully until it devours all possible room for encounter with the beloved. The other always remains extraneous and a stranger. But relationships are nourished on participation, on being able to share the secret areas of the soul with one's partner, on facing the fight for existence together. If they are confined to silence, to dark remoteness, they end up by becoming sickly and slowly dying as in the case of the relationship between the land surveyor and Frieda.

Twenty-eight

The Mute Passion

The analysis of a novel inevitably forces the interpreter to make choices. One dwells on certain details rather than on others, and this choice indicates the approach which has been used in reading the work. In the vast plot, the interweaving of situations and characters, only some of them are given particular significance. One can never emphasize enough that every reading is a reconstruction of a work. The imagination of the reader superimposes itself on that of the author so that the reader's *Weltanschauung,* and above all his secret inner world, become one with the world of fears and desires that the written page reveals. We have read *The Castle* as the summons to a journey to the abode of the Other, of Otherness. The failed outcome of K.'s search, of his attempt to escape from the narcissistic sphere in which he lives, turns this last novel of Kafka's into a bitter confirmation of the impossibility of relating. No bond truly can fill the deep solitude of the individual, who is destined to wander a stranger in a gelid reality.

Love and relationships remain inaccessible to the writer, who continually reaffirms his pessimistic view of Eros. The surveyor's failure is already foretold in the first chapters, by the way in which he experiences love. K.'s encounter with Frieda, in fact, takes place in silence, in the inability to speak.

> He would have liked an intimate talk with Frieda, but the assistants hindered this simply by their importunate presence. (Kafka 1922b, p. 48)

And a little later it is Frieda's turn to be mute:

"I belive I know what you mean," she said, and she clung to his neck and tried to say something else but could not go on speaking. (Kafka 1922b, p. 49)

This moment in the novel, when the desire to communicate finds no possibility of coming out, is very significant for our thesis. However great our desire to open our souls to the beloved, it is inevitably destined to remain frustrated: one is left mute before the Other and, in fact, it almost seems as if one's voice breaks.

The breaking of the voice, the turning mute in the presence of the beloved, is a widely used literary motif. In the verses of Sappho (1958, p. 39), which were taken up again by Catullus and Racine, the sight of the beloved excites a terrible commotion in the lover: her voice breaks, her sight dims, there is a rumbling in her ears while her whole body breaks out in a cold sweat. This experience is not far from what happens in the presence of the divine. The numinous, the thing that is totally other seems to "alter" the being who receives the revelation. The stupor felt by the soul in this case is the dismayed marveling in the face of what is totally different from herself. In the eyes of the lover, the object of love, due to the violence of his manifestation, is a daimon. The intensity of the experience is connected to the being whose appearance allows the daimon to manifest itself in all its terrible power. "God is everything that exceeds us, that got the better of us" (Yourcenar 1957, p. 50). From a psychological point of view, God is nothing but Otherness made absolute. In the concept of divinity are synthesized the inaccessibility and terrifying power of the love object. In reality the lover is confronting the power of her own unconscious. The reciprocal interest that connects two people activates a very profound sphere. The Other has succeeded in penetrating the most intimate core of the soul, activating ancient experiences. The relationship with the other provides the relationship with the source of emotion. The soul is put face to face with itself. Moses must cover his eyes before the burning bush in order not to be blinded. And faced with the divinity, as with the beloved or with the violence of one's own emotions, one's voice breaks. There seem to be no adequate words for what one feels. There is nothing else to be done except, like Job, to put one's hand before one's mouth and keep silent.

307

Thus in the XXXIII Canto of his Paradise (1987 p. 346, vv. 121–23), Dante expresses what he felt in the presence of the divinity:

> How weak are words, and how unfit to frame
> My concept—which lags after what was shown
> So far, 'twould flatter it to call it lame!

In Judaism the name of God is not to be pronounced. Gardena imposes the same prohibition on K., telling him not to name Klamm, the village's phallic divinity. For the inexpressible the only code seems to be silence. All of us will have found ourselves at some time unable to speak, to suffer a kind of block, an inner barrier that stops words from flowing freely. I do not refer here to those banal conversations in which we are moved to hold a dialogue. It is not the common daily word without a deep significance which I have in mind, but the "heavy" word, so deeply steeped in meanings as to become dense, like the white dwarfs, those stars which before exploding concentrate their entire mass in a highly reduced volume. When one is in the grip of strong emotions, one is experiencing something inexpressible in words, however banal it may be for others.

In the novel this inner impediment is projected outward onto the two helpers. In their presence K. is not able to speak to Frieda confidentially, to express his feelings for her. Since Artur and Jeremias can be considered the surveyor's alter egos, personifications of his infantile side, the difficulty they express is contained in the archaic aspect of emotion, in its still undifferentiated form.

In his essay on schizophrenia, Searles (1965a, pp. 305–306) emphasizes how what is truly destructive for the psychotic is precisely the chaos of his inner world. His reactions are an uncoordinated jumble of ambivalent feelings that may explode from one moment to the next with tremendous fury, just as on the contrary, and just as suddenly, they may be repressed and inaccessible. The fragmentation of the ego produces many varied personalities, disassociated among themselves and each of which personifies a different feeling. This psychic structure sometimes can cause the interweaving, for example, of plural emotional relationships, in that each of these fragmented parts is projected onto a different person with whom it is experienced. To maintain control, the ego must block the reunification of the fragments, even if this defensive maneuver results in a further alienation of the subject. It is in the moment when the emotion presents itself in all its ambivalence, in all its polyhedral facets, that the voice disappears, that an adequate code for translation is lacking. The individual is a ready prey for the irruption of the unconscious. An archaic and undifferentiated emotion remains far from contact with consciousness so that it is deprived of that cultural modeling that allows the individual to translate his inner world into a language comprehensible to others.

The civilizing work of culture creates a channel for the legitimate expression of inwardness. Generally, the adult has learned this code and is able to control the flow of emotions and prevent them from overflowing into perilous agitation. Thus, for example, violent rage is blocked by rational control and keeps us from killing our adversary, translating perhaps the homicidal impulse into a more or less verbal aggression that can range from subtle irony to open insult.

One of the spheres in which the human being generally loses this control is that of love. Love is letting go of the emotions, is living with the other the entire intensity of our sentiments from the most violent and destructive anger to the most unrestrained desire, to the greatest tenderness. In the case of love we are dealing with an overturning of that social convention which forces us to keep tight rein on our feelings, because it is that which allows us to be always ourselves, to show the other what we really feel, which determines the degree of our involvement and thus the importance of the relationship.

The problem of the inability or impossibility of expressing oneself becomes much more complex when it ceases to affect a single situation limited in time, but involves all of one's deepest experiences.

In this case, not being able to speak reveals a radical difficulty in making contact. In the case of K. as of any other person afflicted with this block, the words silently accumulate deep down in the soul. A terrible frost seems to have struck the subject, petrifying him and thus enclosing his feelings in impenetrable crystals. Emptiness and darkness mix together in the silence while the soul goes into spasms striving to find the code of expression. But, by a kind of awful spell, each attempt is followed only by silence.

Many films of Ingmar Bergman contain long moments of silence while the camera frames the protagonist's face in close-up, leaving to the expressions that one gradually manages to decipher there the job of explaining the implicit. In a recent film by the Turkish director

Tevfik Baser (1987), *Forty Square Meters of Germany*, very little dialogue is used throughout. An almost total absence of words expresses the drama of incommunicability between a Turkish immigrant and his young wife whom he, from jealousy, keeps locked up in their apartment. He is incapable of understanding her world, of respecting her needs and desires.

This is the dramatic experience of silence that we find constantly in the pages of Kafka. The theme of silence, of the lost voice, recurs obsessively in many of his writings and dominates between the lines of his diary and his letters. Josephine the singer, the mouse heroine of one of his stories (Kafka 1971) slowly loses her voice until she is entirely mute and so forgotten. Behind this metaphor hides not only one of Kafka's final symptoms — that not being able to proffer words, the cruel nemesis of the unconscious — of the tuberculosis of the larynx which was going to kill him, but above all, his profound inability to give voice to his soul, his feelings, to find a channel of communication.

But to understand what determined his flight into silence one has to read "The Silence of the Sirens" (Kafka 1971). The writer rewrites the myth of Sirens introducing a significant variant. It is not with their song that they fascinate Ulysses but with their silence.

> Now the Sirens have a still more fatal weapon than their song, namely their silence. And though admittedly such a thing has never happened, still it is conceivable that someone might possibly have escaped from their singing; but from their silence certainly never. (Kafka 1971, p. 431)

The relationship with the women is conveyed by silence, that is, by the apparent impossibility of verbalizing what one feels. In his eyes the women appear like distant creatures possessed of a mysterious and fearful power. They do not speak, do not reply, like Felice who was stingy with her letters to the tormented Franz. It is in silence that their seductive power exists. Silence fascinates, captivates, because it is a challenge to find a meaning, a hidden message in the mute attitude of the person. Kafka's acute sensitivity was probably marked by the aloofness of his mother and the authoritarianism of his father. He was not able to reabsorb the negativeness of his family circle, which he continued to experience as a distant, unreachable emotional sphere.

It is hard to delineate a precise chain of causality in the complex existential network that becomes a deep unease in the face of life, in a bigger or smaller permanent wound. Often, we only manage to define a network of connections. Then we notice how in relations thus structured, the communicative potential of the word, which synthesizes an important part of everyone's capacity for relations, becomes damaged. The coldness of the mother, when accompanied by particular psychological conditions in the child (a basic weakness of the ego, a more acute sensitivity and greater need of love) that make it more difficult for him to integrate the trauma, can create the fracture, and in extreme cases, the loss of all codes, verbal and non-verbal, directed toward the other.

In fact, if the other continues to withdraw, to refuse herself, all openings and tools of contact, of intimacy, of union, are experienced as a mortal danger. Nothing is left but to take refuge in silence, in one's own distance and inaccessibility. The relationship with feeling and the capacity to express it is a relationship with one's own soul, which passes by way of the Other. A child can only live out its feelings if he has someone near who is able to understand and accept them. If this condition is lacking, the child will be obliged to react to his feelings in secret, preferring to renounce them and not experiencing them at all.

With this observation as a point of departure, it may be possible to penetrate the obscurities of psychotic language, which is a matter of saying and not saying at the same time. The language of schizophrenics is marked by the inability to express one's experiences in words. Rather than finding expression in words, the emotions come out more often sensorially as hallucinations and delirium. What the psychotic lacks — and to a lesser degree than prepsychotics — is a common code, shared and thus objective, with which to express her inner world. Her constant withdrawing from the other, her aloofness, make it impossible for her to differentiate herself entirely, to escape from her symbiotic universe.

No objectivity is necessary at the primal relationship level. The newborn child's first manifestations of sounds are experienced without the knowledge that a linguistic code exists. They are "acoustical material" emitted by his body, which goes to encounter that of the other, of the mother, just as her words touch the child's body and mind. Their function is that of "acoustical milk" (Maffei 1986, p.

204). These first sounds require no translation. It is the mother's love, her empathy that deciphers their meaning, allowing her to fulfill the desires they express. The acquisition of language, instead, implies the child's capacity to picture to himself another being different from himself. In order to speak, it is necessary to be convinced that the other, to whom our words are directed—another who is different from us and with whom the relationship is not symbiotic—can understand what is being said and is conditioned by it (Maffei 1986, p. 242). Verbal communication, unlike the nonverbal kind expressed by body contact, presupposes a distinction between one who speaks and one who listens. It is necessary that the child be discovered as a separate entity, as an individual, and above all, that she has recognized the Other in her imaginary world, clarifying to herself her position with regard to this otherness.

The word, in fact, represents, "the passing of body language beyond its own limits, the discovery of space and the non-I" (Resnik 1972, p. 117). To communicate means to bind, to make contact, to establish a relationship between two entities, and this implies a clear distinction between subject and object. The language of the psychotic, on the contrary, does not presuppose any listener as an independent being, as someone other than himself. The voice that is born from inwardness remains a prisoner of the subjective fantasy that it would like to project to the outside. The symbiotic model leaves no room for otherness, for the inevitable distortion that occurs when the message is received and translated into the listener's interpretive categories. What the schizophrenic wants to transmit is the totality of his own subjectivity, but keeping it unaltered and impervious to the changes that the other, with his own sensibility, might bring to it.

The word ought to sum up the totality of a being in the communication of an experience and an emotion. It is no longer only a message, by means of which one can express together with an event the experience that accompanies it, but it is the Word, that is to say the illusion, the hope, the dream of a total communication that abolishes the borders between the I and the Thou. Faced with this immense task, the voice withdraws in fright.

The psychotic's misapprehension lies in thinking that any inner experience is inexpressible. But becoming mute only imposes the task of deciphering the message on the other. It is the other who must find the key, a means of communication. In this challenge, a desperate plea for love is often hidden. "If you love me, if you really want me," it says silently to the one nearby, "it is you who must seek the key to my world, who must accept me for what I am, who must understand me without asking me questions." This is a subtle, difficult game, often exhausting, that can have various outcomes in different cases and different contexts.

It is difficult if not impossible for a couple having a relationship of this kind, both of them being involved in a web of affection, to escape from the trap of metacommunicating silence, revealing and clarifying to themselves and the other the deep dynamics that cause this kind of communication. The passing of one partner to a different level of communication would imply the rupture of the homeostatic situation. An activating of the imaginary, which finds no equivalent in the response of the other, is one of the most subtle ways of annihilating the partner. To be constantly dealing with a lover who never speaks, who does not show his feelings, who always lets the partner carry the burden of deciphering what he feels, possibly using small gestures such as a tone of voice, a particular position of the body, the way of touching or embracing one, certainly constitutes a strong and repeated stress. The mind can never relax, one can never entirely let oneself go, because one is obliged constantly to keep on the lookout for the signals the other sends in order to know what is happening.

The impossibility of verifying the correctness of one's intuitions can create the sensation of slipping slowly, but always more intensely and inescapably, into madness. Searles (1965b, pp. 246–49) lists many of the possible ways in which one can drive the other crazy, from provoking opposing aspects of her personality to stimulating and frustrating her at the same time or by a rapid alternation of her needs, up to sending her signals that put her in a double bind in that the verbal messages contradict the unconscious ones. Thus one undermines one's partner's confidence in the credibility of her emotional reactions and disqualifies her capacity for making correct judgments of reality. If having to face silence is a dramatic situation, it is just as tragic not to be able to speak, as we have seen. Not to be able to offer words means to have overloaded the other with significance, with projections; it means to have transformed him into a divinity before whom, shaken by terrible tremors, one can only be mute.

Within an emotional relationship it is often the man who covers his emotions with silence. In the eyes of a woman, her partner's silence is understood as a distraction, being absorbed in other thoughts, or else finding her company uninteresting to the point of having nothing to say. What, in reality, he is going through at that moment is an intense emotional experience for which he has no words. Having loaded the feminine with significance he can only be silent in her presence.

It is probable that the great distance from which one's life has been emphasized and analyzed makes it difficult in many cases, especially for men, to develop an adequate code of communication. In "normal" situations, during the first stages of life, which set an indelible mark on the psyche, a male child finds himself immediately in a relationship with otherness, whereas a girl is received into a relationship of identity, of resemblance. Unless there are unconscious feelings of rivalry, rejection, or hatred of the infant, the mother, as a woman, ought to be able to realize a very deep understanding of her little girl because of their identical bodies and psychic structures, because of those common features that constitute the female.

This is something that is not available to the male child. The differences between him and the mother create an unbridgeable distance that can be experienced as rejection, as separation. From the very first he finds himself immersed in a reality which cannot entirely understand him and with which he cannot entirely identify. This very early fracture marks his inability to communicate. The sphere of communication is in great part something alien to him. But what is alien is also disquieting; it inspires awe, fear.

So then, it is evident that a man's detachment is in many cases not dictated by the desire to annul the woman he loves, to make her suffer by his silence, but is instead the expression of a real inability to relate. The solution quite commonly adopted by many people is a schizoid attitude that rejects all intimate and deep contact with the other. The only possibility of getting out of this critical situation is to learn the language of communication. To rediscover words, for men as well as women, means abandoning the illusion of total communication, which leads inevitably to the failure of the relationship by making it ever harder for the individual to express experiences verbally.

Twenty-nine

Sexuality and Encounter

The innkeeper disapproves of the bond that is arising between K. and Frieda. Gardena tries to protect Frieda from a man she considers unsuitable, a foreigner who doesn't love her and is only using their relationship in order to reach the Castle. In the long conversation between the land surveyor and Gardena, this new personage takes shape who embodies many of Kafka's fears concerning the feminine.

One can connect the name Gardena with the German terms *Garde* and *Gardist,* which mean the guard. French, too, has similar words: *garde* or the guard, and *garder* or to guard, to have custody and thus to detain, maintain, conserve. Gardena seems to be the one who detains, conserves, and bars access to something. If we join these different meanings to the psychological features of the character, we become aware that she is a personification of the Great Mother archetype.

According to Neumann (1956, *passim*) the feminine presents an elementary character that tends to contain, to block the development of what she has borne as well as a transforming character that impels to movement and change. The work of the innkeeper connects Gardena to the positive aspect of the feminine character. She is the one who receives and nourishes, the uterus that gives life. As soon as he arrives in the village, K. seeks shelter in her inn. But during the conversation with the land surveyor, the woman's agitating and terrible face is revealed. The hostess places herself like a barrier or a gate between K. and Klamm, appearing almost in the guise of a Castle guard.

If the Castle and its mysterious lord, Count Westwest, represent the west, sunset, death, this precociously aged woman who guards the entrance recalls the mythical Old Woman of the West. Setting in the west, the sun is immersed in the womb of the subterranean world, which devours it. In many myths the Old Woman of the West personifies the witchlike and voracious image of the Fearsome Mother. In Melanesia the guardian spirit is always a woman, a monster from the subterranean world who guards the entrance to the land of the dead (Neumann 1956, pp. 159–76). K.'s getting lost and arriving at the village can be considered a journey to the Underworld, a venturing into the world of shadows, of the images that populate the psyche.

The land surveyor has already encountered the first of the guards: the son of the gatekeeper, Schwarzer, the "black devil" who has barred his way. Gardena is the second of a long series of obstacles he will find along his way to the Castle. If Schwarzer, with his actor's face, is an image of the collective, an incarnation of the persona, the hostess of the inn seems instead to personify the frightening faces that the Mother archetype takes on in the masculine imagination. K. in some ways resembles the lost Snaporaz of Fellini's *City of Women* (1979).

Like the film, Kafka's novel seems to be a long gallery of female characters, each one different from the other, all of them enigmatic, ineffable, and as allusive as a metaphor. Frieda, Pepi, Olga, Amalia, Gardena, the hostess of the *Herrenhof,* the mysterious woman nursing a child, the mother of Hans Brunswick, and Gisa, the schoolmistress, can all be read as a journey through the myths and obsessions of the male imagination. For the fifty-year-old Snaporaz as for the land surveyor, the feminine is always otherness, difference, ungraspable. It is a foreign sphere with which there can be no communication, no encounter, except perhaps for very brief moments. All relationships, all attempts at dialogue only end in emphasizing this hiatus. Both men are curious, fascinated, but above all frightened by the feminine sphere.

Both Snaporaz and K. fail to succeed in recognizing their own feminine aspects which, constantly set at a distance by projection, change into an accelerating, menacing fantasy. Gardena represents the voracious aspect of the unconscious — even though this side of her is mitigated by her role as a provider of nourishment. She marks the limits of the underworld. Gardena's presence seems to protect against the irruption of other more dangerous "mother" phantoms, even more devastating and fatal. It is possible to say of her what Kafka wrote in a story (1971, p. 207) apropos of the tomb of the great ancestor:

> For my family this tomb represents the frontier between the Human and the Other, and it's on this frontier that I wish to post a guard.

The tomb is one of the elementary negative characteristics of the feminine. Gardena can be considered a *container* who changes into a tomb at the end. She is a custodian of the order and the tradition that has always regulated the life of the village. There is no change or development in her. Acceptance of the norm is incarnated in her person. Gardena represents an eternal principle, always the same and unchanging. In trying to keep K. and Frieda with her, she defends the status quo. If K. let himself be stopped by her arguments and accepted a quiet life without questions, he would, in reality, become the victim of a *uroboric sphere.* By prohibiting him from making contact with Klamm, Gardena wants to keep him from escaping from symbiosis, of gaining access to the Father, to the Law. The constant questioning of himself, the attempt to meet Klamm, to be received by the Castle, can all be interpreted as K.'s effort to differentiate his own identity.

In her second conversation with K., Gardena allows another glimpse of the strange world to which she belongs. There seems to be a total lack of contact between the lords of the Castle and the villagers. Their relations are regulated by a cold and complicated corpus of bureaucratic norms. To some degree this distance is reduced by the sexual relations the officials have with the women of the village. The common feature of these encounters is that they take place whenever a call is received from one of the officials. Characteristic of them all is their distinct asymmetry, the lord–slave situation, in which the power exercised over the partner replaces all spontaneity, all chances for dialogue. Reciprocity seems to be unthinkable. Thus sex is the only way of filling the immense gap between the partners.

If, at first sight, it might seem that the only thing happening is a coerced gratification of a need, when one looks closer one sees that the urgently important function of sex is to make contact. The body has a primal role in our evolution. It is body language that establishes the syntax of the relationship. The flesh patently predominates over the word from birth to death, unchangingly, in every fundamental experience, because it refers back to the primal sphere, the world of the Mother. To choose body language means to go to the roots of existence. If we suppose that the particular type of relationship connecting the village women with the officials is based on a disturbance that leads to the erecting of a "castle," a barrier of distance, a narcissistic closure between oneself and one's partner, then what means can be considered the most appropriate for encountering otherness than a return to the origin of the defect, to the origin of every form of relationship?

A therapeutic encounter with another individual — especially if he is a psychotic or borderline case — is the best of all situations for verifying the importance and the reality of this problem. There is in fact an area of the personality that cannot be reached with words, with pure and simple interpretations. Only the real presence of the therapist, his sharing of the patient's experience, his warmth and capacity for making contact, synthesized at times in the simple and essential language of the body, in the tender gesture of a caress, for example, can manage to reach the other's suffering and drive out the pain, as if it were a frightened animal that blows and wounds had forced to hide deep in its den.

Balint (1968, p. 22) calls this area of suffering the *original defect.* What the patient perceives in this case is not, in fact, a conflict or a complex, but precisely a "defect," a lack to be made good. It is something that is missing due to the discrepancy between the infant's biopsychic needs and the material and emotional care that the mother gives.

Overturning all the more obvious interpretations, the call takes on a value that goes beyond that of exploiting the partner sexually, bending her to the mechanical satisfaction of physiological needs, and instead becomes a request, a call for help, the spasmodic and unconscious desire for communication.

If the Other is powerful and tremendously agitating because of his mysteriousness, his aloofness and inaccessibility, one must meet him in a situation which allows one to some degree, in an asymmetrical relationship, to keep up the illusion of one's own strength, one's possibilities of dominating and controlling what is happening.

The attempt to make contact with the Other, to throw a bridge across to otherness, is proclaimed and denied at once in the rigid ritual that regulates the erotic encounter. The body appears to conceal and reveal the secrets of the soul. Everything which has been said through caresses, revealed through erotic agitation, through the frenzy and tenderness by which the flesh of the other is possessed, is immediately afterward denied, shrouded again in silence, in secrecy, by the ending of the act. The bodies dress themselves again while the souls revert to their defenses. In such a context the word is impossible. The word is dialogue, permanence, a declared statement, the desire for understanding. Even in its ambiguity, in its possibilities for deceit, it is a translation of the inexpressible, it is—when it is authentic—the admissions of one's wounds, one's limitations, one's fears and desires. The inability of the officials to enter into a relationship is expressed by their limited way of making love. The relationship with the other is connected to meeting an infantile need, without being able to evolve toward new, more mature forms of encounter in which there is room for reciprocity.

It is interesting at this point to understand why the village women submit to such an affectionless kind of relationship and are even proud of it, as Gardena demonstrates when, full of nostalgia, she shows K. the souvenirs of her short-lived relationship with Klamm.

These young women resemble O, the much-discussed heroine of Pauline Reage's novel (1954). O allows her lover to conduct her to Roissy Castle where, for his sake, she performs any erotic acts that the lords and their pages ask of her. Her body no longer belongs to her and becomes the property of others. Branded like an animal, she is sold to another man, but emotionally she remains faithful to the one whose slave she had become. Pleasure originates and is fed in her by subjection, by being for others a purely sexual object, a tool for pleasure.

Many women who go into analysis present the same dramatic inner situation, of which, at the beginning, they are often unaware. In many of these cases I have seen how the alienation from one's own body, from one's own sexuality, which is lived passively and only to please one's partner, hides a deep and extremely remote fracture between feeling and sexuality. One of the causes of this estrangement from one's body is often to be found in seductive behavior on the part of the parents toward the child. By exciting sexuality this behavior creates a conflict between the need of satisfaction and the ego's prohi-

319

bition of incest. Searles (1965b, pp. 245–46) maintains that to excite sexuality in a situation where it would be dangerous for the ego to satisfy it is one way to drive the other mad.

It is not entirely irrelevant that very many schizoid or borderline patients have gone through such a situation in their childhood. Genital immaturity keeps the child from entirely understanding what is happening to her. She instinctively feels the situation to be prohibited and responds to it by freezing her body, abandoning it, not allowing herself to feel. The emotional tie to the seducing parent, the fear of losing his or her love if she should ever reveal her incestuous secret, and above all the fear of going mad, of not being believed or of being held responsible for what happened, all impel her to keep silent. In some cases she will continue to keep the memory of what happened, a memory isolated from the feelings experienced at the time.

Parents who are seductive in a subtle way are not aware of the sexual meaning of their actions. They rationalize their behavior, thinking of it as a series of affectionate gestures. But the child clearly perceives the sexual implications. The parent's unawareness, his acting as if the situation were entirely normal, damages the child's critical capacity and makes her feel mad in fact. These parents exploit the child's need of warmth and intimacy to get from the situation an unconscious sexual excitement which they need all the more intensely, the more their partner — husband or wife — withdraws from sexual intimacy.

A seductive parent is also a rejecting parent. To use the body of one's child for sexual excitement is a violation of his privacy, but above all it is a rejection of him, a negation of him as an independent being. In general such parents are afraid or embarrassed to cuddle their children. They are afraid of an intimacy that makes them feel guilty. The child, left alone with his sensations and fears, reacts more often than not by excessive attachment to the seductive parent whose love he feels the need to secure (Lowen 1967, pp. 94–95). It will take years of analysis before one is able to reveal the "secret" without being suffocated by a sense of guilt or the fear of being mad and, above all, to escape from the incestuous spiral. That original sexual submission, in fact, spoils future relations and coerces us to repeat the learned model of behavior. Sexuality remains a foreign emotion, prohibited, that can only be experienced by letting the other possess one and reliving the old complicity.

The call of the officials is, in reality, an "inner call." If Klamm is a sort of priapic divinity, an Eros, with whom one must form a relationship in order to enter deeply into desire, then his is an invitation to make contact with everything that disturbs and frightens: violence, seduction, dependence, and inaccessibility. The context in which such a confrontation takes place assumes a particular importance. The absence of the officials, their withdrawal from the relationship, ought to compel the women, who have remained alone with their fantasies, to give their attention to the inner *daimon* that possesses them.

From a psychological viewpoint this absence can be brought close to the emotional distance of a parent for whom one is disposed to do anything to ensure the primary need of protection and attachment. But the absence of the parent figure, just like her seductive behavior, can block one's capacity to withdraw from the incestuous tie and change the choice of object. In order to truly unite with the village men, to be their companions, the women ought to abandon the Oedipal object. But one cannot abandon something one has never possessed. The unconscious conjunction with a substitute father must continue until it becomes possible to introject his image. Those who, like Gardena, lose this relationship precociously without being ready for the separation and so for a new, more mature love, seem deeply unhappy, resigned, spent. Klamm's rejection causes the hostess of the inn to grow prematurely old, almost as if the powerful official contained in himself the vital principle, the essence of love.

Being, like all the other officials, an animus figure, he represents that part of the self with which one must make contact in order to reach greater psychic integration. But the women of the village — except for Frieda who manages to leave the father/lover — indicate their inability to recognize and integrate the violence of their desire, the intensity of their sexual experiences, because they remain tied to a relationship of subordination, perceived as oppression, as a law without appeal, like the old *ius primae noctis*. Projected onto the officials, these desires remain cut off from the rest of the personality. In order to live their sexuality they need to be in a subordinate position in which they appear to be without responsibility.

The need to remain in contact with the other, obscure object of desire is shown by Klamm's gifts, which Gardena jealously preserves and proudly shows to the land surveyor. Like all human beings, Gardena needs to feel loved and remembered, or at least to have the illusion of so being. Barthes (1977, p. 75) acutely notes the importance of gifts. A gift is a sensual tool of contact, a kind of third skin that unites lovers. Through this object one gives oneself totally to the other, inasmuch as on an imaginary level one has transferred all of one's being to the gift.

As for Frieda, for K. too the encounter with the other represents an important stage in psychological development. If Frieda with the land surveyor opens herself up to human relations, the latter who—as the novel allows us to guess—has had other feelings, other encounters, sees the little barmaid as offering him a new, regenerating love, a sentiment that will make up for his past and which will allow him to transform his personality. For both of them the relationship has all the flavor of a search.

Each encounter is born of a deep desire, of a search that is part of human nature, a search, however, that reveals itself to be inexhaustible. At the moment in which a human being feels psychologically disposed to fall in love, to encounter someone who can satisfy his most secret needs, he doesn't really have any precise idea of what he is looking for, what object he has in mind. He is only aware of wanting to share his life with another person. He expects this new encounter to fill his soul, his need of loving and being loved. He goes in search of love without really knowing what it is. Perhaps it is the very impossibility of completely fulfilling his desire, making the reality correspond to the dream, that permits the constant deepening of the relations that are established, opening up ever-new dimensions, new knowledge of oneself and the other. No relationship is ever capable of offering that fullness which, once possessed, would be capable of challenging the darkness of existence, conquering every danger, completing, in a word, the human being and compensating for his lacks.

One of the essential characteristics of a relationship is the attempt to take possession of something. To love is almost to rob the beloved of that *something* which she possess and which we need in order to feel complete. What compels us to the search for the other is always a feeling of something missing, something fundamental which we lack, which was taken from us in the past — or which perhaps we never had — and which now we must regain at all costs. It is this sensation that creates the first asymmetry between the one who loves and the one who is loved. By virtue of this mysterious property the beloved is incredibly powerful in the eyes of the lover.

In describing the encounter between K. and Frieda, Kafka uses an extremely significant metaphor. The intercourse of the two lovers is described as similar to a dog scraping and digging in the ground for food. On a psychological level, to look for a relationship is, in fact, the same as to go in search of food. The other is food which we must have in order to live. It is no accident that the hunger artist (Kafka 1971) lets himself die of starvation because he never found the food he was looking for. Solitude, the impossibility of a relationship, the lack of success in finding that love to which one aspired, all force the soul to hunger. At the bottom of this inability we always find the fear of facing the inevitable turmoil that every new relationship generates, and above all to recognize the dark and disquieting ground of the soul: the Shadow.

To love someone desperately means to have found in this other the food one had gone in search of. To be loved corresponds, in fact, to the uniqueness of one's desire. Nevertheless, since the lover himself has shaped the reality of the beloved, he finds he is confronted with himself. And this identity between the beloved and the lover is what creates a secret complicity between the two that makes it possible for the lover to perform the most criminal acts, to transgress any principle and forget the previous vows of fidelity. Those who love are capable of surmounting any difficulty, and despite this of continuing to love.

Frieda's love for K. induces her to bear all trials. She remains alone while the land surveyor goes to visit Barnabas' sisters; she works for him, seems almost to age prematurely, worn out by the burden of her doubts, her jealousy, the unbearable silence of the solitude to which she is abandoned. In giving herself to the beloved man she renounces herself, seems to annul herself, forget her own being, so that only her beloved's being can emerge. Frieda, like many women, has become only "food," she has identified herself with nourishment. It would seem that in the violence of her passion she can only accept to exist for the other and not for herself any longer.

If Frieda annuls herself, K. experiences the relationship as expropriation, as the need of repeatedly nourishing himself, almost devouring the beloved. Thus we can understand Frieda's fears, fears generated by the very violence of her feelings. Kafka imagines the woman kissing her lover with great passion, almost savagely. It is the intensity of her rapture that makes her fear falling into a condition of total dependence. The secret glue binding the union of many couples is the hooking up of two complementary pathologies. While one of the partners lives the relationship in such a way that his companion feeds on him entirely and until he is totally emptied or the relationship ends, the other is on the lookout for strong types, apparent winners, but whose characteristic psychology is to let themselves be dried out. This kind of asymmetry, in which the giving and taking do not balance out at all, seems to be the one behind K. and Frieda's relationship, which leads it to inevitable failure.

Thirty

The Struggle for Life

The Castle is an unfinished novel that was interrupted two years before Kafka's death. Its images can be read as a kind of spiritual testament. Baioni (1962, p. 244) in fact considers the land surveyor to be the final stage in the writer's moral progress. From the moment of the expulsion and condemnation that characterizes the affair of Josef K.-Kafka in *The Trial,* we reach that perennial situation of "arriving at reality," the summation of the writer's human and artistic pilgrimage. K. is in the condition of someone who finally finds himself at the gateway of truth but cannot pass the threshold. After much questioning, after much wandering, he seems to see—like Moses—his goal from afar, his land of Canaan. At this point the enigma of noncompletion breaks in. If the genesis of many of Kafka's works appears conflictual to the point that many are left unfinished and others are only fragmentary, if Kafka himself wanted his works to be burned at his death, if Kafka's writing presents itself as a continuous interrupting and taking up again, the attentive reader will find an incomplete text posing questions for him. In reality, every text, even when unfinished, carries its ending within itself. Kafka was very well aware of this fact, since he noted in his diary:

> However, one should not forget that the story, if it has any justifica-
> tion to exist, bears its complete organization within itself even before
> it has been fully formed. (Kafka 1910–1923, p. 322)

Writing is an activity that has to do with the interminable, the incessant (Blanchot 1955, p. 12). There is a moment in the composition of a work when it seems to exclude its author, to put her aside. It is not fatigue or the setting in of a form of sterility that blocks progress. A work is completed when the artist is no longer detained by it, chained to it, by the imaginary contents, by that part of himself from which he can now feel liberated, since the creative work has contributed to exorcising the demon (Blanchot 1955, pp. 30–40). He is excluded from the work because he can no longer feed it with his inner world. *The Castle* is a work of seeking, of questioning, of a call. Kafka seems to be taking hold of a thread of hope which in the end is brutally snapped off. In his diaries he described his life as a hesitation before birth. With this work, as with his others, he tried to give form to that birth, to the soul's efforts to discover a path. Only by means of literature could Kafka get a grip on existence. A short phrase that he wrote down in July 1914 (Kafka 1910–1923, p. 300) contains the sense of his life: "But I will write in spite of everything, absolutely; it is my struggle for self-preservation."

Writing was supposed to save him from madness, from the disintegration of his soul. Kafka knew he was an outsider, an exile, a person who was lost in this world and who had to find a living space in which to take refuge: this space was narrative writing. The discovery that he didn't know how to live, either by himself or with others, constantly tormented him and always more. That feeling of guilt which appears obsessively in all his writings was a guilt originating in his own nature: the knowledge that he didn't know how to live.

> We are sinners not only because we have tasted of the tree of science, but because we have not yet tasted of the tree of life. Ours is a sinful condition, and that quite apart from any guilt. (Kafka 1954, p. 732)

Like many of Dostoyevski's personages, whom he well knew, such as the underground man, Kafka was a dreamer, an individual lost in his world of fantasy, incapable of action, of actively changing his life. The only space left to him was that of dreams, of inner life.

> My talent for portraying my dreamlike inner life has thrust all other matters into the background; my life has dwindled dreadfully, nor will it cease to dwindle. Nothing else will ever satisfy me. (Kafka 1910–1923, p. 302)

Possibly he hoped to construct a new personality by means of his dream world, but this hope was destroyed by the progressive worsening of the disease that was to kill him. Like the land surveyor, from the very beginning he was excluded from salvation as represented by the mythical Castle. Both K. and Kafka are exiles because they have relegated their feelings to the sphere of exile. More than outsiders to the world, they were foreign to themselves. That desolate and snowy land in which K. finds himself wandering at the beginning of the novel is a region lacking in intimacy, in contact, in warmth, and in which everything one imagines one is about to grasp immediately vanishes (Blanchot 1955, p. 60).

Let us try to imagine the suffering of a person who feels his life to be a continuous hesitation, an attempt that is never realized. Kafka found himself facing a reality that he could not recognize, that he had no categories for recognizing and possessing. The world belonged to the others; for him there was only a little corner, the corner consisting of his diaries and his writings, where he took refuge to watch pulsating life. When one loses the possibility of conquering the world, of living like others, of creating a space for oneself that one thinks one deserves because in some way one must have been destined for it, then the sphere of imagination and the spirit become preponderant. Then the only way of surviving is linked to this dream space and the constant narration of the stories of the soul. The tool of art is used to find a way to reduce hesitation, an answer that can give one the courage to face existence. It is possible that the creative individual cannot manage to adapt herself to a collective solution. She does not see reality in the same way that others do. She knows a truth of her own, a deeper truth, to which she must remain faithful. The price of this fidelity is often that of withdrawing to her private space where her own needs, her own imaginings can find an abode. Kafka knew he had to remain faithful to himself, but in this effort he lacked the courage to carry his truth to the outside world, into daily life.

In his works this personal truth appears as a kind of guilt, and as such it cannot be proclaimed out loud but only whispered obliquely through his work. He remained locked up in that inner world, in everything he had glimpsed there and described so acutely. In the writer the confrontation with the pain of existence was cut off from its working out. Suffering is not transformed and purified within the ambit of a renewed personality, and it only remains blind invocation, incessant testimony. Thus one understands the reason why this last novel was left unfinished. The daimons Kafka had tried to exorcise by writing had been stronger than he was. He could not reach the end of the road that he, like K., had begun to travel. In one of his last letters to Milena he wrote (1920–1923, pp. 228–229):

> It's a long time since I wrote to you, Frau Milena, and even today I'm writing only as the result of an incident. Actually, I don't have to apologize for my not writing, you know after all how I hate letters. All the misfortune of my life — I don't wish to complain, but to make a generally instructive remark — derives, one could say, from letters or from the possibility of writing letters. People have hardly ever deceived me, but letters always — and as a matter of fact not only those of other people, but my own. In my case this is a special misfortune of which I won't say more, but at the same time also a general one. The easy possibility of letter-writing must — seen merely theoretically — have brought into the world a terrible disintegration of souls. It is, in fact, an intercourse with ghosts, and not only with the ghost of the recipient but also with one's own ghost which develops between the lines of the letter one is writing and even more so in a series of letters where one letter corroborates the other and can refer to it as a witness. How on earth did anyone get the idea that people can communicate with one another by letter! Of a distant person one can think, and of a person who is near one can catch hold — all else goes beyond human strength. Writing letters, however, means to denude oneself before the ghosts, something for which they greedily wait. Written kisses don't reach their destination, rather they are drunk on the way by the ghosts. It is on this ample nourishment that they multiply so enormously. Humanity senses this and fights against it and in order to eliminate as far as possible the ghostly element between people and to create a natural communication, the peace of souls, it has invented the railway, the motor car, the aeroplane. But it's no longer any good, these are evidently inventions being made at the moment of crashing. The opposing side is so much calmer and stronger; after the postal service it has invented the telegraph, the telephone, the radiograph. The ghosts won't starve, but we will perish.

One of the keys we have used for reading *The Castle* was that of the relationship. The Castle is the world of the Other, which must be understood and approached if one is to escape from exclusion, isolation, and a sense given to life. K.'s attempts, which proceed parallel to his love story with Frieda, reflect the desire for a relationship, for contact. Kafka did not know how to enter into a relationship. Therefore the hero of his novel can only remain excluded from the Castle. We find ourselves before an insuperable gap that separates us from the other, emphasizing his absence. Frieda abandons K., thus sanctioning the failure of the relationship. The specter of abandonment presented itself constantly to Kafka, inducing him to write to Milena:

> If it's at all possible in this unstable world (where, if one is swept away one is simply swept away and can't help it) — don't let yourself be frightened away from me, even if I disappoint you once or a thousand times or just now or perhaps always just now. (Kafka 1920–1923, pp. 181–182)

Frieda's betrayal leaves K. in a lost condition like the one at the beginning. The land surveyor is alone again, without work, without a house. The relationship with this woman was experienced by him as a return to the climate of first trust and acceptance from which this betrayal now excludes him. K.'s attitude, and his way of understanding a relationship are still immature and infantile. To love in a relationship that excludes the possibility of being abandoned, of being betrayed, is to love in an incomplete way that leaves no room for the Shadow aspect of the personality. In these cases what one desires is not only to be contained in the Other, who can never lie, betray, or desert, whose absolute goodness and perfection makes of her a divine being — and thus something totally unreal — but it also and mostly means being protected from one's own ambivalence, one's own possibilities of deserting and betraying (Hillman 1964, p. 63, *passim*).

Frieda's betrayal is an important test of reality for K. It is as if by way of the pain the land surveyor ought to learn another way of entering into a relationship, different from the fusional type. One proof of fusion is that the love object is asked to proffer a constant presence, since his absence generates a sense of emptiness and of loss, the same sensations that K. had on his arrival in the village. If K. wants Frieda to love him in silence, to be always at his side no matter what he does and without ever asking any questions, the girl also seems to ask her man for a presence capable of warming her and filling her life. But the demands of the land surveyor seem to be distinctly disproportionate to his capacity for offering himself to the woman. K. seems to be asking her to be present in each and every situation, to accept his comings and goings, to understand his difficulties and problems, without her receiving an emotional equivalent, to the point that Frieda in explaining to him the reasons for their separation, murmurs in a heartfelt way:

> "Oh, how much I need your companionship, how lost I have felt without it ever since I've known you, to have your company, believe me, is the only dream that I've had, that and nothing else." (Kafka 1922b, p. 237).

Neither the land surveyor nor Kafka seems capable of giving heed to the needs of the partner and caring about her. A narcissistic personality is often incapable of recognizing and accepting the other. The ideal relationship that Kafka continues to long for in the form of his fictional characters is one of total fusion; but he ends by withdrawing from it in fright since to be so absorbed means to do away with borders and thus result in reciprocal destruction.

> I can't think of any greater happiness than to be with you all the time, without interruption, endlessly, even though I feel that here in this world there's no undisturbed place for our love, neither in the village nor anywhere else; and I dream of a grave, deep and narrow, where we could clasp each other in our arms as with iron bars, and I would hide my face in you and would hide your face in me, and nobody would ever see us any more. (Kafka 1922b, p. 134)

The end of a relationship is always a critical moment in which one imagines one is dying. The absence and the loss of the one we love creates so great a vacuum that it is as if we had been totally deprived of our souls. What is left over is an empty shell, only the outline of what had once been our personality. If the other, in seducing us, in making us fall in love, has robbed us of our soul, now in leaving us he seems to have made this theft final. We have the impression that it is no longer possible to join up again with ourselves without the arms of the beloved. We feel completely estranged from ourselves. We feel as if we no longer know who we are.

Nothing around us makes sense anymore. But to feel so annihilated, the relationship must have reached so deep a level that the beloved is truly unique, irreplaceable, and therefore necessary for life. From the time that Frieda leaves him, the land surveyor will not manage to proceed along the road to the Castle.

Thirty-one

The Guilty Messiah

K. is the man who finds law in wandering, the man "of dissatisfied and altered will, who always passes beyond the goal and always tends to go further" (Blanchot 1954, p. 114). How else can one interpret his renunciation of any possible result, any possible arrangement, which renders his journey void of any final and definitive goal? The myth of the wanderer is perhaps the most universal of all myths. It expresses something more than the simple circularity of a journey. Wandering in itself, the moving around in time and space, evokes the nature of existence itself, whose point of departure is almost lost to memory while the destination is scarcely known. But the adventures of the hero, his wanderings, carry within them another myth equally rooted in all cultures: that of the *test*, which Josef K. represents in exemplary fashion (Fisch 1984, p. 13). Like the bank clerk Josef K., the land surveyor too "is a hero of seeking" (Fisch 1984, p. 13).

In his story — as in that of Ulysses — the archetype of wandering and that of being tested are continually interwoven; each refers to the other and cannot exist without the other. But for K. these myths refer to a continuous inner wandering, to the *voyage of the soul* and its trials. In *Hadrian's Memories* (Yourcenar 1951, p. 111), the Roman emperor calls himself "a Ulysses with no external Ithaca." Similarly, the life of the land surveyor seems to be a constant search for the island in which it will finally be possible to return to oneself. The outsider, the exile, the excluded K. has no fatherland, can never cease wandering, because this inner horizon — the horizon of an absolutely personal K. truth — is never definitely reached.

K. is obliged to choose this impossible road because right from the start he was excluded from taking "all possible ones." He cannot take the normal roads used by others because he has been banned from the world, exiled from himself, condemned forever to the absence of any certainty, relegated to a place where there can never be a true and stable sojourn (Blanchot 1954, p. 115). Kafka's world seems to be under a spell that keeps the subject exiled from himself as well as from grasping anything that is different from himself (Adorno 1942–1953). It is the tragedy of a way of being different, of a solitude, that cannot accept the encounter or the relationship.

Since he is a solitary hero, K. must proceed on his course toward the Castle. Marked by the excess of his desire, by not being able to accept partial answers, he appears to be affected by a romantic passion for the absolute. That constant going too far which makes him neglect all offers is the clear sign of his dissatisfaction that originates in the discrepancy between what reality presents him with and that secret hope, that private dream that no concrete promise can fulfill. His sin is one of hubris. K. is an unquiet man, deeply different from the Josef K. of *The Trial* who, in his indifference, in the apathy of his tranquil bourgeois life, never notices his alienation until the moment of his arrest, and whose final condemnation is nothing but the official ratification of his death of the soul.

From the beginning, K. chooses, abandons his placid daily life, and opens himself to the unknown, to the *call*, in the hope of a renewal and rebirth. If, because of an inscrutable decision of destiny, he is excluded from the land of Canaan, that does not mean that he loses the nostalgia for a possible paradise, that does not mean that he is going to give up his search. Perhaps it is the torment of the knowledge that this place is inaccessible — like the "island that isn't" in Peter Pan — and his desire to reach it that makes his actions tragic. Faced with such a dream, no comfortable compromise is possible.

Many interpretations of Kafka's writings have emphasized the sense of failure that weighs on all his characters: K. does not manage to reach the Castle, Josef K.'s throat is cut, Josephine the singer loses her voice, the dog finds no answer to his questions, the hunger artist dies and a panther replaces him in the cage where he made a spectacle of fasting. Success and lack of success are not two opposing, unrelated factors, however, but rather the two poles of a continuum. Failure does not only mean annulment and the destruction of prospects, because in fully experiencing this sphere of defeat and death, the psyche may reemerge from the wreckage.

Alchemy describes the phases of *dissolutio*, *mortificatio*, and *putrefactio*, through which matter must pass before the *lapis* is formed. The soul must go through destruction and descend to the underworld before rebirth is allowed. We might consider failure not so much as a blockage in the flow of vital energy but as a "desired" condition "caused" by our unconscious, by that underworld which has need of failure to allow for recognition and the activating of a new attitude profoundly different from the preceding one; a new attitude governed by another *daimon* (Hillman 1971c, p. 98, *passim*).

If we analyze Kafka's works attentively, there where others find only death and failure, we might see the germs of a renewal. As Christian Godden points out (1977, p. 107), the fact that the land surveyor falls asleep during the conversation with Buergel in a crucial moment when important facts are being revealed to him, or the granting of a residence permit — in Brod's version — only at the moment of death, does not negate the possibility that K. or a future K. may one day have a better life: that is, they may, after having gone through failure, enter a phase of profound renewal. It is no accident that little Hans Brunswick, who is entrusted with representing that possibility of renewal, declares that he wants to become a man like K. The novel's narrator comments:

> Had engendered in him the belief that though for the moment K. was wretched and looked down on, yet in an almost unimaginable and distant future he would excel everybody. And it was just this absurdly distant future and the glorious developments which were to lead up to it that attracted Hans; that was why he was willing to accept K. even in his present state. The peculiar childish grown-up acuteness of this wish consisted in the fact that Hans looked on K. as on a younger brother whose future would reach further than his own, the future of a very little boy. (Kafka 1922b, p. 144)

The episode of Hans Brunwick plays a fundamental role in the novel, despite its frequently being passed over unnoticed. It is Hans, the child, who represents K.'s hopes, the possibility of rebirth. Hans Brunswick is no exception to the secret logic of meanings in the names of Kafka's characters. An old Czech legend tells of a brave and just sovereign: the King of Brunswick, the hero of a thousand adventures, who will reawaken from the sleep of death in a day of peril when his country will have need of him. In the imagination of the people of Prague, he is the mythical savior whose magic sword can put to flight any enemy.

The figure of the young boy, according to Jung (1940, p. 157), is an archetype who appears in all cultures to indicate a "potential" future, the anticipation of a future development. On a psychological level the appearance of the young boy in dreams and fantasies is the forecast of a personality change. He anticipates the forms that the process of individuation will take by way of a synthesis of the conscious elements of the personality, offering himself as a unifying symbol of the opposites, an "author of totality" (Jung 1940, p. 158). As in the image of the *self*, the young boy seems to express the vital impulse of self-realization. But the child is also the image of a particular psychic condition marked by regression: it is the return to our psychological matrix, to the situation of vulnerability and dependence that distinguishes the beginning of every human being's life. Its appearance on the imaginary level expresses a pressing need to return to our beginnings.

If within K.-Kafka's psychological matrix there is the inability to make contact with one's own soul, with the complex and subtle world of the emotions that appears to be immersed in chaos, to be undifferentiated: and if this condition of nonrelationship with the unconscious, reflected in the relations with the other, is due to a deficit, to a wound inflicted during the primal relationship, the possibility of curing it must go through a return to infancy. In fact, that which returns, points ahead to the goal of finding a solution to one's sufferings, to one's "psychic disorder" (Hillman 1971a, p. 21).

The help that little Hans offers the land surveyor, a help that also includes the possibility of an interview with Frau Brunswick, the incarnation of the Mother archetype, concerns the leading function that the return to childhood has in the process of personality growth and integration. This is perhaps the meaning one can give to the famous evangelical admonition: "Unless you become as little children, you shall not enter the Kingdom of God" (Luke 19:17). But the presense of the child does not only mean growth, development, unlimited expansion, and perfect integration, which annuls the psychic disorder. If the child constitutes a psychic state, then the path he indicates also requires the acceptance, the taking in of our infantile aspects, directed toward an existential model that does not refer to mythical supermen, but to those personalities who have recognized and not denied their fragmentation, their vulnerability.

The end of the novel appears to allude to this return to origins, to the mother. *The Castle* breaks off at the moment in which Gerstaecker, the cart driver, takes K. to his house after having offered him a new job taking care of the horses. In the hut, dimly lit by the fire in the hearth and the light of a candle, Gerstaecker's old mother offers K. a trembling hand and speaks to him in a weak voice. This scene evokes K.'s arrival at the *inn by the bridge*, his need of a refuge, his falling asleep beside the stove. In both cases a maternal, almost womblike ambience is evoked. Whereas at the beginning this refuge is denied to the land surveyor, who is consigned to the servant's room, the last place in which K. is given shelter seems to offer a more permanent refuge.

This warm and hospitable atmosphere, which seems to be a place of warmth and consolation like the maternal bosom, recalls a famous scene of Ingmar Bergman's *Cries and Whispers* (1972). In the film one sees the prosperous servant girl who tenderly holds the dead woman in her arms. While her two sisters, terrified by the dying woman's request for affection, deny her this last consolation and flee in fright when she tries to grasp their hands, the servant girl is the only one who is not afraid. The girl even offers her breast. The maternal aspect of the feminine shows itself by offering refuge even in the face of death. From a psychological point of view, this scene seems to allude to a capacity for acceptance and understanding that is not lacking even in the presence of the most terrible and desperate of conditions: death is exorcised by love.

The final welcome given to K. also contains a reassuring element that ought to nourish the land surveyor and allow him to revive. It would be extremely interesting to know what it is that the maternal-feminine represented by the old lady says to K. The murmured words of the woman which the land surveyor is only barely able to hear and does not clearly understand, perhaps may be considered the last message he receives from the unconscious. If K. only manages with considerable difficulty to make contact with the Mother, the interruption of this tete-a-tete has a meaning analogous to the breaking off of his relations with Milena, who represented for him the possibility of opening up to the unconscious, to the feminine and maternal sphere. In both cases we find ourselves confronting the inability to give heed to one's own inner voice, almost as if the defensive shell smothered the voice to the point of its being inaudible.

The entire development of the novel is already contained in its title. *Das Schloss* in German has a meaning similar to the Latin *castellum*, indicating a "closed space." The fact that German also attributes the meaning of a lock to the term makes us think of a a well-guarded inner space, in a castle of defenses, of a "lock" in fact, which can in no way be opened. The drama of *The Castle* regards a closure, an impenetrability, that cannot be overcome. The closing up of the Self is the closing up of the Other, since anyone who makes himself inaccesible is blocking all roads of encounter with otherness. Significant in this respect is the fact that the story of the emperor's message that can never reach the least of his subjects is contained within another story, that of the Great Wall (Kafka 1971), which from time immemorial the Chinese have been trying to erect along the entire border of the empire to protect themselves from the attacks of the barbarians. *Das Schloss* is the desperate metaphor of a closing up that alienates the individual from himself as well as from others, the metaphor of a solitude does not manage to be overcome.

The novel seems to develop entirely along the line of an opposition, a polarity already contained in words. On the one hand we have *Das Schloss*, the fortress cum lock, and on the other the land surveyor cum messiah. The profession of the hero, in fact, represents a compromise between two Hebrew words: *mashoah*, or land surveyor, and *mashiah*, or messiah (Robertson 1985, p. 228). Kafka, who was well acquainted with the messianic tradition, makes of his hero a kind of messiah, a liberator, on whom the destiny of the village depends, and, in particular, that of the women who turn to him with their hopes, as Pepi confides to K. in their last conversation. The same conception that Hans has of K., according to Robertson (1985, p. 234), alludes to the prophesied coming of the Messiah that has played such a great part in Jewish culture.

But it is a particular messiah to whom Kafka alludes: *The Guilty Messiah* (Baioni 1984, p. 279). One branch of Jewish mysticism sees salvation as being possible only by way of this savior, who takes on himself the destiny of all the guilty, who operates as an apostate, offends the laws of the community, but who for this very reason has the privilege of descending into the realm of the impure to liberate the sparks of the Shekhinah, divine knowledge, from the prison to which it is has been exiled. And yet this messianic hope at times seems to shatter against a wall of absurdity.

The fact of their all being outsiders provides a secret resemblance linking the guilty Messiah of the Jewish tradition, the land surveyor K., and the writer Kafka. For these last two the search for the horizons of truth represents an attempt at redemption and purification. In Kafka's case this redemption takes place by way of the written word. If, as Kafka noted in his diaries (1910–1923, p. 399) on January 16, 1922, "All such writing is an assault on the frontiers," the aim of the writer should always be to go beyond these limits to bring the word back into the realm of the pure, the infinitely pure. But writing is also a withdrawal from life. In his search for truth, for an answer, by way of an inexhaustible series of questions, writing inserts a gap, a deep slash in life. Martin Buber believed he had rediscovered in the Hasidic spirit the basis of Jewish spirituality, thus furnishing the young German-Jewish intellectuals of Prague the fundamental texts for their formation. In Hasidism there is contained the fundamental affirmation of the unity of spirit and matter, of reason and instinct. Buber drew upon a religious vision that accepted the life of the senses as a manifestation of the divine, which is to be found in all things. "No action is preferred. God wishes to be served in *all* ways" (Buber 1955, p. 23). But Kafka does not seem to be able to overcome the fracture that separated him from the earth, from the flesh. The effort to raise himself to purity made him reject the opportunity for transcendence offered by Eros. Love, the erotic, the relationship, remained impure spheres for him. In his attempt to rediscover the profound spirituality of Eastern Judaism, he could not forget all the deep torments of Western Jews. A secularized spirit, perhaps ill with rationalism, is not capable of discovering the divine in things. As the Zarathustra of Nietzsche maintains (1883–1885, p. 6), to commit sacrilege against the earth, that, today, is the most horrible thing.

Forgetful of this, in his siege on the limits the writer does not manage to nourish his search, his thirst for the absolute with an earthly dimension. The fact that *The Castle* is unfinished thus reflects his impossibility of overcoming the torment, of finding a third way in which the search for the horizons of truth does not preclude and conceal those of love.

References

Adorno, T. 1942–1953. "Appunti su Kafka." In *Prismi*. Toronto: Einaudi, 1972.

Agamben, G. 1976. "La passione dell'indifferenza." In M. Proust, *L'indifferente*. Torino: Einaudi, 1987.

Alberoni, F. 1979. "Innamoramento e amore." In *Innamoramento e amore: Le ragioni del bene e del male*. Milano: Club degli Editori, 1982.

Andersen, H. C. *The Complete Illustrated Stories of Hans Christian Andersen*. London: Chancellor Press, 1990.

Apuleius. *L'asino d'oro*. Milano: Garzanti, 1982.

Arendt, H. 1944a. "Franz Kafka: il costruttore di modelli." In *Il Futuro alle spalle*. Bologna: Il Mulino, 1981.

⸺. 1944b. "Franz Kafka: l'uomo di buona volontà." In *Il futuro alle spalle*. Bologna: Il Mulino, 1981.

Argan, C. G. 1970. *L'arte moderna (1770–1970)*. Firenze: Sansoni, 1978.

Arieti, S., and Bemporad, J. 1978. *La depressione grave e lieve: L'orientamento psicoterapeutico*. Milano: Feltrinelli, 1987.

Aristophanes. "Le nuvole." In Acarnesi. *Le nuvole, Le vespe, Gli uccelli*. Milano: Garzanti, 1985 (*see* Loeb Classical Library).

Baioni, G. 1962. *Kafka: romanzo e parabola*. Milano: Feltrinelli, 1976.

⸺. *Kafka: letteratura e ebraismo*. Torino: Einaudi, 1984.

Balint, M. 1968. "The Area of the Basic Fault." In *The Basic Fault*. London: Tavistock Publications.

Barilli, R. 1982. *Comicità di Kafka, un'interpretazione sulle tracce del pensiero freudiano*. Milano: Bompiani.

Barthes, R. 1977. *A Lover's Discourse Fragments*. London: Jonathan Cape, 1979.

Basile, B. 1982. *La finestra socchiusa: Ricerche tematiche su Dostoevskij, Kafka, Moravia e Pavese*. Bologna: Pàtron Editore.

Baudelaire, C. 1861. "The Flowers of Evil." In *Selected Poems*. Harmondsworth, Middlesex: Penguin Books, 1986.

Baudrillard, J. 1979. *Della seduzione*. Bologna: Cappelli, 1985.

Beckett, S. 1952. *Waiting for Godot*. London and Boston: Faber and Faber, 1965.

Bemporad, J. 1978. "Franz Kafka: un prototipo del carattere depressive." In Arieti, S., Bemporad J. *La depressione grave e lieve: L'orientamento psicoterapeutico*. Milano: Feltrinelli, 1986.

Benedetti, G. "Introduzione a una psicoterapia della schizofrenia." In Benedetti, Corsi, Piacentini, D'Alfonso, Elia, Medri, Seviotti. *Paziente e analista nella terapia della psicosi*. Milano: Feltrinelli, 1979.

Benjamin, W. 1934. "Franz Kafka: Per il decimo anniversario della morte." In *Angelus Novus: Saggi e frammenti*. Torino: Einaudi, 1982.

Bernhard, E. *Mitobiografia*. Milano: Adelphi, 1969.

Bichsel, P. 1982. *Der Leser: Das Erzählen*. Darmstadt und Neuweid: Hermann Luchterhand Verlag.

Binder, H. *Der Schaffensprozess*. Frankfurt am Main: Suhrkamp Verlag, 1983.

Binswanger, L. 1956. *Drei Formen missglückten Daseins: Verstiegenheit, Verschrobenheit, Manieriertheit*. Tübingen: Max Niemeyer Verlag.

Blanchot, M. 1947, 1952. *De Kafka à Kafka*. Paris: Edition Gallimard, 1981.

_____. 1954. "Kafka e Brod." In *Da Kafka a Kafka*. Milano: Feltrinelli, 1983.

_____. 1955. *Lo spazio letterario*. Torino: Einaudi, 1975.

_____. 1969. *L'infinito intrattenimento*. Torino: Einaudi, 1977.

Blixen, K. 1952. "Out of Africa." In Dinesen, Isak. *Out of Africa and Shadow on the Grass*. New York: Vintage International, 1989.

Böhme, H. 1977. "Mother Milena: on Kafka's Narcissism." In *The Kafka Debate*. New York: Angles Flores.

Branca, R. 1971. *Il segreto di Grazia Deledda*. Cagliari: Editrice Sarda Fossataro.

Brancati, V. 1949. *Il bell'Antonio*. Milano: Einaudi, 1984.

Brod, M. 1937. *Franz Kafka*. Milano: Mondadori, 1956.

Buber, M. 1927. *Die Erzählungen der Chassidim*. Heidelberg: Lambert Schneider Verlag.

———. 1952. *Good and Evil*. New York: Charles Scribner's Sons, 1958.

———. 1955. *La leggenda del Baal-Shem*. Assisi-Roma: Carucci Editore, 1978.

Bucelli, D., and Fiorentino, M. 1988. "Dostoevskij e la vita interiore." In *Giornale Storico di Psicologia Dinamica*, 23.

Cacciari, M. "La porta aperta." In *Icone della legge*. Milano: Adelphi, 1985.

Calderon de la Barca, P. *La vita è sogno*. Milano: Bompiani, 1983.

Camus, A. 1942. "La speranza e l'assurdo nell'opera di Franz Kafka." In *Il mito di Sisifo*. Milano: Bompiani, 1984.

Canetti, E. 1969. "L'altro processo: Le lettere di Kafka a Felice." In *La coscienza delle parole*. Milano: Adelphi, 1984.

Cantoni, R. *Che cosa ha veramente detto Kafka*. Roma: Astrolabio, 1970.

Carotenuto, A. 1980. *A Secret Symmetry: Sabina Spielrein between Jung and Freud*. London: Routledge and Kegan Paul.

———. 1982a. *Discorso sulla metapsicologia*. Torino: Boringhieri.

———. 1982b. "La frustrazione da nullità." In *Giornale Storico di Psicologia Dinamica*, 11.

———. 1987. *Eros and Pathos: Shades of Love and Suffering*. Toronto: Inner City Books, 1989.

Cerna, J. 1985. *Milena Jesenkà*. Prague: Jan R. Cerny.

Ceronetti, G. *Come un talismano*. Milano: Adelphi, 1986.

Chevalier, J., and Gheerbrant, A. 1969. *Dizionario dei simboli*, vol. I. Milano: Rizzoli, 1986.

Citati, P. *Kafka*. Milano: Mondadori, 1987.

Colli, G. *La sapienza greca*, vol. III. Milano: Adelphi, 1980.

Conrad, J. 1912. "The Secret Sharer." In *Heart of Darkness and the Secret Sharer*. New York: Bantam Books, 1989.

Dante Alighieri. "Paradiso." In *La Divina Commedia*. Bologna: Zanichelli, 1987.

De Filippo, E. 1948. "Le voci di dentro." In *I capolavori di Eduardo*, vol. I. Torino: Einaudi, 1973.

De Martino, E. *La terra del rimorso*. Milano: Il Saggiatore, 1961.

Dickinson, E. 1862. *The Complete Poems*. London, Boston: Faber and Faber, 1991.

_____. *The Poems of Emily Dickinson*, 3 vol. Cambridge, Mass.: Harvard University Press, Belknap Press, 1955.

Dostoyevski, F. 1846. *The Double*.

_____. 1848. *White Nights*.

_____. 1864. "Notes from the Underground." In *Notes from the Underground and the Gambler*. New York: Oxford University Press, 1991.

_____. 1866a. *A Disgraceful Affair*.

_____. 1866b. *Delitto e castigo*. Minalo: Garzanti, 1969.

_____. 1876. *A Gentle Creature*.

_____. 1879–1980. *The Brothers Karamozov*. Harmondsworth, Middlesex: Penguin Books, 1982.

Erbetta, M. "Codex Bezae Cantrabingesis." In M. Erbetta (a cura di). *Gli Apocrifici del Nuovo Testamento: Vengeli, testi giudeo-cristiani e gnostici*. Marietti, 1982.

Euripides. *Le Baccanti*. Roma: Signorelli, 1982. (*See* Loeb Classical Library.)

Fertonani, R. "Introduzione." In Kafka F. *Il Castello*. Milano: Mondadori, 1979.

Fisch, H. *A Remembered Future: A Study in Literary Mythology*. Bloomington, Ind.: Indiana University Press, 1984.

Fiumara, R., Caporali, M., and Zanasi, M. "Il Sé e l'identità." In M. Ciani (a cura di). *Il narcisismo*. Roma: Borla, 1983.

Freschi, M. "Kafka: la scrittura e l'ebraismo." In A. Gargani, M. Freschi, *Kafka oggi* (1883–1983). Napoli: Guida, 1984.

Freud, S. 1887–1904. *The Complete Letters of Sigmund Freud to Wilhelm Fliess* (Translated and edited by J. M. Masson). Cambridge, Mass: Belknap Press of Harvard University Press, 1985.

_____. 1908. "On the Sexual Theories of Children." In *The Standard Edition*, vol. IX. London: Hogarth Press, 1974.

_____. 1914. "On Narcissism: An Introduction." In *The Standard Edition*, vol. XIV. London: Hogarth Press, 1974.

_____. 1929. "Civilization and its Discontents." In *The Standard Edition*, vol. XXI. London: Hogarth Press, 1974.

Fromm, E., Suzuki, D., and De Martino, E. 1960. *Zen Buddhism and Psychoanalysis*. New York: Harper & Brothers.

Funari, E. "Fenomenologia, processualità e struttura nel tema del 'Doppio.'" In E. Funari (a cura di). *Il Doppio tra patologia e necessità*. Milano: Raffaello Cortina, 1986.

Fusini, N. *Due: La passione del legame in Kafka*. Milano: Feltrinelli, 1988.

———. *Nomi*. Milano: Feltrinelli, 1986.

Ganzerli, P., and Sasso, R. *La rappresentazione anoressica*. Roma: Bulzoni, 1979.

Godden, C. 1977. "The prospect of a positive existential alternative." In *The Kafka Debate*. New York: Angel Flores.

Goethe, J. W. 1790. *Faust,* pt. one. Harmondsworth, Middlesex, 1986.

———. 1809. *Elective Affinities*. Harmondsworth, Middlesex, 1986.

Green, A. 1977. "Atomo di parentela e relazioni edipiche." In C. Lévi-Strauss. *L'identità*. Palermo: Sellerio, 1986.

Hall, C. W., and Lind, R. E. 1970. *Dreams, Life and Literature. A Study of Franz Kafka*. Charlotte, N.C.: The University of North Carolina Press.

Harding, E. 1932. *The Way of All Women*. New York: Longmans, Green and Co.

Haymann, R. 1981. *Kafka*. Milano: Rizzoli, 1983.

Heidegger, M. 1927. *Being and Time*. Oxford: Basil Blackwell, 1988.

Heller, E. 1974. *Kafka*. Glasgow: Fontana-Collins.

Herodotus. *Storie*, vol. III. Milano: Rizzoli, 1984. (*See* Loeb Classical Library.)

Hesse, H. 1919. *Demian*. London: Paladin Grafton Books, 1989.

———. 1922. *Siddhartha*. New York: Bantam Books, 1971.

Hillman, J. 1964. "Il Tradimento." In *Senex et puer*. Venezia: Marsilio, 1979.

———. 1967. "Senex et Puer: An Aspect of the Historical and Psychological Present." In *Eranos Jahrbücher*.

———. 1971a. "Abandoning the Child." In *Eranos Jarbuch*, 40.

———. 1971b. "The Feeling Function." In Hillman, J., von Franz, M. L. *Lectures on Jung's Typology*. Zürich: Spring Publications.

———. 1972. "On Psychological Creativity." In *Myth of Analysis: Three Essays in Archetypal Psychology*. Evanston, Ill.: Northwestern University Press.

———. 1971c. "Fallimento e analisi." In *Trame perdute*. Milano: Raffaello Cortina Editore, 1985.

———. 1972. "Three Ways of Failure and Analysis." In *The Journal of Analytical Psychology* 1.

_____. 1979. *The Dream and the Underworld*. New York: Harper & Row.

_____. 1981. *Psychology: Monotheistic or Polytheistic?* Dallas: Spring Publications.

_____. 1982. "Sale: un capitolo della psicologia alchemica." In J. Strud-G. Thomas (a cura di). *L'intatta: Archeipi e psicologia della verginità femminile*. Como: Red Edizioni, 1987.

Hoffmann, E. T. A. 1815. "Die Elixiere des Teufels." In *Gesammelte Werke*, Bd. 1–4 ff. Hamburg: hrsg. v. N. Erné, 1964–1965.

Homer. *The Odyssey* (translation of W. Shewring). Oxford, New York: Oxford University Press, 1990.

Horney, K. 1945. *Our Inner Conflicts*. New York: Norton & Co.

Huizinga, J. 1946. *Homo ludens*. Torino: Einaudi, 1973.

Jacobi, J. 1957. *Complex, Archetype, Symbol in the Psychology of C. G. Jung*. London: Routledge and Kegan Paul, 1959.

Janouch, G. 1951. *Conversations with Kafka: Notes and Reminiscences*. London: Verschole, 1953.

Jaspers, K. 1959. *Allgemeine Psychopathologie*. Berlin, Göttingen, Heidelberg: Springer-Verlag.

Jesenskà, M. 1923. *Alles ist Leben*. Frankfurt: Neue Kritik Verlag, 1984.

Jung, C. G. 1911–1952. *Symbols of Transformation*. In *The Collected Works*, vol. 6. Princeton, N.J.: Princeton University Press, 1971.

_____. 1930. "Some Aspects of Modern Psychotherapy." In *The Practice of Psychotherapy. The Collected Works*, vol. 16. Princeton, N.J.: Princeton University Press, 1966.

_____. 1938–1940. *Realtà dell'anima*. Torino: Boringhieri, 1983.

_____. 1938–1940. *Psychology and Religion: West and East*. In *The Collected Works*, vol. 11. Princeton, N.J.: Princeton University Press, 1969.

_____. 1940. "The Psychology of the Child Archetype." In *The Archetypes and the Collective Unconscious. The Collected Works*, vol. 9, i. Princeton, N.J.: Princeton University Press, 1968.

_____. 1943. "Psychotherapy and a Philosophy of Life." In *The Practice of Psychotherapy. The Collected Works*, vol. 16. Princeton, N.J.: Princeton University Press, 1966.

————. 1944. *Psychology and Alchemy. The Collected Works*, vol. 12. Princeton, N.J.: Princeton University Press, 1968.

————. 1946. "The Psychology of the Transference." In *The Practice of Psychotherapy. The Collected Works*, vol. 16. Princeton, N.J.: Princeton University Press, 1966.

————. 1951. *Aion: Researches into the Phenomenology of the Self.* In *The Collected Works*, vol. 9, ii. Princeton, N.J.: Princeton University Press, 1968.

————. 1952. "Answer to Job." In *Psychology and Religion. The Collected Works*, vol. 11. Princeton, N.J.: Princeton University Press, 1969.

————. 1961. *Memories, Dreams, Reflections*. New York: Pantheon Books, 1963.

Kafka, F. 1902–1924. "Lettere 1902–1924." In *Lettere*. Milano: Mondadori, 1988.

————. 1909–1924. *Lettere a Ottla e alla famiglia*. Milano: Mondadori, 1976.

————. 1910–1923. *Diaries*. New York: Schocken Books, 1976.

————. 1912–1914. *Amerika*. New York: Schocken Books, 1962.

————. 1912–1917. *Letters to Felice*. New York: Schocken Books, 1973.

————. 1914–1915a. *The Trial*. London: Penguin Books, 1953.

————. 1954. *Dearest Father: Stories and Other Writings*. New York: Schocken Books.

————. 1919. *Letter to his Father*. New York: Schocken, 1966.

————. 1920–1923. *Letters to Milena*. New York: Schocken Books, 1962.

————. 1920a. "He." In *Shorter Works*, vol. 1. London: Secker & Warburg, 1974.

————. 1922b. *The Castle*. Harmondsworth, Middlesex: Penguin Books, 1986.

————. 1971. *The Complete Stories*. New York: Schocken Books.

Kaiser, H. 1931. "Franz Kafkas Inferno: Eine Psychologische Deutung seiner Strafphantasie." In *Imago*, vol. XVII. Wien: Internationaler Psychoanalytischer Verlag.

Kernberg, O. 1975. *Simdromi marginali e narcisismo patologico*. Torino: Boringhieri, 1978.

Kierkegaard, S. 1849–1955. *Diario*, vol. II. Brescia: Morcelliana, 1963.

Kipling, R. *Complete Verse*. New York: Anchor Press, Doubleday, 1989.

Kleist, H. von. 1808. "Pentilesia." In *Sämtliche Werke und Briefe*, 2 vol. München: hrsg. von H. Sembdner,1961.

Kundera, M. 1986. "Somewhere Behind." In *The Art of the Novel*. New York: Harper & Row, 1988.

L'epopea di Gilgames. Fratelli Bocca Editori, 1951.

Lai, G. *Disidentità*. Milano: Feltrinelli, 1988.

Laing, R. D. 1959. *The Self and the Others*. London: Tavistock Publications.

_____. 1960. *The Divided Self*. London: Tavistock Publications.

Lawrence, D. H. 1928. *Lady Chatterley's Lover*. Harmondsworth, Middlesex: Penguin Books, 1961.

Lec, S. 1957. *Unkempt Thoughts*. Lec. Leah Salisbury, Inc.

Leonelli, L. *Coccole e carezze*. Milano: Rizzoli, 1987.

Lessing, G. E. 1968. "Eine Dunplik." In Rilla P. (ed.). *Gemammelte Werke*, vol. VIII. Berlin-Weimar.

Liechtestein, H. 1964. "The role of narcissism in the emergence and mantanance of a primary identity." In *International Journal of Psycho-Analysis*, vol. XLV.

Lopez-Pedraza, R. 1977. *Hermes and His Children*. Zürich: Spring Publications, 1977.

Lowen, A. *The Betrayal of the Body*. New York: Macmillan, 1967.

Lukács, G. 1955–1956. "Franz Kafka o Thomas Mann?" In *Il significato attuale del realismo critico*. Torino: Einaudi, 1957.

Maffei, G. *I linguaggi della psiche*. Milano: Bompianis 1986.

Magris. "Una voce dal caos." In E. Pocar (a cura di). *Introduzione a Kafka*. Milano: Mondadori, 1974.

Mahler, G. 1905. "I canti dei bambini morti." In U. Duse. *Gustav Mahler*. Torino: Einaudi, 1973.

_____. 1905. "Il canto della terra." In U. Duse. *Gustav Mahler*. Torino: Einaudi, 1973.

Marchesi, M. *Il meglio del peggio*. Milano: Rizzoli, 1975.

Martin, P. 1959. "The cockroach as an identification with reference to Kafka's Metamorphosis." In *The American Imago*, vol. 16, 1–4.

Masaraki, G., and Morelli, R. 1982. "Contro la legge di gravità." In *Riza Psicosomatica*, 19.

Massa, S. 1989. "L'obesità come manifestazione di sofferenza psichica." In *Giornale Storico di Psicologia Dinamica*, 25.

Miller, A. 1979. *Das Drama des begabten Kindes und die Suche nach dem wahren Selbest*. Frankfurt: Suhrkamp.

――――. 1980. *Am Anfang war Erziehung*. Frankfurt: Suhrkamp.

――――. 1981. *Du sollst nicht merken: Variationen über das Paradies-Thema*. Frankfurt am Main: Suhrkamp Verlag.

Mittner, L. 1960. "Kafka senza kafkismi." In *Storia della letteratura tedesca*, vol. 2. Torino: Einaudi, 1971.

Möller, C. *La speranza degli uomini*. Milano: Società Editrice Vita e Pensiero, 1961.

Monod, J. 1970. *Le hasard et la nécessité*. Paris: Editions du Seuil.

Montale, E. 1920–1927. "Ossi di seppia." In *Tutte le poesie*. Milano: Mondadori, 1984. English translation: *Bones of the Cuttlefish*. Oakville, Ontario: Mosaic Press, 1983.

Moravia, A. *La vita interiore*. Milano: Bompiani, 1978.

Morpurgo-Tagliabue, G. *La nevrosi austriaca*. Casale Monferrato: Marietti, 1983.

Morris, D. 1971. *Intimate Behaviour*. London: Cape.

Natoli, S. *L'esperienza del dolore*. Milano: Feltrinelli, 1987.

Neider, C. 1948. *The Frozen Sea: A Study of Franz Kafka*. New York: Oxford University Press.

Neumann, E. 1933. "*The Trial*: An Interpretation through Depth Psychology." In *Creative Man*. Princeton: Princeton University Press, 1979.

――――. 1953. "The Psychological Stages of Feminine Development." In *Spring*. New York, 1959.

――――. 1954. "Creative Man and Transformation." In *Art and Creative Unconscious*. New York: Pantheon Books, 1959.

――――. 1956. *The Great Mother*. New York: Bollingen Foundation Inc.

Nietzsche, F. 1876–1878. *The Will to Power*. New York: W. Kaufmann.

――――. 1881. *The Dawn of Day*. New York: Gordon Press, 1974.

――――. 1883–1885. *Thus Spoke Zarathustra*. Harmondsworth, Middlesex: Penguin Books, 1969.

Nin, A. 1959. *A Spy in the House of Love*. Harmondsworth, Middlesex: Penguin Books, 1971.

Olivieri, U. "Analisi statistica dei racconti di Kafka." In *Studi Urbinati di Storia, Filosofia e Letteratura*, vol. XLII. 1969.

Otto, R. 1936. *The Idea of the Holy*. London: Pelican Books, 1959.

Paracelsus. "Labyrinthus medicorum." In K. Sundhoff (a cura di), *Sämtliche Werke*, vol. 11. Munchen and Berlin, 1922–1935.

Pascal, B. *Pensées*. London: Penguin Books, 1966.

Pavese, C. 1952. *Il mestiere di vivere*. Torino: Einaudi, 1980.

Pfeiffer, J. 1966. "La passione dell'immaginario." In Blachot. *Lo spazio letterario*. Torino: Einaudi, 1975.

Pirandello, L. 1904. *The Late Mattia Pascal*. New York: Dedalus, 1988.

_____. 1916. "Così é (se vi pare)." In *Maschere nude*, vol. I. Milano: Modadori, 1985.

_____. 1926. "Uno, nessuno, centomila." In *Tutti i romanzi*, vol. I. Milano: Mondadori, 1985.

_____. "Six Characters in Search of an Author." In *Three Plays*. London: Methuen Drama, 1991.

Plato. *Menexenus*. Cambridge, Mass.: Harvard University Press, in Loeb Classical Library.

_____. "Phaedrus." In *Phaedrus and Letters VII and VIII*. London: Penguin Books, 1973.

_____. *The Symposium*. Harmondworth, Middlesex: Penguin Books, 1951.

Poe, E. A. 1842. "The Pit and the Pendulum." In *Tales of Mystery and Imagination*. London: J. M. Dent & Sons Ltd, 1991.

Proust, M. 1896. *L'Indifférent*. Paris: Gallimard, 1978.

Racheli, A. M. *Il luogo kafkiano, architettura evocante, architettura evocata*. Bari: Dedalo, 1979.

Rank, O. 1914. *The Double*. Chapel Hill, N.C.: University of North Carolina Press, 1971.

Raspaolo, D. 1988. "Su una possibile interpretazione della leggenda del lupo mannaro." In *Giornale Storico di Psicologia Dinamica*, 23.

Reage, P. 1954. *Storia di O*. Milano: Bompiani, 1982.

Resnik, S. 1972. *Persona e psicosi*. Torino: Einaudi, 1976.

Robert, M. 1963. *L'antico e il nuovo*. Milano: Rizzoli, 1969.

_____. 1979. *Seul, comme Franz Kafka*. Calmann-Lévy.

Robertson, R. 1985. *Kafka, Judaism, Politics and Literature*. Oxford: Clarendon Press.

Rollmann-Branch, H. S. 1960. "On the question of primary object need." In *Journal of American Psychoanalytical Association*, 8.

Roth, J. 1927. *Fuga senza fine*. Milano: Adelphi, 1985.

_____. 1939. "La leggenda del santo bevitore." In *Il mercante di coralli*. Milano: Adelphi, 1984.

Rouze, M. *Oppenheimer e la bomba atomica*. Roma: Editori Riuniti, 1966.

Rûmî, Gialâl ad-Dîn. *Poesie mistiche*. Milano: Rizzoli, 1980.

Sacher-Masoch, L. von 1870. *Venere in pelliccia*. Milano: Sonzogno, 1986.

Sacher-Masoch, L. von 1906. *Le mie confessioni*. Milano: Bompiani, 1983.

Sappho. "Tramontana é la luna . . .." In S. Quasimodo (a cura di). *Lirici greci*. Milano: Mondadori, 1974a. In English: *Sappho: A New Translation*. Berkeley, Calif.: University of California Press, 1958.

Sartre, J. P. 1943. *L'essere e il nulla*. Milano: Il Saggiatore, 1984.

_____. 1945. "Porta chiusa." In *Le mosche, Porta chiusa*. Milano: Bompiani, 1987.

Sassone, A. M. 1988. "Il diavolo come dimensione desiderante." In *Giornale Storico di Psicologia Dinamica*, 23.

Schierse-Leonard, L. 1982. *La donna ferita: Modelli e archetipi del rapporto padre-figlia*. Roma: Astrolabio, 1985.

Schillirò, C. 1988. "La pulsione creativa: Arte come terapia." In *Giornale Storico di Psicologia Dinamica*, 23.

_____. 1989. "Il nome dell'assenza: Franz Kafka o del castello interioré." In *Giornale Storico de Psicologia Dinamica*, 25.

Schwarz, A. *L'arte dell'amore in India e Nepal*. Bari: Laterza, 1980.

Searles, H. S. 1965a. *Collected Papers on Schizophrenia and Related Subjects*. London: Hogarth Press and the Institute of Psychoanalysis, 1965.

Senzaki, N., and Reps, P. 1957. (a cura di) *101 Storie Zen*. Milano: Adelphi, 1973.

Shakespeare, W. *Hamlet*. Ware, Hertfordshire: Wordsworth Editions, 1992.

Sharp, D. 1980. *The Secret Raven: Conflict and Transformation in the Life of Franz Kafka*. Toronto: Inner City Books.

Shelley, M. 1818. *Frankenstein*. Oxford, New York: Oxford University Press, 1991.

Sophocles. *The Complete Plays of Sophocles*. New York: Bantam Books, 1988.

Spielrein, S. 1912. "Die Destruktion als Ursake des Werdens." *Jahr-buch für psychoanalytische und psychopathologische Fors-chungen* 4: 465–503.

Stutley, M., and Stutley, J. 1977. *Dizionario dell'induismo*. Roma: Astrolabio, 1980.

Terence. "The Self-Tormentor." In *The Lady of Andros, The Self Tormentor, The Eunuch*, vol. 1. Cambridge: Harvard University Press, 1986. Loeb Classical Library.

The Bhagavadgita. London, Boston, Sydney, Wellington: Unwin Paperbacks, 1989.

Trevi, M. *Metafore del simbolo*. Milano: Raffaello Cortina Editore, 1986.

————. "Sul problema dell'Ombra nella psicologia analitica." In Trevi, M.-Romano, A. *Studi sull-Ombra*. Venezia: Marsilio, 1975.

Untersteiner, M. *Sofocle*. Milano: Lampugnani Nigri Editore, 1974.

Valéry, P. 1894–1945. *Cahiers*. Éditions Gallimard, Paris: 1974.

Vattimo, G. *Il soggetto e la maschera*. Milano: Bompiani, 1979.

Watzlawick, P., Beavin, J. H., and Jackson, D. D. 1967. *Pragmatic of Human Communication: A Study of Interactional Patterns, Pathologies, and Paradoxes*. New York: W. W. Norton & Co.

Webster, P. Dow. 1951. "A Critical Examination of Franz Kafka's *The Castle*." In *American Imago*, 8.

Williams, T. 1947. "A Streetcar Named Desire." In *A Streetcar Named Desire and Other Plays*. London: Penguin Books, 1959.

Winnicott, D. W. 1971. *Gioco e realtà*. Roma: Armando, 1986.

Woodman, M. 1985. *Puoi volare farfalla*. Como: Red Edizioni, 1987.

Yourcenar, M. 1951. *Memoirs of Hadrian*. Harmondsworth, Middle-sex: Penguin Books, 1986.

————. 1957. *Fires*. London: Black Swan, 1985.

————. 1968. *L'œuvre au Noir*. Paris: Gallimard. English transla-tion: *The Abyss*, G. Frick, tr. New York: Farrar, Straus and Giroux, 1976.

Index

127–129, 135, 138, 144, 151, 155,
172, 178, 185–187, 191, 193, 198,
208, 210, 212, 217–219, 233, 237,
239, 246, 281, 286, 291, 303,
314, 316, 332
Psyche, 49, 265
psychoanalysis, 27, 48
classical, 23
psychodrama, 208
psychology, 27
psychosis, 128, 137, 143, 186–187,
219, 308, 311–312, 318
psychotherapy, 23
puer, archetype of, 178–179, 208
purity, 79, 82
and guilt, 63–64

Racheli, A. M., 51
Racine, 307
Rank, O., 210
rape, anal, 75
Raspaolo, D., 153
Reage, Pauline, 319
reality, ix, xiii–xiv, 1, 3–7, 12–13,
18–19, 22–23, 29, 37–38, 42, 47,
56, 71, 78–80, 83, 85, 94–95,
103, 105, 108, 110, 126, 130–132,
137, 155, 159–160, 165, 167–168,
229, 234, 243, 245–247, 250
existential, 130
of the soul, 155
psychological vs. objective, 4
rebellion, 166
regression, 43, 134, 153, 185, 204,
334
Reich, 163
rejection, 134, 136–137, 138,
140–144, 151–152, 154, 163–164,
167, 170–171, 176, 181–183, 186,
230–234, 240–241
religiosity, Christian, 21
repression, 162, 187, 202, 211
resistance, by patients in analysis,
35, 48
Resnik, S., 312
Rilke, R. M., 40

Robert, M., 177, 284
Robertson, R., 33, 93–94, 336
Rollmann-Branch, H. S., 222
Roth, Josef, 71, 281–282
Rueckert, 41
Rûmî, Gialâl ad-Dîn, 292
Rye, 210

sacrifice, 131–133, 148, 168, 189,
223
sadism, 73
salt, 217–218
Sappho, 307
Sartre, J. P., 71, 229, 252
Sasso, R., 283
Sassone, A. M., 291
Satyr, 283, 289–290
Schiele, Egon, 247
Schierse-Leonard, L., 264
Schillirò, C., 95, 197
schizoid personality, 115, 257, 320
schizophrenia, 143, 151–152, 160,
308, 311–312
Schoenberg, Arnold, 40, 195
Schubert, 247
Schweitzer, Albert, 120
Searles, H. S., 308, 313, 320
self, x, 48, 53, 56, 63, 79, 109,
114–115, 117, 131, 134, 141,
210–212, 222, 224–225, 247, 321,
334, 336
archetype of, 127
betrayal of, 8, 24, 63
false, 24, 63, 163
self-esteem, lack of, 52–53
senex, archetype of, 178–179
sentiment, 158–159, 196, 204, 237,
240, 257, 265–266, 309, 322
see also emotion
Senzaki, N., 54
sexuality, 5, 53, 71, 84, 172–173,
179, 190–191, 223, 238, 261–263,
270–271, 274, 283–285, 287,
289–291, 302, 317, 319–321
animal, 104